The Poetics of I
Heidegger's Line

Michael Roth

Lensgrinder, Ltd.
Kirkland, WA

This edition ISBN: 978-1-7343428-0-2
Original ISBN cloth 0-8101-1317-1
Original ISBN paper 0-8101-1318-X

Library of Congress Cataloging-in-Publication Data

Roth, Michael
        The poetics of resistance: Heidegger's Line / Michael Roth
        p. cm. -- (Northwestern University studies in phenomenology
& existential philosophy)
        Includes bibliographical references and index.
        ISBN 0-8101-1317-1 (cloth: alk. paper). -- ISBN 0-8101-1318-
X (pbk. : alk. paper)
        1. Heidegger, Martin, 1889-1976. 2. Derrida, Jacques. 3.
Political Science -- Philosophy. I. Title. II. Series.
        B3279.H49R678 1996
        193--dc20

Studies in Phenomenology & Social Philosophy

Lensgrinder, Ltd

Kirkland, WA

In Dedication To...

The one who let me start... Arthur Melnick
The one who kept me going... Laura Haber
The one who let me finish... Annie Pritchard

Table of Contents

Acknowledgments

It would not be enough to merely acknowledge Arthur Melnick for his role in this project: I *thank* him for everything he said to initiate the thinking that developed as this book, most of which he probably doesn't remember saying—making it all the more a gift. In addition, there are other colleagues from my days at the University of Illinois to whom I am grateful for helping to let the project become what it is: David Jacobson for his unfathomable dedication and patience, especially in those early days of the project when I needed to be able to speak in fragments with someone who was able to transform my stuttering into complete sentences. Allen Hance for his continual movement past our disagreements so as to understand my work on its own terms: a true friend of difference. Bert Kögler for his ability to push me on the details so as show me where the real points of contention were. There are no words to describe the importance Bill Vaughan had for this project: a friend and colleague, he continually helped me to see that I wasn't carried away by madness when, in those long discussions of Heidegger, we were each finally able to articulate the poetic thinking that we had so long held on to in silence. Hugh Chandler, who was the first Analytically trained philosopher to take my position seriously as a philosophical approach and, in doing so, made it possible for me to believe that it might actually be one. To Laura Haber I am by far the most indebted for her willingness to let me ramble on when it mattered and for her ability to make insightful comments when I was stuck, proving that she had been listening all along.

Then there were the people who came to the project in those difficult days at the end when the fun stuff had all been done and there was nothing left but hard work. Truly special people for their willingness to help in this way, I must express sympathetic gratitude to Martin Srajek for reading parts of the final draft for the sake of refining it with the concerns of its published form in mind, Heather Kenny at the publisher's office for her patience with my frequent phone calls, and all the people at Northwestern University Press who did things to help this project along without my knowing who they were or what exactly they were doing, since it is ultimately my ignorance of these matters for which I am grateful.

Finally, there are the people who helped in a variety of ways that I am still in the process of discovering and rediscovering, but of which I am completely unwilling to speak: Annie Pritchard, Linda Roth, Harry

Weingarden, and the silent holocaustal voices of my ancestors who continue to burn in me as the sparks and ashes of resistance.

List of Abbreviations

All of the texts listed here are translations existing in English. Although I frequently referred to the "original" in French and German, I relied for the most part on the translations. Because I write and think in/as/through English, a steadfast loyalty to the "original languages" of deconstruction would not have done me any good in the matter of thinking through the project of deconstruction. This method may be inappropriate to a piece of scholarship, but I am not sure whether what follows is a piece of scholarship (and, quite frankly, when it comes to ethics, scholarship is not needed).

Heidegger

ID	*Identity and Difference*. Bilingual edition. Translated by Joan Stambaugh. New York: Harper & Row, 1969.
BP	*Basic Problems of Phenomenology*. Translated by A. Hofstadter. Bloomington: Indiana University Press, 1988.
BW	*Basic Writings*. Translated and edited by D.F. Krell. New York: Harper & Row, 1977.
EGT	*Early Greek Thinking*. Translated by D.F. Krell and F.A. Capuzzi. New York: Harper & Row, 1984.
PLT	*Poetry, Language, Thought*. Translated by A. Hofstadter. New York: Harper & Row, 1975.
BT	*Being and Time*. Translated by J. Macquarrie and E. Robinson. New York: Harper & Row, 1962.
QCT	*Question Concerning Technology and other essays*. Translated by W. Lovitt. New York: Harper & Row, 1977.
TB	*On Time and Being*. Translated by J. Stambaugh New York: Harper & Row, 1972.
EP	*The End of Philosophy*. Translated by J. Stambaugh. New York: Harper & Row, 1973.
WCT	*What is Called Thinking?* Translation by J.G. Gray. New York: Harper & Row, 1968.
OWL	*On the Way to Language*. Translated by P.D. Hertz. New York: Harper & Row, 1971.

QB	*The Question of Being*. Bilingual edition. Translated by J. Wilde and W. Kluback. New Haven: College and University Press, 1958.
DT	*Discourse on Thinking*. A translation of *Gelassenheit* by J.M. Anderson and E.H. Freund. New York: Harper & Row, 1966.
EB	*Existence and Being*. Translated by D. Scott. Edited by W. Brock. Chicago: Regnery, 1968.
WP	*What is Philosophy?* Translated by J.T. Wilde and W. Kluback. New York: NCUP, Inc., 1956.
MFL	*The Metaphysical Foundations of Logic*. Translated by M. Heim. Bloomington: Indiana University Press, 1984.

Derrida

P	*Positions*. Translated by Alan Bass. Chicago: University of Chicago Press, 1981.
D	*Dissemination*. Translated by Barbara Johnson. Chicago: University of Chicago Press, 1981.
OG	*Of Grammatology*. Translated by G.C. Spivak. Baltimore: Johns Hopkins University Press, 1976.
S	*Spurs*. Bilingual edition. Translated by B. Harlow. Chicago: University of Chicago Press, 1979.
M	*Margins of Philosophy*. Translated by Alan Bass. Chicago: University of Chicago Press, 1982.
WD	*Writing and Difference*. Translated by Alan Bass. Chicago: University of Chicago Press, 1978.
SP	*Speech and Phenomena*. Translated by D. Allison. Evanston: Northwestern University Press, 1973.
NANN	"No Apocalypse, Not Now." Translated by C. Porter and P. Lewis in *Diacritics* 14, no. 2 (Summer 1984).
G	*Glas*. Translated by J.P. Leavey, Jr. and R. Rand. Lincoln: University of Nebraska Press, 1986.
G I	"Geschlecht: Sexual Difference, Ontological Difference." Translated by R. Berezdivin. *Research in Phenomenology* 13 (1983).
G II	"Geschlecht II." Translated by J.P. Leavey, Jr. in *Deconstruction and Philosophy*, edited by J. Sallis. Chicago: University of Chicago Press, 1987.

SOR   "Sending: On Representation." Translated by P. and M.A. Caws in *Social Research* 49, no. 2, (Summer 1982).

PC   *The Post Card: From Socrates to Freud and Beyond.* Translated by A. Bass. Chicago: University of Chicago Press, 1987.

Introduction

In what follows, I am working on saying something that cannot be said. Rather, it must be shown, demonstrated, and practiced, so that it comes to pass while one is positioned in its midst. For this reason, the text contains very little—if any—"meta-commentary" or "signposts" pointing the reader back and forth to major events that he or she may find of interest along the way.[1] Any device that pretends to offer guidance in this way is robbed of its referential character not long after its appearance by being transformed into one more demonstrative gesture flattened out in the dynamics of the work. No doubt this will make the task of the reader quite difficult. For not only does this strategy fail to assist readers, it sends misleading signals and deceptive messages in their direction. It is to be hoped that such misconceptions will be dissolved eventually, but that must be left to the deconstructive practices of the reader. The important thing is that deception and misunderstanding (really it may be better to say, "varieties of false or distorted understanding") will be a constant threat to the reader. I will not wave these problems aside with some excuse about how hard it is to read Heidegger and Derrida. Rather, the matter that complicates the text and forces it to demand so much of a reader is ethics. Ethics, I claim, is always demanding and difficult. And what's more, it is terrifying. This last quality is not so much the result of some idiosyncratic element of this attempt at a post-structuralist ethics, rather all of ethics is terrifying to the extent that there is so much at stake in it: the consequences of going wrong may turn out to be abysmal.

One of my many presuppositions is that ethics is hard, and one of my motivations in seeing an ethics within deconstruction, is that historically ethics has been made too easy. One of deconstruction's chief

---

[1] "If any" because, although there are many such remarks as they are traditionally and professionally understood, it should become clear in the course of this introduction that they cannot be functioning in this way "pure and simple." For further consideration of this point, the reader may want to reread this footnote upon completing the introduction, and perhaps after reading each of the chapters of this book — or perhaps at any time the reader is drawn to it.

virtues seems to be its uncanny capacity for making what has always seemed easy immensely difficult. I don't mean that making value-judgments is made more difficult by deconstruction, but that deconstruction can show how easy it is to make value-judgments of any kind, and thus—by deconstructing the judgment as based in the language of "presence"—can force ethics into a difficult region where it can no longer rely on the oversimplification of "practice" achieved by value-judgments or normative claims.

Suppose then that deconstruction sets up some other kind of claims in opposition to the traditionally ethical normative ones. Additionally, suppose that the deconstructive project is the attempt to resolve the difference, to arrive at some kind of a conclusive decision about what exactly differentiates the one from the other. If this is the case, then deconstruction is nothing other than a sickly version of metaphysical attempts at doing ethics. *Différance*, as Derrida delivered it, would be nothing other than an assertion about the relation of something with its other. Suppose, to the contrary, that deconstruction's *différance* is a question. Not an assertion made about this or that in their relation or on their own, but instead a questioning of their relation, *différance* as a questioning of the difference, rather than its assertion: which would really be a redundant project since it has been done many times before by just about every thinker worthy of the name "philosopher." Deconstruction, therefore, becomes the attempt to question the relation between metaphysics and what is other to it. Not to define the two in their relation, for this is the task appropriate to metaphysics, but to make their relation questionable and thus to insert the possibility of something other, not as an assertion, but as a question.

Therefore, this essay essays the heuristic and is questionable at every step. Even the unity of the work presupposed in the demonstrative "this" is open to question—i.e., ontological status (or its privation) must be thought with a question mark. No doubt this is essential to any heuristic structure the aim of which is to provide strategies for learning and inquiry. But it would be dishonest for me to claim that this device ensures the success of what follows. The only success this work has achieved is in the systematic necessity from which each part succeeds the one previous. And it is precisely this element of success that guarantees the ultimate failure of the project. On my reading of the work, it provides a systematic account of the thinking of the "later Heidegger" and the way in which Derrida's deconstruction interprets it. Within this system, it has become possible to articulate the implications for practice arising from the post-structuralist attack on metaphysics. But even this strategy is saturated with limitations, as an essentially anti-systematic program will appear differently when examined with the theoretical gaze of a system. The reader, therefore, will be tempted to view the discussion of the final chapter as prescriptions or normative claims. But as propositions of this kind, the discussion will be disappointing at best, ridiculous at worst.

The logic of the first chapters is derived from a totalization of Heidegger's notion of the world or open region where Unconcealment, *Ereignis*, Difference, Saying, and Clearing are posit(ion)ed as axiomatic. While reading these chapters, it may be tempting to compare Heidegger to previous transcendental and systematic philosophers like Aquinas and Kant (and perhaps the early Heidegger). Some readers, those who wince at the idea of a system, will no doubt be put off by this strategy. Others, the lovers of system, will be troubled no less for they will find a number of ways in which the strategy seems to unravel. Systems do not tend to be strategic, but foundationalist: an axiomatic tactic or strategy borders on the contradictory. On this count, proponents of system will see this work (or at least the thinking it pretends to represent) as a bad imitation of the great works of those other systematic philosophers of the tradition.

The antagonists, on the other hand, might attempt to deconstruct it. They would show how the presupposition of system as strategy necessarily unravels, how it already rips the ground out from underneath before trying to establish it. Furthermore, they would note how the elements that form the parts of this system are themselves hostile (as they might claim both Heidegger and Derrida were well aware) to the possibility of unifying the totality as system demands. I have nothing to say in opposition to the reading of these antagonists of system and hasten to add that it would be an error to think that it is possible to coherently advocate deconstruction without beginning within the systemic. The idea that the systematic is hostile to deconstruction is a self-defeating principle as will become clear throughout the book. The deconstructive position, as I demonstrate it, is that metaphysics attempts to assert a foundation in the midst of abysmal movement, so to speak. If system is essentially hostile to deconstruction in such a way as to make them mutually exclusive, it would be impossible to say why there ever was any metaphysics at all according to deconstruction. Deconstructing deconstruction, therefore, would amount to demonstrating the advent of system in the midst of its deconstruction so as to unravel the very possibility of this systematizing—all of which amounts to an ethical positioning of deconstruction relative to metaphysics.

Deconstructing what is already at work deconstructing itself is not a great accomplishment. Thus any deconstructive reading of this strategic system is on a par with its strategically systematic reading of Heidegger and Derrida: there is nothing extraordinary or original in it except what its readers assert as such. Without putting it into this position, it may more resemble the gentle activity of the casual reader who is willing to let the work guide her through it. That is, she will let herself be overwhelmed by the text where this "letting," or as Heidegger would say *Gelassenheit,* is already a becoming text. This is not passive but patient, suggesting passivity in much the same way that receptiveness does: a passivity that is passionate in its activity, that musters great amounts of force in focusing attention, gathering in, and accepting what has been given. Thus, anyone who has spent a moment listening to another should be in a position to comprehend the activity involved in receiving. I will come to refer to this notion in the fifth chapter as "dedicated patience," and no doubt it will have been an attempt at moving past any strict opposition between the passive and the active. There is a spontaneity or impetus at work in the becoming text of a reader. From the point of view of the reader, such vital tropes make sense. But if the viewpoint is shifted to the text being read, it is the unraveling of the text. The text unravels in reading, which is the meaning of "text" and it is the meaning of "reading."

A text is not merely symbols on a page, or still more basically, lines and loops against a background. The text is at work, it works by opening a pathway that is reading, which reads temporally and spatially, but in such a way that resists any linear univocity. There is too much chaos at work in the reading of the text. You probably will not read what follows in one sitting. It may take you days or weeks or months to read it all. There will be gaps, there will be other events in your life sprinkled between the pages, you will forget things, you will emphasize various segments in relation to the interspersed events. There is dissemination. Not only dissemination, but unraveling, unfolding, unconcealing. The text explodes in its being read, it carries you away from yourself and yet, in some sense, it leaves you intact. The text unravels. You become text in reading, you unravel. There is unraveling.

Whom does "Heidegger" belong to, after all? I have read him, I have tried my best to think along with him. When I think of the coming to pass of the world in *Ereignis*, or the opening up of clearing, it does not follow that I am sitting in a chair with one of Heidegger's essays on my lap. I may be in a park or teaching a class or in a conversation with a friend. So, then, why is that "thinking" Heidegger's? Maybe you have paused in the last few paragraphs. Perhaps it is raining, you may have watched the water touching lightly upon the window and thought about texts unraveling or Penelope's patience. Who do these thoughts belong to? Why would anyone insist on building walls while reading, why is there so much hostility to the otherness of thought? If nothing else, I hope this essay calls into question the notion of "ownness" or of "having one's own thoughts."

If the reader is becoming text, what early Heidegger referred to as Da-sein (a being there, spread out *there* in the world), then reading is always unraveling. The impulse, however, is to push against the veil. I feel it. The veil is that fringe of the text that borders on the "real," the present world out there beyond the textuality of language. The world that yields this "reality," that gives it to the experiencing subject, is only analyzable in thought—and a certain modification of thought at that. Assuming for the moment that "tree" refers to a tree, it nonetheless holds that trees, the objects or facts of analysis, cannot be abstract. Trees, too, are always in the world, absorbing light, making oxygen, ingesting water, spreading seeds. Language need not be a veil that lies between the tree and myself, when I breathe the tree's oxygen I am with it, alongside it, inside it, and it is inside me. This interwovenness of the tree and myself is the textuality that grants us something other than an ordinary or natural conception of language, an epic conception of language as Saying (the Saga of *Sagen* as we will soon see from Heidegger). What philosophers call "ordinary" or "natural" language is no doubt a form this interwovenness takes. But its material is the gesture, the suggestion, the bearing out of relationships. When reading is described as the unraveling of a text, we may understand "reading" as a dynamic movement of any *thing* in the world. It is not only books that are read, but situations and circumstances; even DNA is reproduced by a kind of reading. Reading is therefore a movement of the text, perhaps *the* movement of the text. If the text is a corpus, or perhaps a corpse, its reading is its invigoration, its becoming not-yet dead.

And so reading unravels the system. What follows is a systematic account of the later Heidegger and Derrida, and in being read it will unravel. The conditions of its unraveling are built into the dynamics of its textuality. But texts are also written. It doesn't make sense to talk about writing as if it were something that happened to the text. Rather, writing weaves texts and, to the extent that texts are nothing other than what is woven, writing seems to create texts. Writing as an activity seems to be more like spinning than unraveling. But such appearances cannot deny the role of unraveling in writing. To the extent that words guide textual movement, the mechanical process of writing is receptive, a patient acceptance of the arrival of words. Writing also appears as the unraveling of a text spun out somewhere else, somewhere out *there* in the interstices of language.

Where writing attempts to produce a whole or completed work, it appears to spin and weave. But the whole, so clearly present at each instant of the writing, is being undone just as surely. Assuming for a moment that I am an intending subject, I can say that the moment of creation always appeared as a pure present where a whole was emerging. But, going back and rereading the writing of a given day, I would always discover that the text had eluded me. There was more and less than I had intended to put there, and yet those sentences were the best possible for expressing my meaning at the moment (and if I re-write, where does the moment go?). These problems will be multiplied if more and different readers come to engage this text. The text seems to spin a coherent whole, but it always spins out of control and unravels. Intentions amount to so little in terms of writing: an intending subject is always tragic and perhaps even a little pathetic. Because the text, in writing and reading, is always spinning and unraveling, weaving and unweaving, it is somewhat problematic to speak of texts at all. The text—it is not an unfamiliar word and English speakers have a lot of experience with textiles, fabrics, materials, etc.—suggests a whole or totality woven in a process of interweaving. That is, the text, a blanket for instance, appears unified and whole, whereas the fibers are involved in all sorts of tensions: strands crossing over and under other strands, fibers winding around still more fibers. At the microscopic level, the text appears less like a harmonious whole than like a conflagration of warring factions and tense forces. For this reason, the spinning of the text is always a kind of unraveling. Its order and holism are essentially chaotic and frayed: the blanket is worn.

The logic of the first two chapters is that of a systematic unraveling. From the beginning, they seem to present what Heidegger was, perhaps, unwilling to do: systematically interweaving the important elements in his works written after 1935. In Heidegger's typically short essays there are more hints and suggestions than anything else. It takes a long time reading these many essays to get past the initial feeling that they are somehow all the same, to get to the point where it is possible to discern a coherence in which they each attempt to supplement the others. "Heidegger's Later Thought"—the phrase has a ring of the systematic about it and proponents as well as antagonists of system both use the phrase. But the only systematizing Heidegger seems to have thought possible is the dynamic undertaken by the history of metaphysics. This history seems to have made a system of itself, transformed itself at each of the many relays of its passing into a linear system with monumental figures as axioms and plenty of scholarly corollaries. Philosophy as the queen of the sciences is not only rigorous as to its subject matter, but it must be rigorous as to its historical representation of itself. From a traditional point of view, rigor suggests the preservation of the system of philosophy, not only relative to cosmology or ontology, but *as* a tradition itself.

From this perspective, what Heidegger attacks when he tries to overcome Philosophy is not necessarily the monumental works of individual thinkers like Kant, Descartes, and Aristotle—all of whom are treated with obvious reverence, but the system that they, no doubt unwittingly in some cases, support and even defend. When viewing great historical thinkers from the point of view of texts unraveling, there is nothing to oppose, no tradition of metaphysics as presence to criticize. Opposition, in a strict logical sense, is only possible within the axioms of a systematized tradition. System suggests the fundamental manner in which decidable oppositions are produced, where "decidable opposition" suggests a clarity and completeness regarding the manner opposed (A & ~A) as well as a decision or judgment as to which is to be affirmed (T) and which negated (F) in the system.

However, this system does not exist in some ideal place beyond the philosophical texts that constitute it. The fact that Heidegger can read individual philosophers of the tradition and feel reverence for them does not mean that they, as individuals, are not implicated in the systematicity of philosophy. Rather, system penetrates the works of thinkers and becomes, perhaps, their goal or subject for inquiry. But the particularity of the text, always unravels this systematicity. What Heidegger sees when he reads Kant and Aristotle and others, are thinkers in tension with themselves. Thinkers equally in the grip of their own textuality and the traditional philosophical system: tradition on this reading is nothing other than the transcendental positing of the philosophical figures as axiomatic in the creation of a discipline.[2]

The unraveling of the text and the development of systematic forces along with the attempt to create binary opposition to the dynamic of unraveling are both steps on the way of deconstruction. Opposition is already a particular kind of relationship that arises in *opposition* to the multiple unraveling relations of the text. This double opposition is system itself; it is the absolute of system. System is always conservative or

---

[2]It seems to follow from this that all implication in tradition is a matter of force. To deconstruct tradition, however, is not simply to oppose it. This, as I will go on to describe shortly, only differs slightly from the question concerning the relation between deconstruction and metaphysics.

preservative to the extent that it seeks to stem the tide of unraveling. It does so by opposing force. It may be possible to speak of forces at work in the text, but these forces are more than just opposing forces. There are too many directions (the French *sens* means both direction and sense or meaning) for these impetuses to take to think of them exclusively in terms of a single opposition. Opposition comes out of the first resistant efforts of system. System is therefore essentially reactive insofar as it always responds to, while attempting to terminate, the unraveling of textuality. But it does this through the strategy of presenting itself as fundamental and active, the only true agency in existence. This semblance of system is system itself; the opposition of system to textuality arises out of the appearance of a ground where that ground is the representation of all firmness and stability. Stability understood as active is illusory to the extent that stability is always a reaction to the dynamic of the text. An analogy may be found in the ideals of classical conservatism. The political conservative wants stability but recognizes that it is only possible in politics if the political practitioners keep up with the changes that occur of necessity through the course of time. Conservatives do not advocate standing still, rather the illusion of standing still is the way conservatism reacts to the essential movement of history.[3] This reactive opposition is the rise of force as hostile to the differential otherness of movement. Reactive force gives rise, philosophically or metaphysically speaking, to the discipline of philosophy. When Heidegger opposes the metaphysics of presence, I take him to oppose philosophy as discipline, as force reactive to the deconstructive movement of Being: that is, to oppose tradition as system.

Given the importance this point attributes to the distrust of system, I can now show why this project has to begin where it does and cannot begin (as a "radical" deconstructor might claim) with a programmatic elaboration of deconstructive practices. Since I have had to address the relation to system at the beginning, perhaps it would have been better to show how Heidegger reads the philosophical tradition before doing anything else. Heidegger's thinking is so essentially in dialogue with this tradition that the reasons for his dismissal of it are fundamental to any project attempting to engage Heidegger and develop with him a notion of practice that is no longer guided by that tradition. But it is not tradition that Heidegger opposes. It is not history, either. What Heidegger takes issue with is traditional metaphysics, the history of philosophy. What

---

[3]Cf. *Conservatism in America* by Clinton Rossiter. Cambridge, MA: Harvard University Press, 1982.

gives tradition and history their problematic quality is philosophy, metaphysics as presence, or system: axiomatic or transcendental attempts to build sturdy structures in opposition to the dynamic textuality of the world. I therefore believe that it is possible to situate Heidegger's critique of history and tradition only after I have articulated his relation to system.

But how should I do this? Is it enough to merely describe it as I have done here in these last pages? Or do I have to demonstrate it, show or unconceal it in the process of working through it, in practicing it? The demonstration is not only a simple waving of the hand, but a manifold gesturing, not *a* demonstration, but many. And any demonstration requires that its own possibility be revealed along with it. The demonstration must have the power to show what it tries to show (otherwise it will not have shown it at all, but only weakly approximated it). So this task is doubly difficult and it would seem to require an initial section on method and then a section that demonstrates the overwhelming of system. For it cannot be demonstrated that Heidegger opposes system, since it is through system that opposition exists. "Overwhelming" system is more appropriate to Heidegger's project because the dynamic avoids opposition, instead it breaks through the systematic opposition of traditional metaphysical thinking. A section on method would be equally flawed in that method suggests the manner in which one applies or derives a system. The ground of method lies in principles that determine completely the decisions made in given circumstances. Overwhelming system, therefore, requires the overwhelming of method as well.

The important question for this demonstration, therefore, becomes how to proceed in overwhelming system without opposing system in a systematic fashion? I believe that I have taken my solution to this problem (and I mean to phrase this in systematic fashion for reasons that will become clear), although not found precisely in this manner in either Heidegger or Derrida, right from their texts. I attempt in the first two chapters to render Heidegger's later philosophy systematically. Thus it becomes clear that I solve the problem of this question by treating it systematically as a strategy. The *decision* to solve the problem is already the decision to work through system so as to overwhelm it. The solution as well as the question both arise from my being gripped by the same systematic philosophy that I seek to overwhelm. And overwhelming system amounts to little more than unraveling it to show that the textuality of Heidegger's thinking is already at work in the opposition as the opposed dynamic to which systematic philosophy reacts. The demonstration therefore takes place as a systematic reading/writing of Heidegger's later philosophy and what I demonstrate in the demonstration is nothing other than the de-monstration of system in favor of the many gestures of the demonstration. But I manage to do this without making system into a matter for discussion and thus reducing any systematicity out of it. Rather, I work through system as system, as the formal apparatus of thought instantiated through a reading of Heidegger. The demonstration, therefore, works as the work of textuality replacing method. A demonstration is nothing other than an unraveling and spinning of texts. The validity of the demonstration is that it works, where working does not only suggest the employment and deployment of instruments, but the dynamic unfolding of a textuality that demonstrates the movement of language. The text demonstrates the "Being of Language" by emerging as an example of language at work in the midst of a systematic unraveling.

In the context of expounding "deconstruction," I have heard some philosophers explain that the deconstructor wants to find a place for the other in theory whereas metaphysics does not. On this reading, we learn what is wrong with metaphysics (according to deconstruction) and what is right with the projects of thinkers like Heidegger and Derrida. Right, I say, because *there is* otherness. There is a problem with this handy little description of deconstruction, though: it is false. I say it is false and mean it, literally. It is false in the sense that any statement or assertion is false: it fails to refer, it isn't satisfiable, it won't work, etc. The other is everywhere in the history of metaphysics. In Plato's *Sophist,* otherness is a form called difference which is important because it differentiates one form from the others. All forms participate in the form of difference to the extent that they are different from the other forms. Likewise, all forms participate in the form of sameness in that, while different from the others, they are the same as themselves. Otherness has a place in metaphysics, not only in Plato but elsewhere. So, perhaps deconstruction's problem with metaphysics is not the absence of otherness, but its subordination to identity in metaphysical systems? Difference, albeit important, is still a form for Plato and thus the same as itself. Difference, like all the forms, participates in sameness, the principle of identity rules over its essence.

The form of difference is the same as itself and therefore cannot be difference, "pure and simple." This wresting of purity from difference, however, is not a contradiction, but insures difference. That is, only through the formal nature of difference can it differ from itself and be difference. But sameness is polluted in this way as well. The form of the same participates in difference in so far as it is different from the other forms. Therefore, sameness is not purely and simply the same either, but different. Although this seems to follow from Plato's theory of the forms in *Sophist,* it seems to be a kind of immanent critique of the theory he presents there. Plato says there is a form of difference and sameness. But because there are such forms and that every other form is participating in these forms as forms themselves (the same as themselves and different from the others), the possibility of a form as a pure and simple intelligible entity becomes questionable. The doctrine of forms suggests that the existence of forms is impossible.

Maybe, then, deconstruction attempts to show that metaphysics' attempt to subordinate otherness or difference to identity only succeeds by overlooking the dominion of difference over identity? But this would be only a first step in deconstruction: a criticism of metaphysics that operates within the confines of a metaphysical debate. This conception of difference that has emerged from the first step claims that difference appropriates the ground of metaphysics. "Difference dominates metaphysics" suggests that difference makes everything its own, claims everything that follows from it as its own, as essentially different, from itself, from everything else. Difference appears to be a universal condition or transcendental category. From this vantage point, it seems perfectly plausible to claim that metaphysics is desirable insofar as it wrests identity from difference. This process would be similar to the attempt to create order out of chaos and, by doing so, make the world inhabitable or rational. This movement would necessarily raise the question, "Is that good?" and thus place the inquirer inextricably within the parameters of metaphysics.

The second step of deconstruction would have to attempt a transformation of difference so as to remove it from this interplay with identity. The deconstructor does not wish only to raise difference above identity, but to transform both difference and identity so that they may no longer occur in opposition to each other. Opposition ceases and dissemination occurs. The opposition, according to Derrida and others, is always metaphysical, whereas the multiple transforms all oppositions. But the multiple is subject to opposition as well. Metaphysical thinking has always affirmed that the many opposes the one. The multiple that is in opposition to the one can never transform the metaphysical if this is the case. When Derrida and Heidegger rage against totality or totalization, they are attempting to transform the multiple, to display it in its openness and not as a totalizable quantity. Or so this hypothesis would have us believe.

But this second step, therefore, will not appear much different from the first step. At least not at first. Difference dominates identity, and then the many will rise up to dominate the one. On this reading of the project, however, deconstruction doesn't take place; this isn't even a second step, it is merely the first step taken again. How then can deconstruction take this second step and how can it be described? This is the question of deconstruction, the question that opens the deconstructive problematic. Following Heidegger, it will be enough for the moment to comprehend the meaning of the question and to formulate it thoughtfully. Solving the problem opened by the question will have to wait until the question is pos(ition)ed. This question is the question as to how deconstruction relates to metaphysics. My concern here is with the transformation of any and all metaphysical presuppositions into those of deconstruction; or, at the very least, into doctrinally neutral presuppositions. The question of the transformation is particularly difficult in that seeing metaphysics and deconstruction in opposition such that sameness and difference (or the one and the many) are opposites is to already place their relation in a metaphysical framework.

This leads us back in a circle. That metaphysical framework is the one that proclaims metaphysics as the champion of identity and deconstruction as the champion of difference. It would then be necessary to point out that Plato includes difference as one of the forms and that... well, you know the story.

But surely there must be something equally problematic about trying to think the relation of metaphysics and its other in a rigidly deconstructive fashion. Doesn't this set the standards in an equally biased manner? Only claims presenting deconstruction as a doctrine or theory can contain this question: the same sort of claims which present deconstruction as nothing other than this first step, this championing of difference. Any construction of deconstruction as something that is "nothing other than..." fails to grasp otherness. Deconstruction is not a doctrine, its transformation of metaphysics is not an alternative (to) theory. Rather deconstruction is the pos(ition)ing of the question of deconstruction, and that means that it is the attempt to raise the question concerning the relation of metaphysics and its other. And what is more, it attempts to do so in a such a way as to think not only of metaphysics, but of its other. [4]

---

[4]The reader will surely notice that the problem of the last few paragraphs has only been made worse in this formulation of the deconstructive position. In the context of an introduction, which supposedly summarizes what comes later, it is impossible to say what needs to be said concerning these matters. I only hope that this manner of phrasing it (namely, that deconstruction is *nothing other* than questioning concerning the relationship between

It becomes clear at this point why the first step is what it is. When deconstruction shows that something of the other escapes the metaphysical attempt to subsume it to the logic of metaphysics, it shows us that there is otherness (otherness in a sense that even escapes, to some extent, being the other *of* metaphysics). Deconstruction does not champion difference in this move, it merely shows that *there is* difference (as opposed to the enslaved negation of identity that metaphysics calls difference or otherness). Difference. Something that is not metaphysics, that is different from metaphysics and escapes its logic, something that positions itself differently, that differs from metaphysics, that is not dominated or determined or pre-determined by metaphysics, that is other to it.

The second step, therefore, takes place with the following components in view: a metaphysics that claims universality, an otherness that escapes universality (and therefore threatens it), and the hopes of raising a question as to the relation of the two. But why this last component? Why should anyone question the relation? Is there something revealing about any desire to uncover a relation? Maybe all questioning concerning the relation of a one and an other is metaphysical to the core. Wouldn't a more radical deconstruction merely leave the issue alone, show that *there is* difference and leave it at that? Don't worry about the relation, leave that to the metaphysicians. Derrida says that if you leave metaphysics to take care of itself, it will eventually take care of you.[5] For all his criticisms of Heidegger's conception of the History of Being, Derrida seems to be in agreement with him when he claims that the totalizing nature of metaphysics will not stop, will not leave its other to itself. Metaphysics will coerce from within and without anything that attempts isolation from the metaphysical. Separatists, he seems to claim, repeat the flaws of the demons from whom they are running. That is, if we naively leave metaphysics to itself, we not only risk being attacked externally by metaphysical movements, but we also risk importing the metaphysical into what we had hoped would be different. Derrida says

---

metaphysics and deconstruction), although ultimately a metaphysical formulation articulating a doctrinal understanding of deconstruction, will at least prove a significant heuristic device that will satisfy the reader until the matter is demonstrated in what comes.

[5]For example, in the last lines of "The Ends of Man" when describing the necessary double gesture of deconstruction. Cf. *Margins of Philosophy*. Translated by Alan Bass. Chicago: University of Chicago Press, 1982. Especially pages 134-136.

this is the important lesson learned in the first step of deconstruction: metaphysics will return to attempt to recolonize difference.[6]

The second step of the deconstructive project attempts to render metaphysics impotent in the same moment as it leaves metaphysics behind. Robbing metaphysics of its virility, castrating it (or perhaps only circumcising it as a symbolic warning), amounts to showing that *there is* difference and that there is nothing metaphysics can do about it. But not only that. It also amounts to showing that difference can and must continue to posit(ion) itself in such a way as to resist the sway of metaphysics. Therefore, this step attempts to question the relation of metaphysics to its other without describing some fact in the world regarding the way one thing and some other thing oppose each other. Rather, this step tries to create a relation, it relates to metaphysics in a manner that asserts the other within metaphysics and yet maintains its distance from metaphysics. Difference, on this account, does not seek to overcome metaphysics or dominate it, but to remain inside it as a pesky cipher that splits its purity (removes its foreskin) and remains other to it, outside and alien to its logic. Maintaining a difference from metaphysics and yet continuing to act upon it will not only make deconstruction into something other than the domination *of* difference, but it will force metaphysics into a constant and intense relationship with its other, it will force metaphysics to confront its other as an other, as different from it. This relation, created in deconstructive practice, will not only transform the other of metaphysics, but will transform metaphysics. Metaphysics will no longer be able to take its otherness for granted, it will have to

---

[6]It is fairly accurate to say that Derrida understands the role of metaphysics as roughly analogous to (and exemplified by) the imperialism of a conquering power (an army or a culture). It would be (and was) a terrible error for an isolated people, which becomes (or is) aware of the presence elsewhere of imperialist forces, to believe it can live an insulated life. It is the nature of the imperial to spread out into all the corners of a place, to root out every resource, and exploit them. Imperialism is an international movement and cannot be countered through anything other than an international movement (even if that international movement is carried out on a local level — these are merely battles in what imperialism has already dogmatically defined as a large scale war). This point is illustrated nicely by Theodore Adorno (Cf. *Minima Moralia*. Translated by E.F.N. Jephcot. New York: Verso, 1991. Especially Part One.), when he suggests that isolation from the system of civil society is the way in which "technology" incorporates the "individual" into that same system.

recognize the other, and any metaphysics that recognizes the otherness that confronts it as something other than metaphysical is no longer metaphysics—as Plato, or all the references in his footnote, conceived it.[7]

Here I have formulated a question that the following work requires almost four hundred pages to elaborate. Although it is possible that this asymmetry results from the wordiness of the project, it may be due to the broad strokes of this introductory and oversimplified version. My main concern for this discussion is that it shows the reader the necessity of beginning the project in the way that I have. That is, although I begin with Plato's principle of identity and Heidegger's emphasis on difference, I do not set them up in opposition to each other as metaphysics would. Or

---

[7]Notice that, in the terms given by Emmanuel Levinas in *Time and the Other* (translated by R.A. Cohen. Pittsburgh: Duquesne University Press, 1987.) and *Totality and Infinity* (translated by A. Lingis. Pittsburgh, PA: Duquesne University Press, 1969.), metaphysics saturated by this relationship to the other becomes ethics. Rather, first philosophy, engaged in otherness, becomes ethics. The "field of forces" "beyond being" is characterized by absolute alterity. It is the place where the one comes face to face with the Other (in death and time). Many questions are raised by the introduction of Levinas, only a few of which I can go into here. The absolute alterity of the Other has already been discussed at great length by Derrida in his "Violence and Metaphysics: An Essay on the Thought of Emmanuel Levinas" (in *Writing and Difference*. Translated by Alan Bass. Chicago: The University of Chicago Press, 1978.) where he suggests that this "Hebraism" of absolute alterity runs into as many problems as the "Helenism" of phenomenology's focus on light and presence. Derrida, of course, concludes that "Jewgreek is Greekjew. Extremes meet" (*WD*, 153, cited from Joyce's *Ulysses)*. The problem raised relative to absolute alterity is that the coming of the future (central to Levinas' erotic experience of the Other) can only come in the abyss of the absolute. How can the other remain absolute and yet approach in its otherness? Why wouldn't an absolutely other be completely impossible? Of course, Levinas says that it *is* impossible for just this reason, it is beyond the light of possibility. Despite its so-called impossibility, the Other is written in Levinas' book, Levinas describes or demonstrates the Other. Despite its absolute impossibility, something of the other remains, the other leaves a trace and, therefore, is not *absolutely* other.

Nevertheless, the inclination to place ethics "beyond being," to insert or inscribe the exteriority of the Other in the "there is" of "being," is the opening up of a dwelling place *(ethos)* in the heart of Being, at the "origin" of Being. This renewed placing of the ethical suggests that deconstruction (beginning with Heidegger's later works) is an ethical movement.

rather, I do not do so explicitly. The articulation of their opposition, identity and difference, is a problem that Heidegger and Derrida both attempted to pose, to make questionable. One makes nothing questionable by taking it for granted. Rather, the problem of the granting (the giving of the given) must be raised.

These first two chapters may therefore seem to serve the same function as the first two books of Spinoza's *Ethics,* insofar as they lay out the fundamental and most universal components of an ontology. Only by beginning in this fashion can the relation of textuality and metaphysics be thought in some way other than a metaphysical manner of opposition. Later in the work, this relation will be called the nearness or "ab-solute proXimity" of metaphysics and its deconstruction as textuality. It is only through this thinking of the relation between reactive forces and their being overwhelmed can anything like deconstructive practices be demonstrated. In fact, I want to claim that deconstructive practices are nothing else but attempts to overwhelm or unravel the reactive forces of system and totality. That is, deconstruction is always the providing of examples, the working through of texts, the demonstrating of positions.

At this point one might ask, why deconstruct? "It happens," Derrida said when asked a similar question.[8] If Derrida were speaking in German instead of English at the time, he may have said *"Es ereignet."* Any who want a more systematic answer to this question will be disappointed. I hold that emancipatory practices are mutually exclusive of method. Showing this is essential to the project that follows, but the first signs of the demonstration do not appear in the last chapters when I explicitly take up the matter of practice, but in the opening chapters where I demonstrate the nature of textuality as the overwhelming of system. Only through the demonstration of the unraveling of all systematicity can a pathway for deconstructive practice be opened.

The third, fourth, and fifth chapters try to bring unraveling and overwhelming textuality into the world of human beings. Strictly speaking, they do not extend the first two chapters, but replace them, supplement them, with human concern and practice: the history of philosophy as something other than a discipline, the human body as something other than an individuated subject, and, finally, practice as something other than methodologically committed action. It may still be possible for a reader to finish these chapters and ask, why should I choose

---

[8]During the question period after the paper Derrida delivered at the conference at Loyola University commemorating Heidegger's 100th birthday (September 21-24, 1989).

deconstructive practices over systematic ones? But of course, as I showed in my strategic question that orients the project, this question only pretends to suspend judgment. It is already a systematic question that has decided in advance which approach it prefers. It puts the questioner in the position of a reagent who tries to appear as an agent and thus lure opponents into debate on systematic grounds, to make others into opponents who must defend themselves. Instead, the attempt to overwhelm system should lead us to ask how is it possible that there is so much opposition to textuality? What impetus is being enacted through the reactive force of the metaphysical? No one should try to *solve* these problems, and although it is possible to do so, only an attempt to fit them into a systematic understanding could do so. By turning on metaphysics, its reactionary nature may be unconcealed and the rules of debate and opposition that prevent it from appearing disciplinary and coercive may be overwhelmed. This is not opposition to system since opposing system is already to lose to it.

The task of this book, therefore, is not to produce an alternative to metaphysical examples of ethics, since any such presentation of alternatives is nothing other than an opposition to the systematic in ethics which, of course, makes both ethics and any resistance to its traditional forms all too easy. Instead, I offer an attempt at repositioning the ethical relative to the systematic efforts of metaphysics. By bringing about a deconstruction of system in the midst of the projects of thinkers like Heidegger and Derrida, I am able to let the ethical emerge in the distance between metaphysics and deconstruction, to let it emerge as the questioning of the difference. Working in this way, I carry out a microcosmic examination of the ethico-metaphysical elements of human practice in chapters 4 and 5 for the sake of demonstrating the multiple positions articulated in the event of the overwhelming of system. And it is the manner in which this multiplicity emerges that ultimately makes ethics so much harder than it has been. Technically, then, this is not itself an example of "applied ethics" as some might hope to find, but an ethical treatise in the fashion of the theoretical, systematically deconstructed. But this dynamic, taking place full force in the last chapters, will be totally inadequate to the readers who have not come to challenge the advantage metaphysical thinking has had over human practices: that is, the reader who has not seen the extent to which textuality has overwhelmed metaphysics in the first three chapters.

It is characteristic of systems to express control, through universally applicable axioms, over any and every proposition governed by the system's rules. This application assigns all value, truth-value in the best-known cases of system, but normative value as well. Kant, for good reason, requires that the foundation of any ethics be guided by freedom. He goes on to posit the good will as a freely legislating rational being, but he never questions whether the production of normative legislation is consistent with the notion of freedom. It would be a mistake to see in this query an advocacy of what modern philosophers typically referred to as license whereby an individual's practice fails to respect the rationality of human beings in the expression of their wills. To pose license as preferable to free legislation would be to oppose the system of metaphysics within the rules laid down by that system. Kant understands both freedom and license as modifications of a will, either as rational or as driven by that natural force that he calls "inclination." The question here becomes one of deciding who, or what, is going to be in control of action: reason or nature. Kant frames both rationality and nature within a structure of domination. And, more specifically, a structure of domination dependent on something like a subjectivity that pre-determines the being of entities in the process of apperception. Such a structure is immediately identifiable as metaphysical not only because it recalls the writings of thinkers from Descartes to Kant, but because it displays a pre-structuring of entities that stabilizes them as knowable for an experiencing subject in opposition to more fluctuating and chaotic phenomena that might disrupt such objectivity.

The point here is that even Kant's great conception of freedom relies on a view of subjectivity and experience that regulates and normalizes the world in a way that determines objectivity. Now, as far as this goes, it isn't even an objection to Kant. But recall (as I will do with greater detail in chapter 3) Heidegger's claim that such determinations of entities are also necessarily responsible for framing the subject as that which always corresponds to those possible objects of experience. That is, the objectivity of entities determines the subject as an epistemological entity (determined as a subject). Making a human being into a subject is, therefore, inconsistent with letting persons be free; instead, it indicates their subjection to the authority or control of a systematic taxonomy, it stabilizes human identity for the sake of predictable clear and distinct knowledge which can engage in a predictable clear and distinct world of objects (i.e., the mathematical formulation of everything that exists which rises along with modern calculus is not just incidentally related to the modern concept of the mind as subject and the world as object).

The importance Kant placed on freedom is praiseworthy, but, I claim, it is a component of his ethical theory that overwhelms the metaphysical determinations of subjectivity and will. That is, if we take the kingdom of ends seriously along with its requisite notion of respect for the other, we cannot concomitantly accept subjectivity. In what follows, when I, following Heidegger and Derrida, reject reason, it is reason as a faculty of the subject that is first and foremost being rejected. But it cannot stop there, since this metaphysics of subjectivity contains within it adjacent notions that equally entangle theory. Rules, normative claims, and prescriptions all arise from the modern ethical structure and are implicit in its reactive forces.

Heidegger does not stop with these modern determinations, but proceeds to the technological. Resources and universal imposition characterize the age of technology instead of the objects and subjectivity of the early modern "Age of the World Picture." Here, everything that is exists as a natural resource or human resource or social resource for the sake of production and consumption. Furthermore, human beings become masters of the universe insofar as they fuel the engine of the great locomotive. The universality of universal imposition or *Gestell* attacks even the being of humanity until human resources become subdivided into consumer habits, labor power, unemployment statistics, etc. Making the machine of society run well is the goal of this epoch and its ethics is fittingly pragmatic or, worse, utilitarian. The harmony of the masses, whose numbers are growing, becomes a crucial social concern for which multiple apparatuses are deployed: schools, mass media, culture industry, sports, etc. As the population curve goes up, the need to control people increases and the main concerns of policy become human behavior. Ethics no longer concerns itself with the individual's will, but with their behavior.[9] Theoretically, this control aims at the "general welfare" or

---

[9]Hannah Arendt, in *The Human Condition* (Chicago: The University of Chicago Press, 1958. Pages 41-42.), writes: "It is the same conformism, the assumption that men behave and do not act with respect to each other, that lies at the root of the modern science of economics, whose birth coincided with the rise of society and which, together with its chief technical tool, statistics, became the social science par excellence. Economics—until the modern age a not too important part of ethics and politics and based on the assumption that men act with respect to their economic activities as they act in every other respect—could achieve a scientific character only when men had become social beings and unanimously followed certain patterns of behavior, so that those who did not keep the rules could be considered to be asocial or abnormal." Note that Adam Smith's "invisible hand," which is widely described as the first modern attempt at scientific economics, describes a social movement that is beyond the will or intention of any

"common interest"—Marxists fit into this category as well since they criticize the existence of hegemonic interests for the sake of a "common interest"—for the sake of which regulation and behavioral education is justifiable. Once again, it is for the good of the people and the promotion of freedom, equality, and whatever else you like that such regulations are enacted. Similar to the modern system, and in some ways much more shrewdly (like in the United States where people believe that "common interest" is equal to GNP), the regulations—in the ideal situation—emerge from the individuals' own rational self-interest which is intensely pragmatic. Rational self-control is for the sake of the good. According to the behavioral model, control is the best way to achieve efficiency. Harmony means goodness.

In both the modern and the technological epochs, ethical theories with systematic forms abound. Both attempt to guarantee morality through the control of behavior or action. But is it possible to have anything other than license without control? Is it possible to prevent anti-social behavior without normalization and regulation? If I answer these questions, I fall into a trap.

Now, this introduction is a failure unless readers understand it as a strategic attempt to facilitate their approach to the first chapters so as to let those first chapters facilitate their reading of the last chapters. It's called an introduction although it lacks all the "social" graces that word ought to suggest. It is rude, it does not leave the readers to work through the text for themselves. It is a blatant attempt to formulate a method or strategy for the reader to employ while reading this text, to construct the personality and experiences of a universal reader. To really ensure its success, however, I would have to write a preface that would tell the reader how to read the introduction. And then, perhaps, a colleague or friend of mine could write still another forward so as to tell the reader how to read the preface, and so on and on. It could go on like that forever.[10] I am making this gesture at this time because it is relevant to

------

individual agent in society. The rise of economy and the rise of social behavior (and the rise of capitalism) are simultaneous, and point beyond a metaphysics of the rational will of the subject. Heidegger, on the other hand, seems to suggest that the technological and the Modern are two distinct epochs of History. Yet, the historical evidence analyzed by Arendt suggests that the two "epochs" are occurring right alongside each other. Some of these matters will be addressed in the last three chapters of the project, but many of them point beyond the limits of the text.

[10]A friend, Bill Vaughan, has written in a recent letter to me: "The

the trap I have just encountered. The purpose of an introduction is to prepare the reader for the situations that follow. When the reader comes to certain difficult passages or becomes troubled as to what the point or import of what she has read so far is, she may recall some phrases from this introduction as guidelines for her understanding. Perhaps "values" work in the same way? We learn them growing up, or we come to reflect on them when we're older, during some quiet moments set aside for moral meditations. Perhaps we even spend a large portion of our lives thinking about what sorts of things matter to us and what would happen if we found ourselves in certain situations. Morality, therefore, would function like a system allowing the agent to apply individual laws to concrete particular instances. It seems that we are always being introduced to morality.

And so I will leave off with the entire project of introducing "this project" (Which one? Aren't there several at issue here?). Instead, I will present (make a gift of) this brief passage as an example of the project. After all, I began with a long discussion on the nature of the systematic and the way in which it deconstructs in the demonstrations of thinkers

---

requisite broad contextual believability of your project already compromises it. The frame-story, or history of the text, is theatre dependent. Contexting and prefacing the text is essentially a narrative act. An adventure story portraying the lofty beginnings, subsequent trials and happy destiny of the text. The biography of the text creates it as protagonist whose vicissitudes command a kind of sympathy, an acceptance of the desired interpretation....

"Rabalais' Gargantua reminds me of such an example of mediatory distancing from writing so as to preserve it somehow. There, the opening narrator "Alcofrybas Nasier" recounts the discovery of Gargantua's geneology, implying the presence of those who accept such fantastic stories of court genealogists. So you have the empirical author Rabalais, the implied author, the unreliable narrator, the cynical believers in court genealogies, the implied reader versed in counterfeit, and the empirical reader. Rabalais presents the act of composition as a process of counterfeit just as the counterfeiter presents fabrication as textual mediation."

And so it all amounts to so little. It's worth underlining the very common literary presence of an unreliable narrator: Proust, Dostoevsky, and Twain are all masters of this genre. They teach us to be suspicious of the story relayed through the eyes of a mediator. And so I am becoming suspicious of my own introduction. It has been months since I wrote those chapters that make up this project. I have done and read so much in the interim, I have read them over quickly, I have forgotten much, been oblivious often. I am no longer trustworthy. I cannot privilege my own reading of this text. Let this be a warning to the reader ready to be committed to my reading of the text.

such as Heidegger and Derrida and, perhaps, in this project as well. It is only fitting that such an "introduction" take on the disguise of the system to discuss the systematic. But then, changing shapes (wearing different masks), it is also important that I deconstruct in the course of this introduction not only the systematic, but the possibility of any kind of introduction at all. We arrive at the end, reader and writer, and we realize we haven't been where we thought we were and we haven't wound up where we thought we were destined to be. Lost, we retrace our steps, try to study the example to see what it exemplifies, the demonstration to see what it demonstrates. What we find is only one more example, one more demonstration. It could go on like that forever. Again, if we were fortunate (if fate bod(i)es well for us—reader and writer), we will have begun to like retracing our steps.

Chapter 1
This Weirdness That Takes Place

In this chapter,[1] three features of Heidegger's philosophy will be shown to belong together: *Ereignis*, unconcealment, and difference. The demonstration will be carried out through the process of coming to think the (pre)supposed meaning of this initial, somewhat bold, claim. A demonstration is not only a logical proof or an exhibiting of facts, it is also a public rally in support of a cause or the exemplification of a practical procedure or application. In the latter connotations of the word, the demonstration is a coming to pass of some state of affairs, it is an event. Here, and throughout, demonstrating the belonging together of these three crucial features of Heidegger's philosophy will amount to a slow unveiling of whatever is bold in this first claim. The chapter is divided into three parts resembling a march (since some demonstrations are marches, not rallies): the route begins with unconcealment and then proceeds in a spiraling motion, building support along the way—first from *Ereignis* and then from difference. These three parts belong together just as the components of the march belong together at each step along the way (while only slowly opening to view, since a demonstration is also a manifestation of feeling). But first, it is necessary to give a few remarks on the boldness of this belonging together.

What belongs together, for Heidegger, is *the Same*.[2] Here "the

---

[1]It may be noted that "weird" is "suggestive of or concerned with the supernatural; unearthly; eerie; uncanny" and "of an odd and inexplicable character; strange; fantastic" and, archaically, "fate; destiny" and "one's assigned lot or fortune; kismet." It derives from the middle English *werde*, *wirde* meaning "having power to control one's fate." The Indo-European root is *wer*—and connotes a relation to the German *werthan* for "to become or turn into" and the Old English *weorthan* for "to befall." Notice, finally, that both "this" and "that" function as demonstrative pronouns while "that" also functions as a relative pronoun.

[2] *Die Selbe* in German, which is not to be confused with *die Gleich*. Heidegger's word choice here, as I am about to show, is not accidental or incidental to the point he is frequently attempting to make with the word. In his truly awe-inspiring work on Heidegger, William J. Richardson makes this

Same" is used to interpret the Greek *to auto* which Heidegger traces back to Parmenides, fragment 3: "*To gar auto noein estin te kai einai,*" which Diels/Kranz translate as "thought and being are the same." The fragment is the earliest and most authentic articulation of the principle of identity (*ID*, 27), which "is considered the highest principle of thought" (*ID*, 23). Heidegger derives the principle in its modern form through an examination of Plato's use of it—in *Sophist*—to distinguish existence, motion, and rest. Plato has the stranger say that "they make three in all. And each one of them is different from the other two, and the same as itself" (254d, trans. Cornford in *Collected Dialogues)*. Heidegger thinks this "same as itself," this claim of self-identity which thus separates each of the three from the other two, formulates the principle A=A, the principle of identity which proclaims the self-sameness of everything that is. Before we go astray, believing that A=A means that A "equals" A, Heidegger reminds us that the "=" here must be understood as "is." The self-sameness of an entity is the claim that it is in fact itself, it is in its Being what it is. The principle of identity is really a principle of Being: "With this 'is', the principle tells us how every being is, namely: it itself is the same with itself. The principle of identity speaks of the Being of beings." (*ID*, 26)

This position is concluded with the claim that "to every being as such there belongs identity, the unity with itself" (*ID*, 26). Heidegger understands this to mean that for something to exist it must have an identity; rather, the existence of something is its identity. Suppose, for example, that Being were taken as the absolute subject underlying all else

---

point nicely when he writes in a footnote: "Two different correlates may be called "but one"[Selbe] by reason of the unity of their mutual belongingness (*Zusammengehören*), sc. the correlation which gathers them together. This implies, however, that the difference between the two be preserved, otherwise the duality, and therefore all *cor*relation, disappears. In fact, it is the difference *as difference* that gathers both correlates together.... when two members of a comparison are "same" [Gleiche], however, all difference between them disappears, so that only uniformity results." (*Heidegger: Through Phenomenology to Thought*, The Hague: Martinus Nijhoff, 1967. P. 588.) Although Richardson uses the word "same" to translate "*Gleiche*" and "one" for "*Selbe,*" it is clear to me that he and I are in complete agreement on this matter. I do, however, swap the two translations only because of the potentially dangerous quantitative connotations that the word "one" can have in English. That is, to be one suggests that the things that belong together are not two things, but one and thus joined in just the way Richardson says "*Selbe*" does *not* suggest they are joined—without a retained difference.

(substance), an unmoved mover of all things. It would be the case that anything that could possibly exist would be predicated of this primal Being, a determination of it. What it means, in that event, to be a predicate or a determination of Being would be the self-sameness of the entity; if some predicate of Being were not self-same, then it would, perhaps, be two or more predicates of Being or not a predicate at all.

It follows from this that the principle of identity would not only be the highest principle of thought, but the highest determination of Being. For all the various predicates or determinations of Being—the many—are brought into a unity within Being itself as itself.[3] All that is predicated of Being is and so, insofar as it is, it is the same, identical. Being is the One: "Listening not to me but to the *logos* it is wise to acknowledge that all is one" (Heraclitus fr. B50). Heidegger thinks this is the way that the principle of identity has been understood thus far: first Being as a unity and then any determination of it, each conceived in terms of a self-same unity in accordance with Being as the supreme model. Perhaps now we might attempt a first rereading of Parmenides' fragment: "Thought and being are the same (identical)." Heraclitus has provided the tools necessary for this rereading when he presents Being as the *logos* and, in fragment B50, uses the word *homologos,* translated as "wise to acknowledge." The principle of identity does not only speak through the *logos* to which Heraclitus asks us to listen, it also speaks through the manner of listening that he describes: *homologos* as a unity with the *logos*, being the same as the *logos*. Thought that is the same as the *logos* is wisely acknowledging that all is one: there is a double identity here. First the unity of the all in Being as *logos,* and second the unity of thought (the reader to whom Heraclitus is addressing himself) and Being. Heraclitus

---

[3]Plato, of course, would not agree with this. He says in the same section of *Sophist* that Sameness must be different from Being since "if they were *not* different then to say of two things that they both existed would be to say that they are both the same. In particular, we have agreed that *kinesis* (motion) and *stasis* (rest) both *exist*; but it would be different, and indeed absurd, to say that they are both *the same*." (J.L. Ackrill "Symploke Eidon" in Vlastos' *Plato.* Notre Dame, IN: Notre Dame University Press, 1978). Heidegger, however, is claiming that Being is the same as itself just as motion and rest are the same as themselves. Furthermore, all the predicates of Being are predicates of the selfsame Being, this is what makes the principle of identity the highest principle—even for someone like Plato who sees it as a characteristic of Being—as is evident in Plato's claim that despite the difference between motion and rest, they are both the same in so far as they both exist.

and Parmenides, in this instance at least, are saying the same about the same.

This way of understanding the fragment, Heidegger thinks, conceives the identity relation as "belonging together" with the emphasis on the "together." Heidegger proposes still another rereading Parmenides (and elsewhere he performs a similar reading of Heraclitus) in terms of a "belonging together" that places the emphasis on the "belonging." "Belonging together" is *zusammengehörigkeit*. Looking at this difference in emphasis requires a closer look at the figures of Heidegger's language, but most of my remarks at this point will have to be brief, offering only an indication of what will come later with more detail.

We have seen that the principle of identity speaks of the Being of beings. But even before the principle itself, identity has been speaking. Parmenides's formulation comes prior to the principle and yet it too speaks, saying: "thinking and Being belong together in the Same and by virtue of this Same." (*ID*, 27) We have seen already how some philosophers have understood this saying of identity (i.e., Plato). But such an understanding of the saying of identity is an understanding of the *zusammen:* all is one, the manifold *is* in its unity. Here, the *gehörigkeit* is placed in the background, submitted to the rule of togetherness where what *is* together must of course *belong* together (as though belonging were only an afterthought). Heidegger's reversal of this interpretation begins by suggesting that this traditional interpretation must be misdirected since it fails to listen. And since identity speaks to us, it is something that can only be understood by one who listens to it. When we do not hear what speaks to us, how can we be said to understand it?[4]

But why so much talk about hearing? Where is there any mention of hearing in Heidegger's language? "For the proposition really says: 'A *is*

---

[4]This merely describes Heidegger's question. We may be left wondering how such a "trick" with word usage can function as the single-most important reason for rejecting the entire tradition of metaphysics as the interpretation of the principle of identity as self-sameness or, what Derrida will later rename, presence. The critical question is how does language work? Although the question is suggested at this point, I'm not sure it is adequately formulated. The title of chapter 2 is "This Saying That Encircles." The demonstration there will be directed toward the event of language's movement. I believe we will then be able to see how "meaning" circulates so as to evoke thought. Where meaning evokes thought, language guides the understanding. Failing to listen, failing to belong to what speaks to you, is therefore a failure to think. The problem with metaphysics is that it fails to think. At least these are the highlights of what is to come.

A.' What do we hear? With this 'is,' the principle tells us how every being is, namely: it itself is the same with itself." (*ID*, 26); and "The claim of the identity of the object *speaks,* whether the sciences hear it or not, whether they throw to the winds what they have heard or let themselves be strongly affected by it. (*ID*, 27). What is said can be heard, or not heard, or even misheard; or it may fall upon the deaf ears of those "who never hear what you want." The principle of identity, identity itself, speaks, and in speaking it lays claim on whatever is: and then its claim can be listened to or it can be ignored. But the traditional view that I have rendered above certainly does not ignore the claim of identity. How could anyone possibly think that? The principle of identity is the highest principle of thought, the first determination of Being, it unites thought and Being: when we let the principle lay its claim, our thinking becomes true in the highest sense, it becomes identical with Being. Haven't these "metaphysicians" done just that?

Heidegger would answer with an unequivocal "no." By emphasizing the *zusammen,* the togetherness of a unity of the manifold, and by appending the *gehörigkeit* as an afterthought, the traditional metaphysicians have failed to hear (*Sie haben nicht gehört*). Heidegger says over and over and over again, from *Being and Time* until his death, that we speak because we hear and we hear because we belong to what speaks to us.[5] In this claim, the reader must hear the connection Heidegger is making between *hören* and *gehören:* "to hear" and "to belong." When Parmenides lets identity speak through his fragment, what it says must be listened to. In fact, it lays claim on all who hear and thus lets them hear only where the emphasis is on the "belonging" of the "belonging together" of Being and thinking. It is only when this hearing takes place that the claim has been made at all: the claim is itself the belonging together of listener and what speaks in a way that claims. Listen one more time: "thinking and Being *belong* together in the Same and by virtue of this Same."

No longer is identity, or sameness, a determination of Being; rather, the Same determines Being. The same, what the principle of identity claims, is prior to Being and thought. Being and thought are together, they belong together, in the Same. The Same is now a realm where Being and thinking, Being and man, come together. It is a place of belonging, where everything belongs (where even nothing belongs), and therefore, a place where everything comes together: togetherness is subsumed by belonging. The crucial step in this reversal is that whatever belongs together in the Same is held apart in its coming together. Thinking and

---

[5] Cf. The essay on Heraclitus' *Logos* in EGT, for example.

Being come together in the Same where they belong, but they do not lose themselves in each other. The emphasis on belonging requires that we maintain the distinction of what belongs: thinking together with Being is not the same as thinking belongs with Being. The first collapses the two into a self-same or simple unity, the second holds them apart as two separate elements.[6]

As the result of this discussion, however, any possible meaning of "the Same" eludes us. In the traditional interpretation, sameness was the way that all determination of Being came together under the unity of Being. But in Heidegger's rereading, sameness seems to hold the elements that come under it—or rather, within it—apart; and Being itself, what philosophers always thought as the most universal of concepts or principles, is said to be determined by "the Same." It seems that my effort to clear up the meaning of "belonging together" through a bold claim has created greater confusion than before I began. In the beginning, I claimed that three features of Heidegger's philosophy will be shown to belong together. I now see that this belonging together is the Same and that the claim might then read: three features of Heidegger's philosophy will be shown to be the Same. But "to be the Same" can't be the right formulation since Being comes after the Same and no one of the elements of the claim is Being. Recall that the issue for the Same is *Ereignis,* unconcealment, and difference; Being is not part of the picture and so I will not be able to demonstrate that these three elements *are* the Same. To take Being for granted in this way, to take it as a given instead of marching straight toward the meaning of this giving, is to repeat the mistakes of metaphysics, it is to fail to belong to the bold claim in such a way as to hear what it says.

Instead, I note that the Same is what speaks to those who make an effort to hear it, to belong to it. The bold claim refers to hearing and saying: three features of Heidegger's philosophy will be heard as saying the Same—the Same speaks to those who hear it *as Ereignis,* unconcealment, and difference. The "as" in this claim presents still

---

[6] The first of these positions may be called "Idealism" and, to the extent that traditional philosophy interprets Parmenides in this way, it is idealist. As is the case with Marx, therefore, I would claim that Heidegger thinks all traditional philosophy is "Idealist," including apparently non-idealist views like Hume's empiricism and Russell's logical atomism. The other position is, as I demonstrate in the last three chapters of the essay, the only formulation for a truly materialist philosophy—where "materialism" has a sense that I am going to derive from Derrida rather than Marx.

another problem: is it that the Same is *nothing other* than these three features of Heidegger's thought? This question goes astray in its substantialization of the Same and its desire to create an identity between this *thing* and the other *things* being discussed. But identity is precisely what is at issue here and the Same cannot *be* a thing, because it seems to be that which yields the possibility of things, it is what makes things possible (this follows of course from the fact that the Same determines Being which in turn determines all things that *are)*. The "as" cannot be understood as identity or existence.[7]

---

[7] This marks the beginning of what will become a running confrontation with a popular reading of "deconstruction" as it is practiced by both Heidegger and Derrida (although sometimes it is precisely on the basis of this issue that the two are distinguished). On this reading, Heidegger is thought as a transcendental philosopher who has supplemented the cognition of a subject with some kind of ontological form. The most compelling case in the literature on Heidegger is made by Reiner Schürmann in *Heidegger on Being and Acting: From Principles to Anarchy* (Bloomington: Indiana University Press, 1990). In some ways, the reading I have offered thus far of Heidegger's later writings suggests that I am going to present a transcendental account where the categories of Being are going to be developed as the dynamic at work in belonging-together. But, recalling the introduction, I hold that this "axiomatic" presentation of the "categories" is a strategic starting point which will ultimately incite the deconstruction of system as such, and with it the transcendentalism that I think Heidegger equates with traditional philosophy. First Philosophy, therefore, has always been about making a transcendental move with regard to the Being of whatever is said to exist (a position which Schürmann elaborates beautifully as conditions for agency within the epochs of metaphysics). But, additionally, I hold that Heidegger's response to this move is not one similar in kind with the tradition (i.e., presenting ontological categories that are the conditions of possibility of historical epochs that are themselves enabling conditions for determining entities within that age of history), but instead undermines the basis for making the move at all: that is, the formal conditions of all transcendental formalism. My question for the transcendental reader, therefore, is—following Schürmann—how can there be anarchy (absence of first principles, and hence, first philosophy) if there are categories which ultimately function as principles describing the emergence of the metaphysical at various points in history? Or, more to the point, how can Heidegger's position be explained without making use of the distinction from transcendental philosophy between form and matter, a distinction which Heidegger explicitly rejects? At various points throughout the text I will come back to this point, since it seems that there have been attempts to answer this question, but I have not gone far enough in my project to grant them fair hearing at this time.

But what other way could anyone understand the word "as"? "As" always means *as* something that is, to be *as* something, to be determinate. It seems that I cannot get the bold claim off the ground, I can't even state it as a claim. Once again as a reminder: three features of Heidegger's philosophy will be heard as saying the Same; the Same speaks to those who hear it *as Ereignis,* unconcealment, and difference. The problem is that the "as" follows all hearing, we hear as... Always. The only way to avoid the "as" is to let the matter speak. The claim then becomes: *Ereignis,* unconcealment, and difference say the Same; the Same says *Ereignis,* unconcealment, and difference. These two formulations say the Same. And now a bold claim has been stated.

It is a bold claim not only because it aims at the belonging together of these three features, but because it claims that it is the claim *of* those three features themselves, the claim *of* the Same. But there is a danger here, for it seems that—in stating the bold claim—I have raised suspicions about that same "hearing" that interjects the "as" when I pointed to the problems that occur in all hearing as... After all, it was the tradition's failure to hear that rested at the bottom of Heidegger's criticism. It seems that those who listen must hear what the Same says, and yet what they do hear is heard as the Same, and so it is not the Same that speaks prior to determinate Being, but instead the Same that has come to be determinate. Perhaps this is why Heidegger often refers to a mystery that withdraws in every metaphysical account, the mystery that yields whatever is however it is? Or perhaps it is no mystery at all, but only the result of a reductio that suggests Heidegger's thinking is nonsense? Or perhaps there is some third possibility: I have come upon a wall in thought because some element of it has been taken for granted as given, when no such granting has been made.

From here I will go on to examine the three features of the bold claim, making some effort at setting each of them apart in their distinctness so as to see how they belong together in and by virtue of the Same. This abstraction should demonstrate as much about the individual elements of the claim as about the nature of their belonging together. These two aspects of the demonstration, the setting apart and bringing together of belonging, will be performed hand in hand. At the end of the chapter, therefore, the belonging together of the three features will have been demonstrated and the questions that plague this bold claim will be advanced—which is not to say that they will be solved, although with any luck they shall have gained a new direction.

Unconcealment/Aletheia

Aletheia is a goddess and Parmenides's poem begins with her: first with the journey toward her, guided by her handmaidens, and then she speaks. Aletheia, like the Same, speaks. She is kind and walks hand in hand with the journeyer; there is no threat from her. She speaks only of what is and warns of the nether path, the pathway of seeming and deceit. She is truth and good, pure and radiant—she comes to Parmenides from a gateway opening into the light of the sun. Her words welcome and she praises those who seek her, understanding better than anyone that the path to her abode is not a frequently traveled way (fr. 1). Aletheia is at the end of the path; she is the aim of the journey called inquiry, and she speaks freely to any—or at least to the traveler in the poem, who is presumably no different from any of the others who have made the same journey— who manage to reach her, revealing all her secrets, telling all that is, warning of all that is not.

For a moment it may be useful to participate in these adolescent fantasies that seem to have guided the philosophical tradition from Parmenides to Nietzsche: if Heidegger's *aletheia* were a goddess, what would she be like?

First, her name would be hyphenated, would be separated within itself: *A-letheia*. She would be a goddess with a vagina, a "sex which is not one."[8] *A-letheia* always moves in a twofold manner and her name must appropriate that feature: "*Lanthanein* means to be concealed; a- is the privative, so *a-letheuein* is equivalent to: to pluck something out of its concealment, to make manifest or reveal." (*BP*, 215) This goddess is

---

[8]Cf. Luce Irigaray "This Sex Which is not One" (in This Sex Which is Not One. Ithaca, NY: Cornell University Press, 1985. P. 26): "In addition, this sex organ which offers nothing to the view has no distinctive form of its own. Although woman finds pleasure precisely in this incompleteness of the form of her sex organ, which is why it retouches itself indefinitely, her pleasure is denied by a civilization that privileges phallomorphism. The value accorded to the only definable form excludes the form involved in female autoeroticism. The one of form, the individual sex, proper name, literal meaning-supersedes, by spreading apart and dividing, this touching of at least two (lips) which keeps woman in contact with herself, although it would be impossible to distinguish exactly what 'parts' are touching each other." Parmenides unitary and unmoving Aletheia may be said to resemble the phallus, whereas Heidegger's resembles these parting lips that constantly touch each other. Irigaray deserves more attention on these matters, but this will have to be deferred.

called *A-letheia* because she is tricky, not the forthright friend to the inquirer that Parmenides knew. Wily and deceptive (just like a woman no doubt),[9] she never gives or tells all, always holds something back—concealment is just as much a part of her as is revelation. In fact, this goddess *A-letheia* can only give because she holds back, she is only able to give away secrets because she has secrets to tell: "concealment preserves what is most proper to *aletheia* as its own" and "is older than every openedness of this or that being" (*BW*, 132). And yet she never gives everything away. She always keeps a little something for herself.[10]

Second, this goddess is not the type to wait at home for the arrival of the traveler; instead, she is a traveler herself out on the road among the lovers of wisdom.[11] This is not to say that she is a traveling companion,

---

[9]Not that it matters, but I do not mean to be misogynistic here, although no doubt I am. I think this is a result of engaging in this very type of thought experiment. Making truth out to be a woman no doubt helps us to understand truth in a more concrete form, but it also essentializes "woman" by chaining her to a concept. I am performing this experiment only to engage a tradition filled with experiments such as this.

[10]Both Heidegger and Derrida see complete revelation as quintessentially metaphysical (that is, metaphysics as first philosophy seeks the origin from which the Being of what is can be completely and exhaustively known). In matters of truth, when *A-letheia* does not give everything over to presence (complete revelation ontologically or epistemologically speaking), she is—in some sense—untruth.

[11]This essential element of Heidegger's *a-letheia* is most clearly elucidated in the line: "the essence of truth is the truth of essence" from "On the Essence of Truth" in BW. At this stage of his thought, 1931, Heidegger has not problematized the use of the word "truth" to translate *a-letheia*. Later, he will do so and settle, as an alternative, on unconcealedness. It is my position that Heidegger would make the same claim as in "On the Essence of Truth" with the substituted interpretation of the Greek *aletheia*. This will be demonstrated more fully in what follows. For now, it should be registered that the claim that the essence of *aletheia* is the *aletheia* of essence, where the second essence takes on a verbal form (as opposed to the nominal form of the first part of the phrase), suggests that *aletheia* in its essence is dynamic; and what's more, that it is *the* dynamic par excellence.

This may also be a good time to mention Joseph Kockelmans's book *On the Truth of Being* (Bloomington: Indiana University Press, 1984.) which was instrumental in helping me to see the central role truth as *aletheia* plays in the writing and thinking of the later Heidegger. Kockelmans' suggests, however,

she is not likely to be found hand in hand with any of the inquirers—even the most skilled, even those on the untrodden paths. Finding her, in her constant movement, is not as easy as Parmenides thinks (and he thinks it's very hard!). It is not simply directing oneself toward the light—as though a moth could know truth—for *A-letheia* loves shadows, and finds them even at high noon. The best a Heideggerian traveler could hope for is a sort of respectful distrust of the goddess whose movement cuts across all elements of existence, casting a shadow and shedding light in every direction.

Enough of this, Heidegger did not think *A-letheia* as a goddess, not even as a woman. *A-letheia* is not a proper name for the goddess ruling the boyish passions of Western philosophy, it is only *a-letheia,* unconcealment.[12] Anthropomorphizing truth bridges its distance from metaphysics to its other. The discussion will begin by following the two elements illustrated above: 1) the twofold nature of *a-letheia,* and 2) the dynamic nature of *a-letheia.*

1. The hyphenated word keeps open the root, *lethe,* which often gets passed over in the contemporary understanding of the Greek *aletheia,* where truth is thought in terms of what is revealed, what is as it is in its being revealed, present to us for inspection, for discussion and description. This is to be expected, for what is more natural than to overlook *lethe,* to look past concealment toward what is manifest? *Lethe* is concealment and concealment in the sense of hiding. What hides is concealed from view, it hides itself to conceal itself from the view of those who see. In this hiding, not only is something hidden, but the hiding itself is hidden. It is not that the missing things are lost, are concealed to our view as we look for them, hoping to reveal them for our own use—where

---

that his book is an attempt at offering a "systematic" account of the later Heidegger and that is no doubt what he has delivered. Yet, by placing unconcealedness at the center of this system, he confused me as deeply as he informed me, since he gives an account of truth that did not seem to permit of the systematic. This leaves me wanting to say, perhaps in a way that Kockelmans would be unhappy with, that he and I are in complete agreement with the exception that I have attempted to draw out some further consequences of his project (i.e., the deconstructive of system) which ultimately renders it erroneous while retaining it as an essential first step in the project aimed at understanding the later Heidegger.

[12]This, perhaps, should not be said so quickly and with so little attention as it directly relates to remarks made by Derrida in *Spurs*. It will be handled more completely later in a more suitable context i.e., after more has been said about Heidegger's *a-letheia.*

are those papers? I can't find my pen. We do not even miss what is truly concealed, we don't even think about it, the very fact that it is concealed is hidden from our view. Heidegger's understanding of *lethe,* concealment, is as a double concealment; not only does it hide something from our view, but it hides itself, it hides the fact that it is hiding. Heidegger calls this the mystery, "not a particular mystery regarding this or that, but rather the one mystery—that mystery (the concealing of what is concealed) which generally holds sway as such throughout man's Dasein." (*BW*, 132-3, translation altered)

This concealment, *lethe,* is not merely an accidental feature of *a-letheia;* rather, "it is older than every openedness of this or that being. It is older than letting-be itself which in disclosing already holds concealed and comports itself toward concealing." (*BW*, 132) Any revelation, any manifestation, is revealed out of concealment—concealment is the source of all that is revealed. Although I have been writing all along about concealment, I find that I have always been thinking about concealment in relation to a possible revelation. The concealed and the concealment of it, the mystery, are only concealed because it is possible for there to be revelation. We cannot think of pure concealment; although hiding is the precondition for being found, it is meaningless to hide unless it is possible for someone to find you. If hiding, concealing oneself, is not relative to being found, then it isn't hiding at all—it's merely crouching in a corner behind some shelves, waiting in the bushes, standing silently in the dark.

It might be thought that the understanding of concealment as historically concealed in the interpretation of the Greek *aletheia* is a thinking of pure concealment. But that would be incorrect. When the concealment is concealed, something else is revealed in its place. We do not think the concealment of concealing because we are too busy with what has been revealed out of concealment. When I am busy with a project, the world (as world) within which I am carrying out my project is concealed. This means that the context where entities are encountered is concealed in favor of the few beings with which I am involved in my project. Furthermore, the concealment of the world is also concealed—I do not miss the world, I haven't lost it, it's the furthest thing from my thoughts since I am concerned primarily with my project (the entities revealed to me). Nevertheless, this concealment of the concealed world is not pure, since the world is—in a sense—revealed to me. That is, I am in it, the beings of my project are within the world.[13] The entities revealed,

---

[13]This is only meant as an example. So far concealment is being

have been revealed out of concealment, even when that concealment is itself concealed. This "out of," however, marks a persistent trait of what happens in unconcealment. An entity emerges out of concealment, but concealedness persists in the Being of the entity as it endures in unconcealment. An unconcealed entity continues to exist in unconcealedness and so concealment continues to inhabit the entity in its existence. And so we already begin to see the dismantling of presence in the entity and, therefore, the entity (itself).

In addition to the coupling of all concealedness with a revelation, we note that even when thinking turns itself toward concealment, it cannot think pure concealment (i.e., concealedness itself). Thought's turning toward concealment already reveals concealedness. Concealment ceases to be hidden as concealment when thought turns toward it. But this does not mean that it is revelation, it is the revealing of concealment. The act retains the "as such" of both concealing and revealing and thus erases any possibility of the "as such." This turning toward concealedness, injects it with revealedness so as to dismantle the presence of either term in the opposition revealing/concealing. Likewise, all concern for the revealed entities in the world is fraught with concealment. This dismantling of the "as such" in both revealing and concealing is a turning (or reversing) of the principle of identity which speaks in every "as such."

Heidegger discusses the interconnectedness of revealing and concealing most thoroughly in his essay on Heraclitus's fragment B16 which Diels and Kranz translate as "How can one hide himself before that which never sets [*To me dunon pote pus an tis lathoi*]." He writes:

> Heraclitus thinks the never-setting. In Greek thinking, this is the never-going-into-concealment. In what domain, therefore, does the saying of the fragment take place? According to its sense, it speaks of concealment—i.e., it speaks of never going into concealment. At the same time,

---

discussed abstractly. I am not, in this example, committing myself to any necessary connection of the notion of concealment and revelation to Heidegger's notion of world, project, and entities in *Being and Time*. Furthermore, I don't even want to commit myself to connecting revealing-concealing to thinking—at least not yet. Thinking, at this point, merely functions as a vehicle for making the abstract discussion a little more concrete. For a detailed discussion of the relation between unconcealedness in BT and the later works, see Kockelmans' book (op cit.). At the very least, he gives a thorough account of the problems that must be considered in attempting to draw an analogy between early and late notions of truth as *aletheia*.

> the saying directly signifies the always-enduring rising, the
> ever and always-enduring disclosure. The phrase *to me
> dunon pote,* the not setting ever, means both revealing and
> concealing—not as two different occurrences merely
> jammed together, but as one and the Same. (*EGT*, 112-3)

A-letheia is the belonging together of revealing and concealing; they
are the Same. There is no pure revealing or pure concealing; the two
always happen together, they *belong* together, it is appropriate that they
should happen together. Still, this proclamation of sameness causes some
problems: Plato has taught that motion and rest both exist without being
the same as each other (for they are opposites), which proves that
sameness and Being are not the same in the sense of being identical. Plato
is of course making a plea for difference; he wants to say that difference
is too (as the being of negation, of what formally *is* not). If Being is
sameness, singularity, then there cannot be many things—all plurality
would be illusion, the way of seeming. Heidegger must not be following
the same laws of logic that Plato did, since he wants to preserve plurality
while claiming that all that is, is brought together under the determination
of Being.

A full discussion of this difficulty would still be premature, but some
things can be said now. Belonging together is the way Heidegger
understands the Same. Only what is different can belong together, only
what is spanned by a distance—near or far—can be side by side.
Heidegger would disagree with Plato, he would not think it absurd to say
that motion and rest are the same. Heidegger's notion of the Same is
permeated by difference, it requires it. For the moment, we might take
note of the difficulty that this transcends in Plato. Once again, for Plato,
both identity and difference exist although they are not identical (they are
the Same); although they are both characteristics of one and the same
Being. Or maybe they aren't? It is really a mystery whether identity and
difference are traits of the same or of different beings—the question itself
doesn't make any sense. What could Plato possibly mean when he says
that both difference and identity exist? What does existence mean in this
case? Heidegger, in a sense, has been motivated by this difficulty (recall
that the opening of *Being and Time* is a quotation from *Sophist*). Here we
note that his solution comes through positing Being as determined by
identity and difference in their *belonging* together. He says later in the
essay on Heraclitus, while discussing fragment 123 ("Nature loves to
hide" [Diels and Kranz], "*Physis kruptesthai philei* "): "And so *physis* and
kruptesthai are not separated from each other, but mutually inclined

toward each other. They are the Same. In such an inclination each first bestows upon the other its proper nature." (*EGT*, 114) For two elements to be the Same they must form a relation, a mutual inclination. This mutual inclination, however, is not the result of having been placed alongside the two, as if the relation were only accidentally incurred, but it arises out of a reciprocal bestowing, a giving of the one to the other; a giving that is not merely a gift to be received or rejected according to custom, but a giving of what the other is in itself. Revealing is revealing only because concealing gives its revealing nature to it and naturally the gift is returned—although this is an awkward way of putting this since it is the mutual bestowing that precedes either of the elements.[14]

Heidegger translates this fragment as "Rising (out of self-concealment) bestows favor upon self-concealing." (*EGT*, 114) Notice that *physis* is understood as revealing while *kruptesthai* is understood as self-concealing; but I am going to put off discussion of this for a moment in favor of the bestowing of *philei* understood as "belonging together." Two people in love are said to belong together, and love is often referred to as a gift. The gift of love enjoyed by two people who belong together results in an intimacy unrivaled by any other, any stranger to the relation. The nearness of lovers in intimacy, in sharing a smile or a caress, is an expression of their belonging together; it is their loving relationship. Love speaks of nearness, of being together, of belonging. Heidegger writes: "But Heraclitus is thinking both in closest proximity. Indeed their nearness is explicitly mentioned. Nearness is defined by *philei*. Self-revealing loves self-concealing." (*EGT*, 113) Lovers become lovers when they fall in love and love grows out of a developed intimacy: perhaps a few awkward dates at first, conversations filled with an uncertainty as to how much to say. The intimacy enables the love which in turn gives rise to the lovers, the lovers appropriate their lives as lovers, as partners, out of the intimacy that brings them near to each other.[15]

---

[14]As Derrida points out in *Given Time: I. Counterfeit Money* (Chicago, IL: The University of Chicago Press, 1992), it doesn't make sense to speak about the exchange of gifts. Gifts are those donations which mark the extreme limits of economical exchange. He rightly points out that this bestowing of the two in their relation forces us to ask the question of what "giving" means (giving a meaning to "meaning"?). I will examine this more thoroughly later in this chapter. For the moment, I will only point out this difficulty of giving a definition: I must presuppose what I hope to prove—that there is giving at all.

[15]This example doesn't work in perfect analogy since in the case of two people in love there are two persons who precede the intimacy, who become

This talk of revealing and concealing being proper to each other, of their being near to each other, and of their determining each other will, soon, come to recall *Ereignis*. Likewise, I have shown that difference is essential to this understanding of revealing and concealing in their sameness. We now get a glimpse at what belonging together means in the larger context of this discussion: *Ereignis* and difference belong together with unconcealment, because one cannot venture very far into the meaning of unconcealment without discovering *Ereignis* and difference. Again, a full discussion would be altogether premature here; still another deferral.

Returning to the other elements of fragment 123, Heidegger emphasizes that the relation is not to be understood in terms of an alternating dominance, where sometimes *physis* and sometimes *kruptesthai* holds sway. The two belong together. *Physis* is not "essence" as frequently thought, where essence is the German *das Wesen,* the whatness or quiddity of things. Heidegger thinks *physis* as *wesen*, a verb meaning "dynamic unfolding."

> Rising as such is already inclined toward self-closing. The former is concealed in the latter. *Kruptesthai* is, as self-concealing, not a mere self-closing but a sheltering in which the essential possibility of rising is preserved—to which rising as such belongs. Self-concealing guarantees self-revealing its dynamic unfolding [*wesen*]. In self-concealing, inversely, what reigns is the restraint of the inclination to self-revealing. (*EGT*, 114; translation modified)

Most of this citation is repetition, further support of the belonging together of revealing and concealing. What is new in this repetition is the equating of *physis* with revealing and *kruptesthai* with concealing and the thinking of *physis* not as essence or nature but as dynamic unfolding. Recall the quotation from the beginning of the discussion on unconcealment: "the essence of truth is the truth of essence" (*BW*, 140). This now reads as "the whatness of truth is the truth of dynamic unfolding" where the second use of the word "essence" is now properly understood as the verbal sense of *wesen* which interprets the Greek *physis.*

---

intimate; whereas in Heidegger's discussion, it is the intimacy that first gives rise to the two intimates. Although, one might narrow the gap between example and thought by mentioning that the identity of the persons who have become intimate is redefined in the course of loving—that is, they become "lovers" only through their relationship.

In turn, *physis,* thought in this way, is the same as *to me dunon pote* of fragment 16—the "not ever setting." And, should anyone be tempted to think that Heidegger has defined unconcealment in terms of *physis* alone in the essay "On the Essence of Truth," he adds that "[f]or Greek thinking, *kruptesthai,* though unuttered, is said in *to me dunon pote,* and *physis* is thereby named in its full character, which is governed by the *philia* between revealing and self-concealing." (*EGT,* 114)

Without contriving it, we have entered into the place where the first element of unconcealment transforms itself into the second: the dynamic nature of unconcealment. The twofold nature of unconcealment as revealing and concealing is a twofold movement, rising out of self-concealment.

2. *Physis,* this dynamic unfolding, has been examined previously by Heidegger so as to focus some of the discussion concerning "truth" in "The Origin of the Work of Art." Here too he stresses the twofold nature of *physis* and how the movement of unconcealment is included here in both its moments:

> The Greeks early called this emerging and rising in itself and in all things *physis.* It clears and illuminates, also, that on which and in which man bases his dwelling. We call this ground the *earth.* What this word says is not to be associated with the idea of a mass of matter deposited somewhere, or with the merely astronomical idea of a planet. Earth is that whence the arising brings back and shelters everything that arises without violation. In the things that arise, earth is present as the sheltering agent. (*PLT,* 42)

Arising out of self-concealment is illuminating, the shining of a light out of the darkness; a clearing is opened up by the rising of *physis.* Clearing here recalls a place in the forest where the trees have been removed. The sun, blocked by the towering splendor of the surrounding forest, has suddenly been given over to itself, to its shining; it floods the clearing, filling it with its light made all the brighter in comparison to the dark, cool forest ground spreading in every direction beyond the perimeter of the clearing. What's more, the clearing, a place where the light shines, is also earth. It is a place of cleared earth, the light of the sun shines upon the earth although the earth is revealed only because the ground has been cleared for it. In other words, the earth is revealed in the clearing but it is revealed as the concealing, sheltering ground of the clearing.[16]

---

[16]Cf. TB 65 where Heidegger writes: "The forest clearing (opening) is

The opened part of the clearing, what is set upon the earth, is the world and there is no down to earth way of describing this world:

> It is the temple-work that first fits together and at the same time gathers around itself the unity of those paths and relations in which birth and death, disaster and blessing, victory and disgrace, endurance and decline acquire the shape of destiny for human being. The all-governing expanse of this open relational context is the world of this historical people. (*PLT*, 42)

Heidegger is examining unconcealment in terms of artworks. His claim is that art is the setting to work of "truth" or unconcealment. (*PLT*, 39) In the temple of the Greeks, the world of the Greek people is unconcealed. Where here their world is the "open relational context" that rules their existence together in history.

In *Being and Time,* the world was conceived as "significance," meaning "the relational totality" of "the relational character which these relationships of assigning [for the sake of which, in order to, towards this, in which, and with which] possess." (*BT*, 120) These relations were understood along with Dasein's comportments (where comportment is the German *verhalten* related as the verb form of the German noun *Verhaltniss,* which can be translated as "relation"), where projects and equipment are at issue. That is, first and foremost, Dasein is its projects, Dasein's Being-in-the-world is having projects. But all this is already to speak incorrectly since we are making it sound as if there are entities called tools and events that exist and can be called projects when they enter into specific relations. A project evolves *out of* certain kinds of

---

experienced in contrast to dense forest, called 'density'(Dickung) in older language. This substantive 'opening' goes back to the verb 'to open'. The adjective *licht* 'open' is the same word as 'light'. To open something means: To make something light, free and open, e.g., to make the forest free of trees at one place. The openness thus originating is the clearing. What is light in the sense of being free and open has nothing in common with the adjective 'light', meaning 'bright' — neither linguistically nor factually. This is to be observed for the difference between openness and light. Still, it is possible that a factual relation between the two exists. Light can stream into the clearing, into its openness, and let brightness play with darkness in it. But light never first creates openness. Rather, light presupposes openness. However, the clearing, the opening, is not only free for brightness and darkness, but also for resonance and echo, for sounding and diminishing of sound. The clearing is the open for everything that is present and absent."

relationships. That for the sake of which all things are carried out, that for which all comportment is meant to assist, is called Dasein. Dasein relates with such and such for the sake of itself, comportment projects itself so that something may be done for Dasein. Tools are used in order to accomplish this and these tools are involved *in* environments *with* other tools. Again, the world is nothing other than these relationships and it is these relations, set into motion by their constant signification of each other that constitutes "objects" and "subjects." Dasein is not a subject, it is a relation, so too the world is not an object but a totality of relationships.

In Heidegger's later work, the holism or totalization of worldly relations falls by the wayside for the sake of open-endedness where the relations go on and on without *telos,* without organizing principle. This marks a significant turn in Heidegger's project, as the opening of the earlier totality insures the move away from transcendental conditions of the world (organizing features of the totality) and toward a concealment that constantly defers the meaningfulness of the world. The open region is the place (the Da of Dasein perhaps) where all these relationships, all the historically determined relationships of a people, come to pass or happen. And in fact, it is the coming to pass of these relationships in a certain historical fashion that *is* the very Being of that historical people which Heidegger is describing. This coming to pass of relationships determining the people is what Heidegger calls the destiny of that people.[17] Here destiny, *schicken,* is sending into openness, the manifestation through bestowal or giving of the open region, of lightening. The Greek world is the world where certain kinds of relationships come to pass, where people build temples for the goddess Athena, where rich adolescents lounge in the Mediterranean sunshine and talk philosophy with wiser, older men, while their slaves toil in the privacy of their homes laboring under the strain of heavy marble, building temples for the gods perhaps. And the Roman world differed from the Greek world not *because* the relationships were different, but the differences in the relationships *are* the difference between the Roman and Greek worlds.

"World is the ever-nonobjective to which we are subject as long as the paths of birth and death, blessing and curse keep us transported into Being." (*PLT*, 44) As long as Dasein is alive, as long as it is Da-sein, it is in the world comporting itself, entering into relations that make it be Dasein; better yet, Dasein emerges out of those very relationships. And

---

[17]Coming-to-pass is the way that many translators have rendered *ereignen*—the verb form of *Ereignis.* This should be kept in mind, although it will not be discussed in detail until later in the chapter.

here, once again, Heidegger understands these relationships not only as relations but as pathways, pathways stretching between..., a way from here to there that makes it possible for the traveler to arrive at a destination (the location of which is no doubt open-ended).

Physis emerges out of self-concealment as earth and world where earth is the ground upon which the relationships of the world are fostered. It is tempting to link the world with revealing and the earth with concealing, but Heidegger warns against it. "By contrast the temple-work, in setting up a world, does not cause the material [the earth] to disappear, but rather causes it to come forth for the very first time and to come into the Open of the work's world." (*PLT*, 46). The sheltering, concealing of the earth is not the concealing half of the movement of unconcealment. Rather, the earth presses forward into the clearing when the world is opened up; and, in fact, the earth is revealed as earth for the first time in the light of the clearing. Within the forest, the earth is covered over with leaves and debris fallen from the trees; it is concealed as earth just as the light of the world is concealed by the trees. The earth, in fact, shelters the world. The world comes forth so as to be set back into the earth and the earth comes forth so that it may shelter the world.

In the matter of artworks, Heidegger describes earth as the "the massiveness and heaviness of stone," "the firmness and pliancy of wood," "the hardness and luster of metal," "the lighting and darkening of color," "the clang of tone," and "the naming power of the word." (*PLT*, 46) The temple is built out of stone, the cottage out of wood, the saber out of metal, the ritual paint has a hue, the hymn sounds forth, and the language is written with ink. The marble of the temple is concealed when the worldliness of the temple opens up. When I walk into it and feel its grandeur, absorb the life of the people who worship there, I am oblivious to the stone as such that has been carved into walls and ceilings. A better example might be in the paint used on the finished canvas of some master—the material quality of the paint withdraws in favor of the face that is *there*. And yet the worldliness of the face in that portrait rests on the paint brushed across the canvas stretched out on wood. Heidegger writes: "The work moves the earth itself into the Open of a world and keeps it there. *The work lets the earth be an earth*." (*PLT*, 46)

The work lets the earth be an earth and the world be a world because it is the place where truth is set to work—unconcealment happens here. This is why I am spending so much time discussing world and earth in the work of art when the intended aim was to discuss the twofold movement of unconcealment. The earth and the world belong together in the work of art. But still this is only half of the story.

The earth is revealed, but it is also concealed in the sheltering of the world. I have made it seem as though the paint and the canvas and the wood were the earth upon which the world of the portrait is set. But in fact, these items were produced as well. The stretcher bars and the blank canvas were fashioned out of "raw" materials and as such set up the world of the laborer who produced them. Similarly, there are equally productive relationships that can be discussed all the way back in the process of creation of these earthly goods. "Earth thus shatters every attempt to penetrate it." (*PLT*, 47) That is, every effort at penetrating the earth reveals a world that sets back deeper into the earth. The way in which the earth is brought forth into the openness of *physis* is as the self-secluding, as that upon which the world is set.

> World and earth are essentially different from one another and yet are never separated. The world grounds itself on the earth, and earth juts through world.... The world, in resting upon the earth, strives to surmount it. As self-opening it cannot endure anything closed. The earth, however, as sheltering and concealing, tends always to draw the world into itself and keep it there.... The opposition of world and earth is a striving. (*PLT*, 49)

I already claimed that the earth and world are not strictly analogous to the movement of unconcealment. It is still unclear what grounds this claim. It appears that the self-concealing earth is revealed as such in the setting to work of truth, and that in the essay on the artwork the revealed world is infected with concealment since the beings that are revealed in the world are also concealed. And in fact Heidegger tells us that entities, things within the world which come to be only within the world, can only be concealed after they have entered into the open clearing. (*PLT*, 53) So revealing comes out of concealing and, in the process, concealing itself can be concealed or revealed. Likewise, in revealing, concealment of what has been revealed can still occur. This is beginning to sound more and more like an analogy. Heidegger even says that "[t]his happening [of truth] we think of as the fighting of the conflict between world and earth" (*PLT*, 57).

But there is a problem and it presents itself in each of the passages that suggest the analogy. Here, the separation, the nearness, of earth and world is the distance of strife—of *polemos*. Earlier, I showed that the relation between revealing and concealing was characterized by love or harmony: *philia*. This striving between earth and world is described as a battle, as an ongoing struggle between the revealing tendencies of world and the concealing tendencies of earth. (*PLT*, 49) Thus, the movement of unconcealment as the twofold character of truth is the result of the tension resulting from the proximity of two such incompatible neighbors. The spark of unconcealment is the fiery passion of turbulence that burns between them, within the expanse of their great differences. Is this the image that Heidegger is trying to achieve? Is he trying to set the stage for an analogy between world/earth and revealing/concealing through the images of a tension filled romance? But such romances usually burn so bright only for a short time; don't the lovers eventually exhaust themselves, or die of a spent love and the emptiness that remains? All such marriages of tension and harmony are saturated by finitude.

Later in the essay, he begins to talk of the relation in terms of a game: "Truth happens in Van Gogh's painting. This does not mean that something is correctly portrayed, but rather that in the revelation of the equipmental being of the shoes, that which is as a whole—world and earth in their counterplay—attains to unconcealedness." (*PLT*, 56). Is the battle between the lovers just a game they play to keep their romance alive? This is a serious kind of play, the kind of play where the players are staking their lives, their destinies. They play with each other and with themselves for the sake of maintaining their relationship. The game they play, the tension they live through, the intimacy they share: they belong together.

Revealing and concealing as world and earth are in play, conflict, love. This intimate relationship seeks out, among other things, works of art. I mentioned earlier that "truth happens in Van Gogh's painting" of some peasant shoes. Heidegger described this happening as the "epuipmental being of the shoes" becoming unconcealed, arising up out of its concealment. This work of art does not merely portray correctly the appearance of some shoes, but it clues a viewer into the Being of the shoes as equipment worn in the world where the peasant works the earth. We are now turning from the abstract consideration of the twofold movement of revealing-concealing that is unconcealedness to what is revealed and concealed in that movement. The conflict between the moments of this movement yields the Open clearing where entities are as they are. It is in this way that we can say that the clearing is a world set upon an earth.

> The openness of this Open, that is, truth, can be what it is, namely, this openness, only if and as long as it establishes itself within its Open. Hence there must always be some being in this Open, something that is, in which the openness takes its stand and attains its constancy. In thus occupying the Open, the openness holds open the Open and sustains it. (*PLT*, 60-1; translation modified)

The conflict of revealing and concealing, the striving that is its dynamic unfolding, is always the unfolding of an Open region, of a clearing. The Open, the place where entities reside in their being as they are, is occupied by the openness of unconcealment's movement, it is possessed by it. Unconcealedness must result in an Open region and the entities existing within it. Unconcealedness is, therefore, always a bringing forth of things that are (*Seienden*). And even if what is brought forth in unconcealment is destined to retreat into concealment, something else will be revealed in its place. Furthermore, any entity that is brought forth into the open is constantly enmeshed in the conflict (occupied by/with it), and there is always a danger that it will recede into concealment. That is, the life span of something that exists is nothing other than the play/conflict/harmony of these relations.

Unconcealment does not exist beyond the world, only to descend into it occasionally in great works of art and during special events — it does not sit in mastery from on high, but is in the midst of everything: an immanent dynamic. "[T]here belongs to it what is here to be called establishing" (*PLT*, 61), where this establishment is the setting up of the world upon the earth. Heidegger wants us to see that the "clearing of the openness and establishment in the Open belong together" (*PLT*, 61). That means, very simply, exactly what I have been saying all along in various ways: the movement of unconcealment is the happening of the world set upon the earth, and the world is only the relationships that make up all that exists within the world — tools, theoretical entities, plants, beasts, human beings, etc. Despite suspicions that Heidegger is somehow deeply connected to the thought traditionally attributed to Parmenides, it seems that Heidegger's view of the way of truth as unconcealment is as far from the statesman of Elea as it could be. This notion of unconcealedness is an affirmation of a ruling flux, a fluctuating *arche* or ground that is dynamic — a constant exploding of dynamite reminiscent of Heraclitus's "The lightning bolt drives all things." All there is, is the constant tumbling and unfolding of *a-letheia* where *a-letheia's* tumbling is understood as the bringing forth of entities into the world from out of concealment. All the entities that are brought forth continue to reside within/as the flux (be occupied by it), within/as the rift between world and earth where they are involved in the conflict between revealing and concealing, where their standing in the Open, their being revealed, is permeated with a negativity that constantly threatens it. This serious game of love that is a constant striving threatens to destroy the intimacy of all that has come near in favor of some further liaison of unconcealedness.

In "The Question Concerning Technology" Heidegger discusses a sentence from Plato's *Symposium* which he translates as "Every occasion for whatever passes over and goes forward into presencing from that which is not presencing is *poiesis*, is bringing forth." (*QCT*, 10)[18] Heidegger understands *poiesis* not as poetry, in the sense that Plato's usual translators have of the word, but as this very process of bringing forth. Heidegger says: "*Physis* also, the arising of something from out of itself, is a bringing-forth, *poiesis*. *Physis* is indeed *poiesis* in the highest sense" (*QCT*, 10). All along I have been discussing *physis* and unconcealment as though they were strictly interchangeable. Now I see that *physis* is the highest form of *poiesis*, where that signifies the bringing forth of the Open from within the conflict between revealing and concealing, world and earth, so that it may reside there.

Henceforth we must remember that *a-letheia* is poetic and its poem is the twofold movement of unconcealing that brings forth entities in their existence, so that they may come to rest in the Open region where the world nestles down onto the earth in a constant striving that threatens all that resides *there*.[19]

Ereignis/Aletheia

Ereignis is a common word in German where it means "event," "occurrence," or "incident." Something is always happening, *Ereignis* is "what happened;" it is used much like *Geschehen*. No doubt, Heidegger is aware of the everydayness of this word and it is precisely because of it that he adapts it to the specialized sense that it has in his work. Heidegger writes in a fragment of "The Principle of Identity" that was not included

---

[18]Michael Joyce translates in the *Collected Dialogues* of Plato (Princeton, NJ: Princeton University Press, 1961): [Poetry is] "calling something into existence that was not there before." (*Symposium* 205d)

[19]Ultimately these last pages (and much of this discussion on *aletheia* and *physis*) redefine the verbal meaning of *wesen* which will continue to occupy a crucial place in the project ahead. *Wesen* is no longer the whatness of some one individual entity, but a movement characteristic of the world/earth, revealing/concealing. Because this movement is open it does not permit of the present identity of an entity that is as such (i.e., participates in some form or is some form itself), but challenges all coming to pass of the "as such" for the sake of a dynamic unfolding. Instead of talk about what an entity is in its essence, we might now speak of the way something happens, the manner in which it is occupied by the dynamic of the world/earth and *a-letheia*.

in the English translation by Stambaugh: "Das Wort Ereignis ist der gewachsenen Sprache entnommen. Er-eignen heisst ursprünglich: er-äugen, d.h. erblicken, im Blicken zu sich rufen, an-eignen" (*ID*, 100-1). A rough English rendering is: "The word 'Ereignis' is taken from natural language. Originally er-eignen means [N.B. Coming-to-pass calls or evokes originally]: er-äugen, that is to say, er-blicken, to see or catch sight of, to call to oneself in looking, an-eignen, to en-own, ap-propriate."[20] This fragment defies translation, it is no wonder Stambaugh left it out. *Eräugen* doesn't exist anymore although *Äuge* is the common word "eye" and "er-" is a common enough prefix (one might translate *eräugen* as "to behold"). In this passage, there is an implied connection to *Augenblick* — implied through the use of *er-blicken* to elaborate *er-äugen* — which means "moment" or "blink of an eye." This word recalls *Being and Time* and the description of authentic (*eigentlich*) Dasein's temporal ecstasis contrasted to the inauthentic mode of presence as a simple now point called *Gegenwart*.[21]

Although they are synonymous in daily German, Heidegger will want to distance *Ereignis* from *Geschehen*. *Geschehen* is related to the family of *Geschichte*, meaning "history" — *Geschehen* is what happens in history, an historical event or occurrence; while *Ereignis* is more than history, it remains throughout history, it announces the coming of history — future and past. But Heidegger doesn't want the distance to stretch too wide. History and historical events are still very near to *Ereignis* which may be said to come to pass in/as/through history.

---

[20] Translation by A. Hofstadter in "Enownment," in Spanos, *Martin Heidegger and the Question of Literature* (Bloomington: Indiana University Press, 1979).

[21]Consider each of the following two passages: "When resolute, Dasein has brought itself back from falling, and has done so precisely in order to be more authentically 'there' in the 'moment of vision' (*augenblick*) as regards the Situation which has been disclosed" (*BT*, 376). and "In resoluteness, the Present is not only brought back from distraction with the objects of one's closest concern, but it gets held in the future and in having been. That *Present* which is held in authentic temporality and which thus is *authentic* itself, we call the *"moment of vision" (augenblick)"* (*BT*, 387). Compare these to the following from Kierkegaard's *Philosophical Fragments:* "And, now, the moment (*Øieblik,* meaning eye-blink as well). A moment such as this is unique. To be sure, it is short and temporal, as the moment is; it is passing, as the moment is, past, as the moment is in the next moment, and yet it is decisive, and yet it is filled with the eternal. A moment such as this must have a special name. Let us call it: *the fullness of time."*

Geschichte and *Geschehen* are connected to Heidegger's understanding of *schicken*, "to send" as in "*Ein Brief zu schicken*" (to send a letter). *Schicken* in turn suggests *Schicksal* and *Geschick* ("destiny" and "fate"). Here, destiny and fate cannot be separated from the connotation that they are kinds of sending. Destiny is the arrival at a destination of a letter sent by post. Furthermore, this letter sent by public post is something that has happened, an event that has occurred. The story *(Geschichte)* of our history *(Geschichte)* is a batch of letters sent so as to arrive in/as/through time.

Recall a passage from "The Origin of the Work of Art" cited in the last section on *a-letheia* concerning the meaning of "world":

> It is the temple-work that first fits together and at the same time gathers around itself the unity of those paths and relations in which birth and death, disaster and blessing, victory and disgrace, endurance and decline acquire the shape of destiny for human being. The all-governing expanse of this open relational context is the world of this historical people. (*PLT*, 39)

The paths and relations of the place known as the expanse of an open region are shaped in the form of destiny. The shape of the world, the figure it takes, is that of destiny. The relations, paths, and practices of an historical people, the practices and activities that govern their lives are sent and occur as having been sent; they are what has happened, happen, and will happen to this people. This destiny of the people, what has happened to them, been sent their way in the paths they have taken, is the world within which they *are*. And this world is nestled into the earth as the openness of the Open which has been brought forth into and by the twofold movement of *a-letheia*.

Ereignis is related to *eigen,* meaning "own" and "proper" with clear connotations of *eigentum* meaning "property" or "a possession." *Ereignis* is also related to *ereigen* meaning "to prove" or "to show" in the sense of a demonstration (Grimm's lists it as the Latin *monstrare)*. And lastly, it is related to *eignen* meaning "suitable" or "appropriate" where appropriate may be understood both as "proper" and as "to acquire." Along with all these connotations, *Ereignis* must also be thought as "event" and it is usually translated as "event of appropriation" so as to reflect some of these relationships. In the event of *Ereignis,* entities are brought forth and they are brought forth into their own, becoming what they are. Bearing these multiple meanings in mind, reading some of Heidegger's writing on the matter should help.

Heidegger understands the sending of the world, what emerges in unconcealing, as a gift. The destiny of a people is their living in the world opened up within/as/through this missive. "In unconcealing prevails a giving, the giving that gives presencing, that is Being, in letting-presence." (*TB*, 5) Presencing is given in a gift that lets-presence: Being ("Being means presencing") is given in the Open in/as/through the entities that exist *there,* the beings that are *there* ("To let presence means: to unconceal, to bring to openness"). Contrary to a traditional notion of Being as the original substance or first principle of which all else is a determination or modification, Heidegger thinks Being as the datum of a giving, as given—a gift. Thus, when Heidegger says he wants to discover the meaning of Being or what evokes Being (*was heisst Sein?)* or the truth of Being, he is asking after the giving of Being. What gives Being? Why *is there* Being at all and not rather nothing?[22]

In this last question we must read the "is there Being" as though it were written in German: "*gibt es Sein?*" Heidegger says that "Being *is* not. It gives Being as the unconcealing; as the gift of unconcealing it is retained in the giving. Being *is* not. It gives Being as the unconcealing of presencing." (*TB*, 6) "There is Being" is always "*es gibt Sein*"—it gives Being. Being is brought forth in unconcealing and rests there in the rift where revealing is in strife with concealing; and this Being is always given along with entities that are.[23] But Heidegger is not concerned with

---

[22]This troublesome paragraph addresses the entire problematic of *Being and Time* and its relationship to other, later, works written by Heidegger. I'm not sure how much of this problem is essential to the matter at hand, but my understanding of the early Heidegger focuses on the variety of hints he gives for a path beyond (sic) Being. The historical determination of Being and its coherence in a meaning (not unified but adjusted to some significant context) gestures beyond the presence of what is as such and toward the giving of what is, how what is comes to be as such, the meaning of the as such, and thus the mission giving embarks on to construct what is as such.

[23] Although a reference to the German is required to make this point, I don't think any great weakness is demonstrated in the ability of English to speak the language of thinking: in fact, if I my project were to reread *Being and Time*, I think this point of triangulation between English, German, and thinking would allow a turning that Heidegger claimed could not take place in BT, perhaps precisely because he was writing it in German. That is, "there is" allows—through its connection to both *es gibt* and *Dasein*—a turn from any humanism of the thinker to an anti-humanism of Being. The conclusion may be that all turning, all thinking, all deconstruction requires the movement of more than one language so that the difference can be unconcealed in thinking. What made Heidegger think, therefore, that Greek and German

Being—he says that is the province of metaphysics, the given ground of a first philosophy that has forgotten its own meaning, that has forgotten what evokes it and what gives it. Metaphysics fails to come into its own. For Heidegger, the *es* of *es gibt* is what matters most of all for thinking (*On Time and Being* is entitled "*Zur Sache des Denkens*" in German—toward the matter of thought).

Heidegger wonders in this essay if perhaps it isn't time which gives Being. He entertains this notion long enough to see that if it is time that gives Being, it must be a multiple giving. He says that if it were the case that time gives Being it must do so in a three-dimensional fashion, as having been, as being, and as will be. This threefold dimensionality leads him to see that there must be a fourth dimension to keep it all together, and that that dimension is really the giving that we were after in the first place. He calls this first dimension of time, the dimension that gives time in its threefold movement, the "nearing nearness" because "it brings future, past and present near to one another by distancing them" (*TB*, 15), and he says it has the character of "denial and withdrawing" where that means that the advent of the present is denied so that the future could come forward while the present escapes into the past. Time, like Being, is given by the "it" of "it gives" and "this giving proved to be the sending of Being, as time in the sense of an opening up which extends." (*TB*, 17) "The It, at least in the interpretation available to us for the moment, names a presence of absence" (TB, 18). And then on the next page:

> Simply by thinking the "It" in the light of the kind of giving that belongs to it: giving as destiny, giving as an opening up which reaches out. Both belong together, inasmuch as the former, destiny, lies in the latter, extending opening up.... What determines both, time and Being, in their own, that is, in their belonging together, we shall call: *Ereignis*. ... Accordingly, the It that gives in "It gives Being," "It gives time," proves to be *Ereignis*.

Heidegger does not think there is very much to be said about *Ereignis*. It

---

were such great languages for thinking was that they were the languages *he* was employing and not some essential element of the natural languages themselves, as he claims in various places. Derrida may therefore be likely to draw a similar conclusion to Heidegger's with the exception that French and German would be substituted.

withdraws from view in favor of/for what it gives. There is no experience of *Ereignis,* the experimenter is among what has already been appropriated: Being, time, etc. No visible exchange takes place between the taking subject (*vernehmen* suggests taking and perception) and the giving reality (i.e., the data of experience). *Ereignis* does not mark an exchange between persons and things. *Ereignis* is always eluding us, and yet we are constantly confronting its "effects": what has come to *be* in/as/through it. We are on familiar ground, however, when we read of destiny and opening up. These suggest the movement of *a-letheia* and the bringing forth that is its perpetual task. *A-letheia* is not what is opened up, rather it is the opening up, the coming-to-pass in/as/through which opening up happens (takes place). And what is thus opened up comes to rest in unconcealment; it trembles there in the tension of the rift that continues its struggle in the nearness. *A-letheia* is never shown, *is* nothing. "Only what *aletheia* as opening grants is experienced and thought, not what it is as such." (*TB*, 71) Instead, it is constantly showing the world and the Open, only to withdraw from view in doing so. And this showing is *Ereignis,* this coming into its own of the world upon the earth as Being, time, entities, Dasein, etc. is an event, it is gift-giving without exchange: the presentation of a gift where the presenter then withdraws, a present given in absence, etc. Unconcealment dynamically unfolds as the Open where Being and time reside, where they linger as gifts. The dynamic unfolding of Being is given in/as/through *Ereignis.* Heidegger has told us that a "giving resides in *a-letheia*" and this giving is called *Ereignis.* The play of presence and absence, the nearness of the near—intimacy of what is other itself—says "the Same in terms of the Same about the Same." (*TB*, 24).[24]

---

[24]Of course, Derrida has done all of this already; except I'm never sure if he thinks he is doing it *with* Heidegger. The meaning of the giving, the impossibility of *giving* a simple and pure *account* of giving, and the withdrawal of all giving from any economical exchange is all focal in Derrida's discussions in *Given Time.* Notice also, and I will come back to it later, that there is also a question being raised as to what remains, what continues to reside in the open, what rests there for the moment. Unlike the economical, the gift leaves a residue, something remains without having been used up or exhausted. This calls into question all that is said to be exchanged within the general economy outlined by the giving of the gift since the economical is surrounded by a trace or residual that erases the possibility of total exchange (i.e., we're left wondering whether there is anything like "Being" at all). Furthermore, this also demonstrates the impossibility of viewing such an "economy" as transcendental idealism. After all, the gift as residue becomes a condition for the impossibility of Being. What's more,

Ereignis ereignet and unconcealedness unconceals. These phrases say the same. There is the struggle of *a-letheia,* its intimate nearness, and what is (opened) in/as/through this struggle. The struggle opens up while what is opened—in its openness—resides in the strife. The moment *(Augenblick)* of opening, a moment that unconcealment cannot unconceal with/out, comes to pass in/as/through the event, *Ereignis. Ereignis* stretches across the battlefield and resides (resonates) in the striving that goes on there. *Ereignis* is not a secondary attribute or modification of unconcealment, rather the movement of unconcealment sends what is in/as/through the Open; and this sending comes in/as/through *Ereignis. Ereignis* strives and sends, unconcealment strives in revealing-concealing: the dynamic emergence of sending. "The event of appropriation is that realm, vibrating within itself, through which man and Being reach each other in their *wesen* (verbal), achieve their active *wesen* by losing those qualities with which metaphysics has endowed them." (*ID,* 38)

"Man and Being" are both given in/as/through *Ereignis,* they each come into their own there, rising up out of self-concealment so as to belong together, appropriately reaching out for each other as if to take each other's hand. Reaching out their hands as if to give or receive a gift, they vibrate. We have felt this unsteadiness before. This shaky uncertainty which Heidegger has thought as the agitation of the striving, concentrated into a repose that appears as the stability of an Open place, is the push-pull of *polemos/philia* where revealing and concealing play out together their reciprocal roles (*PLT,* 57). The vibrating region is the trembling flow of time's unfolding, coming into itself, be-ing.

"Being and man" belong together in "an identity whose active essence [*wesen]* stems from that letting belong together which we call the appropriation [*Ereignis].* The essence of identity is a property of *Ereignis.*" (*ID,* 39) *Ereignis* gives the Same, proper to it is the essence of identity. The play on words is veiled in the English. When Heidegger calls the essence of identity a property of *Ereignis,* he is saying that "*Das Wesen der Identität ist ein Eigentum des Er-eignisses.*" (*ID,* 103) And this follows soon after his having asked the question "What does appropriation have to do with identity? Answer: Nothing. Identity, on the other hand, has much, perhaps everything, to do with appropriation" (*ID,* 38). Identity is belonging together and appropriation is here considered as

---

Derrida says the withdrawal of the gift is its impossibility, suggesting that it is the impossible condition for the impossibility of Being. All possibility amounts to nothing in the works of deconstruction.

a letting-belong together. I have already said many times that components belong together because it is appropriate that they should be together. We now see that this belonging together of the sameness of identity is determined, or allowed to occur, in/as/through *Ereignis*—this happening is a letting happen. Identity as belonging together does not determine *Ereignis,* but is determined by it: the principle of Identity comes to be as the highest principle of Being in/as/through *Ereignis.* The givenness of identity attains its foundation in a giving that is the Same, where this suggests the impossibility of foundations and the "as such"—the impossibility of identity.

Ereignis shows itself in what it lets belong together, what it lets be the Same. Let us recall that the belonging together of revealing and concealing was given out of the striving between them. Once again we see that *Ereignis* wedges itself into unconcealment. It spans between the two terms as the battleground of their trembling movement. *Ereignis ereignet,* the happening of what happens, says "the Same in terms of the Same about the Same." (*TB,* 24) This phrase means something new in this repetition. The happening of what happens is a tautology, it is the Same in/as/through itself, and it speaks, it speaks the same, the letting belong together, and it speaks the dynamic unfolding of identity in/as/through belonging together.

> What happens in the history of Being? We cannot ask in this manner, because there would then be an occurrence and something which occurs. But occurrence itself is the sole happening. Being alone is. What happens? Nothing happens if we are searching for something occurring in the occurrence. Nothing happens, *Appropriation appropriates.* Perduring the opening out, the origin takes the parting to itself. The appropriating origin is dignity as truth itself reaching into its departure. Dignity is what is noble which appropriates without needing effects. The noble of the worthy Appropriating of the origin is the unique release as Appropriation of freedom, which is unconcealment of concealment—because it belongs to the ground-less. (*EP,* 79)[25]

---

[25]The word for dignity is *Würde* which resembles *wurde,* the preterite tense of *werden* meaning "to become." Becoming is frequently used as a temporal notion or as a result of the higher unity of determinate Being that synthesizes Being and Nothing. We have already seen that this dignity of the origin can have no such connotations. It might however be linked to the

Nothing happens, *Ereignis ereignet.* We can no longer naively write this as the happening of happening. Happening itself is the movement of *Ereignis,* it is event. Being does not happen, rather Being *is* and nothing *happens.* But certainly the principle of identity is, isn't it? And the Same happens? But *Ereignis* has no effects to speak of, is not responsible for the production of possible beings or possibly self-identical entities that are in so far as they are as such. How can the axiomatic principle of identity be said to result from the sameness of *Ereignis* and Unconcealment when Heidegger says nothing results from *Ereignis's* happening. That nothing results from *Ereignis* no doubt follows from the fact that nothing happens there. To think *Ereignis* in terms of the production of effects or the making of determinations or modifications or whatever is no doubt to think *Ereignis* in terms of what is, to think what happens as essentially metaphysical. The question of giving raised in/as/through *Ereignis* is the question of the relation of metaphysics and its other, the relation of the principle of identity and the Same.

In the second half of the previous quotation, we hear the first talk of difference in connection with unconcealment and *Ereignis.* "Perdurance" is *austragen* or "carrying out," which indicates the migration of what is into the Open from out of a concealed abyss (groundless origin). This migration is a becoming other, the becoming other of the origin. A pure and simple unitary origin could never accomplish the perdurance of sending, since the one perfect and unmoving source (Parmenides's Being, for one) could never be said to become other. Any movement toward otherness separates the agent (the one who acts) from the destination (the other place where one is not now) and the point of departure would be groundless (it would be impossible to get there from here). There would have to be an additional component to interact with the first one so that it may change from its stasis into its other through movement (or as movement). This third thing, however, is already the otherness of the first and so would, in turn, require an additional reagent to enable it to connect with the first one. And so on and on. The third man is always deferred, his necessary presence makes presence in movement impossible. The way out is a divided origin. An origin that is parted, that has taken difference right into itself, that has been cracked open so as to yawn like an abyss. And this is precisely what *Ereignis* as happening accomplishes. This will be handled more fully in the next section, but something of it had to be

---

notion of becoming as seen in "becoming what one is" vs. "coming into one's own."

indicated here so as to suggest abysmal *Ereignis:* groundless because it is not firm, it is not a solid foundation upon which one can be certain and steady in all one's cognitions. *Ereignis* is an abyss—a groundless ground—because it does not demonstrate the same self-present completeness of a self-evident first principle. In fact, it is always other from itself; it takes the parting or dividing of the carrying out right into itself and this is what makes it possible for it to happen as the giving that sends.

But isn't it the case that, since revealing and concealing belong together in their striving, the movement of *a-letheia* must be understood as occurring *in Ereignis,* something that has come to pass, that has been allowed to belong together and is now subject to the metaphysical principle of identity (as opposed to Heidegger's "inverted principle of identity" which I am calling "the Same" or "belonging together")? It is true that the separate moments, revealing and concealing, are properties: when I describe revealing/concealing as unconcealment I am naming *what* comes to pass in/as/through *Ereignis.* But I also, in that event, present *a-letheia* metaphysically as two separate moments. When I name unconcealing in terms of the (/), however, the naming inhabits the strife that is the mutual bestowal of the one and the other, the tension that is their reciprocal struggling against and in favor of the other. Revealing and concealing suggest something to me regarding the belonging together of Being and thinking. The self-identical terms Being and thinking (like revealing and concealing, etc.) are not identical to each other, and it is as self-identical contraries that they come to be together. This is the character of so-called binary opposition in metaphysics. The logic of unconcealment informs us that belonging together as the Same is a dynamically emergent region that precedes the contraries that evolve out of it as organizing principles. In unconcealment, revealing/concealing are not oppositions in any sense of the word, they are inseparable, they are the strife between them, they are their own interplay. There is no revealment ever without concealment, and vice versa; that is the precise nature of the one word phrasing of this movement, unconcealment as *a-letheia*—where the dash holds *lethe* and *aletheia* together inseparably.

But I am speaking a little too naturally and uncritically about this evolution of contraries from the dynamic unfolding. Two givens belong together, and Heidegger says explicitly that they belong together in the Open. The givens are pretenders to the throne of this realm, no doubt, but they are involved in the realm, which makes their pretensions possible— their proximity to the throne enables them to set themselves up as organizing   principles   (*arche*).   Only   what   has   emerged   into unconcealment can belong together. The principle of identity as the "principle" of the Same where the two are said to *belong* together depends on the two being able to emerge out of the strife and then being set back into it. Time and Being belong together in the extended region of the Open, thinking and Being as well. In this movement, the leap of the Same gives and is given along with the principle of identity. If I am tempted to say that the relation of the principle of identity to the Same is one of belonging together (as opposed to the relation of a cause to its effect or vice versa), I will beg the question. Belonging together says the Same, the one cannot explain the other.

Heidegger writes: "In *Ereignis* vibrates the active nature [*wesen*] of what speaks as language, which at one time was called the house of Being." (*ID*, 39) Also recall, for a third time, that *Ereignis* "*speaks* the Same, etc." *Ereignis* is a vibrating region and what vibrates there is the *wesen*, the dynamic unfolding, of what speaks. But it is *Ereignis* that speaks, it speaks the Same. The dynamic unfolding is the unconcealing of... Of what? Of what speaks there? No, what speaks there is *Ereignis,* and *Ereignis* vibrates in/as/through dynamic unfolding. Speaking is proper to *Ereignis,* and what is spoken enters into unconcealment *in/as/through* language, while what enters into unconcealment is what rests in the Open after having emerged from unconcealment in its striving.

What emerges first and foremost, perhaps, is the principle of identity where principle is *der Satz. Satz* may be "principle" or it may be "sentence," or even "proposition" (in the strict sense). The principle of identity acts as a leap carrying us beyond metaphysics and into its *ab-grund,* its abyss. The principle as the first sentence spoken by unconcealment and *Ereignis* is the way back to them from the metaphysical tradition that has pushed them into oblivion. In this sense, the problem that opens regarding the relation of the principle of identity to the Same is the question concerning the movement from metaphysics to its... well, its Other. The principle of identity is beyond metaphysics in so far as it speaks of the abyss with a human voice, because it is already language, it arises in the dynamic unfolding of what speaks as language. By starting with the principle of identity as metaphysics understands it (i.e., Plato in *Sophist),* as a characteristic of Being, we are able to perform an "inversion" that gets to a principle of identity beyond metaphysics and which can then, in turn, be used as a springboard into the abyss that floats beneath the ground of all metaphysics.

Heidegger thinks the relation of identity to the Same is as important as any relation can be. This makes the difficulty we've had in sorting through this relationship all the more pressing. Even attempting to think this move as an inversion is problematic, in that inversion is a typical move in the traditional logic of metaphysics. Two self-identical things are in question in the performance of an inversion. *A-letheia* and *Ereignis* speak the Same, they let what belongs together belong together in the opening expanse that their dynamic unfolding unfolds. The relation of the abyss to what belongs in/as/through it is *the* question of Heidegger's later thought. If metaphysically determined concepts and components are at least part of what belongs there, then the relation of the abyss to what belongs cannot be thought metaphysically. The frequent glossing over of this relation in my essay has been accomplished through the use of the word "speaks." In chapter 2, I will show how "speaking" specifically articulates this relation.

The section on *a-letheia* concluded with the statement that unconcealment results in a bringing forth known as *poiesis* where the standard modern translation is "poetry." Heidegger, I will show later, thinks this is no accident and that it tells us something about poetry's essence. In this section, we have seen a continued development of unconcealment, and a new development of *Ereignis,* in terms of tension, strife, vibration, and something arrived at in a spring. Consider that the German word *dichten,* which means "to compose" or "to write poetry," belongs to a family of words signifying various modes of poetry and the poet. What is interesting in this word (*dichten)* is that it also means "to make tight." Presumably what is tight, like a drum, can be made to vibrate or perhaps is already vibrating in the tension of its being stretched out. Trampolines, when tight, provide an excellent spring for jumping, bouncing, leaping up to the sky and, obviously, away from the ground. Tight and making tight also mean "securing," in the sense of battening down something so as to hold it fast—the loose and the slippery are made tight, secured. Friends can be tight: they are intimate, close friends. "We're tight," we say while crossing our fingers. "Like this." And tight also means "drunk" as in inebriated, overcome with the frenzy that alcohol brings. Or perhaps tight means "cheap," keeping a relentless grip on valuable currency; or "snug" as in "a tight fit" where everything is pressed together in an absolute proximity.

All this only in passing and to be taken up in more detail later: Aletheia the poet demonstrating tightness.

Dif-ference/A-letheia/Er-eignis

"Heidegger and difference" might suggest "Ontological Difference" or "Ontico-Ontoligical Difference," where the difference between Being and beings is made questionable. Most all commentators[26] are in agreement that Heidegger dropped the word "ontological" in the later works because of Heidegger's further development along the way toward what may be said to lie beyond the ontological—the way toward what takes place outside metaphysics. This observation, as far as it goes, is correct. Heidegger becomes increasingly explicit about the possibility that there is something that differs from Being/being, something that defers the traditionally accepted ground. Nevertheless, Heidegger creates difficulties for following him along this way by referring to that realm outside metaphysics as Being itself, a Being that is beyond the ontological. Thus, at one point, Heidegger is calling the features of this thesis outside of ontology (*Ereignis,* unconcealment, and difference): Being itself, the source of all that presences.

In "Letter on Humanism" Heidegger writes: "For the 'it' that here 'gives' is Being itself. The 'gives' names the essence of Being that is giving, granting its truth. The self-giving into the open, along with the open region itself, is Being itself" (*BW*, 214). As should be apparent when comparing this passage to the passages cited in the previous section from *On Time and Being,* something very noticeable has changed between the 1947 *Letter* and the 1962 lecture. The passages are particularly revealing in that the context seems to be identical: the "it" of "it gives" or *es gibt.* The move is, of course, from "Being itself" to *Ereignis,* but it is not so obvious what kind of steps Heidegger's thinking is taking along this way. That is, does something not yet thought come to be thought in the move toward *Ereignis?* Better yet, does "Being itself" say the Same along with *Ereignis?* These questions call upon me to re-read Heidegger's *Letter* along with the recently published *Beitrage Zur Philosophie* which, written in 1936-38, already begins to think the meaning of *Ereignis* as what may be said to lie outside Being. Tracing the development of Heidegger's use of the term "Being" and its relation to what is present in Being as well as its relation to what belongs together in the giving over of what is would be a book length project all on its own.[27] At this time, I can only continue to formulate the hypothesis that Heidegger from the 1920s through the 1960s is asking after the sending or giving that

---

[26]Richardson, for example, writes in a footnote on p. 15 of his book that "the word 'ontological' has become for Heidegger suspect. Cf. *Gelassenheit,* p. 55. In the later years, even the "ontological difference" becomes simply *the* difference (*US,* 24)."

[27] Actually, without going as far as that, Schürmann does a pretty good job of sorting out these developments in Part Three of op cit.

discloses what is in its Being. This prolonged meditation leads him through frequent twists and turns regarding the manner in which giving/sending takes place. At first, Heidegger allies himself with the traditional preference for understanding this most essential (meaning *both* essence/quiddity *and* dynamic unfolding) movement as Being. Later on, he begins to see the problem that results from thinking this outside as Being when the role of Being is intimately wed to what is in the open that has been sent or given. That is, if Being lies in the open as the Being of what entities are there, and if Being gives entities over to themselves as the beings that they are, in what sense can Being be said to lie between Being and beings in the open region cleared in the giving/sending of what is? In what sense can Being *be* the outside of itself and thus, not *be* at all? This, as I am about to discuss, is the question of difference that Heidegger is finally able to raise explicitly in the course of the 1950s.

Even in his use of the word "Being" to refer to this matter at the origin of all instances of Being's coming to presence, however, Heidegger has already begun to point beyond the Being of ontology. He talks of Being's master name, of the one word that will get us past the various instances of presence that have been called Being throughout the history of Western metaphysics. The master name is supposed to point to the unique source of all instances of Being; it is supposed to gesture beyond metaphysics and back into its ground. But this ground, as I have shown, is an abyss; and pointing into an abyss is really pointing nowhere at nothing, hardly even pointing at all—a gesture that doesn't quite happen. It seems, then, that talk of the master name is destined to spin its wheels (might I say that this talking of master names is the destiny of metaphysics itself). To the extent that the master name is the way in which each great metaphysical thinker has thought the Being of beings, the master name is the name given to giving itself, to Being itself (according to the *Letter)*. In this understanding of Being itself, there persists a substantialization of giving, a substantialization that giving cannot maintain: giving doesn't take place when it is held in place by the heaviness of substance.

The problem lies with "Being." The focus on Being clutters the movement outside it, makes metaphysics impossible to escape. Beyond Being lies nothing, nothing at all, and there cannot be any gesture directed toward it (rather, the direction of the gesturing will always be indirect). In fact, it is the desire to point directly at the source of Being (to refer to it) that conceives the nothing that may be said to lie outside Being within the rules set forth in Being. This desire directly ties such an inquiry to the methods and logic of metaphysics (or ontology). Heidegger's effort to step—or leap—toward the outside of metaphysics is an effort to move along the way of what may be said to lie outside of Being. In this matter, in so far as this is the case, it is correct to point out that dropping the word "ontological" in "Ontological Difference" is evidence of an attempt to step beyond Being. But that is only half of the story.

In dropping the word "ontological," Heidegger's thought about difference undergoes a change as well. Difference is no longer merely concerned with Being, it too has stepped beyond Being and is no longer merely the difference between Being and beings where the aboriginal Being (*Ursein)*, the source of the two components that belong together, resides. Heidegger writes in "The Anaximander Fragment" concerning "usage," translating *to creon,* which Anaximander says is the governing ruler (*arche)* of all that comes to be, much like the threefold components I am developing here work in Heidegger's thought: "The word 'usage' is dictated to thinking in the experience of Being's oblivion. What properly remains to be thought in the 'usage' has presumably left a trace in '*to creon.*' This trace quickly vanishes in the destiny of Being which unfolds in world history as Western metaphysics" (*EGT*, 54). Being's oblivion, I take it, is the source of all Being's historical instantiations, here still conceived in terms of Being and yet already gesturing away from it. *To creon* is a master name, no doubt, but as such it contains a trace of what is thoughtworthy in it—its source. This trace withdraws in the sending of Being that establishes itself as the history of metaphysics. It is the nature of a trace to vanish, it is the withdrawal of what is presencing. This trace that traces the realm outside what is sent as the Being of Western metaphysics, is a vanishing difference.

Within/as/through this trace, difference is pushed back into that forgotten realm that philosophers have been trying to gesture toward with a unique master name, and which makes the possibility of assigning a master name impossible. Difference steps between any pointing and makes it a pointing at nothing, at the no-place between two places, the abyss.[28] And just so we do not think that difference is just a master name that assures its seat upon the highest throne of rule by being the word that supplants any possible naming other than its own un-naming, difference is divided by being interwoven together with unconcealment and *Ereignis*—both of which resemble "difference" insofar as they are un-

---

[28]A major way in which this becomes clear is that Heidegger does not speak merely of the difference between Being and beings, but of the difference between Being and time, thinking and Being, revealing and concealing, etc. I will show how the step beyond the "Ontological Difference" to the "difference as such" is the generalizing of difference for its role in letting belong together.

words (words that do not name any-thing). Heidegger writes in the same essay:

> The oblivion of the distinction, with which the destiny of Being begins and which it will carry through to completion, is all the same not a lack, but rather the richest and most prodigious event [*Ereignis*]: in it the history of the Western world comes to be borne out. It is the event of metaphysics. What now is stands in the shadow of the already foregone destiny of Being's oblivion. (*EGT*, 51)

The trace that remains in the destiny of Being is the trace of *Ereignis* which happens or traces throughout history, and which is always withdrawing into concealment in favor of what it grants, the destining of Being. And not only is it difference and *Ereignis,* but it is unconcealment too since what traces is what disappears and appears together, what is absent in presencing and presences in absence.[29] This stepping outside of difference (and the *Ereignis* and unconcealment with which it interweaves beyond as the beyond) sets us off on our way in this section; it settles nothing, it only sets us in motion.

In the essay "Moira" concerning Parmenides's fragment 8, 34-41, Heidegger writes:

> As such [the subject of the sentence "*To gar auto noein estin te kai einai*"],[30] the Same reigns. Specifically, it reigns as the unfolding of the twofold—an unfolding in the sense of disclosure. That which unfolds, and in unfolding reveals the twofold, allows taking-heed-of (thinking) to get under way toward the gathering perception of the presencing of what is present (Being). Truth, characterized

---

[29]All this talk of trace should bring Derrida to mind since he has done so much with trace in his writing. Derrida frequently suggests that Heidegger's thought of *Ereignis* gets beyond metaphysics and often talks about the "traces in Heidegger's thought" (*Spurs*), but I have never seen him draw the two together. Cf. footnote #10 for how unconcealment is more of a trace in Heidegger's thought than Derrida admits—perhaps this is what stops him from making the connections between trace and *Ereignis.*

[30]In this return to Parmenides' fragment 3, Heidegger is claiming that, contrary to the typical reading as "Thinking and Being are the Same," "the Same" must be read as the subject of the sentence to which thinking and Being are applied as two predicates. This does not depart at all from the use made of this fragment in the "Aletheia" essay.

as the disclosure of duality, lets thinking, from out of this duality, belong to Being. What is silently concealed in the enigmatic key word *to auto* is the revealing bestowal of the belonging-together of the duality and the thinking that comes forward into view within it. (*EGT*, 95)

And this should be read along with: "Could the unfolding of the twofold consist in this, that a shining which illuminates itself comes to pass (*ereignet*)? The Greeks experience its basic character as disclosure (*Entbergen*). Correspondingly, disclosure reigns in the unfolding of the twofold. The Greeks call it *Aletheia.*" (*EGT*, 93)

In an essay further elaborating the belonging-together of thinking and Being, Heidegger is significantly blurring the lines that divide the components at stake in my thesis. The Same reigns; it rules over all that endures, all that has been revealed and is now present in existence. Thinking belongs to Being and therefore can come forward as "thinking" out of the duality revealed in this belonging-together. Thinking only steps forward as itself from within the duality that it forms with Being. Presumably, the equivalent claim could be made about all that belongs-together: time and Being, man and Being, beings and Being. As what rules in all these different components, the Same is the disclosure or unfolding of the twofold, it is that out of which the two components come into their own as what they are. The unfolding which reveals the twofold is the letting belong-together of the twofold. In these passages, Heidegger is not only thinking of the Same but of *a-letheia* and *Ereignis.*

It is "duality" that is given first. The twofold unfolding unfolds duality, and this duality is more than just a relation that arises after the relata that join together in it. Recall that thinking was said to have come out of the duality, as though duality were given first and thinking emerged only later. This duality, Heidegger writes, has been forgotten—it has receded into oblivion throughout the history of metaphysics in favor of those relata that emerge out of it. The history of metaphysics, we have said, is the variation in modes of Being that have held sway in the Open throughout time. Here Heidegger calls history "the destining of the duality" (*EGT*, 98) where we can only understand the duality as the various ways Being has presenced in relation to the beings and thinking that are also "there" with it in the Open. This duality, as the historical sending of Being, is not revealed as such: it has been concealed.

"Destiny altogether conceals both the duality as such and its unfolding. The essence of *Aletheia* remains veiled" (*EGT*, 97). Dualities are revealed: Being and thinking, time and Being, man and Being; but duality as such is concealed along with its unfolding. The suggestion here is that the essence of *Aletheia* and the duality as such and its unfolding are not separate in some sense. When the one is concealed, so is the other. Perhaps the second sentence of the passage is even supposed to paraphrase or repeat the clause in the first sentence. The duality as such is the essence of *Aletheia.* And the essence of *Aletheia* was the striving between world and earth, revealing and concealing out of which unconcealment unfolded its components. The intimate strife of *Aletheia* is the duality as such and the movement (tension or agitation) of its unfolding.

This makes perfect sense since out of this striving at the heart of *a-letheia* came the Open where Being and thinking were said to reside. Now we understand that opening up of the Open as the duality as such unfolding into the twofold out of which what can be said to belong together will emerge (i.e., Being and thinking). This movement strikes me as the moment when the letting belong-together happens—that vibrating region out of which such twofold components can come into their own. The realm of striving, loving, and interplay is the region of the duality and its coming to pass. Duality as such, the unfolding of which is concealed, is a twofoldness without two components: the essence of a twofold, without their presence. It is the possibility that there is two (*es gibt)*. It is difference.

Being and beings come to pass out of their difference. The *between* of the difference between Being and beings is difference. Rather, there is Being and beings in the difference between them. This claim suggests that the relata emerge from their difference and that difference is itself the dynamic of differentiating that occurs in the giving of what is in the Open. The unconcealing or withdrawing appropriating of what unconceals in an event, is the giving of difference, the differentiating giving of what comes to pass as what it is in the open that lies there without itself Being as such. No longer a simple negation of what is, difference emerges as a component of giving/sending.

What is the Same, what belongs together as a duality, is also different (*EGT*, 88). Unlike self-present identity encountered in the principle of identity as Plato formulated it, Heidegger's notion of the Same is a holding apart of components that are together. It equally speaks of a unity and a plurality, a one and a many, a same and a different. The duality that is implied in sameness is prior to the relata that are said to be twofold, the duality is the difference out of which what is different is able to emerge. This duality as such that has receded into oblivion in the history of metaphysics is difference, the difference between Being and thinking, Being and time, Being and man. The between is not something which opens up when these elements come into proximity of each other. The between is first. I will proceed to untangle this, to clarify it as best I can; and then I can put all that has come so far into a format that will demonstrate the thesis that has guided this essay so far.

Difference is *Unterschied* in German. Heidegger develops this notion in the essay "Language":

> But neither are they [world and thing as two components that belong together] merely coupled together. For world and things do not subsist alongside one another. They penetrate each other. Thus the two traverse a middle. In it, they are at one. Thus at one they are intimate. The middle of the two is intimacy — in Latin, *inter*. The corresponding German word is *unter,* the English *inter-*. The intimacy of world and thing is not a fusion. Intimacy obtains only where the intimate — world and thing — divides itself cleanly and remains separated. In the midst of the two, in the between of world and thing, in their *inter,* division prevails: a *dif-ference*. (*PLT*, 202)

The middle, which is an intimate place that joins the world and the things that are within it, is a place between: a division that prevails between the two components, where *unter* is the between of intimacy and *schied* is the division. I can say that the components are intimate only because intimacy stretches out between them. When we talk about dif-ference we are talking about the intimacy in the middle between components, and we are talking about it as though it were outside, beyond the components, and it was from *out* of this realm that the components emerged (all emerging is a coming out from, an ecstatic movement).

Earlier we saw that Heidegger sees the moments of unconcealment as arising out of a reciprocal bestowing of favor which interpreted the Greek *philia. Philia* spoke there of intimacy and nearness. This striving that was characteristic of unconcealment is the intimacy of dif-ference, the middle place between any two components. It is easy for us to think revealing and concealing as two ordinary opposite components that reside in an intimacy out of which they arise. This is the language Heidegger himself has frequently fallen into in order to describe the nature of revealing and concealing. They have clearly been set up as opposites much like world and things or thinking and Being. We also saw that "unconcealment" is the one word rendering of this twofold movement that is analyzed, broken down, into the opposition revealing *and* concealing.

Furthermore, we saw that two components can be said to belong together only after they have come to reside in the strife (or intimacy) of unconcealing—after having come to presence out of it. The striving of revealing/concealing unfolds two components that belong together because they come to reside in the striving of unconcealment.[31]

We now see that the same is said regarding dif-ference. That the components come out of the dif-ference so as to reside there implies that this dif-ference is the striving that yields those components that come to belong there. Or rather, we might also say that this striving is the dif-ference out of which components emerge *as* different. And both striving and dif-fering are, in this formulation, being said to let belong together what belongs together. This is precisely the event that Heidegger has described as *Ereignis*. I have revealed here an element of my inquiry that I have tried hard—perhaps unconsciously—to suppress until now: whenever I make an effort to think one of the elements of the thesis, the other two immediately creep onto the stage and show themselves as well. This is characteristic of their interwovenness. Although it seems as though I am making headway on these matters, I want to continue to speak

---

[31]This mistaking revealing/concealing for an opposition, something Heidegger even does on occasion, is perhaps intrinsic to the very act of trying to think *about* un-concealment. If un-concealment speaks as revealing and concealing, it is already giving over what it says to the world of language and Being—the world, the world in which I write and think. We are seeing that all three of the elements under discussion are characterized by the *lethe,* by their being concealed (which is already to place them into a determinate framework). This suggests that the very project in which I am currently engaging (and that Heidegger engaged for all his life) is in vain, since all revealing of what is concealed by thinking plays into the hands of some metaphysical understanding of Being and origin. This crack in the foundation at the beginning of this essay is not a flaw, however, it is the very reason why this essay is being written. That is, I am seeking—in the long haul—to demonstrate that the difficulty is in the language we use to suggest these matters. We cannot refer directly to the threefold elements of the abyss (point to them) because they are what makes all such pointing possible, they underlie all such pointing and any effort at pointing has already departed from this origin (ab-origin) never to regain it with the use of the very thing that marks its departure.

In this case, I must work in a circle so as to get back to what underlies the point(ing) of departure. Beginning in the right place and making the right steps are the essential aspects of this project—the success or failure of what follows depends on it.

of dif-ference: my aim is not only to demonstrate the belonging together, but to open a path for the sequel.

Dif-ference, in English, is derived from the Latin *dis* and *ferre* meaning "apart" and "to carry," respectively. Dif-ference is a carrying apart, a carrying of something away from something else. We must also recall Heidegger's *inter,* which matters so much in the grasping of dif-ference as intimacy, which means "between." *Interesse* is the Latin word that has come to be understood in English as interest. Inter-esse is "to be between" or to be in the middle. Heidegger writes: "Interest, *interesse,* means to be among and in the midst of things, or to be at the center of a thing and to stay with it" (*WCT*, 5). When someone is deeply interested in something we often say that he is carried away by it. To be carried away with something is to be so thoroughly engrossed in it that one can be said to be in the middle of it, or that he is centered on it. "Can I call you back, I'm right in the middle of something." We also say of someone that he is self-centered, carried away with himself. When someone is in the middle of a crowd and the crowd surges in some direction, the person at the center is likely to get carried away by the crowd. Being carried away, being in the middle, intimacy, and the between are all relationships or connotations that arise in considering "dif-ference."

In the second essay of *Identity and Difference*, Heidegger pursues the question, "where does the 'between' come from, into which the difference is, so to speak, to be inserted?" (*ID*, 63) He is discussing here the difference as such between Being and beings, emphasizing that "Being as well as beings appear *by virtue of the difference*" (*ID*, 64), and has posited their revealment as "overwhelming" and "arrival." Being is sent, given by the it of *es gibt,* so that its being given results in its coming into unconcealment where this coming is a coming-over (*Überkommnis,* coming over, overwhelming). Being's coming is an overwhelming of what arrives (*ankunft* from *ankommen*), something that is in the coming over of Being. These are beings, entities, *Seienden.* Being comes over unconcealedly, it is revealed in the Open: "beings arrive as something of itself unconcealed only by that coming-over" (*ID*, 64). Being can only overwhelm if there are beings arriving to be as such in this overwhelming. The revealing of Being as that which overwhelms is the revealing of beings as that which arrives in so being overwhelmed (coming into Being): between this overwhelming and this arriving there is a difference.

> The difference of Being and beings, as the differentiation
> of overwhelming and arrival, is the perdurance (*Austrag)*
> of the two in unconcealing keeping in concealment. Within

> this perdurance there prevails a clearing of what veils and
> closes itself off—and this its prevalence bestows the being
> apart, and the being toward each other, of overwhelming
> arrival. (*ID*, 65)

Difference is perdurance where *Austrag* is "carry out of" from
tragen meaning "to carry." What comes in the overwhelming arrival can
come only because it has first been carried away from its place of origin.
A post office employee, the one who delivers the mail, is called a carrier,
he carries the letters that are destined to arrive at a household or place of
business. These letters bring news from afar and place demands on the
recipient who might be overwhelmed by the messages. But contrary to
what some critics of Heidegger have claimed, the mail is not some letter
sent once every few thousand years (like some process that sets a whole
epoch in progress and guides it from the beginning toward its end where
the message sent at the beginning will wither and the epoch will come to
an end); instead, the mail comes every day—even, in our case, on official
holidays and Sundays. [32]

Difference is therefore the dynamic of sending. All sending takes
place in the way of sending. In *Letter,* Heidegger thinks Being as that
which sends itself into the open destination where entities come to be.
But, for Being to give itself, its giving must be a differing of itself from
itself. There can be no Being *itself* if Being is that which gives itself to
itself. Rather, the self-giving of Being, is the residence of dif-ference
within Being, a difference that differentiates Being from itself. In other
words, what traditionally lies outside of Being, what traditionally differs
from Being, comes to reside in Being as that which gives or sends entities
as they are into the open. The movement of giving/unconcealing/taking
place is a movement of differentiation that places the outside inside Being
and thus destroys the possibility of Being itself outside of Being and
beings. Rather the outside of Being and beings, their difference, gives

---

[32] John Caputo sometimes suggests this in his mixture of Heidegger and
Derrida presented in *Radical Hermeneutics* (Bloomington: Indiana
University Press, 1987) as does Werner Marx in his *Heidegger and the
Tradition* (Evanston: Northwestern University Press, 1971.). Although their
presentations of the position, unlike the much more careless work of others,
do not in the least merit the polemical nature of the criticism I have made
here. In fact, they both make the position look quite attractive as a further
elaboration of the transcendental reading of Heidegger that I mentioned
above.

them from the outset, overwhelms, sends them to their destination so that they may arrive there.[33]

Austrag is linked to the coming to presence of Being and beings through the unconcealing keeping in concealment that is characteristic of their overwhelming arrival. Being and beings come into the Open, the clearing that prevails in dif-ference in/as/through *Austrag,* out of the twofold movement of unconcealment. They come to rest in the Open region opened up in/as/through unconcealment. Here the opening shows/gives (itself) as a prevailing characteristic of *Austrag,* of the carrying away that is dif-ference. This thinking of dif-ference as *Austrag* and unconcealment as an opening up of the Open (all of which can be said to happen, *er-eignen),* is that wherein Being and beings come to reside. A chief argument earlier for the impossibility of a unified origin at the foundation of all that is was that out of the singularity of the self-present oneness, any transcendence would be impossible. Now we see that Heidegger's threefold elements of thinking are the transcendence within which all that belongs together comes to be together, into relationships. There is no more need to talk of the problem of transcendence.[34]

We saw in the previous citation that dif-ference as the carrying out from, or away from, opens a clearing where the two components are bestowed as being apart and being toward each other. This clearing is, as

---

[33]I take this as an important first step along the way of positing the question concerning the relation of metaphysics to its other (deconstruction). It may be said at this point that metaphysics is given, that the ground is given, and that the dynamic outside the ground, that gives the ground, is the giving of the ground itself. Giving, therefore, is the relation of metaphysics and deconstruction. But not only giving, we have also caught a glimpse of the way giving inhabits what is given. The relation I am trying to posit is therefore one of giving and inhabiting. This theme will occupy an important place throughout this project.

[34]Transcendence is used here to suggest any movement beyond or to the outside. In *Being and Time,* transcendence is the ecstatic temporality of Dasein, the standing outside of itself of Dasein in/as/through time. This claim further develops the larger theme that Being itself can no longer be said to give itself since the possibility of giving itself is given over to Being by the incision of a difference within Being, the inhabiting of Being by difference. Difference gives itself Being so that Being can give itself to the entities that are. This forces Heidegger to think the outside that difference presents within the region opened up as metaphysics. It follows, finally, that the Being of metaphysics is called into question by the presence of difference (non-presence) in the midst of what is.

the discussion of transcendence shows, within the difference where that difference is the striving of unconcealment—it is perhaps the span or expanse, between or within the difference itself. Only because this Open region has been cleared within the difference of unconcealment can what belongs together reach out within its belonging. And this reaching out requires that they be set apart before moving toward each other in this mutual reaching. The letting happen of this reciprocal reaching is *Ereignis*. What is appropriated to itself in the Event of *Ereignis* is a reaching out between two components that belong together. The coming out of the middle point between is a coming into one's own as a component in the relationship of belonging together. This emergence out of dif-ference is characterized as *Ereignis*. In this context, the richest example might be: the inside and the outside only come to be (as a metaphysical binary) because the inside comes out of the outside and the outside is on the inside.

I mark this interweaving beyond of the threefold outside with hyphens that hold each of the words apart so that the other two may be inserted in the middle: un-concealment, *Er-eignis,* dif-ference. The hyphen is always in the middle of the word and it always opens up the word so that something can happen in the space that stretches out between the syllables. The hyphen spans the center of the word and carries the two components of the word away from each other, out of the middle, it places something from outside inside the word. It is a common charge against Heidegger that he is carried away with the hyphenization of words. Rather than defending Heidegger from this criticism by demonstrating the importance of the hyphen, I am offering him up completely to the charge. Yes, it is absolutely true, Heidegger is carried away with hyphens, the hyphen is being carried away itself, it is this same carrying away.

With the proper insertion of the hyphen, I am ready to address the thesis one more time in an effort to bring this chapter to a close through an articulation of where it leads. I repeat that: *Er-eignis,* un-concealment, and dif-ference say the Same; the Same says *Er-eignis*, un-concealment, and dif-ference. Despite a momentary doubt, we saw that both of these formulations must be maintained. The first lays claim to the saying of the principle of identity, where *Satz* is a sentence spoken as language. The second lays claim to the leap that must be made from the principle of identity to that which speaks it, where *Satz* is a leap.

We have seen that the thinking of any one of these three features has immediately led to the thinking of the other two. This is not to say that they *are* the Same, rather that when we speak of one, we are speaking of the other. In other words, all speaking done by these three features is a speaking of the same language, a saying of the Same; and all saying of the Same language is a speaking that comes from all three of these features. Their speaking is done together as though speaking required the interweaving of these three features—as if without this weaving between them, there could be no speech.

But this speaking which now comes to the fore as the interweaving of the three features is not without problems of its own. I use the word "speaking" as though I know what it means, as though it is significant for me and carries great weight. I act as if it is the answer to the inquiry, when in truth it raises more questions than it answers: questions about the logistics of this interwoven uttering that says the Same and is said by it. Furthermore, recall that the whole problematic was cast into doubt right from the outset because we needed to let these three features speak without hearing it as something that exists, and yet I said that the traditional approach to the principle of identity became suspicious because of its insistence on subsuming belonging (*gehören*) to togetherness (*zusammen*). I said that the problem with this view was that it failed to hear, *hören,* and then I said that we had to avoid hearing only ourselves in favor of hearing what is said.

The manifold problems here threaten this inquiry with danger, a danger that lies deep within it and lurks in every word uttered—it is a trailing danger that silently assaults the movement of the discussion, waiting to pounce at any moment. It is the danger of lapsing into vanity, into futility, into utter non-sense. The danger of having set out on a path that does not lead anywhere and cannot, by its very nature, have any direction. The awe-ful something which stalks this project is the very silence it seeks to demonstrate; and the fear or anxiety which runs ahead (*vorlaufen*) of this beast that follows is the yearning of a reversal where pursuer and pursued will change places—perhaps they already have and we have been moving in a circle all along. The danger *is* dangerous because its precise nature is unknown. Is it vicious? Is it virtuous?

We should venture forward into the danger without hoping to subdue it (if it is the vicious kind that needs subduing we are lost), but to befriend it, to get on intimate terms with it. If it is vicious, our befriending it will demonstrate its becoming otherwise; if it is virtuous, it should readily accept our offer of friendship. In either case, we continue and have no choice in these matters—what forces us to continue is bigger than we can manage: a stake in a game that holds life itself at bay. And we move on now in the direction that is opened up for us at this time, in the direction of speaking.

Chapter 2
This Saying That Circles

Recall the bold claim as it currently reads: *Er-eignis,* unconcealment, and dif-ference say the Same; the Same says *Er-eignis,* un-concealment, and dif-ference. The discussion in chapter 1 did not result in an exhaustive formulation of the claim. Instead, it opened it up to its boldness: it merely suggests without concluding. On the one hand, hearing, insofar as it connotes belonging, has been missing from the traditional understanding of the principle of identity; and this was developed in conjunction with the concern that we resist a certain kind of hearing. On the other hand, any familiarity with a common-place notion of "saying" became questionable. What remains, then, is an aporia of the ear and an ambiguity of the mouth. Regarding the aporia and the need to retrieve a deaf tradition without hearing (and yet, one might add, without being deaf either), only a preliminary investigation is possible during these steps in the demonstration. And these preliminary remarks will be no more than the residue of the inquiry into the other matter: the ambiguity of saying.

Immediately, it should be noted that saying should not be confounded with human speech. In the bold claim that seems to govern this essay, "saying" is the verb in both clauses of the claim. It would only be slightly misleading to add that no other verb (except a synonym, if there are any) could replace "saying" here. Furthermore, "saying"—as it is used here—could not be given to any other subject. We might observe, then, that "saying" is appropriated from the English language by this bold claim and to it: the boldness of the claim is no doubt that it claims "saying." It is for this reason that translators of Heidegger have appropriately capitalized the word: saying here is Saying.

"Saying" replaces "Language" in Heidegger's thinking beginning in 1953/4 with "A Dialogue on Language."[1] The two words are roughly

---

[1] Richardson attributes this change, on p. 633 of his book, to Heidegger's increasing awareness of the metaphysical implications of the word "language." In the following sections, I will be supporting this reading in more detail. It is also interesting to note that Richardson translates *Sage* as

synonymous, but a key ambiguity is dispelled by the shift. In the essay "Language" of 1951, we see two phrases juxtaposed to each other: "Man speaks" and "Language speaks." These are not identical. *Die Sprache sprecht* (Language speaks or, literally, language languages) is reminiscent of the Heideggerian tautologies, all of which evoke the Same. The other phrase, *Der Mensch spracht,* does no such thing—it speaks in a different way. The shift, therefore, dissolves the possibility of confusing the workings of Language with the workings of human speech. The two are related, of course, but they are not identical, and separating them may be the necessary preliminary stage for bringing them together. This shift in terminology, however, confuses as much as it clarifies. The move to Saying from Language veils the tautological quality of Saying. This confusion is furthered by the bold claim which presents the three elements as though they were the subject of the sentence to which Saying is the verb. The bold claim of this essay, however, attempts to restore Saying to its place of tautology.

What makes this restoration possible is the undermining of the subject-verb construction that takes place in the reversal of the second clause relative to the first. In the previous chapter, this reversal was described in terms of a principle that becomes a leap (*Satz* to *Satz*) where the former reminded us of the principle of identity and the latter of the leap out of traditional metaphysical thinking. The tautology is not evident in the repetition of a noun as a verb (*Ereignis ereignet, Sprache sprecht,* etc.), but in the reversal of a clause that only seems to repeat what has preceded it (it should be noted that a verbal presentation of a noun does not *identically* repeat what it follows). Repetition of this kind is the tautology of the Same that has been working throughout this essay: the Same as the belonging together in unity of what is different. Still, the repetition of a clause over and against the repetition of a noun as verb cannot be thought as mere tautology, but can be thought as an economy of tautology. The bold claim preserves the tautological quality of Saying by inserting it (or, more accurately, letting it be *ex*-perienced as *in*-serted) in an economy *of* the Same.

According to these developments, two revisions must be made in the bold claim: *Er-eignis,* un-concealment, and dif-ference Say the Same: the Same Says *Er-eignis,* un-concealment, and dif-ference. I capitalize "Saying" so as to highlight its appropriate relation to the rest of the claim;

"aboriginal utterance" which suggests the sort of abysmal economy that I am here trying to develop.

and I replace the semi-colon with a colon to highlight the repetition of the bold claim.

Even still, a danger remains in this formulation. It is not a danger that can be dispelled by reformulating the claim. Instead, facing this danger requires a deeper look at the repetition occurring in the claim's inversion. The problem of a faded tautology seems to have been evaded by developing tautology as an economy (a plurality of relations rather than a single simple relation). With this economy, danger persists in the claim's grammar. Above, I suggested a disadvantage to the bold claim's resembling an assertion presenting a subject and predicate and inverting itself by merely switching the position of the subject with that of the predicate. As inverted assertions, the bold claim presents—as existing in Being—a nexus or economy of concepts that relate in various fashions, a relation that is inverted within the bold claim (this would be an economy of exchange no doubt). This making-present of the economy of the claim through exchange goes against everything articulated in the first steps of this demonstration. In other words, the bold claim makes present the elements that are supposed to "say" all coming into presence. For instance, how can un-concealment as the tension between revealing/concealing as world/earth be made present? A laborious effort has been made to show how this economy is precisely outside the Being of what is purely present, of what has come to be as such.[2] How could the claim present what excludes and precedes all presence? How could an economy without identity suffer from the equations necessary for exchange?

For the most part, the response to this dilemma will be the task of the following chapter. It is possible, however, to begin by offering some introductory remarks. The relation of *Er-eignis,* un-concealment, and difference to each other and to the Same cannot be equated to the relation between a subject and a predicate. The key flaw in the analogy is the copula. Typically, a verb used in such a sentence will imply the copula, the Saying of the Same implies *is* Saying the same, for example. But this

---

[2] So, in terms of the development of system, at this point the economy is transcendental where the material conditioned by the conditions of possibility are, strictly speaking, the matter of transcendence. I take it that at this point, my reading of Heidegger is roughly in line with the very common reading found throughout the literature (i.e., Schürmann, Caputo, Kockelmans, and Marx as suggested in the previous chapter). But I have not finished yet, and the key move comes when the transcendental no longer conditions transcendence, but collapses into it. This will have taken place by the end of this chapter as noted in the introduction.

is not the case here. There is no Being in the bold claim, the bold claim is not claiming anything concerning Being. Perhaps the primary difficulty is the conjugation of the verb "to say." Rather than "Saying," the claim offers "Say" and "Says." Conjugation implies Being and it implies a subject that precedes the verb and a predicate that succeeds it.

Furthermore, the conjugated form of the verb suggests, in this context at least, that there is a realm of the three elements that serve as subject and that pre-exists all Saying. As though first of all and before anything else there were the nexus of the three (what we might synonymously call the Same) that Say. This is basically an anthropomorphism where a common understanding of speech as an activity performed by a human organism is abstracted to the most "universal" level. This linear reading of the claim describes a source that is articulated through an active verb and is common to the tradition of which Heidegger attempts to step outside. The implied "is" of the verb and the linear progression from subject as agent of activity to the activity itself are correlated within a larger body of "metaphysical" claims. And the structure of *this* essay facilitates such understanding of the matter. After all, the first chapter lay out the weirdness—this nexus of elements outside pure Being, and the second chapter shall proceed true to form by discussing Language as the effect of this source (its transmission). This progression does not differ from any thinking that begins by positing a ground before going on to derive the determined elements from it.

It is not trivial, therefore, to move away from conjugated formulations of "to say." In fact, the move away from genetic developments proceeding from an origin is the movement of deconstruction emigrating outside of metaphysics while remaining inside its structure (perhaps like a virus); it is the eccentricity of metaphysics' outside. "Saying," which will now replace "say" and "says" in the bold claim, must be understood as an eccentric circling:

Er-eignis, un-concealment, and dif-ference
Saying
the Same:
the Same
Saying
Er-eignis, un-concealment, and dif-ference.

All along it has been tempting to view "Saying's" position as stationary within the claim. Nothing could be more natural: the subject and predicate change positions while the verb remained where it was. This sedentary understanding of "to say" belongs to the metaphysical understanding of the bold claim. In the new formulation, the economy circles, a circling interweaving the components: Saying surrounds the Same and is surrounded by its components. This circulation is an economy, an economy of the Same, of Saying, etc., where all circling is seen as a repetition that fails to identify each instance of the movement, fails to exchange one moment for another. True to this revised (or repeated) form of the bold claim, this chapter, which runs the risk of being read as a linear effect of the first chapter, circles back to what has preceded it. Therefore, the concern here will not only be with Saying, but with Saying as it plays within the weirdness that appears to have introduced it, but may just as easily have been introduced by it.

From what has been said thus far, two sections of the upcoming chapter can be delimited: (1) the circling back of Saying will attempt to elaborate "Saying" in terms of its relationship to the three components of "weirdness" from chapter 1, while also developing the circularity of Saying and revealing its immanence to the movement of "weirdness;" and (2) the opening up that occurs in this circular movement demands attention—"opening" was mentioned in the first chapter and is intimately connected to the circling back of Saying, yet it also merits a separate discussion as "opening" can be the articulation of a dimension where what is can come to be. Such an opening, which takes place in the weird circling of Saying, dynamically unfolds in/as/through a call that lays claim to whatever is capable of hearing it (i.e., stepping into the Open—making one's way into it—and dwelling there, ears raised to listen).

The Circling Back of Saying

"What is Saying?," it might be tempting to ask at the outset of this way of thinking; and the answer, "Saying is..." would be elicited. But the response trails off as a non-answer: "Saying is nothing, Saying *is* not." In the first chapter, I demonstrated other ways in which this formulation occurs. *Er-eignis,* un-concealment, and dif-ference, likewise, *are* not. They are *this* weirdness *that* takes place—demonstratively, they are that in/as/through which all taking place takes place. This occurring was likened to the sending of what *is* from nothing. In his essay on "The Nature of Language" Heidegger equates this sending of what is with a granting. All that is, is granted, given over like a gift. Saying is the grant, it is the giving over of what is given in Being, of all that is (*OWL*, 75). Because Saying grants what is, we cannot properly discuss Saying in terms of what it is. To do so would be to describe it in terms of the part of it that is present, while ignoring that part of it that is absent or in transition. It would be like making an object out of Saying so as to describe it in its objectivity, while ignoring the aspects of it that are objectifying. In this case, describing what Saying *is* amounts to speaking *about* it where "about" should remind us of the German *gegen*, which is the base of the word *Gegenstand*, object. "Saying" that is an object does not speak, it says nothing.

> *Inquirer*: Speaking about language turns language almost inevitably into an object.
> *Japanese*: And then it really vanishes. (*OWL*, 50)

At the beginning of the essay on "The Nature of Language," Heidegger talks about undergoing an experience with language so that "in experiences which we undergo *with* language, language itself brings itself to language" (*OWL*, 59). Earlier in the same essay, Heidegger had opened the discussion with some remarks about the undergoing of an experience at all, about how undergoing an experience with something, anything, is a being overwhelmed and transformed by that something. More specifically,

> to undergo an experience with language, then, means to let ourselves be properly concerned by the claim of language by entering into and submitting to it. If it is true that man finds the proper abode of his existence in language—whether he is aware of it or not-then an experience we undergo with language will touch the innermost nexus of our existence. (*OWL*, 57)

Rather than speaking about language, we must take up our residence within language and let language bring itself to itself there. Presumably, both of these moments of the experience will happen together: our experience with language will not only deliver us over to language, but will bring language to itself. This suggests some remarks Heidegger makes elsewhere regarding the reflexive nature of language.[3]

---

[3]"We would reflect on language itself, and on language only. Language itself is—language and nothing else besides. Language itself is language. The understanding that is schooled in logic, thinking of everything in terms of calculation and hence usually overbearing, calls this proposition an empty tautology. Merely to say the identical thing twice—language is language—

Contrary to the claim that language is something speakers learn to use to express their conscious thoughts and of which they, through age and practice, can gain a certain amount of control, Heidegger sees language as that place where we are *already,* where we have been born and will dwell all of our lives—whether we realize it or not. Properly speaking, then, it is language which speaks: language is not, rather language speaks.

> "Language is language." This statement does not lead us to something else in which language is grounded. Nor does it say anything about whether language itself may be a ground for something else. The sentence "Language is language," leaves us to hover over an abyss as long as we endure what it says. (*PLT*, 191)

Language, like weirdness, brings us into an abyss. The undergoing of an experience with language brings us into language such that language comes to itself (I might say, anticipating what is to come, that language comes into its own) as groundless. Entering into and submitting to the reflexive being (as in *wesen*) of language is hovering over an abyss; one might even say that groundless language is abysmal.

Already we are beginning to experience the circling of language: Language, without ground and not a ground itself, comes from nowhere and goes nowhere. And yet, Heidegger has told us, our entrance into language is a coming to be where we already are. It is because we live within language that our experience with language leaves us hovering over an abyss. Furthermore, since language touches us in the heart of our existence when we undergo an experience with it, our very existence becomes abysmal—a circling within language. We have looked into the abyss and it has looked back at us. But lest we become frozen with dread, we must slow down and retreat a little as we have already advanced too far, too fast, along the way.

How is it that here I have been writing about language when this discussion began with Saying? Heidegger repeatedly tells us that language, as he is concerned with it in his later thought, is not the everyday use of language commonly referred to as human speech: "To say and to speak are not identical. A man may speak endlessly, and all the time say nothing. Another man may remain silent, not speak at all and

---

how is that supposed to get us anywhere? But we do not want to get anywhere. We would like only, for once, to get to just where we are already." (*PLT*, 190) From the essay "Language" originally published in the German edition of *Unterwegs zu Sprache.*

yet, without speaking, say a great deal" (*OWL*, 122). Here speaking refers to human speech, to the movement of mouths and the voicing of sound; it is a very specific activity that makes up some part of most humans' lives. Saying, on the other hand, is not such an activity or practice and has little to do with the voice and the movement of various organs. But it is still not quite time to speak of Saying.

Human speech as voice is not merely "the articulated vocalization of thought by means of the organs of speech. But speaking is at the same time also listening" (*OWL*, 123). That is, quite simply, we do not merely invent our speech *ex nihilo* each time we perform an act of utterance; rather, we come to our speaking lives through a language that is given to us and already developed. Our speaking, therefore, is more a sculpting of language to particular circumstances than a creative invention without matter. Both the form and matter of language pre-exist our instantiation of variations of it. "Speaking is listening to the language which we speak. Thus, it is a listening not *while* but *before* we are speaking" (*OWL*, 123). It is not that we are listening to ourselves speaking in a perfect self-present system; rather, we have listened to language before opening our mouths, and it is such listening that enables us to open our mouths in the first place as a response to what we have heard. Quite plainly, we speak language because we listen to language. And, before the charge of contradiction can be shouted, I add that the speaking of language following upon all listening to language is what Heidegger has called the speaking *of* language (*die Sprache sprecht)*. Language speaks in/as/through any human speaking of it which follows upon its having been heard. When we respond to the language that speaks to us, we speak in the manner of speaking that has been given over to us in our hearing. It follows that we are always speaking within the confines of a language that comes to us and to which our own speaking is a response: "the speaking of a particular language."[4]

Insofar as we are not aware that language is speaking to us and enabling us to speak it, we may mishear what has been said to us. In this mishearing, language continues to be spoken, albeit badly. Again, mishearing might be thought in terms of speaking about language mentioned above. Precisely what speaking about language is (aside from

---

[4]This phrase is intentionally ambiguous as it implies both the ordinary conception of a particular language user's ability to speak that language and the language itself that is speaking in the response. Also, the idea of a "manner" of speaking has to be left ambiguous at this stage. It shall be developed and explained further in what follows.

being precisely what we are doing here and shall have to resolve shortly), can be seen in all speaking that devotes itself to the objects already present in a perceptual field without heeding the process by which that object comes to reside in the field. Thus, an interpretation of one kind or another takes absolute authority over the being of the entity in question—the entity is understood in terms of its presence as a direct result of a language that speaks in terms of presence (i.e., as propositions about entities that are already there to be spoken about). In our present case, language, spoken in ignorance of its speaking to us is equivalent to the chatter of fools who can be told nothing as they live a life destined to make its own mistakes. A language all the time speaking speaking speaking without pausing to listen, without pause for letting the process that works through language come to pass (er-eignet) so as to surpass any special and exclusive emphasis laid on the particular words spoken and the authority of those who have spoken them.[5] The presence of language in its being misheard is, therefore, not only that it is an object for linguistics but that in the daily speaking of it we have no concern for hearing what speaks to us in/as/through language, but only in our speaking of language that drones on in conversation and foibles that needn't take place or, at the very least, which drown out the proper speech of language itself that we are, after all, mishearing.[6]

We speak because we hear and proper hearing is the hearing of what is essential to the speaking of language (*EGT*, 65). Essential to the speaking of language means the essence of the language that speaks through us, since the "of" is taken as an objective genitive. The essence of language is Saying. "Yet *language* speaks. Language first of all and inherently obeys the essential nature of speaking: it says. Language speaks by saying, that is, by showing" (*OWL*, 124). "*The essential being of language is Saying as Showing*" (*OWL*, 123). Leaving aside for the moment the introduction of the new term of showing, we can remark that Saying is the essence of language and, therefore, of all speaking— although Heidegger works the argumentation in the opposite direction. We speak because we hear language which speaks to and through us in its essential nature as Saying. There are entire languages that lead to

---

[5]For example, a language of reference and intention.

[6]It is noteworthy that in French *entendre* signifies both hearing and understanding. In that case, language as something that must be listened to is also what must be understood and all mishearing is misunderstanding. In so far as speaking depends on hearing/understanding, it should be more apparent that speaking can nevertheless go on even if we have misunderstood—in fact, it happens all the time in daily talk.

mishearing, where mishearing is the manner of hearing proper to them. A language commonly called "objective" or "representational" is one such example, at the very least because it requires the objectification of what renders all objects present.[7] These are languages and manners of hearing where the essential nature of language as Saying is not heard. In this case notice that mishearing gains its "mis-" from its relation to Saying and not from its relation to language.[8]

Earlier I equated language with Saying when comparing the work of 1951 with the work of 1957. Here we see that the equation is not a simple one. All speaking says; language insofar as it is speaking says. That contradicts the view that sometimes human beings speak without saying anything. This is absolutely crucial to the elaboration of these elements:

> Speaking *qua* saying something, belongs to the design of the being of language, the design which is pervaded by all the modes of saying of what is said, in which everything present or absent announces, grants or refuses itself, shows itself or withdraws. This multiform saying from many different sources is the pervasive element in the design of the being of language. With regard to the manifold ties of saying, we shall call the being of language in its totality 'Saying'—and confess that even so we still have not caught sight of what unifies those ties. (*OWL*, 122-3)

Here we see that there is a new category distinction that is being employed by Heidegger which leads us to see a false inconsistency. Human speech is not identical to the speaking of language, that has been said already. And although language speaks through us in being listened to by us, our speaking is not the speaking of language (i.e., in its essence). Language, as demonstrated previously, is speaking before any human beings ever open their mouths. The speaking that has its essential dynamic in/as/through Saying is the speaking appropriate to the being of language. When language speaks essentially it is *also* Saying. Our speech can only fail to say when it has misheard the essential speaking of language. There

---

[7] Support for this claim will be the focus in much of chapter 4.

[8] All talk of essences here might be understood in terms of the verbal *wesen* described in the previous chapter. *Wesen* was described as "dynamic unfolding" where that suggests the unconcealment of the open. Saying, therefore, as the essence of language, implies that the essence of language is dynamic unfolding. Demonstrating or *showing* this will take place in what follows.

are, then, languages that are prone to mishear in that mishearing is an erring or oblivion to the Saying that goes on in language as its essence. All languages that are not essential are misheard: mishearing is a failure to hear the essence of language, which is not to say that the essence doesn't continue to speak through them, only that it is not listened to. Despite the fact that I am using the same word for human speaking and language's speaking, I am not referring to identical phenomena. This should make clear the claim that "language speaks" and "Saying" can be equated without running the risk of contradicting ourselves in the subsequent claim that some languages speak without Saying anything, or leave Saying unsaid in what they say. We shall not be fooled into thinking that because Saying is the dynamic unfolding of language it is somehow something other than language. The reflexive nature of language, that all we can say is that language speaks (appropriately), leaves no room for an Other to the essence of language. It might be tempting to say along with Rorty that language is all there is (*es gibt)*, thus emphasizing the equation of the essence of language with the speaking of language (in all its forms and manners determined as such by their oblivion *or* heeding of the essence), but of course we would have to immediately go on to add something Rorty misses: language is not all there is.[9]

Now that the sought after terms are a *little* more clear, it is possible to begin to focus on the Saying that was to have been our theme in the first place. Returning to the passage cited from "The Way to Language," notice the familiar characteristics ascribed to Saying within which "everything present or absent announces, grants or refuses itself, shows itself or withdraws." Within Saying, worlds are being made through the revealing/concealing of things within them. This reference to revealing/concealing recalls *a-letheia* and hence the other components in the nexus. Saying is more than mere language—English or Swahili for example—it is the world or significant context within which all that is comes to be and ceases to be. This nonlinguistic, "existential" nature of Saying is what leads me, initially, back to the components that I have already covered in the essay. To get at the Saying of language, I must now circle back to where I have been already so as to examine the dynamic

---

[9]This immensely charged claim should barely make sense; it is a claim that, hopefully, rests on the boundary or frontier of sense. It is only because language is and is not all there is (and hence is Saying), that there can be anything like multiple manners of speaking and hearing. The strangeness (or weirdness?) of this claim will have to be unravelled slowly in what is to come.

unfolding of Saying in/as/through *a-letheia, Er-eignis,* and dif-ference. I shall continue along this way momentarily.[10]

---

[10]In fact, I can only continue and not begin this circling because I showed that, in the midst of the discussion, I had already begun this circling back. The circling back, therefore, can be said to have slipped into the project without being explicitly invoked. All the while, thus far, I have been speaking—pretty transparently—*about* language and Saying. Yet, in the midst of this objectification, the text has been carried along from underneath, so to speak, by a current that forced me to circle back to where I have already been. Circling back is something that took place (*er-eignet*) within the movement of speaking about Saying. This requires a few marginal "methodological" observations.

At the end of "Time and Being" Heidegger, after discussing the *Er-eignis* that gives time and Being, writes: "The lecture has spoken merely in propositional statements" (*TB*, 24). This final sentence of the lecture seems to undermine much of what has taken place throughout it. He is claiming to have addressed the *Es gibt* of *Er-eignis* in terms of the given presence that resides at some distance from the withdrawing event. Yet he must admit that something of the matter for thinking has taken place in the lecture, if only in an obscure and elusive manner. *Er-eignis* does reside in this lecture, despite its being covered over by the propositions that Heidegger uses to reveal it, it resides as covered over (as lying underneath, so to speak). It might be argued that there are other essays where Heidegger does not speak in such propositional form and so better accomplishes the Saying of the event. Such essays as "Language in the Poem" and "Remembrance of the Poet" perhaps. These essays are obscure, elusive, and beautiful—deeply poetic, yet they make for difficult exposition in the format I am currently organizing. Furthermore, a manner of speaking or writing that follows the manner of Heidegger's essays, may not be suitable for the needs of this project (after all, if they were, why not just read Heidegger—a question I highly recommend to the reader.). As a result, it would seem that the underlying manner of "Time and Being" is what is required here. There is, therefore, throughout this text, a subtext that constantly pushes toward the surface, attempting to dismantle the text itself (to de-structure or de-construct it). If such an approach is to be successful in hearing the matter for thinking, it must circle constantly from underneath. Such a circling will undoubtedly continually attempt to replace the inquiry at the beginning. The final chapter of this essay will bring us, hopefully, full circle back to where we began (i.e., the matter for thinking). Therefore, whenever I discuss the necessity of the movement of this essay, I am gesturing toward the underlying circling that is constantly carrying the project along and back to where it began, to where it already is.

Before doing so, I'll make some last remarks on the quotation above and the points it raises for consideration along the way. First, it is impossible not to feel a certain unity in Saying and therefore to understand it as a ground of all that is. In the passage, Saying is dispersed into a multiplicity of modes where their unity is not caught sight of. All the modes of Saying are just that, modes *of* Saying, which is presumably the self-same Saying for each of the modes. What that means and how the self-same is constituted *as such* are beyond our scope at the moment. The future attempt at gaining this insight will be made more difficult since the self-sameness of Saying is not grounded in or the ground of anything. This first concern suggests the abysmal nature of Saying in its various modifications. Second, I cannot help but latch onto the word "totality" in Heidegger's phrase and be reminded of his use of the word "totality" in *Being and Time* while discussing the being of the world as significance. "Totality" no doubt closes the system of Saying without being aware of the bonds that keep the system closed (i.e., the unity that has not been caught sight of). At first, this concern may seem like the previous one, and many of its implications *are* those of the first concern. Nevertheless, there is this reference to *Being and Time* which lets me think of meaning as a property of Saying. Meaning was a totality in *Being and Time* and it made up the Being of the world within which all that is came to reside. Another way of putting this is that all that is is meaningful or, negatively, there is no nonsense. But that, pardon the play, is absurd. There certainly is non-sense and the history of human beings and the world is not only a history of meaning, despite the clear implications of this in *Being and Time*. It is almost certain that it was the totalizing quality of meaning that led Heidegger to drop the term from his thinking in the subsequent years after *Being and Time*. Totality, for Heidegger, implied presence, closure and an oblivion to the dynamic unfolding of language and the world. Therefore, connected but not identical to the concern for unity in the phenomenon of Saying will be the concern for any reduction of Saying to a totality such as meaning, which becomes one mode of Saying among others and not Saying itself, which Heidegger might have implied in the passage cited.

The citation seems to imply that Saying is a complex unity or closed totality of various modes of Saying. Neither this nor the possibility that Heidegger held this view throughout his later work should be taken for granted. Heidegger's admission of ignorance following the labelling of Saying is a provocative hint that appearances of unity can be deceiving.

Saying and *A-letheia*

This conjunction has been suggested already in the hendiadys of "Saying *or* showing" and throughout Heidegger's work of the fifties. Hendiadys, from the Greek meaning "one through two," is a form of belonging together; the words combined in the conjunction are the same: "'To say,'[*sagen*] related to the Old Norse '*saga*,' means to show: to make appear, set free, that is, to offer and extend what we call World, lighting and concealing it. This lighting and hiding proffer of the world is the dynamic unfolding of Saying" (*OWL*, 93, translation altered). All that human beings have come to think they know about language must be bracketed at this moment of discovery in/as/through Heidegger's text. He is not here concerned with reference or sense, structure or sign; but with Saying as showing understood as the lighting/concealing of world, the opening up of un-concealment. Earlier we came to see this movement as a striving and, recalling this strife seen equally as intimacy, love, and struggle, we are not surprised to see that same phenomenon referred to as a Saga. My dictionary tells me that a Saga is on the one hand "an Icelandic prose narrative of the 12th or 13th centuries recounting historical and legendary events and exploits," and on the other hand "any long narrative."[11] We have already seen connections of un-concealment and *Er-eignis* (appropriating event); and so it should therefore only be a slight advance to see how the taking place of their nexus is a Saga, the Saga of the world. Saying as showing is built into the movement of *A-letheia*, revealing and concealing. I might even claim that Saying as showing is *the* movement of *A-letheia*.

It should be obvious from the preceding, however, that these matters run aground when it comes to presenting them in formulas. Saga, Saying or showing, cannot *really* be built into the movement of *A-letheia*, nor can it really *be* the movement of *A-letheia*. The first phrase suggests a distinction that doesn't prevail—Saying is not something over and against *A-letheia* to be built into it, to happen alongside it. Nor can we compare the existence of each of the elements, *A-letheia* and Saga, so as to see them as identical in the way I have done in the second phrase. Heidegger

---

[11] "My dictionary" is the American Heritage Dictionary. I selected it because it is the most "grocery store" type of dictionary (they sometimes have one on a shelf with bestsellers near the cashier). That is, I intentionally used the dictionary that would give me the most ordinary meanings of words relative to everyday English for the sake of discovering the still very prominent connections between essential Saying and vernacular English.

recognizes this difficulty and so provides thinking with a "guide-word" to lead it into the relation between *A-letheia* and Saga:

> The being of language: the language of being.
>   Two phrases held apart by a colon, each the inversion of the other. If the whole is to be a guide-word, then this colon must indicate that what precedes it opens into what follows it. Within the whole there plays a disclosure and a beckoning that point to something which we, coming from the first turn of phrase, do not suspect in the second; for that second phrase is more than just a rearrangement of the words in the first. If so, then what the words 'being' and 'language' on either side of the colon say is not only not identical, but even the form of the phrase is different in each case. (*OWL*, 94)

This guide-word is not new, as it recalls the phrase from "On the Essence of Truth" discussed in chapter 1: "The essence of truth: the truth of essence." This phrase began an effort at understanding the nature of *a-letheia* as the dynamic movement, thought by Heidegger through his reading of Heraclitus, as *physis*. I called *physis* dynamic unfolding when rendering in English the term *wesen* from the second clause of the guide-word: dynamic unfolding is *nothing other* than the movement of *a-letheia*. "The being of language: the language of *a-letheia*" is the way to say, following Heidegger, this guide-word.[12]

The essence of language: the Saying-showing of *a-letheia* as dynamic unfolding. The circle inversion of the clause is the most natural thing on earth. It is almost impossible to avoid this circling. The bold claim circles, the guide-word circles, the essence of truth circles, and now, this most recent effort at restating the guide-word circles. This circling that might be called an inversion, if the speaker gives way to certain tendencies in language, is an effort at avoiding a hierarchy that yields a ground to one element in the nexus and renders the other elements derivative. By circling, dynamic unfolding or un-concealing in/as/through

---

[12]The link raised here between showing and *a-letheia* (and which quickly disappears now that we read it as a link between Saying and *a-letheia*) suggests that showing—as in what happens in phenomenology and in the articulation of Saying—is not a gesturing toward what is present in front of an observer and thus can be made present to another who is following along with the observer's gesture. I am claiming that the showing of the gesture that goes on in all Saying is a showing that un-conceals where absence and hiddenness is just as dynamic an impetus as is presence.

language, neither element gains the primordial upper hand: the two equally lay claim to each other. But this is not an expository technique of a writer trying to make his point clear. Rather, it is the circulation of an economy of the Same, it is a movement of *a-letheia* in/as/through Saga; or, better still, economizing (itself), Saying (itself). And still better: the essence of language: the Saying of un-concealment.

Un-concealment occurs in virtue of the striving between revealing and concealing. Earlier I referred to this striving of revealing/concealing as nearness. Heidegger further substantiates this circling of Saying within un-concealment through a discussion of the nearness of Saying:

> The guide-word gives us a hint on this way [into the neighborhood of poetry and thinking], but not an answer. But that hint-where does it point? It points only to what defines the neighborhood of poetry and thinking as a neighborhood. Neighborliness, dwelling in nearness, receives its definition from nearness. Poetry and thinking, however, are modes of saying, indeed preeminent modes. If these two modes of saying are to be neighborly in virtue of their nearness, then nearness itself must act in the manner of Saying. Then nearness and Saying would be the Same. The demand to think this is still a flagrant imposition. Its flagrancy must not be softened in the least. (*OWL*, 95)[13]

Nearness is distance, or lack thereof, between (i.e., differing or separating) revealing and concealing. This distance is absolute in the sense that it is never overcome by proximity or a fading into the distance. It is the striving where revealing and concealing are in tension, thus enabling the world and earth to open up and come to rest upon each other in the strife. All un-concealing is an un-concealing out of the nearness or of the nearness. This nearness recalls the belonging-together of the Same where the two elements are neither identical nor separate members of an oppositional pair. Instead they form a unity in their difference, a oneness through two (hendiadys) which has been called a pure relation or relation as such.[14] It is the same feature that is now being attributed to Saying in

---

[13]For the moment, we will have to settle for an understanding of poetry and thinking as indiscriminate modes of Saying. A more detailed discussion of the specific qualities of these "preeminent" modes of Saying will occupy us later.

[14]And therefore, is neither oneness nor two. The possibility of singularity and binarity (and plurality for that matter) can only be understood as an effect

so far as all the modes of Saying belong together (what Heidegger is calling dwelling in the same neighborhood). The so called "unity" of Saying that Heidegger posits without catching a glimpse of it reveals itself in/as/through nearness.

Referring to nearness, and Saying as nearness (which, as Heidegger says awkwardly, are the Same), as a unity, is more than a little curious. Nearness can only be called a unity in so far as belonging-together could be called a unity and belonging-together, as suggested by Heidegger's reversal of the Parmenidean principle of identity, which led to a pure and singular unity of all that is. Instead, I want to claim that there is an understanding of nearness in so far as it relates to Saying and an understanding of nearness as it relates to un-concealment. And this means that Saying dynamically strives: opens and hides such that the opening and hiding strive. Recall that world and earth are in tension; they do battle and let a clearing open and set itself to rest in the tension filled battlefield. The clearing, however, is neither the pure presence of revealment nor the pure absence of concealment; instead, clearing, in a sense, is the tension of the striving between world and earth, revealing and concealing. The tense "source" of all this opening and hiding of un-concealment is what Heidegger calls "nearness." The nearness strives and is in tension. Nearness is the gap that enables the opening up of the Open within the striving of world and earth—as the striving of world and earth. And because nearness includes distance, the striving opens in a multiple fashion, meaning that there are many different possible combinations or modifications of the open that can come to rest within the striving: the possibilities of the Open are open-ended.

Nearness as striving characterizes Saying as well as un-concealing. Saying opens up or articulates itself in terms of multiple modifications of Saying. These modes of Saying are neighbors; they dwell together in the neighborhood of the Same, since they are articulated within the same Saying. Saying articulates various modes of Saying because it is nearness, likewise un-concealment and the various modes of openness which have previously been called epochs or worlds. If nearness in Saying were presence or absence, then there could be no multiplicity of possible modes, since complete revelation would leave no room for an additional

---

of such a difference. Equally "nearness" is not a spatial concept (nor temporal) but it is only because there is nearness that time and space can be understood in any of their various modes. This will come up later on in discussing Derrida since it is my position that this notion of "nearness" is comparable to Derrida's thought of *Differánce* which is the possibility of all time and space and hence disrupts all presence based on a conception of the present as self-present.

mode aside from the present one (or whatever was generated out of it at its end) and complete concealment would leave no room at all, not even for one single mode of Saying.

Concealment is an essential element of Saying just as it is in un-concealment. We saw with un-concealment that all revealing came out of concealment but only so far as we understood concealment as intimately tied together with revelation and not some detachable pure phenomenon. In terms of Saying, the concealment that plays with all revelation is the stillness of silence. Silence is not a mode of Saying, rather it is an interwoven dynamic feature of all Saying; nor is silence or stillness a complete absence of all Saying, rather all Saying is permeated by a stillness that inhabits it. As I said in this chapter's introduction, even those who keep silent can say a great deal since silence, essential to all Saying, is inhabited by Saying.[15] "The soundless gathering call, by which Saying moves the world-relation on its way, we call the ringing of stillness. It is: the language of being" (*OWL*, 108). *This* stillness, resting in the nearness of Saying, enables the multiple modifications of Saying; and stillness requires that any effort at hearing differences in the various modes concern itself just as much with what the Saying leaves unsaid as with what the Saying says.

This discussion might just as well have been framed in terms of "relation" as indicated previously. The nearness of striving as the opening up of the open in un-concealment could just as well be thought as the relation "as such." Likewise, Heidegger refers to the Saying in terms of relation: "Language is, as world-moving Saying, the relation of all relations. It relates, maintains, proffers, and enriches the face-to-face encounter of the world's regions, holds and keeps them, in that it holds itself-Saying-in reserve" (*OWL*, 107). Relation as such is frequently allied with difference and so will come up again in the section devoted to it. What matters here, however, is the way that relation is demonstrated as being universal to all that happens within the world. Since the world is relationships, relation as such is essential to the opening up of world

---

[15]There is a type distinction that is being glossed over here for the sake of brevity. Silence as stillness is not the same as the silence that is a failure to utter a sound: Stillness is not Saying at all (even if it never can be separated), whereas the silence of soundlessness is still a Saying. Although human beings can be silent by not making a sound, they can never be still, although stillness inhabits them insofar as they hearken to any Saying. The two types are being used as roughly analogous here, but only for the sake of a clarifying example. I will come back to this in due time.

in/as/through relationships. Likewise, language understood as relationships would be equally dependent on dynamically unfolding relations that enable the opening up—which is nothing other than the coming into relation of the various relationships that say language (or the world). In this process, relation itself gets concealed in favor of the related elements.[16]

By looking briefly at nearness and relation we have gained, aside from seeing the connections of Saying and un-concealing (both of which might be called showing), a few insights toward better understanding the movement of un-concealment and, hence, Saying. When I refer to the opening up of Saying as articulation, I am making note of the way relationships come into relation through the movement of Saying (i.e. the saying of Saying). Furthermore, I acknowledge that such coming into relation will happen in a variety of modes. For example, using the text of *Being and Time,* some modes of relation are equipmental (ready-to-hand) while others are theoretical (present-at-hand). In addition, some modes are technological, others poetic or thoughtful. These modes of relations, saying, un-concealing, or nearness all strive together in the Same, where this may not imply that, opposed to it, there is some place outside the Same: even concealment occurs in/as/through the Same.

In addition, I made some gestures toward a better understanding of the connection between the striving of world and earth and the Open that opens up in this battle. The discussion of this phenomenon in the first chapter made it seem as though the open region or clearing was a result of the strife, some effect of the economy (perhaps a depression in it). The initial absence of the Open within the bold claim no doubt contributes to this misunderstanding. Although the majority of this discussion must wait until the second part of this chapter, I can make an effort now to clarify

---

[16]It is worth mentioning that the previous passage describes something held in reserve or held back in the world moving relation of Saying. Of course, what is held back is frequently alluded to in discussions such as those on stillness, nearness, and *Er-eignis;* but it is important to recall the remarks made about giving and the economy in chapter 1. An economy in which something is held back, or kept from circulation, is an economy without totalization and closure. That something is held back in the circling of Saying suggests that there is a gift in language that is not to be exchanged, not to be given back, not to be taken into account. This also suggests that the circling of Saying cannot come full circle in the perfect reflexivity of a closed geometrical shape. Circling is not a circle, it is not the closure of a circle, it is a dynamic movement, a movement where gaps are opened up, where continuity is not perfect. It is more like swarming. This theme will become more important in the chapters that follow this one.

the small steps that have been taken thus far. The striving of world and earth, revealing and concealing opens in what I'm calling clearing or world where this second use of "world" differs from the first, which cannot be taken from the context created by its tension with the earth, i.e., the movement of un-concealment. Rather than saying that this world opens up out of unconcealment (which really would be absurd since the world is unconcealed), I must say that the world opens up in/as/through un-concealment; and, likewise, in/as/through Saying, where both are understood in/as/through the Same. In short, the world opens up in/as/through the Saying of the Same. And since the world does so in the context of a dynamic striving akin to both Saying and un-concealment, the movement of *A-letheia* or the saying of Saying is the opening up of the world. When Saying circles back so as to Say in/as/through un-concealment, the world opens up the circling back of Saying *that* unconceals. The circling back that occurs in the movement from the first phrase to the second is an opening up; recall that these are Heidegger's words when referring to the colon. The circling back that moves forward into the second phrase of the guide-word as well as the bold claim is an opening up of the world.[17]

Saying and Dif-ference

I am avoiding a precise repetition of the sequence in the first chapter so as to dispel any possible error in thinking that there is some organized pattern for interrelating the components of the economy of the Same.[18] In

---

[17]In some ways, Heidegger's 1944 study of Heraclitus' fragment B 50 regarding the *Logos* is a clearer exposition of this relation of Saying and un-concealment to the Open. Most notably because of his discussion of *Logos* as laying or bringing to lie together, where what is brought to lie together can be said to be a gathering. In this account we become more aware of the obviously intimate relation between the movement of laying out something and its being gathered together as laid out. Likewise, I might take note of the close correspondence between any unfolding and there being an opened region, since any unfolding is already an opening up. This essay will occupy my attention in the second part of this chapter. Cf. *Early Greek Thinking* pp. 59-78.

[18] Since the axioms of a system are all equally axiomatic, it doesn't seem to matter in what sequence they are derived, because they are not derived from each other. Nevertheless, they usually interconnect where the material of their interconnection is the system itself. (For example, Kant's descriptions of the interwovenness of the equally axiomatic categories of the

the section on Dif-ference In chapter 1, I demonstrated the close connection of Dif-ference to *A-letheia* and *Er-eignis*. I showed that it is impossible to separate them and that this was a significant characteristic of their nexus or economical movement. In the preceding section on Saying and *a-letheia,* some readers might have been led to believe that only un-concealment as Saying was under consideration. Such a reader must now recall that all un-concealing dynamically unfolds in what takes place (where taking place is a translation, i.e., the one Hofstadter uses in *Poetry, Language, Thought,* of *Er-eignis)* and that only what is two-fold may be said to unfold. The two-fold, of course, is another way of saying dif-ference. As a reminder: "Specifically, [the Same] reigns as the unfolding of the twofold—an unfolding in the sense of disclosure" (*EGT*, 95).

On the one hand, the twofold plays in the economy of the Same such that it is bound up with the configuration that gives what is to the Open. That is, the twofold is interwoven with the dynamic unfolding that takes place so that all determinate events can happen. On the other hand, all that happens within the economy of the Same (where happens is understood as derivative of the taking place of *Er-eignis)* expropriates that dif-ference so that dif-ference may be said to inhabit the Open. All this means that dif-ference is not only part of the nexus that gives (*Es gibt*), but that it is opened up along with the gift.[19] And this, of course, may be said of all

---

understanding in the world of posited objects.)

[19] The line I am developing will begin to problematize the difference between opening and the Open (what has been opened in opening). Heidegger, in a conversation with David Krell (recounted in his *Intimations of Mortality*. University Park, PA: Penn State Press, 1991.), draws a sharp distinction between the two. Only on the basis of this distinction, Krell suggests in interpreting Heidegger's remarks, can the question concerning the possibility of metaphysics be thought. But, perhaps in a way that opposes both Heidegger and Krell, I want to argue that only to the extent that this distinction has been understood as the origin of metaphysics can the deconstruction of metaphysics take place. This means that ultimately the distinction Heidegger makes between opening and the Open is the distinction that all First Philosophy is attempting to delimit (evidence for this comes at least in part through the discussion of Heidegger's growing awareness that "Being" is essentially the metaphysical understanding of the economy of what there is (*es gibt*). I also hold, and will be attempting to demonstrate throughout the rest of this chapter in one way or another, that this constitutes the metaphysical move extraordinaire in terms of a transcendental understanding of difference. My note here suggests how aware I am that the transcendental reading of Heidegger is justified by a careful reading of his

the components of the nexus in much the same fashion. Un-concealment is both the dynamic unfolding of revealing/concealing and the Open region within which all that is revealed occurs. This is a further demonstration of the circling that goes on within the Same. But it should not be concluded that this movement of dif-ference in both the giving and the gift (along with the other components) is the "presence" of dif-ference in the gift. Rather, it would be better to say that the dif-ference dif-fers in the gift and that un-concealment un-conceals in the gift, etc. In other words, these components are not origins that give over what originates in them and then are left behind in a teleological or developmental progression. The origin, if this word continues to have meaning, is carried along in/as/through the giving of the gift.[20]

I put off discussing circling within the Same until some groundwork had been done. Quite without noticing it, however, gestures were being made toward circling while discussing un-concealment, since all discussion of un-concealment forced discussion of the Opening region or clearing. Ultimately, this opening of the clearing is *nothing other* than the revealing/concealing of revelation and concealment. In other words, the dynamic unfolding of *a-letheia* is a process that both pre-dates and post-dates the procedure. Put still another way, I might say that the economy of the Same not only opens up in clearing, but continues to play itself out in/as/through the opening up of clearing. It is to be hoped that this characteristic of the economy of the Same will be better clarified in what is to follow as, I believe, the unfolding of dif-ference best lends itself to this feature of the Same.

Dif-ference, like un-concealment, is intimately tied to the taking place of the opening clearing. When Heidegger discusses dif-ference in his essay "Language," he constantly discusses it in terms of the dif-ference between world and thing. He writes: "Being the middle, it first determines world and things in their presence, i.e., in their being toward one another, whose unity it carries out" (*PLT*, 202). This merely reiterates a point from the earlier section on dif-ference where I demonstrated that dif-ference is not a relation after the fact between two phenomena, but that it is an initial determination out of which related phenomena come

---

text. And yet, perhaps against even Heidegger, I want to argue that this element of his thought is in tension with its other concerns regarding the deconstruction of metaphysics. Cf. chapter 5 of Krell's book for his implied criticism of any reading such as the one I am developing.

[20]This topic, discussed too briefly here, will be opened again in more detail in the third chapter.

into relation. "The dif-ference for world and thing *disclosingly appropriates* things into bearing a world; it *disclosingly appropriates* world into the granting of things" (*PLT*, 202-3). We can see, therefore, that it is dif-ference out of which world and thing unfold. They unfold together bearing a necessary relation to each other, but they are given elements (data) emerging from the dif-ference that rests between them.

> The dif-ference is *the* dimension, insofar as it measures out, apportions, world and thing, each to its own. Its allotment of them first opens up the separateness and towardness of world and thing. Such an opening up is the way in which the dif-ference here spans the two. The dif-ference, as the middle for world and things, metes out the measure of their presence. In the bidding that calls thing and world, what is really called is: the dif-ference. (*PLT*, 203)

In this passage, Heidegger explicitly connects dif-ference to the Opening region, a clearing that opens up as the components of world and thing are given from out of the dif-ference. The dif-ference measures out the dif-ferent components such that they are given over into the Open. But the unfolding of the two-fold dif-ference into the Open does not stop there with the coming into their own of the dif-ferent elements; rather, the dif-ference retains itself within the Open thus holding the two apart in their dif-ference. It isn't as though the dif-ference is a transcendental source that grants its determinants once and for all. Instead the granting itself retains a constant measuring off by the granting nexus.[21] Dif-ference cannot merely grant world and thing and then let them subsist in a presence that pits the one over and against the other. The granting by dif-ference in fact requires that dif-ference continue to govern the relation of world to thing as they come to rest opposite each other within the Open. This is what Heidegger means when he says that dif-ference is called in the bidding that seems to go out to world and thing. That is, although it may seem that the dif-ference is what does the bidding while world and thing answer the call and come into the Open, in fact it is the dif-ference itself that answers this call in that it is maintained within the Open,

---

[21] Without the continuing effectiveness of the opening in the Open, there could never have been any metaphysics at all, although this continued effect is forced into oblivion by the metaphysical thinking that fails to hear and thus constitutes as an Open region pure and simple. Cf. chapter 4 and the discussion of Derrida throughout for further elaboration of this line of thinking.

between world and thing, and therefore allows them to reside there as dif-ference.

It is only a very short step from here to a full blown consideration of dif-ference in terms of language. Heidegger has already, in the previous citation, laid a foundation for this by speaking of dif-ference in terms of bidding. He continues on this route in the following pages of the essay:

> The primal calling, which bids the intimacy of world and thing to come, is the authentic bidding. This bidding is the nature of speaking. Speaking occurs in what is spoken in the poem. It is the speaking of language. Language speaks. It speaks by bidding the bidden, thing-world and world-thing, to come to the between of the dif-ference. What is so bidden is commanded to arrive from out of the dif-ference into the dif-ference. (*PLT*, 206)

In this passage, it is the world and thing that are called in the Saying of language. This is not inconsistent with what we saw previously regarding dif-ference as what is bidden, since this call reaches to world and thing within dif-ference. World and thing are being bidden from out of the dif-ference, but they are not being asked to leave. Instead they are being called into their own within the dif-ference so that they may come to fully reside there. The call rings out to dif-ference and calls what resides there out to dif-ference. Dif-ference is both the recipient of the call and that to which the call bids haste. What then calls to dif-ference, bidding forth into dif-ference?

Heidegger says it is dif-ference that calls, that does the bidding. "In stilling things and world into their own, the dif-ference calls world and thing into the middle of their intimacy. The dif-ference is the bidder. The dif-ference gathers the two out of itself as it calls them into the rift that is the dif-ference itself. This gathering calling is the pealing" (*PLT*, 207). Dif-ference not only receives the bid, but does the bidding in such a way that what is bidden is commanded to come forth into the dif-ference. This nexus or economy of dif-ference recalls the self-reflexive being of language in that it suggests that dif-ference is a universe unto itself, acting as every necessary role in the economic life of the Open. Yet, just as the self-reflexive nature of language (language speaks) nonetheless has room for the rest of the economy of the Same, this citation opens a gap through which the other elements of the nexus can enter: the stillness.

"The dif-ference lets the thinging of the thing rest in the worlding of the world. The dif-ference expropriates the thing into the repose of the fourfold" (*PLT*, 206). For now, it is enough to say that the fourfold suggests the world. Heidegger aims in this passage at characterizing the relation between dif-ferent components: the two are bid together to come out of the dif-ference and reside in the dif-ference. This coming to rest is a repose where repose is stillness: not the complete absence of motion, but "as the stilling of stillness, rest, conceived strictly, is always more in motion than all motion and always more restlessly active than any agitation" (*PLT*, 206-7). Heidegger is attempting to approach the rest that occurs in dif-ference when two phenomena that belong together reside within the tension of their dif-ference.[22] It is the tension of equal and opposite forces that hold the two in a constant stand-off and make them appear to be at rest when in fact they have arrived at a heightened form of motion making itself impotent in its striving expenditure. This hyper-agitated stillness is the vibration of *Er-eignis* and the striving of un-concealment. Through this element of dif-ference, its economy circles.[23]

Once again, stillness has emerged along the way toward the nature of Saying. Previously, I equated stillness with the concealment of Saying, the unsaid that accompanies all Saying. Stillness now reveals itself as dif-ference. "Language speaks as the peal of stillness" (*PLT*, 207). This suggests that language speaks as the unfolding of the dif-ference now presented more concretely as the pealing of stillness. Dif-ference is what speaks to itself and yet this auto-affection giving rise to world and thing is a stilling, a bringing into stillness of world and thing—not a stillness that results from the tension between world and thing, but that makes their entrance into the dynamic possible. Heidegger has called this bidding of dif-ference a gathering call or peal. In the movement of dif-ference, there is both a peal and a stillness. I take it that peal and stillness are meant to

---

[22] The word "rest" will come, throughout the discussion of Derrida and the "ethical" later in the book, to suggest notions such as remainder, residue, resistance, what is left over, etc. The point here is that the effectiveness of difference in opening up the world is saturated with something left over, something that remains held back in coming to rest in the Open. This remainder or residue, the resonance of the deconstructive within the metaphysical, not only suggests how metaphysics comes to be but how the deconstruction of metaphysics can take place. In what will only make sense after the reader has passed through the final chapter, opening and the open are—of necessity—in ab-solute proXimity to each other.

[23]Recall for now that *dichten,* to compose or poetize, suggests "to tighten." The tightening of the poet may therefore lead to some interesting connections to this stillness and its manners of strumming (vibrating, striving, agitating, etc.,). These connections will come back to develop poetry as a mode of Saying in the last chapters of this project (cf. chapter 5).

contrast: when Heidegger says that language or dif-ference is the pealing of stillness, he is making a claim of the form that revealing/concealing is the essence of truth (*a-letheia*).

Language is an unsaid saying, just as *a-letheia* is a concealed revealing and dif-ference a pealing stillness. Once again there is a similar pattern developing in dif-ference. Dif-ference, like un-concealment and Saying, opens up. What it opens is a region within which it can reside as dif-ference. Only because dif-ference draws world and thing out into the open where they can rest as dif-ferent from each other, does dif-ference gain a place where it can come into its own as dif-ference. Rather than dif-ference fading away after the advent of world and thing, it is in the moment of their arrival into the open that dif-ference really opens itself up, as the dif-ference that it may be. In the discussion of dif-ference, this tendency of the economy of the Same to open a clearing and then reside there gains greater clarity. To think of world and thing as coming into the open in such a way that they would not reside in their dif-ference is to think of a world and thing that are not dif-ferent—and this is absurd. World and thing come out of dif-ference and are maintained by it within the dif-ference while at the same time maintaining it as the upholder of their own appropriate being.

This opening and residing in the open by dif-ference should make the analogous case of un-concealment and Saying more clear. Saying does not merely subside once the open region is articulated; for that would be the complete withdrawal into silence of what has been said. Likewise with un-concealment, which would merely be concealment if it were to withdraw in the moment of opening. But all of these forms of pure absence are impossible—as any pure absence is.

Dif-ference as the pealing of stillness is the dynamic movement of language as Saying. Dif-ference rounds out the circling when conceived in terms of Saying. The pealing of stillness suggests a loud burst of noise—as if from a bell or thunder—coming out of the stillness returning to it, bidding what is there (i.e., *es gibt)* to come forth and reside in the stillness. I don't think it would be possible for thinking to be more circular than when it is forced to think the being of dif-ference as the pealing of stillness. This circular movement which opens up in clearing where world and thing will come to rest is *nothing other* than Saying as showing. All Saying is characterized by dif-ference which means that all Saying moves in this circle.

A comment Heidegger makes that perhaps draws this character of language into a more concrete context occurs in the "Dialogue on Language":

Japanese: Then there would only be a speaking *from* language...
Inquirer:...in this manner, that it would be called *from out of* language's reality, and be led to its reality.
J: How can we do that?
I: A speaking *from* language could only be a dialogue. (*OWL*, 51).

This exchange follows the dismissal of all speaking about language as an object. Speaking from within language, and thus letting language speak through us, is always a dialogue. But not just any dialogue where there are two participants talking to each other—it has to be a dialogue in which Saying takes place. That is, it would have to be "a dialogue that would remain originarily appropriated to Saying" (*OWL*, 52). A true dialogue, therefore, is one that moves in/as/through the circling of dif-ference such that dif-ference stretches and spans the opening between the participants, drawing them into the pealing stillness where they can come into their own as speakers of a language. A more complete discussion of this will have to be put off until the discussion in chapter 4 of mortal speakers and the use of human language within the economy of the Same.

Another feature of dif-ference that will have to be put off, but that has been suggested already, is a more concrete articulation of the world-thing relation. For now it suffices to say that world and thing open up together from within the economy of dif-ference (or the Same) and reside there. All determinate beings in their Being come to rest in the play of the Same and, like the relation of Saying to the nexus demonstrated in the first chapter, are not merely derivative components grounded upon a generating origin that has been left behind.

Finally, a few remarks about the role of unity and totality are possible. Insofar as the circling is a circling of dif-ference, it is nearly impossible to conceive of it as a simple unity. Dif-ference cannot be a unity, since it sets all unity at odds with itself, brings it into a tense striving where it can never attain a peaceful rest. Unity constantly dispels itself in the face of dif-ference. Nonetheless, it seems possible to conceive the unity of Saying in terms of a structural totality permeated with dif-ference. That is perhaps the most common representation of this view and the one suggested by Heidegger, on some readings of him, in early works like *Being and Time*. The image of a circle certainly adds to this interpretation since a circle is most obviously closed. But this circling experienced in dif-ference and the Same is not a closed circle (and hence, one might argue, not a circle at all), since I have argued from the outset that this circle's circling is an opening up. If the Open region that gets cleared in the movement of the nexus is truly an *open* region, it must lack all closure, and that means it may not be conceived as a totality. The circle image must be understood in terms of the repetition described in the introduction to this chapter. What is repeated in this sense is what has circled back in an open-ended fashion, meaning that it has occurred again but differently: a repetition is the same as what it repeats—in Heidegger's sense of the Same. The circling of the Same is a circling that doesn't get anywhere and yet doesn't remain in one place either. This introduces the notion of "way" that is crucial to Heidegger's thought and which will be handled in the following section on *Er-eignis* as Saying. It is because circling is a way that it cannot be a totality.

Saying and *Er-eignis*

The first connection of *Er-eignis* to Saying may be noted in the granting each evokes. *Er-eignis* gives whatever is given in the *es gibt* or "there is" since all granting lets things come into their own. Likewise, Saying as the dynamic unfolding of dif-ference gives or sends all that is into the Open where it comes into its own:

> If our thinking does justice to the matter, then we may never say of the word that it is, but rather that it gives—not in the sense that words are given by an "it," but that the word itself gives. The word itself is the giver. What does it give? To go by the poetic experience and by the most ancient tradition of thinking, the word gives Being. Our thinking, then, would have to seek the word, the giver which itself is never given, in this "there is that which gives." (*OWL*, 88)

"The word" suggests Saying, altered so as to fit the context of Heidegger's discussion of the poem "Words" by Stefan George that ends with the lines: "And so I renounce and sadly see/Where word breaks off no thing may be." It is because Saying grants Being that there can be nothing beyond Saying. In the essay *On Time and Being* we saw the same construction relating Being to the "*es gibt*" in the sense of an appropriating event that lets all that is come into its own existence.

Mention of giving, Saying or *Er-eignis,* will no doubt suggest destiny—where destiny is the sending of a message that is the dynamic unfolding of language, the way language works. All opening up of a clearing is a sending or destining of a message born out into the open by a messenger, the description of which will have to be delayed. "All true language, because assigned, sent, destined to man by the way-making movement of Saying, is in the nature of destiny" (*OWL*, 133). In the destiny of language, there are already signs that human speech is the destination of the sending of Saying that takes place appropriatingly. Yet, for the moment, I am not interested in discussing any particular destiny of language. Instead I want to focus on the overarching being of language as destiny, as the opening of a world in/as/through which things and mortals dwell, of a region inhabited by whatever belongs there. It is in this equivocation that the fundamental ambiguity of "language" throughout Heidegger's works is most clearly demonstrated. At times he suggests language as a synonym for Saying, as the overall "unity" of all individual modes or historical occurrences of human speaking. Here, on the other hand, I am arguing that language is used in the later essays to refer to the individual modes of world within which all that is may be said to abide. This use of the term accords roughly with his use of the term "epoch" or "world" in a specialized sense (i.e., the world of the Romans or the world of the Greeks which is juxtaposed with earth).

The destining of Saying, therefore, is a coming to pass of un-concealment as the striving between world and earth, where striving is the relational rift implying dif-ference. Earlier we saw Heidegger refer to this as the movement of all that is, in whatever way that it is (historically, culturally, etc.), where movement is *bewegen*—which will later remind us of way-making as it was described in the nature of language as destiny (where what is sent makes its way to a destination). Saying as an appropriating way where an opening takes place is the letting come into its own of an historical epoch governed by a message.

The granting, giving, or sending that is the taking place of *Er-eignis* or, supposedly, the Saying of language, has already been caught sight of in this essay. *Er-eignis,* like dif-ference and un-concealment, opens in the sense that *Er-eignis* as letting belong together and as the Saying of the Same in terms of the Same about the Same opens up in/as/through a clearing where what comes to pass comes into its own.

> The moving force in Showing of Saying is Owning. It is what
> brings all present and absent beings each into their own, from
> where they show themselves in what they are, and where they
> abide according to their kind. This owning which brings them
> there, and which moves Saying as Showing in its showing we call
> Appropriation. It yields the opening of the clearing in which
> present beings can persist and from which absent beings can
> depart while keeping their persistence in the withdrawal. (*OWL*,
> 127)

This coming into its own *that* takes place in *Er-eignis* is also a key feature of the movement of language, where what Says is what releases what is into its own proper being. The owning quality that bridges *Er-eignis* and Saying couples with the movements demonstrated in language, dif-ference and the determining or granting quality of language when it comes to the relating of world and thing. World and thing come out of the dif-ference and come to rest there in their dif-ference. They are able to come out and come to rest together because they belong together. Insofar as world and thing belong together, they may be said to have been allowed to belong together by the Event of Appropriation, which in letting them belong together lets each of them come into their own within their dif-ference. The rising up out of dif-ference and coming to rest in dif-ference which un-conceals world and thing in their ownness is Appropriating Event, *Er-eignis*. That is to say, it is the Saying of the world-thing.[24]

Yet again, however, we are confronted with Heidegger's circular rendering of things. Appropriation yields the Open but not as the effect of a cause nor as the consequence of an antecedent: the giving of "it gives" is not a logical relation. Juxtaposed to this feature, Heidegger accounts for the Appropriating of the Event in terms of Saying:

---

[24] Looking ahead so as to look back to this point, it may eventually become possible for the reader to understand this sentence as the first articulation of the erosion of the transcendental nature of the bold claim. To the extent that Saying speaks in/as/through the thing, the thing is *nothing other* than Saying. Note that I continue to abide by a metaphysical formulation of this point (i.e., nothing other), although it is perhaps now easier to see how the "nothing other" of the thing is undermined by the deconstruction at work in the economy of the Same.

> What is yielding is Appropriation itself—and nothing else. That Appropriation, seen as it is shown by Saying, cannot be represented either as an occurrence or a happening—it can only be experienced as the abiding gift yielded by Saying. There is nothing else from which the Appropriation itself could be derived, even less in whose terms it could be explained. The Appropriating Event is not the outcome (result) of something else, but the giving yield whose giving reach alone is what gives us such things as a "there is," a "there is" of which even Being itself stands in need to come into its own presence. (*OWL*, 127)

Er-eignis is yielding at the opening of this citation, it yields all that is in its presence. Then, after dismissing any possible temporal (having a being that is *within* time) understanding of *Er-eignis,* Heidegger claims that it is yielded itself by Saying. This circle circles once again in the passage when Heidegger says that *Er-eignis* is not the outcome of something else but is that from which all else is given. Now presumably this "all else" does not include Saying since Saying shows *Er-eignis.* In this passage, Saying and *Er-eignis* are circling around each other, each laying claim with equal force to its role as the yielder of the all giving yield: neither comes first, nothing is first.

Er-eignis occurs along with the economy of the Same as the taking place of the clearing within which world and thing come into their own. This element of Saying as owning is not only characteristic of the taking place of the Open, but it is characteristic of what takes place within the Open. That is, the Event comes to pass in some way that world and thing, say, are allowed to belong together, but this letting belong together does not abandon the Event that enabled it to occur; rather, in the continuing abiding of the world and thing in their belonging together within the Open, the taking place of the Event of Appropriation continues to take place. Whenever there is world and thing, there is *Er-eignis.* For a thing to come into its own it must continue to own up to its appropriate being; and for this a continual appropriation of the Appropriating Event is necessary and, in a sense, given.

We have continually seen a stillness residing in the core of Saying, and the Saying that Appropriates is no exception to this. "Silence corresponds to the soundless tolling of the stillness of appropriating-showing Saying" (*OWL*, 131). A soundless tolling is a pealing stillness. This stillness of Saying as appropriating and showing (*Er-eignis* and un-concealment) interweaves among all the various components within the economy of the Same. It is the concealed, the withdrawing mystery that permeates the nexus and is carried along with it in all its coming to pass. This interweaving of the stillness in the silent pealing of Saying adds weight to some of Heidegger's remarks that might otherwise have been overlooked in their gravity: "Time's removing and bringing to us, and space's throwing open, admitting and releasing—they all belong together in the Same, the play of stillness, something to which we cannot here give further thought" (*OWL*, 106). The context of this discussion is a placing of both time and space within the resting stillness of the Same— something expressed in the tautological phrases: time times and space spaces. This passage certainly captures the attention of the reader, for its remarks on time and space place them within the economy of the Same and not as determinate givens by that economy (as will be claimed in the essay *On Time and Being* and further discussed later on), but it may be overlooked that this passage equates the economy of the Same with the play of stillness and the resting of time and space within the Same is a resting within the stillness. Stillness, as the overarching play that I have been referring to, perhaps in a somewhat computational vocabulary, as the economy of the Same, resides within all Saying as the silent concealing that withdraws within all that presences in the movement of way-making previously alluded to as a circling that opens up in destiny.

Frequently Heidegger develops stillness alongside nearness. Once again, nearness arises in Heidegger's discussion of *Er-eignis* as Saying. In "The Nature of Language" Heidegger speaks of the drawing near of the nearness that "is itself the occurrence of appropriation by which poetry and thinking are directed into their proper nature" as modes of Saying (*OWL*, 90). He follows this shortly afterward with an iteration of the way-making of Saying and *Er-eignis* that opens up a world where mortals are able to dwell along with things: "But if the nearness of poetry and thinking is one of Saying, then our thinking arrives at the assumption that the occurrence of appropriation acts as that Saying in which language grants its essential nature to us" (*OWL*, 90). The neighborhood of poetry and thinking as modes of Saying is Saying itself equating Saying with nearness, since nearness is the essence of all neighboring. The appropriation occurring in the opening up of Saying is the drawing into the nearness of whatever is brought forth in that opening up or appropriating. No doubt mortals and things are among that which is brought into nearness through the opening up that comes to pass (*er-eignet)* in the owning of Saying.[25]

---

[25]Nearness, I take it, is the later Heidegger's word for transcendence. Because the nearness is the dimension of all dwelling, it is the case that all that dwells or abides within the world rests alongside (and thereby in nearness to) whatever else is there. The things that thing within the world and the

This drawing quality of Saying as nearness is called the "design" of language where design translates the German *"Aufriß"* and clearly reminds us of the rift (*riß*) so deeply linked to dif-ference and the striving of un-concealment. Heidegger says that the design is the unity of the being of language and this unity, no doubt problematic at this point, is strictly linked to the drawing of language as stillness and nearness:

> The design is the whole of the traits of that drawing which structures and prevails throughout the open, unlocked freedom of language. The design is the drawing of the being of language, the structure of show in which are joined the speakers and their speaking: what is spoken and what of it is unspoken in all that is given in the speaking. (*OWL*, 121)[26]

The reference to what is unspoken recalls stillness and, likewise, the claim that the design is the "whole" of Saying recalls that the design evokes nearness, since Saying itself, generally considered as the overarching Saying of the Same, is equated with nearness itself, the neighborhood within which all modes of Saying dwell. It is significant that Heidegger does not talk about unity or totality here despite the fact that he is talking about the prevailing structure of the Open as design. The language is in fact free of any totalization, since he lets the Open remain without bound when he invokes its nature as freedom recalling the terms Heidegger used to discuss the Open region in "On the Essence of Truth." The whole of the design is not a unity or totality, but a set of "traits" which prevail throughout the Open (these traits are perhaps what I have been calling "components" or "elements" in the nexus or economy of the Same). The fact that the structure of the Open is conceived in terms of design (*Aufriß*) — the base of which is rift (*Riß*), evoking dif-ference — should alert the reader to serious difficulties in referring to this region as a unified totality. As a drawing, the design is such that its marks and sketches can

---

mortals that are essentially in the world may be said to lie in nearness with each other, hence making all relations and interactions possible (and hence enabling all interpretations to occur).

[26]"Der Auf-Riß ist das Ganze der Züge derjenigen Zeichnung, die das Aufgeschlossene, Freie der Sprache durchfügt. Der Aufriß ist die Zeichnung des Sprachwesens, das Gefüge eines Zeigens, darein die Sprechenden und ihr Sprechen, das Gesprochene und sein Ungesprochenes aus dem Zugesprochenen verfugt sind." (*Gesamtausgabe* Band 12, *Unterwegs zur Sprache*, p. 240.)

continually pull things into un-concealedness from out of nothingness so that they may reside there.

This reading of the passage relies on a play with language exclusive to English. On the one hand, mortals and things are drawn into the nearness by the appropriating event of Saying. On the other hand, the design is a drawing of the structure of the open clearing. The design is a drawing that draws all that is into it — and it is best perhaps to leave this sentence ambiguous so that it does not reify itself into a statement that represents. Not only, however, does the design draw such that all is drawn into the Open, but the design itself withdraws in this drawing and it withdraws precisely because the design is a silent one, unspoken and still. The unity of Saying as design, nearness, stillness withdraws in its drawing that structures the Open in/as/through which everything that is drawn there takes place. Perhaps it is the withdrawing of the unity that does the drawing just as a sinking ship draws water into the space it opens as it goes under.[27]

As the reader may have noticed throughout this chapter, I have been struggling to express this same phenomenon with regard to all the various features of the Same. I want to let this version of Sameness appear in its own terms, without letting it seem to be merely another in a long series of metaphysical accounts of the Being of beings. Within the history of philosophy, the various accounts of the ground of all that is frequently posit that ground as a transcendental source of determinate being. In these cases the worlding of the world leaves behind the ground when it constitutes a realm of particular objects that are nothing other than the actualization of their conditions of possibility. But in Heidegger's account, the world — read: open clearing — retains as resting within itself all dynamic unfolding and never ventures beyond that. The difficulty in grasping this is certainly complicated by the format of this essay. The

---

[27]Heidegger's German here (cf. previous footnote) is consistently to draw as drawing with ink or lead (*zeichnen*). I am, of course, letting draw mean both sketching and pulling (*ziehen*). What is drawn is drawn near just as the pencil must rest near the page in order to draw. Both forms of drawing seem, however, to indicate a spur. The spur that breaks water, that draws it aside and the spur that incites something forward, that spurs it on no less than the spur of the stylus that sketches. Later in this essay I believe it will be possible to link these notions together more extensively through Heidegger's works and any possible understanding of them in English. The other kind of drawing, the kind Heidegger isn't using here, suggesting to pull is common throughout *What is Called Thinking?*.

manner of presentation is constantly battling with itself in its effort to say the taking place of Saying. Each segment or section of the essay breaks off from the previous section and the one that is to come, thus breaking up the whole of the project into a multi-staged linear procedure with a clear beginning and a definite ending place. For instance, I spoke before of the nexus of the three components and of how the discussion must circle back; but why not, after all, just include a discussion of Saying along with the discussion of the nexus? It now appears, in addition, that there are difficulties in discussing owning, dif-ference, and un-concealment in a separate section from the one on things arriving within the world as the grant of Saying. Once again, it makes sense to wonder why I do not mix everything together in a way more faithful to the matter itself?

Of course, many other elements placed later in the project are curiously absent from these beginnings, and it would be just as pertinent to ask why they have not been included right from the start. No doubt, this project needs to have already begun at the outset. But this is impossible and may not be achieved, not in any manner: not in conversation, not in a lecture, and not in a written treatise; the always already of the beginning is an impossible condition. This limit of the origin is a factical one, it is a trait of all that is, and the desire for an original presence of the possibility of an always already is no better than the desire for a neat and orderly linear progression stemming genetically from the source. No better here in the sense that it equally instantiates the metaphysical urge for totality, completion, and unity within which all else can be subsumed. Rather than doing everything all at once, in the same place and the same time in pristine perfection; I, following Heidegger and Derrida, resign myself to the limits of being original and move along the way. And since the use of the word "way" strikes a chord in this apparently self-conscious examination, there is some progress in understanding the circling of the circle. All circling of the economy of the Same is making way.[28]

---

[28]An extremely important distinction occurs here but cannot be developed further until later: the always already of the origin (its being limited in its originality) may be evoked as either a condition of possibility or as an impossible condition of impossibility. The first alternative suggests the logic of Kantian transcendental idealism while the second alternative suggests the undecidable logic of deconstruction. Ultimately, however, the move from the one to the other is only a first step in the deconstruction of metaphysics. A second step is the coming to rest of the conditions within the material of the world. On this basis, I hold that Rodolph Gasché in his *The Tain of the Mirror* (Cambridge, MA: Harvard University Press, 1986) has stopped short in his

Recall that the book from which the majority of this discussion comes is called *On the Way to Language.* Throughout the essay "The Way to Language" Heidegger emphasizes that the move into the essence of language so as to come to terms with language is a making way toward language. But this way-making is not the search for a goal or result, both of which have little to do with the Appropriating Event or the Saying that yields: "This verb [*wëgen],* used transitively, means: to form a way and, forming it, to keep it ready. Way-making understood in this sense no longer means to move something up or down a path that is already there. It means to bring the way...forth first of all, and thus to *be* the way" (*OWL*, 130). Way-making is the opening up of the way where the way stretches out in/as/through the economy of the Same. "The way is appropriating" (*OWL*, 129). It is tempting to recall Heidegger's curious sentence from *On Time and Being*: "Appropriation appropriates. Saying this, we say the Same in terms of the Same about the Same" (*TB*, 24). This saying is the making of a way where thinking moves along the way that opens up the being of language. Thought can only make way for the Saying of language—which is nothing other than the way understood in the sense of circling—because Saying has first of all made way for thinking.

"This way-making puts language (the essence of language) as language (Saying) into language (into the sounded word)" (*OWL*, 130). When I speak, if my speaking is appropriate to the Saying of language, I am speaking along a way that has been opened up by the Saying of language itself. Once again, much of this discussion will have to be put off until the discussion of mortal speakers in chapter 4, but what matters now is that the Way and way-making describes the economy of the Same or the Saying of language so as to evoke and articulate the circularity at work in what is taking place throughout this project.

If we understand this whole economy, the Saying of language that un-conceals dif-ference appropriatingly ("The saying that comes to pass and governs in the duality is the gathering of presencing, in whose shining what is present can appear" [*EGT*, 93]), as the way-making of the way, then we will have gained our first foothold for entering into the circling back that characterizes the project thus far. We make our way, step by step, opening the path as we go along it. And it is not accidental that way-making signifies taking steps. The withdrawing design is concealed and

---

description of what is truly revolutionary in the deconstruction of metaphysics as Derrida demonstrates it. This issue will become more central to the project during the last three chapters once Derrida's work is elaborated so as to supplement the discussion of Heidegger developed thus far.

so a key component of the dynamic unfolding of Saying is hidden in mystery and oblivion. In order to take hold of the withdrawing movement of Saying, thought must take a step back, where "back" (*zuruck*) recalls going along the way toward what has been withdrawn, what has been taken back (*zuruckziehen*). Of course, this "toward" also suggests a way, as making-way.

The way is the "unity" of Saying; it is the design of Saying, that which structures the Open through its destiny; it makes a place for itself, opens a way, as destination. This withdrawing unity which, understandably enough, eludes Heidegger (since its nature is elision, if it doesn't elude you it has doubly passed you by) is no real unity at all. The design is a rift, a dif-ference, a striving tension in the nearness of the stillness that rests within motion. To say that design is the unity of Saying and the Same, the play of stillness, is equivalent to saying (within a certain metaphysically determined language that requires the phrasing of everything within logical constructs) that the only unifying feature of all modes of Saying is their lack of unity, their dif-ference. But this is a hollow representation of the withdrawing unity of the design of Saying. It is much better to call it a way.

Heidegger says that way is the proper word for Lao Tze's *Tao* commonly translated in terms of reason and *logos*. Similarly, way, as the Saying of the Same, evokes the Japanese *Koto ba*, where *ba* means petals or flowers and *koto* means "the *Er-eignis* of the lightening message of grace," where grace is that which *gives* delight or *Iki*: "the beckoning stillness" which draws by manner of its calling. *Koto ba* as the Japanese Saying of language is the blooming of the clearing, appropriating all who listen to its beckoning call:

> *Japanese*: In our ancient Japanese poetry, an unknown poet sings of the intermingling scent of cherry blossom and plum blossom on the same branch.
> *Inquirer*: This is how I think of the being-toward-each-other of vastness and stillness in the same Appropriation of the message of un-concealment of the two-fold. (*OWL*, 53)

The economy of the Same plays on in the Japanese understanding of language. There is no unity of Saying, properly speaking; rather, Saying says the Same throughout its various modes. Heidegger's response to the Japanese poetic saying of language is a Saying of the Same: belonging together, vastness (nearness), stillness, *Er-eignis*, message (destiny), un-concealment, two-fold (dif-ference). It should be obvious by now, if not before, that all Saying as *Er-eignis* is a Saying of the entire (I won't say

unified) play of the Same. Likewise with all that has come previously in
the description of Saying as un-concealment and dif-ference:

> But language *is* monologue. This now says two things: it is
> language *alone* which speaks authentically; and, language speaks
> *lonesomely*. Yet only he can be lonesome who is not alone, if 'not
> alone' means not apart, singular, without any rapports. But it is
> precisely the absence in the lonesome of something in common
> which persists as the most binding bond *with* it. The "some" in
> lonesome is the Gothic *sama,* the Greek *hama,* and English *same.*
> "Lonesome" means: the same in what unites that which belongs
> together. Saying that shows makes the way for language to reach
> human speaking. Saying is in need of being voiced in the word.
> But man is capable of speaking only insofar as he, belonging to
> Saying, listens to Saying, so that in resaying it he may be able to
> say a word. That needed usage and this resaying lie in that absence
> of something in common which is neither a mere defect nor
> indeed anything negative at all. (*OWL*, 134)[29]

Language speaks in monologue *and* dialogue, the self and the other,
the play of the Same where all belonging together is a "unity" of dif-
ference.[30] This can't even be called a totality since it is without limit and
without center. Language certainly is not a system, since it is in

---

[29]There is much in the previous citation that has yet to be handled: 1. the
resaying that follows upon the belonging to Saying; 2. the needed usage
which binds mortals with the Saying of language. We have caught glimpses
of these traits in what was just discussed, but I will not deal with it in detail
until the following sections. Any criticism of this mode of operation, as
should be clear from the remarks made in the text above, should not neglect
to grapple with the nature of the way. I claim that partial suggestions and
indications of what needs to be dealt with are part of being along any way at
all. At any given moment along a path, there are signs — so to speak — that
direct one's attention ahead along the path and not just at what is currently
visible alongside the way. In fact, it is of the essence of the way that there be
indications of what is lying ahead — otherwise, it wouldn't be moving along
at all.

[30]Where unity is the unity of a design or *Aufriß* recalling the rift of dif-
ference: "The rift of dif-ference makes the limpid brightness shine. Its
luminous joining decides the brightening of the world into its own. The rift
of dif-ference expropriates the world into its worlding, which grants things."
(*PLT*, 205)

movement; it is the rest of stillness that is movement itself. The relational open context of language makes all totalizing of the Same impossible. How could anything with a dynamic that includes concealment and concealedness be rendered in a totality that implies the presence of everything in the totalization? Completeness is an important element in any totality and Saying—as the play of stillness and economy of the Same, never completes itself: the withdrawing trait of concealedness makes completion impossible, language is inexhaustible. There is no unity or totality of language in the strict sense; and yet the claim continues to hold: reflexive language is the Same, a way.[31]

I continue now, as promised, to the gathering where things and mortals belong, in order to further demonstrate the Saying of the Same.

Saying as Gathering into the Open

Recall Heidegger's saying: "Here, we assume, is the essential nature of language. 'To say,' related to the Old Norse '*saga,*' means to show: to make appear, set free, that is, to offer and extend what we call World, lighting and concealing. This lighting and hiding proffer of the world is the essential being of Saying" (*OWL*, 93). The world, that which is set free, is freedom itself: "Freedom was first determined as freedom for what is opened up in an open region" (*BW*, 127). There will no longer be any temptation to think this setting free or opening up of the Open or World as an effect that results from the process of un-concealment, et al. Neither shall there be a time lag between the Same that circles and the Open that opens in the circling, since time itself opens up along with the open

---

[31]It might be interesting to note that this understanding of way as a non-unified Same is a complete inversion of the traditional reading of Parmenides. If Nietzsche inverts Platonism according to Heidegger, it might be tempting to say that Heidegger inverts Parmenides in the division of the sphere. All the traits of Parmenides way of truth have been reversed and yet there is a similar sort of circling. In Parmenides the circling was static, it was the shape of the truth in its pristine perfection—self-present Being itself. For Heidegger, however, the circling or spherical quality of *a-letheia* is movement. In fact, aside from movement, there is no shape at all to the way—at least no shape as understood in terms of a static form. All figures in Heidegger's reading of the Same have to be understood as the outlined design of a trace or spur that lingers only momentarily (in neither presence nor absence) as the movement continues to pass by. In this sense, it is only through the inversion of Parmenides that the way of *a-letheia* becomes properly a way.

region/world/clearing/freedom. The circling of self-referential Saying, a Saying only concerned with the Same, is — so to speak — an opening up of world, a setting free of what is allowed to belong there at rest in the Open. The open is sometimes referred to as "unconcealedness," which recalls the tenuous distinction between the movement of un-concealment and the Open itself which is un-concealedness. The idea of showing, un-concealing, freeing, opening doesn't make sense without a show, un-concealedness, freedom, the Open.

Although what follows is dangerous for any clarification of this element of language as Saying, it is an important pathway given the existing need to make way for the Open — the meaning of this need must be deferred. From the previously mentioned discussion of George's poem we may read:

> Where word breaks off no thing may be.
> 	The word's rule springs to light as that which makes the thing be a thing. The word begins to shine as the gathering which first brings what is present to presence.
> 	The oldest word for the rule of the word thus thought, for Saying, is *logos:* Saying which, in showing, lets beings appear in their "it is." (*OWL*, 155)

The gathering is the opening up of world and it is in the lightening of this clearing that all things come to be — this world is the dif-ference where world and thing rest. The oldest name for this gathering is *logos* and Heidegger discusses this word, as Heraclitus used it in Fragment B 50, in detail in a 1944 lecture. Looking at this lecture will assist us in getting a better idea of how to think this weird opening up of Saying and thereby come into a relation with the Saying of language that is necessary for any appropriate speaking from it.

Logos is full of danger since the history of Metaphysics is committed to a certain understanding of this Greek notion. *Logos,* aside from being the oldest European word for Saying, was also a word for Being. By this I mean that the *logos* was an historical interpretation of the meaning of Being and thus the ground of all that existed in so far as those who did philosophy within a specific historical epoch understood it.[32] *Logos*

---

[32]This safe manner of phrasing this could probably go a little further out on a limb without coming into danger of falling. Philosophers are not superior beings and probably act as mouthpieces for the general understanding of the

refers, therefore, both to Being and to the essence of Being, as the Saying which gives Being in the circling of the Same. Consider the following:

> *Inquirer*: You are right: only, the insidious thing is that the confusion which has been occasioned is afterward ascribed to my own thinking attempt, an attempt which on its own way knows with full clarity the difference between "Being" as "the Being of beings," and "Being" as "Being" in respect of its proper sense, that is, in respect of its truth (the clearing). (*OWL*, 20)

Being in this second sense is the dynamic unfolding of Being also said by the oldest word of Saying, *logos,* and which was once called "the Truth of Being" (what I've been calling the economy of the Same and the play of stillness). On the other hand, the Being of beings has also been thought under the rubric of *logos* in what has become the traditional understanding of Heraclitus's rendition of a particular stage in Greek thought (i.e., a specific mode of Saying). How did these two very different uses of *logos* come to pass?

It is the existence of these two distinct uses of *logos* that is the danger that threatens the current discussion. And yet, it will only be possible to see this distinction through the discussion itself. A trial by fire, so to speak. In order to prepare ourselves for this danger, however, it will be necessary to go into more depth in understanding the distinction itself and precisely what is at stake in it.

There are in fact several distinctions that need to be made clear along the way. There is *logos* as Being as Saying, on the one hand, and *logos* as Being as grounding all that is on the other. The common element "Being" existing on both hands of the distinction clearly presents a confusion that spells possible disaster. During his work in the 1950s, Heidegger becomes increasingly aware of this confusion and takes several steps toward dispelling it. A good example can be found in the 1955 *The Question of Being*:

---

historical epoch within which they dwell, even if they have a sort of singular position as the first and perhaps only of those in that time period to make the understanding explicit.

> This belonging together of summoning and hearing which is
> always the Same, could that be "Being"? What am I saying? It is
> no longer "Being" at all if we try to think fully and completely of
> "Being" as it is fated to hold sway, namely as coming to presence
> or dynamic unfolding [*Anwesen*], in which way alone we refer to
> its destined essence. Then we should just as decidedly have to
> drop the singularizing and separating word "Being" as to drop the
> name "man." The question as to the relationship of both revealed
> itself as inadequate because it never reaches into the realm of what
> it would like to question. In truth, we can then not even say any
> longer that "Being" and "man" "be" the same in the sense that *they*
> belong together; for in *so* saying we still let both be for
> themselves. (*QB*, 77; translation altered).

The first noteworthy element of this lengthy passage is the
introduction of scare quotes around "Being," which is a new development
in Heidegger's texts. Heidegger senses the difficulty with Being through
the difficulties raised by its relationship with "man." Heidegger realizes
that, since he has understood belonging together as a relationship of dif-
ference where dif-ference precedes what differs, Being asserts a certain
priority in this relation if it is conceived as the Same itself. Being
suggests, therefore, both the relation and one of the related components.
And yet it could not be one of the related components if it were said to be
the relation itself, since the related component is such only out of the dif-
ference in Appropriation. Being would therefore have to both precede and
follow the Appropriation. "Being" becomes a given (datum) determined
in the giving of the Appropriating dif-ference (*es gibt*). Performing this
adjustment of "Being" reveals it as given and thus opens up—for the first
time perhaps—the possibility of reaching into the realm that all
questioning seeks, a realm where "man" belongs together with "Being"
and is not excluded from it in a polar opposition to "Being," a realm which
grants both as belonging together. The reaching that results from this
freeing from Being is a reaching out for what has always already been
reaching out for us.

The two hands of this distinction are now a little clearer, reducing
the danger somewhat. Being, remaining only in its metaphysical form, is
the ground of all that is. This metaphysical conception of Being
encounters Being as the Being of beings. In this ground, a certain form of
the dif-ference has come to presence, namely the dif-ference as it has
given itself over to metaphysics. Because metaphysical inquiry is
likewise concerned with making explicit the Being of beings as ground,
there is a difference that permeates all metaphysical inquiry. This

difference is always understood in terms of the present grounds and beings that are grounded and thus not in its dif-ference as such. Metaphysics, although it represents Being and beings in terms of their difference, is oblivious to the dif-ference as such out of which Being and beings are appropriated. This is precisely the mark of metaphysics, that it has received the difference and lets it operate essentially in its thinking about grounds and all that is grounded while failing to think this dif-ference as a giving of the ground.

When one speaks of an epoch, there is talk of the destining of the Same where one component of that destiny is dif-ference. The relation appears within the world of that epoch as interpreted in a certain way, although the interpreters may be unaware of their interpretation (i.e., it is not explicit as an interpretation). In a metaphysical epoch, the dif-ference is interpreted as grounding, where the relation of Being and beings is one of a ground to its constituents or of a first cause to its effects (the German *Grund* also means reason, so that giving the ground or the cause of something is giving the reason why it is as it is). In such an epoch, Heidegger says, the grounded beings take account of the ground that grounds them. As the grounded beings that take account of the ground, these beings account for the ground. One might even say they ground it: Being always has its beings and beings never are without Being. In this way, all relations within such a metaphysical epoch are conceived in terms of grounding.[33]

---

[33]"The onto-theological constitution of metaphysics stems from the prevalence of that difference which keeps Being as the ground, and beings as what is grounded and what gives account, apart from and related to each other; and by this keeping, perdurance is achieved" (*ID*, 71). Therefore, it becomes possible to see metaphysics as the transcendental move performed in/as/through an epoch for the sake of establishing the conditions for the possibility of existents within that historical age. Heidegger's move, I hope to be in the process of showing, is not to perform still one further move so as to get behind "Being" with his talk of "the weirdness" but to deconstruct the reified structure of Being within an historical epoch for the sake of revealing/concealing its givenness. Thus new categories are not established, but rather a dwelling in the abyss where no categories can be, where no-thing is. This should become clearer throughout the next few chapters. Notice that this would undermine the view of those commentators who claim that Heidegger's deconstruction results in nothing other than one more epoch of metaphysics. Derrida sounds this way sometimes (i.e., in *The Post Card* et al.), but I think John Caputo in *Radical Hermeneutics* (Bloomington, IN: Indiana University Press, 1987) makes the best case where he more or less accepts Derrida's attack on Heidegger. It should be noted that, unlike Caputo,

Where *logos* is conceived metaphysically as the ground of all that is within that historical epoch, it is understood as a mode of the difference that is forgetful of dif-ference as such. When it does so, it functions as the universal presence of all that is present in Being. It is a form of the *logos* that does not give all that belongs together in an Event of Appropriation, rather it rules over all that is present in its domination of what is—it becomes a law of existence. The principle of the ground, here understood as *logos,* is present in all that must follow its grounding guidelines. "Nothing is without ground" means that there is nothing other than what is grounded, and so grounding itself is not essentially permeated by concealment and withdrawing. All that is, is present to the mind and supported by a reason or ground.

Logos as Saying, on the other hand, would be an abyss. It would be without a ground and so, according to the principle of the ground, would be nothing at all. To the contrary, it would be that which gives Being as *logos* as Ground along with any other mode of the dif-ference that is possible. It would be the dif-ference itself, *Er-eignis,* itself, etc.[34]

The historical epoch closely associated with the understanding of the *logos* as Being and ground is the age surrounding the thinking of Heraclitus. Heidegger attributes monumental status to the Eliatic's thought in this early stage of metaphysics. And this is precisely the fulfillment of an awareness of the danger that awaits inquiry into Heraclitus's thought as a manner of getting at the open clearing as Saying. If there is hope for displaying *logos* in/as/through Saying, then it must certainly be difficult to do so through an examination of someone so closely connected to *logos* as ground and Being. Yet, *logos,* as the word for saying understood by metaphysics since Heraclitus (as word, meaning, human speech, etc.), yields a decisive moment in that history. *Logos* as Being and ground is also "saying" and "meaning." In that case, *logos* is the interpretation of the dif-ference that understands saying

---

I do not spend much time on the texts in which Derrida is explicitly offering a reading of Heidegger. I think Derrida is never further from Heidegger than when he is actually reading him, and—on the other hand—never closer than when he isn't. Caputo's reading is no doubt colored by his willingness to accept Derrida's word regarding the relation between the two thinkers.

[34]Much more will be said concerning these matters of metaphysics in the third chapter which introduces Derrida in his relation to Heidegger. At this point, it is still an open question whether or not any thinking can properly be said to escape metaphysical thinking altogether, and perhaps it is best to think that there will never be a time when it is not an open question.

metaphysically for the first time (and therefore not as Saying). Because of this weird relation between Being and saying within the *logos,* it provides the best point of departure for a journey into the Open; but for precisely this same reason it makes it the most dangerous of journeys.

The following section will be divided into two parts corresponding to the two matters raised in these introductory remarks: 1) the opening of Saying as Logos, and 2) The open clearing as perdurance, which will lead us to a closer examination of the relation of thing and world (as well as some other modes of the dif-ference). The first of these matters will be riddled with difficulties and dangers that will force us to retain a keen eye on the distinction between the *logos* that circles and the *logos* that grounds whatever is. The second of these matters will carry thinking, perhaps for the first time, closer to the earth. In fact, the determination of things within the world will bring thinking closer to the sky, mortality, and immortality: there will be call to discuss the fourfold, often called the movement of nearness.

The Opening of Saying as *Logos*

According to Heidegger, the translation of fragment B50 that he cites at the beginning of his essay on Heracleitus in *Early Greek Thinking* (59-78) is a typical one. It reads: "When you have listened not to me but to the Meaning, / it is wise within the same Meaning to say: *One is All*" (*EGT*, 59). Reading this standard translation with a fore-knowledge of Heidegger's style in such matters may surprise the reader. After all, *logos* will show itself as the Open clearing and the casual reader might expect, as in some of the earlier works, to see a link between the clearing and the notion of meaning. And yet, recall that Heidegger only gives familiar understandings of such matters in order to show how far off the mark they have wandered.

Nothing seems more natural than speaking about the clearing in terms of meaning, where meaning implies both the background of intelligibility that Heidegger attributes to sense (*Sinn*) and to the relational significance of world (*Bedeutsamigkeit*). Frequently, I have implied that the Open is that within which things come to presence, that is—in a way—become intelligible and thus available for human experience. I have also shown how the Greek temple in the essay "The Origin of the Work of Art" un-conceals the worldly contexts of significant relations within which one's life and thought can properly be said to *be* Greek. Furthermore, since the clearing has been consistently linked to the destiny of the Same as an historically determined region (i.e., as the region within which history takes place), isn't it perfectly familiar and coherent that the progression of history should be understood as a history of meanings?

All this is natural, easily understood and, best of all, it is completely consistent with the common reading of the early—and familiar—work. Significance, as the relational structure of the world (and clearing), is thought in *Being and Time* as a totality; and, although Heidegger does use words such as "disclosure" and "resolve" (*entsclossenheit* meaning disclosive) so as to suggest openness, any talk of this totality as the Open has not yet emerged and will only do so in the 1931 essay "On the Essence of Truth."[35] The opening of the Open, the "freeing" of it from the closure of totality in *Being and Time,* does mark a significant change in Heidegger's thinking, regardless of whether it can be turned into the one single most important advance in his thought throughout his career. This change turns away from the emphasis on significance as a relational totality within which Dasein, the "essence of human being," may be said to lie as the sole unifying feature. That is, all the relations of the world in *Being and Time* are said to be "for the sake of" Dasein which, therefore, rests at the center and circumference of this closed structure called "world" or "lightened clearing" (*Lichtung,* cf. *BT,* chap. 5, esp. 171, 182-88). The opening of the clearing in/as/through an Open region transforms any emphasis on Sense (*Sinn*) which might have led us to view clearing as a projection of Dasein within which all possibilities may be pursued. Dasein's context projects intelligible relations on this view. In the later work, the essence of human being is dismissed from this central role of projection and such projecting, insofar as it is discussed at all, is given over to the circling of the Same destined to arrive and overwhelm the clearing (i.e., by clearing).

Nonetheless, the notion of Sense (*Sinn*) does not suggest pure presence in the way that meaning (*Bedeutsamigkeit*) does.[36] Sense

---

[35]This is the essay which some interpreters, like Kockelmans, think is the key essay of the so-called "turn" from the early to the later Heidegger. In so far as the "there" of Dasein in *Being and Time* is equated with the clearing (i.e., Dasein's understanding is its being cleared) and insofar as the clearing is the clearing of "Being," it is a natural point of transition if the supposed "turn" is a move from focusing on Dasein to focusing on Being.

[36]My translation of these two terms, as should have already been noted, follows the more widely used translations of thinkers such as Frege and Husserl. This differs from the translators of *Being and Time* who use the words "meaning" and "significance" respectively for "*Sinn*" and "*Bedeutung*."

connotes projection and so—since projection is movement—carries with it a negative placing of itself outside the domain of what is immediately *there* (i.e., the authentic and inauthentic modes of world that we see in *Being and Time,* both of which are thought in terms of totality and significance). Sense, in that case, isn't as alien to Saying as meaning is. The difficulty with Sense is that it may suggest a human source of intelligibility through its other meanings (such as "mind"); this suggestion frequently—perhaps without justification—leads critics to charge Heidegger with idealism. Although it is the case that Being never *is* without Dasein, it is also the case that Dasein has its own intelligibility disclosed to it only through the intermediary of the Sense of Being, where Sense implies something like the later "grant" or "give." This self-understanding of Dasein which becomes explicit through the existential analytic is precisely what enables Dasein to gain an explicit understanding of Being and then Time. The mechanism of the "turn" already lies within the text of *Being and Time,* even if it hasn't been completely executed.[37]

It is not within the parameters of this essay to do a close survey of *Being and Time* and how it introduces the later thought. Still, if there were time to do such a thing even within the narrow context of this current discussion of Saying, I would probably begin with the curious phrase from § 6 of the introduction where Heidegger discusses the destruction of the history of ontology through a reawakening of the question concerning the sense of Being. In the last paragraph of this section he mentions the constant possibility of always finding a more original beginning and more universal horizon "from which we may draw the answer to the question, '*Was heißt Sein?*'" (*BT*, 49). The possibility of this constant deferral of the ground is what requires the reawakening of the question concerning the Sense of Being. The relation between the calling of (*heißt)* and the Sense of Being, which is already nestled into a significant section of the early work, suggests a good deal of what goes on in the later work and especially the aspects of it that have been discussed in this project (Cf. *Was heißt Denken?).*

---

[37] I argue in this in more detail in a paper called "Anxiety and Death: the hinge in *Being and Time.*" Essentially, my line is that the middle two chapters (I.6. and II.1) of the early work function as a hinge that allows the second division to become a retrieval of the first division by folding back onto it like a door swinging on a hinge. I "argue" that this repetition, if read carefully through the dynamic at work in care, disclosedness, anxiety, and being towards death, does involve itself in the turning that is the overwhelming of metaphysics.

Regarding Sense as Saying we need only wonder how non-sense would fit into the picture. Within all Saying lies the unsaid, the stillness out of which the pealing rings. Certainly the unsaid is not *more* essential than what is said in Saying, but it is crucial. Likewise, all talk of Sense would have to be equally talk of non-sense. The Open clearing would be open precisely because it would not be closed off by sense, but would include non-sense, where such non-sense as that which escapes intelligibility is precisely that which is hidden from any human understanding while continuing to permeate everything that is understood. The tendency at this point is to begin thinking that non-sense is *said* all the time. A person might speak non-sensically such that others cannot understand, and perhaps some people even speak without understanding themselves. Yet this historically occurring non-sensical speaking is precisely what I want to call meaninglessness, where the absence of meaning is nevertheless something which occurs, which happens: following others we call it absurdity. On this reading, meaning and absurdity become cultural world notions that belong to specific modes of Saying or language and not to Saying as such or the dynamic unfolding of language. Both meaning and the absurd occur in/as/through clearing and, therefore, the openness of the Open cannot be interpreted solely as meaning. Sense, however, permeated with non-sense is a better early approximation of Saying. It is to be hoped that this excursus prior to the discussion of *logos* will help us to steer clear of some of the difficulties that will arise from a self-evident familiarity with things.

Heidegger attempts to understand *logos* by understanding the verb *legein*: a typical move for him since the verb as the word's movement is more worthy of emphasis than the noun and more richly suggests the matter at hand. *Legein,* before its more current meanings of talk, say, or tell, implied (like the German *legen)*

> to lay down and lay before. In *legen* a "bringing together" prevails, the Latin *legere* understood as *lesen,* in the sense of collecting and bringing together. *Legein* properly means the laying-down and laying-before which gathers itself and others. The middle voice, *legesthai,* means to lay oneself down in the gathering of rest; *lexos* is the resting place; *loxos* is a place of ambush [or a place for lying in wait] where something is laid away and deposited. (The old word *alego*, archaic after Aeschylus and Pindar, should be recalled here: something 'lies upon me,' it oppresses and troubles me.) (*EGT*, 60)

There is a lot that is remarkable in this passage. First, I have to emphasize the togetherness of *legein* where what is laid out in *legein* is laid out together and where this laying out is, in a sense, a bringing to rest. We hear suggestions within *legein* of a gathering laid out as a resting place (of things presumably). And this takes us far afield from the familiar understanding of *legein* as "to talk." Even still, Heidegger is not merely content to present this somewhat unusual interpretation of *legein* without thoroughly considering the ordinary understanding of the word. In fact, the major part of the discussion of the fragment is ordered by Heidegger's effort to see how Greek speakers got from the "original" meaning of *legein* to the now "ordinary" meaning of it. As usual with Heidegger, the explanation of how an ordinary understanding of a word develops is a supporting demonstration of the primordial position of an alternative understanding.

This demonstration begins with a deeper examination of *legein* as laying where "to lay is to gather" (*EGT*, 61). Here "to gather" is the German *lesen,* which means not only gathering but reading. Reading is a predominant sort of gathering "in the sense of bringing-together-into-lying-before." All reading gathers writing so as to shelter meaning. The importance of reading as an example is that, first, it indicates a preliminary connection of laying to saying, and, second, sheltering emerges as significant in gathering. What is gathered is brought into a sheltering place where it may reside, come to rest.

Sheltering is the German *bergen* which also means hiding or concealing. The connotation of *legein* as a hiding place where an ambush is planned clearly indicates this. Furthermore, *bergen* recalls the root of the German *Unverborgenheit* which suggests un-concealedness or *a-letheia.* The combination of all gathering with a sheltering is nothing other than the twofold rendition of un-concealment as revealing/concealing, which additionally signifies a rendering or unfolding of the clearing. Heidegger's summation and emphasis of this point marks the key claim that this chapter must demonstrate: "However, *lesen* thought in this way does not simply stand near *legen.* Nor does the former simply accompany the latter. Rather, gathering is already included in laying. Every gathering is already a laying. Every laying is of itself gathering." (*EGT*, 62) There is more to the intimacy of *lesen* and *legen* than the relation of revealing to concealing where laying corresponds to revealing and gathering to sheltering or concealing. Rather, the intimacy informs us that all un-concealing is a coming to reside or rest in un-concealedness. This coming to rest immediately recalls the rest of stillness that underlies all Saying. All abiding or coming to rest is a fragile and temporary moment of repose which something that comes into the Open takes for a while there (it whiles away its time there). The resting in the Open is not a sign of permanence, of the abiding something's stability to remain forever, but a sign of its relationship to stillness, to the unsaid from which it has come forth and to which it eventually returns. Rest indicates the fragility of what abides in the Open, not its stability; it is a feature of dynamic finitude and not eternal stasis or presence. In terms used previously, I might say that Saying is the opening of a clearing, or that the circling of the Same is the clearing of an Open region, where this region is the resting place for all that abides and, as such, is both sheltering and revealing.[38]

The movement of laying, as a dynamic unfolding of what is brought to lie, gathers together what is brought to lie; and what is brought to lie by this laying are the things that exist in the world where human beings come into contact with them. The world, as open clearing, is a place where things lie before us, gathered there and sheltered by/within the world. When I look around in my study and out my window, I see things gathered here and there. Of course, I do not actually see the world and the laying that brings the world forth, but I do see the things and through the things the world is borne. But this should not surprise me since the world is what shelters the things that are gathered here and, since sheltering is the concealing of *bergen*, I cannot *see* sheltering, although I can certainly experience things as what are sheltered.

Heidegger turns from *legein* as laying to its historical development into talking or speaking. "Saying [what we have been calling speaking] and talking occur essentially as the letting-lie-together-before of everything which, laid in unconcealment, comes to presence [i.e., dynamically unfolds]" (*EGT*, 63). According to my reading, this says nothing more than that the essence of human speech and language is in Saying as the circling of the Same. And yet, while this connection links saying to laying, it also separates them. After all, it changes the saying as human speaking into Saying as dynamic unfolding, et al. Heidegger, for the moment then, has not told us how the ordinary conception of speaking has come from laying, but rather has informed us as to the essence of speech that lies in Saying as the gathering *logos*. He has, as I claimed he does in other works, moved the essence of human speech away from any merely human determination (like vocalization or expression) and into the realm of language itself.

Although this substantiates the previous claims regarding the being

---

[38]This passage introduces for the first time in its greatest clarity the notion of finitude in the whole matter of thinking. The role of finitude will occupy a central role in this project in chapter 4.

of language as Saying, it does little to advance the understanding of the gathering clearing as essential to Saying; except, perhaps, by giving a slightly better account of the circularity of this movement of Saying that opens up along with a better account of why the movement is not a linear procedure grounded in some first cause.

Laying out as the bringing to lie of things can be characterized as determination, but not in the sense of an effect. Saying does not cause things to come into the Open; rather, it lets them come into the place where they belong. Developed here is a sketch of the characteristics of "tautological" thinking, where what is tautological is what belongs to the Same in the sense that it is an dynamic element of the economy of the Same. The items that are given over to tautology are few in number: *Er-eignis,* dif-ference, un-concealment, and Saying, of course, but also time, space, world, and thing. The opening of the clearing is a tautological movement—and this says no more than that the opening is the movement of the Same. Yet I hasten to add to our understanding of this by recognizing the role of things within the nexus. It may be said that the opening of the Open is the thinging of things: where thinging recalls *Bedingnis,* meaning determination. Thinking the nature of determination in the sense that things are determined in/as/through clearing is nothing other than thinking the Same. The thinging of things that dif-fers within the dif-ference from the worlding of world takes place (*er-eignet*) in/as/through the circling of the Same.

I am afraid that it is an error to understand the Open as Saying. It is important to avoid speaking *about* the Open, making it into the object of a representation which is then described.[39] When this is done, the Open withdraws: the opening is always withdrawing as the sheltering region of the things that are revealed within it, but in representation even this withdrawal withdraws. Statements that represent objects can do so correctly because a relation occurs between the statement and the object, a relation that enables a knower to see the object as present even when all that remains is the statement. Heidegger asks in many different places ("On the Essence of Truth" and *Gelassenheit,* for example) how such relations are possible. He always answers the Same: a statement may represent an object only because an Open clearing enables such a relationship to occur. The possibility of relationships occurring, in a

---

[39]It may be important to avoid this, but I am pretty confident that I will continue to objectify the Open throughout this part of the essay. The point I have to bring out, though, if it is possible in this manner of presentation, is that even when we are speaking about the Open, we are doing so from out of the Open. Even where the clearing is obscured, it continues to clear.

sense, pre-exists any particular relations that unfold. The Open is therefore a zone or region of capability, a place of being able to... Recall the descriptions of the components of the Same as enabling from chapter 1. What is more, this enabling of the representation of objects is only one mode of enabling to which there are coupled many others. Tools, unlike objects, exist differently in the Open, likewise with things and beings. And to each of these will correlate a separate mode of Saying. Representation in the form of statements or propositions is not, contrary to the traditional view, an after the fact appending of the word (or statement) onto the thing that exists over there; rather, the statement itself represents in such a way as to let the object stand over there for the first time.[40] This should supplement the passage: "Perhaps these names are not the result of designation. They are owed to naming in which the namable, the name and the named occur altogether" (DT, 71).

Designation would be the appending of a word onto a thing, and it is here contrasted to Heidegger's position which asserts that the thing or named thing, the name as the word, and the namable or the capability of naming all come to pass together in the Same moment. The namable is the underlying open clearing that enables all relations of things to words to take place in the naming that occurs as Saying. Insofar as Saying opens a region, it enables things to come to lie there and it also enables language as an interpretative naming to come to lie. This notion of language is not merely human speech, but all forms of interpretation given above, including the down to business handling of tools which needn't involve talk in its relationships with the necessary things. Likewise, representation, occurring in statements and propositions, is also a modification of interpretation where interpretation is the giving of an "as" structure to an entity: being as object, as tool, as thing, etc. are all types of determinations of the "as." This typology will further determine the manner in which particular things will be seen; that is, what they will be seen as being: we have previously referred to this typology as the modes of Saying. A mode of Saying is a manner in which the relationships of the open clearing occur and hence a manner in which the beings relate to language within the Open. Representation would be a mode of Saying in which the statement and the object would arise out of a certain kind of

---

[40]Represent is *vorstellen,* object is *gegenstand.* The roots are related: *stellen* meaning "to stand" in the sense of to set up or place and *stehen* meaning "to stand" in the more familiar sense of standing. Heidegger wants to say that the object is made to stand by the representation which sets it up and hence lets it be an object.

relation—a relation described in English as "present" and in German as "standing."

This discussion furthers the effort to understand the way that Saying determines the open clearing, but it remains to be seen how Saying does this. This is precisely Heidegger's concern when he wants to get from the original meaning of *legein* as laying to the more common meaning as speech. At this time, I will turn back to the essay on Heraclitus and take up where I left off.

After coming upon Saying as underlying all speaking, Heidegger turns toward hearing. He begins by pointing out that since saying is not vocalization, hearing cannot be the receiving of sounds, the mere reverberation of sound in the ear. If it were, he says, sound would probably go in one ear and out the other. And he points out that sometimes what is heard *does* go in one ear and out the other when he says "that happens in fact when we are not gathered to what is addressed" (*EGT*, 65). Hearing, like saying, is gathering, only it is a gathering of oneself in response to the claim laid upon thought in the laying out of *legein*. Hearing is a receiving of the essential in what is said where the essential can only be the Same. We gather ourselves in hearing as a response to what has been laid out before us in the gathering, which must mean that we are gathered together within it, we too—when we hear properly—are drawn into the gathering. He writes in an oft-quoted phrase:

> We do not hear because we have ears. We have ears, i.e., our bodies are equipped with ears, because he hears. Mortals hear the thunder of the heavens, the rustling of woods, the gurgling of fountains, the ringing of plucked strings, the rumbling of motors, the noises of the city—only and only so far as they always already in some way belong to them and yet do not belong to them. (*EGT*, 65-6)

It is not pure sound that enters the ear and then becomes intelligible to the one who hears. Rather, hearing is always a matter for things. There are no pure sense data of sound; what we hear is already a sophisticated existent thing like a motor or thunder. This articulates the notion of hearing as gathering, since we are told that things are gathered in hearing, things that have been brought to lie there. But even these things are not pure things, but things that exist in the world among other things and that come to take up residence in the world through their relational contexts *as* what they are. Hearing as gathering is therefore a form of interpreting beings as whatever they are. In this case, it is necessary to admit that there are various modes of hearing, probably corresponding to the various modes of Saying.

Hearing is not some separate element of the gathering open clearing that results from the laying out; it is woven into the very dynamic. All laying out that gathers, gathers unto it a hearing. This step of thinking is ambiguous. It seems as though Heidegger is concerned with hearing as something mortals do. Nonetheless, it would be a mistake to understand hearing as an activity of mortals, just as it would be a mistake to claim that the modes of Saying are human activities. The inversion that takes place in the sentence regarding the ear is essential for the step back from human action to the opening up of the clearing. Just as Saying is not human speech but the dynamic that takes place in/as/through human speech, hearing takes place in/as/through human employment of the ears. Although Heidegger relies on a common understanding of hearing to get his point across, he may be moving beyond that ordinary understanding in the same gesture. When Heidegger describes hearing as a gathering of what is addressed in the claim of the *legein* (i.e., gathered by the claim making hearing into a gathering of the gathering), he is not making the crucial step from Saying to human speech as it is heard, but is informing us about the dynamic unfolding of Saying.

> We are all ears when our gathering devotes itself entirely to hearkening, the ears and the mere invasion of sounds being completely forgotten. So long as we only listen to the sound of a word, as the expression of a speaker, we are not yet even listening at all. Thus, in this way we never succeed in having genuinely heard anything at all. But when does hearing succeed? We have heard [*gehört*] when we belong to [*gehören*] the matter addressed. The speaking of the matter addressed is *legein*, letting-lie-together-before. To belong to speech—this is nothing else than in each case letting whatever a letting-lie-before lays down before lie gathered in its entirety. Such a letting-lie establishes whatever lies before us as lying-before. It establishes this as itself. It lays one and the Same in one. It lays one as the Same. Such *legein* lays one and the Same, the *homon*. Such *legein* is *homolegein*: One as the Same, i.e., a letting-lie-before of what does lie before us, gathered in the selfsameness of its lying-before. (*EGT*, 66)

It is not possible to overestimate the importance of this paragraph to my project. It begins by emphasizing the impossibility of hearing pure sound. There may be a way to point out pure sound, but it is not hearing—perhaps some method of thematic analysis based on presence, the representation of a pure object: a sound bite. This sort of pointing out is not genuine hearing, in that it is a method of interpretation that fails to hear or mishears.[41] Successful hearing, on the other hand, is a belonging to what is addressed where the addressed is the gathering of what is brought to lie before the address, the open clearing. I have mentioned already the etymological connection of hearing and belonging, but now it comes forward as particularly important. Since hearing is gathering in such a way as to be drawn into the gathering of *legein,* the way in which hearing is a way of belonging must express itself in terms of what belongs in the gathering of hearing to the gathering of *legein.* The two forms of gathering may be said to belong together, to be the Same. Hearing, as belonging together with the Same (being the Same as the Same), is understood by Heracleitus as *homolegein.* Since I have read *legein* as the Saying of the Same, *homolegein* is the Same as the Same. It appears that the Same has doubled in the taking place of all hearing belonging to the Same. Although I quickly add that this doubling of the Same is nothing new; the Same has always already been this doubling, right from the very beginning, from the very first word uttered here or anywhere.

The hearing that belongs to *legein* does not speak for itself in a way that would block or interrupt the Saying of *legein.* The doubling is not a

---

[41]Two parenthetical comments are needed: 1. It may be possible that a scientist who develops a theory of sound based on its being a pure sense datum is in some sense hearing, but that is not to say that hearing itself is an earful of reverberating sound bits. The scientist may be perfectly well describing how ears work without saying what hearing is in the essential fashion Heidegger has in mind here. The description of the workings of ears may properly hearken to the call of the *legein* that lets ears be as things. But again we should not confuse the description of ears working — even if it is phrased in terms of hearing — with the description of hearing. 2. The claim in chapter 1 regarding the failure to hear of the tradition should be clearer after this discussion. The tradition, for example, represents the objects of the objective world in just the way that sound data theory represents sound: beings that stand over and against human thinking. Such representation and all theories based on it would therefore fail to hear while still being interpretations of entities (i.e., hearing them in some "as" fashion). Similar claims could be made about traditional thinkers who have interpreted entities differently in their being. This project of showing how traditional thinkers fail to hear in this way (that is, fail to belong to what speaks to them concerning the matter addressed) would be what Heidegger calls the destruction of the tradition or what Derrida calls the deconstruction of the tradition. Either way, it is not a task to be carried out in a footnote, so I will come back to it in the next chapter.

separating of the one from the other; instead, they remain appropriate to each other, linked through their dif-ference, striving together as such. In this sense, hearing as belonging does not hear in such a way as to hear as... where the "as" implies the Being of what is. Rather than a hearing *as,* it is a hearing *of* the Same. This does not mean that the hearing is not or no longer an interpretation of the Saying, only that interpretation and hearing are expanded beyond the realm of the as-structure connoting Being. If hearing doubles the Same and hearing hears the Same as Being, then it has heard falsely, for I have demonstrated again and again that the Same *is* not while *granting* all that is. It is nowhere near the right time for discussing this crucial matter regarding the nature of interpretation beyond an as-structure. Yet it has become possible to see that this discussion lies ahead as that trait of the way that explains the possibility of beginning this project as I have done so.[42]

---

[42]Notice that the German word for "to interpret" is *Auslegen* where *legen* is the word Heidegger explicitly links to the *legein* of *Logos. Auslegen* and the derivative *Auslegung* meaning interpretation are crucial to the analysis of *Being and Time* and refer to the "as" structure of something that has been made explicit in its Being as it is regardless of whether the interpretation is authentic or not. It follows, therefore, that within the framework of *Being and Time* it would be nonsense to suggest that there could be a form of interpretation that outstrips the "as" structure. Yet, I have found nowhere in the works of Heidegger dated during the 40s, 50s, and 60s any evidence supporting this framework. In fact, I notice a very telling lack of references to notions of understanding and interpretation (where interpretation is an explicitation of understanding in which what is determined in an "as" structure is determined in accordance with some pre-explicit understanding of the thing interpreted). The interplay of interpretation and understanding is usually thought of as hermeneutics and the project of Heidegger in the early work is frequently called hermeneutical. But references to hermeneutics in the later work, are always in terms of messages being sent out into the open and not in terms of an understanding essential to Dasein. This change of emphasis, where hermeneutics becomes an element in the movement of the Same instead of a feature of Dasein's existential structure (an existentiale), is another major component in the division usually referred to between the early and the later Heidegger. Therefore, I take it as an open question whether it is intelligible to speak of a form of interpretation, *Aus-legung,* that escapes the "as" structure connoting Being. Recall that *Auslegung* means laying out and you will already see that the laying out taking place in a *homolegein* that doubles *legein* is a form of interpretation that outstrips Being since it is this doubling interpretation that grants Being within the Open in the first place. A

Homolegein was translated in the familiar version of Heraclitus's fragment as "the same Meaning" but it has elsewhere been translated as "acknowledge" or "agree." In Heidegger's reading of the fragment, the translation is "proper hearing," where "proper hearing occurs essentially in *legein* as *homolegein.*" (*EGT*, 66) Heidegger recognizes that this translation may be odd. This doesn't mean that he doubts the appropriateness of it, only that he understands there may be some question as to whether this "remains appropriate, if only in the most remote way, to what Heraclitus named and thought in the name *ho Logos*" (*EGT*, 66). Following Heidegger's demonstration may help support some of the claims I am making.

Heidegger notes that the fragment opens with a negative warning, telling the listener what should not be done. What should not be done, Heraclitus says, is for the listener to listen to the words of the speaker. "Heraclitus begins the saying with a rejection of hearing as nothing but the passion of the ears" (*EGT*, 67), where this signifies the idiosyncratic thinking of the individual human speaker who expresses himself in one way or another. It is not the representation of a subject that is to be heard, but something else, something far more grand and worthy of thought. And this something else, this most thought-worthy of things, is the *logos*. Heraclitus, therefore, is dismissing one kind of hearing in favor of another. And this does not conflict in any way with the familiar translations of the fragment: "When you have listened not to me but to the Meaning."

Homolegein is precisely what occurs when this proper hearing takes place. When the *logos* has been listened to, there is *homolegein* as a modification of *logos*. It is worth emphasizing this point with respect to certain charges brought against Heidegger that I will discuss in a moment:

> As such, the proper hearing of mortals is in a certain way the Same as the *Logos*. At the same time, however, precisely as *homolegein,* it is not the Same at all. It is not the same as the *Logos* itself. Rather, *homolegein* remains a *legein* which always and only lays or lets lie whatever is already, as *homon,* gathered together and lying before us; this lying never springs from the *homolegein* but rather rests in the Laying that gathers, i.e., in the *Logos*. (*EGT*, 67)

---

more complete demonstration and an examination of the consequences of this feature of the later Heidegger will be carried out in due course. I wonder, ultimately, whether the early *auslegen* doesn't become the later *austragen*, discussed in the next section.

I call this a "doubling" of the Same, based on an earlier remark in
Heidegger's text, which I have described in the gathering of the *legein*
that is *homolegein* as being gathered in/as/through the initial laying that
gathers. In gathering, therefore, there is not only Saying, the economy of
the Same, and the opening up in circling, but there is hearing belonging
to this same nexus. Slowly but surely more and more attributes of this
gathering are compiled, making it increasingly possible to experience
these phenomena as part of the familiar world within which human being
takes place. As yet, however, the investigations have not taken us far
enough to view this more thoroughly.

In this context, Heidegger explains hearing and Saying (*logos*) in
terms of gathering and laying, not the other way around. Furthermore, the
essay on Heraclitus attempts to go beyond talk of meaning and sense.
Likewise, it suggests that language is not essentially human or necessarily
expressed in sound or print. Rather, language speaks in the way of
gathering. Saying means nothing more than a laying that gathers, or an
opening of a clearing. It will become evident in the following pages that
Heidegger thinks words and human language have a special status among
gathering or opening up, but this may not be taken for granted and must
be demonstrated.

Recalling the text, Heidegger points out that something happens
when there is *homolegein* and that something is "*sophon estin*." "When
homolegein occurs, then *sophon* comes to pass" (*EGT*, 67). *Sophon*
ordinarily suggests "wisdom," but Heidegger probes deeper to look into
what may be said to lie in all wisdom. The wise thing to do is always that
which is indicated by circumstances. A wise action is therefore on the
way toward what is called for by a situation. Such "appropriate" behavior
is called "skillful," "*schickliches*," and "*geschickt*" respectively. These
words have familiar connotations: destiny and fate—the delivery of a
message into the open. And in fact, Heidegger goes on to interpret *sophon*
as the fateful (*geschicklich*). When proper hearing occurs, the fateful
comes to pass. This means that when proper hearing is attuned to the
claim of the *logos,* a message is delivered in/as/through the Opening. In
short, the open opens up, the gathering is laid out, and so on.

The messenger of the Gods is Hermes. The message is what is sent
fatefully in Saying and the messenger is the proper hearing that bears the
message into the open, opening it—blazing a trail so to speak—as it does
so. "Hermes is the divine messenger. He brings the message of destiny:
hermeneuein is that exposition which brings tidings because it can listen
to a message" (*OWL*, 29). Saying lays claim on the open by calling out its

message, and that message is borne in/as/through hearing it. All that exists in the open is determined (be-thinged) by the message sent in Saying and gathered in mortals. This recalls the way a relation enables the things that relate to do so. The message, as the message of dif-ference, is the relation everything in residence there takes up relative to whatever else there is. The mode of Saying that guides the gathering is a particular message of Saying.

The fateful comes to pass in proper hearing. "Where, and as what, does the fateful presence?" Heidegger asks. "The fateful comes to pass insofar as One is All," Heraclitus responds (*EGT*, 68). Heidegger criticizes the traditional understanding of this part of the fragment. He claims that the familiar understanding is that the message of the *logos* is that "One is All." That is, in proper hearing the fateful comes to pass: One is All. On this reading, absolute truth is established. The one message of the *logos,* for now and forever, is that One is All. Heidegger's alternative is that "*Hen Panta* is not what the *Logos* pronounces; rather, *Hen Panta* suggests the way in which *Logos* essentially occurs" (*EGT*, 70). This is a crucial difference. Recall that I said I was going to be on the lookout for the understanding of *logos* as one in a series of master names for Being. The traditional understanding of Heraclitus, the understanding that sees the call of the *logos* as being "One is All," would be a reading that claims the *logos* as a master name for Being, the single and first basic enabling condition of everything that is. When Heidegger criticizes this in the tradition and interprets Heraclitus as saying that the *logos* occurs essentially insofar as One is All, he is rejecting any understanding of the *logos* as a master name for Being, as the ground of all that is.

The One is the unique one which unifies all that is assembled in the gathering. The gathering of the *logos* is therefore characterized as the unique unifying feature of all that is brought to lie. The All refers to what comes into the unique one gathering that unifies. What is unified in the gathering is everything. At this point it might be tempting to see this as an ontological ground. The gathering is a unique one within which all that comes to pass comes to pass. It would seem that this is the unity of Saying that Heidegger claimed had not been seen historically. But Heidegger does not stop at this point. He reminds us of the essential dynamic of laying that includes sheltering. This links the laying that gathers and shelters to the two-fold movement of un-concealment, since the laying is both revealing and concealing; then he goes on to emphasize the "*lethe*" at the heart of un-concealment, and which enables all multiplicity or *Panta.* Although he insists on the unifying nature of the *Hen* in this discussion, he also calls this unified *Hen* a "carrying out," such that we are reminded of the *Austrag* that occurs as dif-ference. To overcome the apparent inconsistency in this, we need only recall that the unity of Saying is not the unity of what is said in Saying, but unity in the Saying of Saying, the laying out of the gathering. And this evokes *nothing other than* the circling of the Same implying the reflexive nature of Saying to which there is no outside (and, strictly speaking, no inside). The *Hen* is a One but it is, in its context, a One among One and a unity saturated with dif-ference.[43]

Heidegger clarifies this by demonstrating that the fateful is not *homolegein* as proper hearing, but the unique One of the gathering (according to Heraclitus in fragment B 32: "Wisdom [*sophon*] is one and unique"). And he supplements this by showing that the *Hen Panta* describes how the *logos* essentially occurs thus suggesting that the *logos* and *Hen Panta* are the Same: "*Hen Panta* says what the *Logos* is. *Logos* says how *Hen Panta* essentially occurs. Both are the Same" (*EGT*, 71). It follows that the *Logos* is the fateful itself. When the *Logos* is properly heard, the *Logos* as the fateful gathers in a laying sheltering. This does not mean that the *Logos* is one such message among others, but rather that it is *the* sending of messages; it is destiny, the Saga of Saying.

The unifying feature of the One is understood in traditional metaphysics without dif-ference. The unique One is interpreted by the tradition as the gatherer of many diverse instances of the unique. The One gets understood as the universal over and against all that is particular. "The *Logos* grounds and gathers everything into the universal, and accounts for and gathers everything in terms of the unique" (*ID*, 69). This universal One that gathers the All and, as such, *is* the All where everything is present in the One (perhaps through participation, as in Plato), becomes the essence or idea. And it was probably through linking essence, understood as quiddity, with *logos* that Aristotle could see essences as nothing more than names. Nominalism derives from the metaphysical interpretation of the *logos*.

Heidegger invokes Heraclitus' fragment B 64, "But lightning steers all things," in an effort to articulate the meaning of destiny. He shows that destiny is the message that brings all things toward human being, gathering and laying them out in assembly. Through the sending of a message, "each being can be joined and sent into its own" (*EGT*, 72). The thinging of things that bears out the worlding of the world comes to pass in destiny; that is, the coming into their own of things. The owning of

---

[43] Cf. Schurmann's discussion of *Hen* on pp. 177-179 of op cit. In a very short discussion, he does a great job showing the same tension between the traditional and deconstructive reading of the Heraclitus fragment.

things, demonstrated previously, occurs through Saying as destiny in the *Er-eignis* of what belongs in the cleared gathering. Heidegger mentions the Heraclitus fragment not only to show that destiny is another way of naming the coming to pass of all present beings, but also to link the *Hen* and the *logos* of the previous fragments to the lightning bolt that steers all things moving in this appropriate fashion. "'Lightning' appears here as an epithet of Zeus" (*EGT*, 72).

It is important that Heidegger link the Zeus mentioned to the nexus of *logos, Hen,* and destiny, because of additional remarks in Heraclitus' fragment B 32. These remarks support the claim that the lightning steering things belongs to the lightning god himself: "The One, which alone is wise, does not want/and yet does want to be called by the name Zeus" (Diels and Kranz translation). This support is necessary, since Heraclitus does not say that it is Zeus's lightning that steers all things. But this is not a problem, right? After all, what could be more obvious than to link the lightning bolt to the lightning god? Still, when dealing with Heraclitus, the lover of wisdom who is best known for his flowing rivers and dancing fires, the equation of a process or event such as lightning with a noun or agent such as Zeus is not as obvious as it might be with some other thinker. Nevertheless, the link is there to the extent that both are, in various places, described as the steering of all that is. In that case, Zeus could be said to name (and not name) the lightning itself.

Heidegger challenges the Diels-Kranz understanding of the fragment by claiming that "*ethelo*" translated as "does not want" means, in fact, "is not ready." What then is the unique One *logos* not ready for? "*Legesthai*" indicates that it is not ready to be assembled under the name "Zeus." This is, for Heidegger, the key to the connection between *logos,* saying, talking, and naming. *Legesthai,* derived from *Logos,* suggests "*onoma*" meaning "to name," where what is named is Zeus.

> To name means to call forward. That which is gathered and laid down in the name, by means of such a laying, comes to light and comes to lie between us. The naming (*onoma*), thought in terms of *legein,* is not the expressing of a word-meaning but rather a letting-lie-before in the light wherein something stands in such a way that it has a name. (*EGT*, 73)

Naming is essentially related to *legein* and *logos,* in that it too suggests laying and gathering, and yet it is not relevant to the laying and gathering as One unique movement (in the sense Heidegger has been developing throughout the essay). Rather, naming as a laying out in the clearing (i.e., a lightening or, perhaps, lightning) is a particle of the *legein* that gathers the clearing itself. What is named is a thing that appears within the clearing, a small copse within the larger clearing.

This should already indicate why Heidegger thinks Heraclitus has told us that the unique One is both ready and not ready to be named Zeus. The *Hen* is not one being among others; it is not something which appears within the Open. It therefore cannot be properly said to have a name, since names are always related to entities occurring within the Open. Yet, the fragment tells us that the unique One also does admit of being named Zeus. This occurs in so far as the *Hen* appears as *Panta,* everything that is in Being, all entities that are. Insofar as the unique One is all things that have come to presence, it admits of being named and hence is ready to be named Zeus. One way to phrase this is that because the clearing is both lighting and concealing; it both renders and does not render itself up to naming. This leads to some additional questions that might be worth looking into when the time is right: Since things bear out world as world grants things, isn't it the case that all things have as part of their essence an element of the unnamable, a bearing that is the un-named clearing? What about all the names given throughout this essay, each supposedly designating some element of Saying that opens up in the sense that Heidegger gives to the unique One; isn't it the case that such components are not ready to be assembled under their given names? To what extent are these components ready to be assembled under these names?

Heidegger raises a number of questions as the essay on Heraclitus draws to a close. The bulk of the questioning is aimed at whether the laying or saying of the gathering sheltering is a mortal behavior. Heidegger seems concerned as to whether this is all an anthropomorphizing of the movement of the Same. He does not pursue these questions at this time but he goes on to describe how *homolegein,* as proper hearing linked to the behavior of mortals, and *legein,* as the Saying of the Same, have a more primordial origin in the "simple middle region between both" (*EGT*, 75). This more primordial origin is called dif-ference. I take it that it is because of this common belonging together in the dif-ference that mortal behavior as proper hearing and the *logos* are able to resemble each other in the first place. This would imply that not only is Saying not an anthropomorphic cosmology, but that the similarity of Saying to mortal behavior is indicative of the relation that joins them and from which they both arise as belonging together. Because Saying and hearing are not merely saying and hearing, but a belonging together in/as/through the circling of the Same, they suggest more than merely mortal elements that have been universalized to encompass everything that is.

The last items of interest in Heidegger's very rich twenty page essay on the *"Logos"* are some remarks he makes in a brief conclusion concerned with the nature of language. He begins by asking what happens when the Being of beings in their dif-ference is brought to language, and goes on to discuss what bringing to language means. He says that it means "to secure Being in the essence of language" (*EGT*, 77). This iterates the point I made regarding the revelatory and concealing power of Saying. But Heidegger uses this meaning to set up his claim that the "*ho Logos*" within Heraclitus's thinking plays a crucial role in enabling this element of language, as the secure place of Being, to become explicit. Yet Heidegger claims that Heraclitus did not himself think language in this manner. Certainly the Greeks saw that *logos* was a name for Being, but they did not think its relation to language in any explicit fashion. Here "language" indicates human language, which is not yet speech, insofar as it is naming (a calling forth of what is named, a gathering of what is in the open) or the gathering of some part of the gathering open—i.e., the copse in the clearing. Heidegger turns to criticize the Greek conception of language by showing how they thought language as tongue, sound, and voice. He claims that this conception of language is what he has been calling language as expression, which is derivative of language as "the gathering letting-lie-before of what is present in its presencing" (*EGT*, 77). Language as naming need not be exclusively allied with the tongue or the voice since such naming goes on within the cultural language world of a people even where the utterance is lacking in favor of a practice or a sensation, etc.[44]

If the Greeks did not think language in this way, how could Heidegger discover language as such in the writings of a Greek thinker? This is how retrieval or repetition (*wiederholen)* works as a way of reading (*lesen)*: it looks at the explicit elements of a fragment so as to discover the concealed or silent elements there (in other words, the familiar and the primordial). The Greek words Heraclitus has used are written names, in the sense Heidegger gives this word, but they are names that designate phenomena that are both ready and not ready to be named. In this slippery contact of designation, the unsaid may be disclosed through what is said. In fact, it is the striving or tension of all that is unsaid with what is said that *is* this slippery contact of designation that makes retrieval possible, since retrieval is nothing other than the taking place

---

[44]It may be that there is some form of vocalization or speech that is most proper to the nature of language as naming what is gathering together in the laying of Saying. The examination of this form of "speech"—so to speak—will be put off until later.

again of the Same—the revealing/concealing tension embodied (or bethinged) in words that name. Heidegger claims that the Greeks, although they did not think the essence of language in the manner of *logos* as Saying, did dwell in such an essential determination of language when they thought of Being as the *logos*. Because they dwelled in such a way, the fragments they have left us (at least this one by Heraclitus) are well suited for retrieval. Their words may fail to make explicit that which is most worthy of thought, but the words cannot help but betray the underlying practices that reside within the thought-worthy. Practices too have a naming capacity insofar as they make up the world of a people; and such practices are likely to find their way, in subtle forms, into the people's speech. Greek fragments are thus retrieved when we cease to hear what is spoken in them in favor of what is said (and unsaid) in their Saying.[45]

Much has been said in this discussion of Heidegger's essay on Heraclitus's *logos* fragment that requires further examination. Still, I hope this section has clarified the open clearing as Saying. Mortals have been introduced in the preceding and, as a result, the project will never be the same. The mise-en-scène of mortality remains critical until the bitter end. At this time, the way in which mortals fit into the workings of the gathering demands an account. But this can only take place slowly and in the right context; so, now, let's turn to the section I promised regarding the thinging of the thing. I will demonstrate that this component in the Same is important for the inscribing of mortals into the gathering clearing, as well as for articulating the role of language as gathering letting-lie-before us (of things through naming).

The Open Clearing as Perdurance

It became evident that the clearing is the clearing of perdurance (*Austrag*) in several different places. Perdurance is "carrying out" and recalls the dif-ference from which the call of Saying comes, to which it calls, and as the destination of what is called. The manner of perdurance, as a modification of Saying and dif-ference, is therefore essential to all that goes on in the clearing. In fact, the Open region clears in accordance with a manner of perdurance, suggesting that there is a mode of clearing specific to the various forms of perdurance, Saying, hearing, etc. All these

---

[45]This provocative but overly terse line of thought will occupy a significant part in what follows. One way to understand the remainder of this project is as the unravelling of what has been merely suggested here.

modes are modifications of the Same, although not all of them can be said to double the Same. That is, say the Same of the Same. The *logos,* and the type of hearing that responds to it, presents more than one possible mode of perdurance. A good way to clarify this might be to recall the discussion of belonging at the outset of this project.

Recall that the traditional mode of belonging together as an interpretation of the *"to auto"* in Parmenides's fragment on Being and thinking was criticized for its failure to hear, where hearing suggests belonging. Instead, the tradition understands the Same in terms of togetherness and unity without difference. Heidegger would be sure to point out that in both cases "belonging" is a part of the experience. In that case, both interpretations hear; but one interpretation fully understands hearing as hearing by recognizing that it occurs because in essence what hears belongs to what speaks to it, what is said in Saying. The other reading hears, but hearing takes a backseat to togetherness; it is not essential. Thus, in this mishearing, the *Hen Panta* is considered to be the message of the *logos* and not the way in which the *logos* gives its message. In this case, hearing goes astray in hearing togetherness as the message of the *logos* and not as the gathering manner in which the message is sent or carried.

The gathering of the *logos* that gives the message of the Being of what is as the unique One is the universal concept of all that is gathered in it.[46] Metaphysics begins here and mishearing the *logos* is metaphysical hearing, which means that it is a mode of perdurance, of dif-ference forgetful of the dif-ference. This means that dif-ference as *"Austrag"* is carried out in this metaphysical mode of hearing, but that the carrying out is overlooked in favor of what is carried out in it. The message of the properly heard *logos* presents itself in such a way as to appear in its presence as the metaphysically heard *logos* cut off from its process of coming to presence, from its opening up. This interruption of sending favors an eternal scheme of things prevailing without end and transcending all time. In fact, it is usually conceived as the determining ground of all time: time is grounded upon the eternal foundation of the present in its presence as the universal Being beyond which there is nothing.

---

[46]Cf. *Being and Time,* page 21: "It is said that 'Being' is the most universal and the emptiest of concepts. As such it resists every attempt at definition. Nor does this most universal and hence indefinable concept require any definition, for everyone uses it constantly and already understands what he means by it." It is at this point, Heidegger says, that the obscuring of the question concerning the Sense of Being occurs; and it is based on this obscurity that he seeks to reawaken a concern for the question.

The hearing that differs from metaphysical hearing, what is it called? Is it hermeneutical hearing as suggested above? That is, a hearing that is not a receiving of some message that is present here for us, but a hearing that bears a message, is a messenger carrying the message. Proper hearing, in that case, cannot be attributed automatically to "man" or "human being." Instead, proper hearing, insofar as it can be called hermeneutical relative to the bearing of the message of Saying, is not the dynamic unfolding of "man" or woman or human being or humankind, but of the messenger. The messenger carries the message only so long as there is proper hearing and the call of Saying to be properly heard.[47]

All this, so far, amounts to little more than a review. But it is a review that draws together what was done separately, and thus, as a sort of repetition, carries the demonstration forward through suggestions and hints it makes concerning the way (in other words, the suggestions and hints are themselves way-making).[48] The message bearing of the

---

[47]It should have been clear from the citation made in the introduction to this section, that Heidegger thinks the name "man" is given up with "Being" as metaphysical determinations, as part of the tradition of metaphysics. As for the name of human being, it too has difficulties in much the way that Dasein does, since both incorporate "Being" within themselves—this has been problematic since the dismissal of "Being" as a term of the Same. "Humankind" might be acceptable because of its implications of Earth, mentioned by Heidegger in the care fable of *Being and Time,* but this will have to be developed explicitly in what follows. For the moment, messenger is the only word I can use, although it too may slip away at any time.

The introduction of hermeneutics as a form of hearing, and thus as a mode of interpretation is first seen in *Being and Time* when a mode of the "as" structure is called hermeneutical. In that case, however, the "as" was an interpretation that arose through a comportment (*Verhalten*) within an equipmental totality (i.e., the world as significance). The problems we saw previously with the conception of meaning and significance in *Being and Time* would then carry over into the conception of hermeneutical interpretation: the world as a totality with a center in the "for the sake of which" that denotes Dasein is a closed unity that resembles the gathering of the *Logos* understood metaphysically. I hope this is enough to distance the two uses of "hermeneutic," although I don't expect to have fully conveyed the full sense of the problem this difference raises.

[48]In chapter 3, when Derrida and his relation to Heidegger will become more focal, I will take a closer look at the nature of hints and gestures and their relationship to signs. For the moment, consider the following passage which will come back later in more detail: "**J**: You are thinking of hints as

messenger who hears what is said in the call of Saying has become familiar to us and, as such, we may overlook some of the more obvious problems such matters raise. Most importantly, we need to ask what comes to pass in this message bearing, and we cannot stop at the frequently accepted answers such as world or gathering stillness or an opening up. We must move closer into the world so as to let it appear in its worlding. The only way it can do so, Heidegger says, is in its belonging together with the thing that bears out the world in being granted by the world. "By thinging, things carry out world. Our old language calls such carrying *bern, bären*—Old High German *beran*—to bear; hence the words *gebaren,* to carry, gestate, give birth, and *Gebärde,* bearing, gesture. Thinging, things are things. Thinging, they gesture-gestate-world" (*PLT,* 200).

The world opens up and clears a gathering place. But, as is evident whenever I try to make the point, such opening up of the world does not take place at some time only to be followed, later, by the arrival of things in that region or gathering. Rather, the worlding of the world, or opening up of the Open, takes place along with—belonging together with—the thinging of things, where this means nothing other than the coming to pass of things into their own as things. Not only does the Open clear in the Saying of the dif-ference or perdurance, but things are owned in this same Saying. The Saying is just as much a Saying of things as a Saying of world.

Things, therefore, are already beginning to suggest (gesture toward) some kind of relationship with hearing, and thus with the message-bearing carried out by the messenger. Things, like the messenger, are what they are only insofar as they carry out something. The world that a thing carries and the message that the messenger carries are the Same. This does not mean that things carry out the messenger who carries the message, or that the messenger carries out the things which carry world, reminiscent of Locke's description of the Indian myth of the world resting on the back of an elephant resting on the shell of a tortoise which stands on who knows what. Rather, carrying out comes to pass in various modes such that each mode belongs together as a mode of the carrying out of the

---

belonging together with what you have explained by the word 'gesture' or 'bearing.' /**I**: That is so./ **J**: Hints and gestures, according to what you indicated, differ from signs and chiffres, all of which have their habitat in metaphysics./**I**: Hints and gestures belong to an entirely different realm of reality, if you will allow this term which seems treacherous even to myself" (*OWL,* 26). I include these lines here so as to hint at the relation between gestures, hints and things which I am about to examine.

Same. All that is carried out in such modes is the Same. Where the carrying out is in oblivion and Being as present ground of all that is becomes the message of all hearing, the messenger which carries that message is "Man" and the things that carry that message are "objects" that "Man" represents. Heidegger talks about this in several places, most notably in "The Question Concerning Technology." In the context of technology, Heidegger explains a particular mode of Saying in which things are understood in a certain way, material resources, which he calls standing reserve (*Bestand*). All that is, is standing reserve, raw materials waiting to be exploited and employed in the machinery of mass production and consumption. Heidegger refers to two dangers in this mode of Saying (called Enframing or *Gestell)*: on the one hand, "Man" understands everything as a natural resource requiring the ordering process of production and, as a result, comes to see himself as the orderer of such production and then, finally, as just like the things he orders. The things condition man to be as they are, to become a material resource—a labor force, human resources, etc. On the other hand, man, as threatened by *Gestell* exalts himself as "the lord of the Earth." This causes man to understand everything that is in the world as his own product. "It seems as though man everywhere and always encounters only himself" (*QCT*, 27). Man conditions things to conform to his own vision of himself. He is the producer and all he sees everywhere is product (i.e., commodities).

This mutual conditioning of things and the messenger stems from each having a place within the Open that is given over to them in a certain mode of Saying. The messenger and things both carry out world, the first through proper hearing as has been shown. The way in which things carry out world (I might just as well say the way in which world grants things, since I have said that they belong together and so looking at one already evokes the other) is the next step along the way. This proves crucial to the question concerning the more precise nature of message bearing. We need to discover how thing carries out world and world grants thing in order to understand message bearing, because the message borne out in various modes corresponds to the thinging of things in those modes. When proper hearing attunes itself to the message of Saying, it is attuned equally to the thinging of things that carry out world in their being granted in the message: "As the calling that names things calls here and there, so the saying that names the world calls into itself, calling here and there. It entrusts world to the things and simultaneously keeps the things in the splendor of world. The world grants to things their presence. Things bear world. World grants things" (*PLT*, 201-2).

We saw in the previous section that naming was a gathering

response to the *logos* as Saying. The calling that names things here and there is the naming that responds in proper hearing. The calling that names the world is the Saying itself, calling into itself, evoking world out of it, it is the opening up of a cleared gathering. These two forms of calling, of course, belong together as the naming of things and the naming of world, just as the thing and the world belong together. In fact, these two sets are only one set. The calling of world and thing is the world and thing. Talk of naming things may sound familiar since it is this naming that derives from the *logos* and yields the ordinary understanding of it. Talk about the naming of the world that Saying does, however, is unfamiliar. How can Saying name at all when naming is the task of the messenger? Such naming is carried out by the messenger but only insofar as the messenger responds to, properly hears, Saying. Heidegger says that Saying names the world and by this he means that Saying lays out the world in a gathering. The naming of the things, however, is a copse within the gathering: naming within the open, responding to it. And yet even this naming strives to be a proper hearing of the naming of Saying as Saying makes its way to language. When things are named, they are not named arbitrarily with invented sounds or pictograms, rather they are named through Saying's coming into language heard by the messenger and evoking a response.[49]

"In the naming, the things named are called into their thinging. Thinging, they unfold world, in which things abide and so are the abiding ones. By thinging, things carry out world" (*PLT*, 199-200). And so the carrying out of world is also a carrying out of the message of Saying. Things and messengers are working together in the carrying out of the messages they bear. Things need the messenger to bear out world because only through the naming that calls the things into their own can the thing thing. And naming, although it stems from Saying, requires that Saying has come to language and that language has spoken. For Language to speak, it needs "us." Therefore, the thing needs this same "us" to thing and carry out world.[50] Heidegger says in many places that "we" speak

---

[49]This appears to contradict a central principle of structuralist linguistics which claims that the sign is arbitrarily fixed to its signified (although once fixed it carries a certain necessity in its relation with other signifiers). It does not however involve a contradiction when one recalls that a name is not a sign. As a brief example in prelude to a more complete discussion later: the use of a hammer for hammering is not arbitrary, but in accordance with its name. The name is not the sound or mark used to represent or signify the thing, it is the thing's relation to other things and hence not necessarily voiced or given over to a vocabulary at all.

[50]Who "we" are is an incredibly important and difficult question to

because we hear and we hear because we belong to what calls out to us.[51] When speaking speaks in response to proper hearing, it names things. And all proper hearing commands such a response, to hear and not respond is not hearing at all: the messenger must be dead.

Much earlier, in "Hölderlin and the Essence of Poetry," Heidegger describes "man" as a conversation and language as essentially conversation. (*EB*, 277) The being of "man," even at this early stage is language as conversation. The conversation later gets thought as dialogue and this dialogue is the back and forth between Saying and hearing. This conversation is both man (now called the messenger) and language. In this conversation, worlds open up and things are given names. We have already seen that Saying is a dialogue, but it is new that the messenger is the dialogue as well. Consider however, that the claim that "we" speak because "we" hear and "we" hear because "we" belong to what calls upon "us" to speak could just as easily be applied to Saying itself. Saying speaks in language and it speaks because it hears as messengers and it hears because it belongs to what calls out to it, itself as reflexive circling.

This overkill of emphasis is meant to make a difficult point as clear as possible. The common understanding of Heidegger's claim that things are brought into their own when naming brings them forth is usually one Heidegger would find ridiculous. For instance, when Rorty says that all there is is conversation and means it in the sense of a bunch of people

---

explore. Certainly we are messengers as proper hearers and speakers. Yet speakers are not, by Heidegger's own words, merely those who speak some human language like English or German, but those who perform the naming of things — which means to gather them within the opening of the clearing, and it does not seem to me that one needs vocal chords or the ability to speak in the ordinary sense to do this. Heidegger frequently refers to these listeners of language as mortals and that will have to be explored in what is about to come concerning the fourfold of which "mortals" form a part. I use the word "us" here because Heidegger does in "A Dialogue on Language" and because it is a fair bet that, at the very least, any one reading this essay will be included in the "us." Beyond that, the word — at the moment — has to stand in the most general of ways for, roughly, mortal hearers who bear the message of Saying.

[51]"If we are to think through the nature of language, language must first promise itself to us, or must already have done so. Language must, in its own way, avow to us itself — its nature. Language persists as this avowal. We hear it constantly, of course, but do not give it thought. If we did not hear it everywhere, we could not use one single word of language." And see the previous section for the countless citations implying hearing that derives from belonging.

talking and talking and talking, never (in Heidegger's sense) saying anything, he is making a point that separates human being infinitely from the being of things—as Heidegger understands them—even if Rorty thinks that he is drawing them closer together into a certain linguistic idealism. The naming of things by the messenger does not happen in some mental faculty called imagination as a product of fancy, it is in strict and necessary accord with the Saying of the Same which circles on the way of belonging together with proper hearing as the essence of the messenger.

If this naming does not linguistically construct the thing, then how does naming, and hence thinging, come to pass?

> Language, Saying of the world's fourfold, is no longer only such that we speaking human beings are related to it in the sense of a nexus existing between man and language. Language is, as world-moving Saying, the relation of all relations. It relates, maintains, proffers, and enriches the face to face encounter of the world's regions, holds and keeps them, in that it holds itself-Saying-in reserve.
>
> Reserving itself in this way, as Saying of the world's fourfold, language concerns us, us who as mortals belong within this fourfold world, us who can speak only as we respond to language. (*OWL*, 107)

Some of this has been gone over before in a different context. The gathering which is world gathers in fourfold fashion it would seem. And this fourfold is, at bottom, a fourfold relation. Insofar as Saying opens as this fourfold, it is the relating of this fourfold relation—as demonstrated previously regarding the world itself, not yet thought as fourfold. Yet there is a holding back in this relating, and that holding back is the withdrawing of the world that was already discussed. The thing comes forward out of the world's fourfold and, although it carries out the world in such coming into its own, the world itself hides from view. The fourfold continues to be borne within the thing, but as concealed. This too has already been shown in a different context when we spoke of the concealed in naming the unique One which was both ready and not ready to be named Zeus.

Saying opens up into a fourfold region borne out by things that are named by the messenger who bears the message of Saying in the calling that opens up. But here there is no talk of messengers, only of mortals where mortals belong within the fourfold as one of the four. Heidegger is here equating mortals pretty clearly with human beings and he says in the following paragraphs after this passage that man is mortal because he experiences death *as* death which is something animals do not do (*OWL*, 107). But before the stance this project has taken on human being is condemned as a misreading of Heidegger, we will have to make our way through the fourfold and the thing that things there to see how it occurs and whether this claim of Heidegger's is consistent with his other claims about proper hearing and the messenger. It is not an uncommon criticism to make against Heidegger that he takes too much for granted regarding the role of human beings in his later thought.[52]

> Stillness stills by the carrying out, the bearing and enduring, of world and things in their presence. The carrying out of world and thing in the manner of stilling is the appropriative taking place of the dif-ference. Language, the peal of stillness, is, inasmuch as the dif-ference takes place. Language goes on as the taking place or occurring of the dif-ference for world and thing. (*PLT*, 207)

And,

> The thing is not 'in' nearness, 'in' proximity, as if nearness were a container. Nearness is at work in bringing near, as the thinging of the thing. (*PLT*, 178)

The play of stillness and nearness both come to pass in the thinging of the thing, in the moment when the thing comes into its own as thing bearing world, where world is the fourfold region. Stilling is the agitated

---

[52]Derrida is the most prominent example when, in his "The Ends of Man," he explicitly makes this criticism. But a reader as conservative as William Richardson also makes the criticism in a sort of unknowing, implicit way when all his discussions concerning the being of man in the later Heidegger take place with reference to the analysis of *Being and Time* concerning Dasein. This is probably the most common form of the difficulty. Many commentators of varying stature make this same assumption without grasping the full extent to which an existential analysis of what was called Dasein would have to be reworked after the turn away from Dasein. Kockelmans notices the reformulation transforming "Dasein" into "mortals" but doesn't go into any depth to discover the difficulties leftover from this shift.

essence of all rest where rest is the staying of what has been owned in the Open clearing of the world. And it is the pealing of stillness that occurs in language. Likewise, nearness characterizes all that we have seen so far. It is the distances spanning in the intimate between where what belongs together strives: revealing/concealing, world/thing, dif-ference, *Er-eignis* itself as nearness. All these reminders show that in dealing with the fourfold regions of the world borne out by the thing, we are dealing with the Saying and circling of the Same, the play of stillness, nearness drawing near—all of which belong together, all of which move within the economy of the Same: "The four are united primally in being toward one another, a fourfold. The things let the fourfold of the four stay with them. This gathering, assembling, letting stay is the thinging of things. The unitary fourfold of sky and earth, mortals and divinities, which is stayed in the thinging of things, we call—the world" (*PLT*, 199).

The world that is borne out in/as/through things is the fourfold regions of sky and earth, mortals and divinities. This world grants things in that, as the world, it is the play of stillness out of which the things come into their own as things. But this "out of" cannot be thought literally. The things do not come out of the world, separating themselves from it in the grant. Rather, they bring the world that grants them with them for the first time; the things come from the world and then rest within it, carrying it with them all the while. This mutual occurring, this intimacy of world and thing penetrating each other, is the dynamic unfolding of dif-ference and Appropriation. A closer look at this is accomplished by looking at the texts Heidegger devoted primarily to the fourfold regions of the world and their play of stillness in nearness.

In "Building Dwelling Thinking," Heidegger gives a compact description of each of the four regions of the world. Each description is followed by a sentence that tells us that when we are thinking of the one region just described we are already thinking of the other three along with it which is the way I described the belonging together of what occurs in the Same. To think of one element in the nexus of the Same is to think of all the elements. Likewise with the fourfold. Regarding the descriptions themselves, they are not exactly the best place to start, since the descriptions of earth and sky are far from clear and the descriptions of mortals and divinities are problematic, even if intelligible from our current position. In the essay "The Thing" Heidegger works through the fourfold using a specific example; this should prove a better starting point.

This essay begins with the explicit purpose of moving into the nearness, where nearness is what the cutting of distance accomplished in the modern world of technology has failed to give us. Heidegger claims that things are what is most near to us and are the only way in which nearness can be encountered, since nearness does not let itself be directly grasped. He turns to a specific thing lying nearby. He calls on a jug to be the mediator between ourselves and the nearness into which we want to find our way. And this jug, he says, is a thing in that it is a vessel for holding something. It is not a thing because it has been produced or crafted into a specific shape. Rather, and this is somewhat surprising, the thing has been crafted and shaped the way that it has, because it is a vessel for holding something. This craftsmanship based on the being of the jug as vessel is not some Platonic producing in accordance with the idea where the idea is present in the maker's mind. The presence of the idea in the maker is a representation of what stands before him. In the full nature of standing forth, however, there predominates first a laying out where laying out means that what stands forth as an object must first have been laid out into the gathering. When we question concerning the vessel nature of the jug, we are not asking about the representation of an object but about the laying out of the vessel into the gathering, and so, the coming into presence of the jug.

It is not the shape of the jug that holds as a vessel, rather it is the void or emptiness of the jug that does so. The liquid held in the vessel, rests between the sides and bottom of the jug, between the sides is the emptiness of the vessel, the void of the jug. Only as shaped emptiness can a jug hold liquid and, without the shaped emptiness, the jug is merely clay. This void becomes visible to us, not when we represent the jug, but when we fill it. In going toward the jug in this fashion, however strange, Heidegger takes it that he is on his way to the thing *qua* thing which means its being as a vessel. And this is not to be arrived at through a representation, since such representing does not hold anything, only vessels can hold. "Man can represent, no matter how, only what has previously come to light of its own accord and has shown itself to him in the light it brought with it" (*PLT*, 171). The essence of the jug is nothing human, it is a gathering of Saying.[53]

The jug holds in the manner of taking and keeping. The jug receives or takes into it what has been poured into it and, in so taking it, it keeps

---

[53]I might remark in passing that this suggests that the mode of Saying proper to representation is derivative upon the mode of Saying proper to naming things, since a thing must first have been gathered in its laying in order for it to be brought to stand opposite. Only because things thing can objects be represented and, therefore, brought to stand opposite. One other way to understand this is that transcendence as such (the relation of the Same) precedes and enables all modes of intentionality.

it. The unity of this holding as taking and keeping occurs in the pouring out of what is held. The vessel has taken in and kept what it is holding so that it may pour it out in the giving of a libation. This does not happen in a sequence of steps in the life of the jug; rather, the being of the jug as jug is the taking and keeping that pours out a gift. In this pouring out that consummates the jugness of the jug, the earth and sky, mortals and immortals dwell. Heidegger relates the earth to the rocks and springs that give the liquid that has been poured. If it is water or wine, it has somehow been brought from the earth. And likewise, the sky would have played a role, in the raining down of the water and shining of the sun where the sun warms the earth and makes it a place for water to dwell. Similarly, the jug is poured by mortals for the quenching of their thirst or in a ceremony that is dedicated to the gods, where the jug gives a gift that is set aside for the immortal divinities.

Each of these four dwell together in a unity within the holding vessel of the jug. The being of the jug as jug, the nature or dynamic unfolding of the jug, is as the fourfold in this way. The jug bears out the fourfold by staying the four regions in their belonging together. The appropriation or coming into its own of the jug is the bringing together of the fourfold that belong together. "At one in thus being entrusted to one another, they are unconcealed" (*PLT*, 173). This un-concealment of the fourfold in their belonging together is the thinging of the thing. The thing gathers the fourfold together so that they can stay together for a while in this thing (while away their time in the Open as the thing/the opening up of the thing). This gathering is the coming into its own of the thing, but it is also the appropriation of the fourfold in/as/through the thing.

In "Building Dwelling Thinking," Heidegger considers the example of a bridge. A much larger thing, but a thing no doubt, and so it must equally stay the fourfold. The bridge swings out across a stream or river and joins two banks together. It gathers the earth in itself by spanning the stream and joining the sides. The swinging across of the bridge sways through the air of the sky up over the stream. The bridge is for the use of mortals who dwell on either side of the stream. And somehow, the bridge brings the mortals before the hale of the divinities where it "gathers, as a passage that crosses, before the divinities—whether we explicitly think of, and visibly give thanks for, their presence, as in the figure of the saint of the bridge, or whether that divine presence is obstructed or even pushed wholly aside" (*PLT*, 153). I quote this in full because I don't know what it means. No doubt, this absence of the divinities from my thinking of bridges is what constitutes me as a modern man who can only be saved by the reappearance of the god. (*Der Spiegel* interview)

But this might not be the only explanation for why the divine being

of the bridge escapes me. It could also be that the effort at making explicit
the gathering of the fourfold in each thing is an immensely difficult
process and requires a certain amount of elasticity in the awareness one
has of the various regions. That is, I wonder if maybe the examples
Heidegger gives of the fourfold regions aren't just that, examples that still
do not reach into its essence. Recall that things bear out world and do so
in the fourfold. Each thing, therefore, carries with it, in its dynamic
unfolding, a similar gathering of elements to those we have seen in the
jug and the bridge.

   Consider the following from "Poetically Man Dwells":

> What is the measure for human measuring? God? No. The sky?
> No. The manifestness of the sky? No. The measure consists in the
> way in which the god who remains unknown, is revealed *as* such
> by the sky. God's appearance through the sky consists in a
> disclosing that lets us see what conceals itself, but lets us see it
> not by seeking to wrest what is concealed out of it concealedness,
> but only by guarding the concealed in its self-concealment. Thus
> the unknown god appears as the unknown by way of the sky's
> manifestness. This appearance is the measure against which man
> measure's himself. (*PLT*, 223)

The god is hard to see in the bridge thing because it is the nature of the
god to be concealed, even its revelation only comes in the form of
concealment. What is concealed in this way has withdrawn, where
withdrawal is what comes to pass in the event of Appropriation where
things come into their own. In the lighting of the sky, the god appears as
concealed. This means, that when the light of the Open shines as clearing
upon the earth the god withdraws in favor of what has manifested itself.
This is the same withdrawing that draws all that resides in the Open and
it is an essential element of the clearing that gathers. It is this withdrawing
god that offers the measure which must be taken. Measure-taking is
poetry. Poets are those who take measure of the god who withdraws in
the sky above the earth upon which the poet dwells. The way in which
such measuring is taken is a special kind of taking, it "does not consist in
a clutching or any other kind of grasping, but rather in a letting come of
what has been dealt out" (*PLT*, 224). The poetic measure-taker who
dwells on the earth is the proper hearing messenger.

   All talk of mortals has been transformed in Heidegger's essay into
talk of poets, where poets are human beings. It therefore seems right to
infer that the poet taking measure of the withdrawing god in the light of

the sky above the earth is the mortal who knows death as death in the previous discussions of the fourfold. In this discussion, over and against the discussions of the jug and the bridge, naming returns as the key component of the thinging of the thing in the fourfold. The poet is the one who calls things forth with names. Things that never were before, now come to be through the naming of the poet. Insofar as the poet is the caller of names, she is the one who takes measure. Hence, the naming that calls forth a thing into the gathering that it bears with it, is a naming that comes from within the fourfold through the intermediary of the mortal poets who properly hear the withdrawing gods and their measure.

A problem arises. Heidegger's only examples of things are artifacts, things that occur through human effort. When we make the shift to mortal poets, however, the things that could come forth bearing world might well be "the flowers of the hedgerow" or the "springhead in the dale" (*BT*, 100). Earth and sky, mortals and immortals may be said to belong together in the thinging of these things as well. When we turn to understand the naming that calls these things forth as the measure-taking that takes place on the earth beneath the sky, we move away from the strange examples of the fourfold that seem to ignore their own poetic nature, their nature as naming that gathers things into the carrying out of world. The naming that gathers in the thinging of the thing is essential to the thing, regardless of what kind of thing that is, but it is not the only element in its dynamic unfolding. Where naming is the response to proper hearing by the poet, it is the role of mortals in the fourfold bearing out of world by thing. The withdrawing god who gives the measure to which the naming is a response are also essential: likewise the light of the sky and the ground of the earth. Remember that the world that opens up does so as a clearing where that clearing is a place in the woods where the light can push to the earth no longer covered with trees. In that forest clearing, the poet dwells along with the retreating god from whom measure is taken. And all these fourfold dwell in the Open as the Open, their relation is the clearing of the clearing where things thing and naming names this relation.

What gathers in the region of the fourfold as a thing is not only a human artifact, therefore, but all kinds of things. Whatever the poet can call forth is gathered there in the gathering of the open clearing or fourfold region. And such things, because they are gathered as names that measure the withdrawing gods and rest on the earth under the sky, bear out world. Named things carry the world within themselves and keep that world as their own. In fact, to speak as I have, implying that the thing is an effect of all this fourfold drawing near, is to misspeak. The fourfold elements only come together insofar as they let things be, as they grant them into the Open and are carried out into the Open by them. The carrying out is the opening up of the Open where the fourfold and the things first come to rest for a while in their circling belonging together.

The things named by the mortal messengers, insofar as they bear out a world that is fourfold with one such fold being those mortals themselves, are not passively called into their own gathering manner as the call and hearer decide. These things be-thing (determine or condition). The poetic mortal hearers name the things as the things must be named, the things come forth bearing the world that grants them but they are not completely malleable to the world's creation, they condition that world and make it be as it is by abiding in it. In this sense, the mortal messengers who do the naming are not creators, but guardians. It is their task, in naming the things that come into the Open, to stand guard over them and assure their residence within the world as the things they are: "If we think of the thing as thing, then we spare and protect the thing's presence in the region from which it presences. Thinging is the nearing of world. Nearing is the nature of nearness. As we preserve the thing qua thing we inhabit nearness. The nearing of nearness is the true and sole dimension of the mirror-play of the world" (*PLT*, 181). The mirror play of the world is the relation, the belonging together in stillness, of the four regions within the world. The coming forward of things is the, albeit indirect, approach of nearness. When mortal messengers hear properly, when they respond to the commanded call of the Saying of the Same, they let things come to be as the things that they are and so act in a doubling response to Saying. This is called a step back.[54] It is a step back, but it is a step along the way.

Because the world that is a fourfold region is gathering itself, it certainly cannot be said to be made up of regions understood as things. This means that the earth that is a component of the fourfold cannot be the earth that is a thing. Likewise with mortals, gods, and the sky (or heavens). We can't understand these regions of the world as literally elements, where elements are already understood as sub-groups of gatherings taking place within the larger gathering itself. When I claim that the withdrawing god is the measure and the mystery, I claim to be

---

[54]"The step back does, indeed, depart from the sphere of mere attitudes. The step back takes up its residence in a co-responding which, appealed to in the world's being by the world's being, answers within itself to that appeal" (*PLT*, 181-2). As both a step back and step along the way, therefore, this is not one further deduction of metaphysical categories, but an elision of the metaphysical, its disruption for the sake of resituating oneself in/as/through the site in which whatever there is comes to pass. The step back will become a central element later in the project. Cf. chapter 5 below.

rescuing the fourfold from any "regional" understanding of them, where this would mean a category of things. Without mystery, there are no things. Without the clearing there are no things (clearing understood as light(en)ing the ground). Without mortals there are no things. This does not mean that mortals, lighted grounds, and gods are three separate elements that all must be part of some recipe for the thinging of things. Rather, they all belong together in the circling of the Same, where the mirror-play (the play of stillness or of essential unfolding) among them enables things to come forward in such a way that they bear out the play that grants them.

In this sense, we see still more clearly how naming—where naming calls the thing into the open—is even less a naming that assigns a rigidly denoting sign. Naming does not mean signing at all, where signing is the attaching of a sign to an indicated thing, or even the attaching of a signifying sound or mark to a signified concept or idea. Naming is calling the thing forth, and it also means "being properly called forth by the thing." Naming works in response to the movement of the rest of the fourfold, it works along with un-concealment, dif-ference, *Er-eignis*, nearness, stillness, Saying, etc. "To think 'Being' means: to respond to the appeal of its presencing. The response stems from the appeal and releases itself toward that appeal. The responding is a giving way before the appeal and in this way an entering into its speech" (*PLT*, 183-4).

Things cannot therefore appear separate from the response to the call that occurs in the message bearing. Rather, this response to the Saying of the Same is the thinging of things. Furthermore, however, the hail itself is not separated from the thinging thing. The withdrawing gods which offer the measure from which the poets perform their naming are equally essential to the coming to presence of things. Without this call, things could not have anything like an own to come into. The measure that is taken is a measure of the Appropriate Being of the things. The calling is the owning of the things as the properly hearing messenger lets them be. This advancing of the call into a response that lets things come occurs in the sky or heavens that move above the earth. The withdrawing gods appear as withdrawn in the light of the sky that opens up a clearing on the ground of the earth. Once again, these four regions are not separate, but they belong together in such a way that any one evokes the others. There would be no sky without earth, mortals without immortals, etc. The things that advance in the Open draw the four regions together in their being drawn into the Open. The design that draws these things is drawn into the things during the drawing. They appear, however, in the shape of the thing, while withdrawing in their own way.

It is because the thing gathers the fourfold world into unconcealedness that the name which gathers the thing can not completely *be* the name of the thing. A thing rigidly designated by a name would not be a thing at all. It would be an object. Things always escape such labels in favor of the names they are given. Every name, therefore, conceals a mystery, and this is the mystery of the Same. Within each of these names, the thing guarded and preserved by the name as the gathering that the thing/name is within the open clearing, there occurs or takes place (*ereignet*) a circling that not only permeates the name, but the thing as well. Heidegger remarks on the fitness of the Latin word *res* for the thing. *Res,* like the German *Ding,* refers to "a contested matter." "To be sure, the Old High German word *thing* means a gathering, and specifically a gathering to deliberate on a matter under discussion, a contested matter" (*PLT*, 174). And then "the Roman word *res* designates that which concerns somebody, an affair, a contested matter, a case at law" (*PLT*, 175). The idea of contestedness in the thing means that there is something altogether unsure about it. It isn't like the notion of object where certainty is the ideal of any representation of it. Rather, certainty is not possible in the case of the thing. Things are slippery, they are being deliberated, people are concerned about them, causes are developing. There might even be demonstrations in favor of the one or more positions in the contest. The thing, because it is contested, is in need of demonstrations and it is during such demonstrations (*while* they are taking place) that the thinging of the thing — as contested — will take place. Essays, like this one or that one, are things; or better yet, things essay.

The essay "The Thing" was undertaken in an effort to arrive at the nearness which eluded all technological development that has sought to close the distances in the modern world. The nearness of the play of stillness which takes place in the ringing of the stillness that is the Saying circling of the Same, approaches as the thinging of the thing where that thing is elusive and mysterious, not at all the object of certainty that the modern technicians are investigating. The point of such a project is not to pin everything down into "the rigid groove of a univocal statement," but to let "the vibration of the poetic saying" vibrate in the bringing forth of things into the Open where they belong, and where all that belongs together there with it can be borne in a preservation that will let it remain for a while.

> When we say mortals, we are thinking of the other three along
> with them by way of the simple oneness of the four.
>
> Earth and sky, divinities and mortals—being at one with one
> another of their own accord—belong together by way of the
> simpleness of the united fourfold. Each of the four mirrors in its
> own way the presence of the others. Each therewith reflects itself
> in its own way into its own, within the simpleness of the four.
> This mirroring does not portray likeness. The mirroring,
> lightening each of the four, appropriates their own presencing into
> simple belonging to one another. Mirroring in this appropriating-
> lightening way, each of the four plays to each of the others. The
> appropriative mirroring sets each of the four free into its own, but
> it binds these free ones into the simplicity of their essential being
> toward one another.
>
> The mirroring that binds into freedom is the play that betroths
> each of the four to each through the enfolding clasp of their
> mutual appropriation. None of the four insists on its own separate
> particularity. Rather, each is expropriated, within their mutual
> appropriation, into its own being. This expropriative
> appropriating is the mirror-play of the fourfold. Out of the
> fourfold, the simple onefold of the four is ventured.
>
> This appropriating mirror-play of the simple onefold of the
> earth and sky, divinities and mortals, we call the world. The world
> presences by worlding. (*PLT*, 179)

The fourfold: the circling of the Same; the circling of the Same: the fourfold.

This is an all too brief discussion of these matters which require more time and the introduction of additional explanatory elements. This must be deferred. It is important to have the germs of these ideas in mind as we step into the next stage along the way, but the bloom of these elements can come only in the last two chapters where I will develop the notion of poetic dwelling of mortals within the Open clearing of the fourfold gathering.[55] The last part of this chapter tried to serve as a demonstration of the nearness of the lived experience of mortal hearing messengers to the Saying of the Same laying a gathering sheltering things.

So, there is a gathering where all that is gathered lies within the

---

[55]At such a point I will be able to deal in detail with the differences in a dwelling that measures and one that does not, where such measuring will be explained as an "openness to the mystery" which is opposed to a dwelling that doesn't even know that there is a mystery to be open to (that is, a dwelling that is oblivious in the previously mentioned sense of a concealing of the concealment). It should be noted, however, that the way this may be said will be drastically transformed in the steps between here and there.

gathering, where that gathering comes to pass as the un-concealing, differentiating, taking place of things that are named in response to Saying. The gathering is gathered in various modes, where the mode of each gathering has a corresponding modification of each of the elements in the economy of the Same. The modes of the gathering are the epochs of history and various modes of existence that share space on the earth at the same time in history: they are cultural as well as historical in so far as the timing of time and the spacing of space are elements in the economy of the Same so modified. Heidegger refers to these as modes of Saying where this has an all-inclusive effect suggesting that each mode of Saying has correspondent modes of gathering, un-concealment, *Er-eignis,* world, time, space, hearing, etc.

The opened clearing is a jointed world *(fugen)* where joints are the articulations of Saying in all its modes. Saying makes its way to human speech through the thinging of the thing, small gatherings within the clearing. Because language speaks within the clearing and because mortals speak, their relationship to the modes of Saying is through their language. "When mortals are made appropriate for Saying, human nature is released into that needfulness out of which man is used for bringing soundless Saying to the sound of language" (*OWL*, 129). Within the clearing, human language is the most immediate connection to the clearing. The names human beings utter daily instantiate the modes of Saying within which they dwell. This means, not only that humans have certain stylistic preferences that bring out their personalities in some psychological fashion, but that their way of speaking is their way of living within the Open and thus the way that the economy of the Same circles in/as/through them. This means that uttered names evoke (belong together with) the sorts of "entities" populating the human world. If humans speak in propositions, they live among objects that stand out. If they speak in poetry, they live among things that are contested matters withdrawing and revealing their abysmal movement. Poetical dwelling implies poetic speaking.[56]

---

[56]It doesn't necessarily follow from this that all speaking in poetic dwelling will be in some form of verse. Heidegger admits in several places that some forms of prose are more poetic than many poems. Likewise, since conversation and dialogue have already been privileged, it is safe to say that some forms of conversation will be poetic. A more complete discussion of this feature of language will be put off until the chapter on poetic dwelling. A major part of that portion of the essay must involve the way in which living with others can occur as poetic Saying.

I hope this discussion was sufficient in introducing the important issues for what follows and in covering the issues of primary concern. This includes the dynamic unfolding of the general economy that characterizes Heidegger's thinking of Saying and the economy of the Same. If the reader has been able to follow the way in which this nexus is developed within Heidegger's works, then the first two chapters of this essay will have succeeded in their goal. The next chapter is an interlude from what follows and precedes it; and it is made necessary by Heidegger's own proclaimed project. Heidegger claims that the economy we have just uncovered attempts to escape the realm or mode of Saying that is called metaphysics. He says in numerous places, from *Identity and Difference* to *On Time and Being*, that it is by no means obvious or certain that any such escape from metaphysics has been accomplished or is possible; although Heidegger seems pretty much convinced that it is desirable, since metaphysics has reached its final stage in the nihilism of technology which threatens "the world" and all that gathers there. It is at this point of entry, a point of entry that Heidegger has woven into his text (his corpus), that Jacques Derrida supplements the demonstration. This is also the place in which the systematic rendering of the Heideggerian project shall come to pass in an abysmal swarming rendering the systematic impotent. But I will leave it to the reader to decide whether this is the essential dynamic of the display of the Circling of the Same or, instead, merely the deconstruction of "Heidegger" performed by Derrida.[57] What follows will be an effort to introduce Derrida's thinking on these matters of metaphysics, its escape, and what comes after it; but this will be done in the context of Heidegger's concerns regarding the escape. I shall be attempting to explore the zone of thinking that is "über die linie."[58]

---

[57] In matters of scholarship, the difference between these two projects would be absolutely crucial. It may surprise the reader to learn, therefore, that I really don't care which interpretation is given to my project and I have no argument to make in favor of one or the other. I've always imagined that Heidegger scholars would respond to this work by saying "that's not Heidegger" while Derrida scholars might respond by saying "that's not Derrida." In the end, the project of a deconstructive ethics need not concern itself with such issues, however interesting they may be for extraneous reasons.

[58] This original title of Heidegger's 1955-6 open letter to Ernst Jünger, published as "The Question of Being," could be translated as: concerning the line, on the line, across the line, or above the line. Heidegger claims that Jünger's sense in the book he wrote with this same title is "across the line." In his own essay, however, Heidegger wishes to change the emphasis to

"concerning the line." This change in emphasis is important considering the theme of the essay is nihilism. An essay that goes over the line would be seeking to transcend or go beyond nihilism. When Heidegger makes his concern only one about nihilism, he is proclaiming his own desire and need to stay within the confines of nihilism. This may suggest, upon first reading, that Heidegger does not wish to transcend nihilism at all where nihilism is associated with metaphysics and technology. Such a discussion will be taken up in the third chapter where the emphasis *I* wish to give to the title will have to be demonstrated along the way.

Chapter 3
Turning *and* Circling

Marking the middle of the way, it is time to consider the turn— to turn our attention toward it. [1] Turn? Which turn is it that I am proposing to consider? The turn from Dasein to Being, from Heidegger I to Heidegger II, from Heidegger to Derrida (as promised for this chapter), from exposition to criticism, from metaphysics to its other? From what do we turn away and to what shall we turn? Shall we turn away only to return to the same old thing, make the "from" and the "to" a matter for the Same (or do we risk insulting our host by returning its gift?)? If we were to proceed with these questions, what unforeseen turn would this project be forced to endure? Would this path of investigation lead us to the turn or merely set us off on a perpetual turning, a sort of eternal re-turning? Is it my turn to venture into this labyrinth of Heidegger scholarship? By what sorry turn of fate has this way led to such a morass of positions and uncertainties? How could everything possibly turn out?

---

[1] The italics of the "and" suggest some comments by Gilles Deleuze which anticipate what follows. Deleuze writes: "This is it, the double capture, the wasp AND the orchid: not even something which would be in the one, or something which would be in the other, even if it had to be exchanged, be mingled, but something which is between the two, outside the two, and which flows in another direction." AND "In the TV conversations *6 times 2* what were Godard and Mieville doing if not making the richest use of their solitude, using it as a means of encounter, making a line or bloc shoot between two people, producing all the phenomena of a double capture, showing what the conjunction AND is, neither a union, nor a juxtaposition, but the birth of a stammering, the outline of a broken line which always sets off at right angles, a sort of active and creative line of flight? AND... AND... AND..." (from *Dialogues* by G. Deleuze and C. Parnet. New York: Columbia University Press, 1987. pp. 7 and 9-10) This understanding of the "and" will come to suggest the logic of the supplement displacing the logic of identity which would name this chapter: "Turning *as* Circling" (or "Turning is Circling": notice that the French for "is" [est] and for "and" [et] are pronounced the same).

155

To avoid this morass (entanglement in the turn), I will turn to the from-to structure of the turn. From-to movement leaves behind and pushes beyond. Even when a turn is a return it may move in this way. It would be impossible to return if one had not already left behind that to which one returns. This involves going beyond as well since what returns is not a new arrival, it is a renewed approach, a move beyond what is left behind only to return with new eyes, a renewed position. It is apparent that all overcoming works this way, moving from-to. And yet the *meta* of *meta ta physica,* of metaphysics, asserts the beyond. The ground of all that presences is beyond what is present. Substance can appear only in the formed content of an entity, substance itself never appears, it is beyond appearances. For Aristotle to speak of substance, he must move *from* the world of appearance *to* the ground beyond.

Heidegger is critical of the metaphysician's project. A possible examination of these suggestions (the inquiry into why metaphysics is problematic and why it is so important for contemporary theorizing to, by any means necessary, avoid it), might be just the catalyst for setting off the turn from Heidegger to Derrida. But how can I examine this matter in this way without begging the question? The from-to structure is a metaphysical one, the metaphysical relation extraordinaire (the one that furnishes the discipline with a name), and the establishing of a tradition (Heidegger-Derrida) on its basis is antithetical to both thinkers' criticisms of metaphysics and its traditions. Is the critique of metaphysics a matter for metaphysics? Is it justified to let metaphysics, the defendant in this case, stand as prosecutor as well? After working so hard to avoid begging this question in the first two chapters relative to the move between the principle of identity and the circling of the Same, should the logic of metaphysics ultimately overwhelm the project?

In a nutshell: the critique of metaphysics is intimately connected to a critique of the metaphysical tradition but not because of some quirk in the critique, instead this stems from the dynamic of all metaphysics: metaphysics is its history and its traditions.[2] Furthermore, Heidegger raised the question of this critique in the Introduction to *Being and Time,* a critique he called the "destruction of the tradition." Jacques Derrida takes up this position which he *both* attributes to Heidegger and claims has escaped him. That is, the destruction of the tradition is not a project

----

[2]And not only "its" history and "its" traditions, but history and tradition as such. It will eventually become evident that "metaphysics," according to Heidegger, is not an intellectual discipline among others but the movement essential to Being.

directed under the authority of Martin Heidegger, but a dynamic particular to language itself. What can this possibly mean?

To some extent, this is the difficulty of "begging the question" that I have suggested. Derrida's attempt to take up a position that Heidegger occupied without being a disciple of Heidegger, is the project of what is called tradition. But how can we understand tradition between two, three, or many thinkers who claim to be destroying or deconstructing tradition? This question repeats the claim that a simple move *from* Heidegger *to* Derrida will only resurrect the tradition being destroyed, metaphysics. Such reasoning is surely vicious and circular.

But circling is not unfamiliar to this project and does not instill terror in a deconstructor as it might a logician or epistemologist. A possible problem with the central figure of chapter 2—or any circling at all—is its closure, its being closed off as a completed whole or totality. And of course all newness and weirdness is effectively barred from such a totality. Yet, that circling there is essentially opening and it is in/as/through this opening that there is (*es gibt*) any world at all. And not just any world, but many worlds, cultures, historical epochs, etc. A closer look at this characteristic of circling will assist us in gaining a better insight into the problems that are raised by the attempt to deconstruct tradition, history, and metaphysics.

Earlier, I arrived at a completely contradictory and almost sense-less position regarding the essence of language. In that context we claimed that "the reflexive nature of language, that all we can say is that language speaks (appropriately), leaves no room for an Other to the essence of language." This led to the contradictory claims: "language is all there is" and "language is not all there is." The strength of this contradiction is increased by the claim that there is no room for an Other to the essence of Language. The movement of language appears to have become contradictory and it seems that there are only (*es gibt*) contradictions. This is just the sort of irrationalism with which people have been charging Heidegger all along. But worse than irrationalism, it demonstrates Heidegger's failure to recognize the Other—just the sort of position that one would expect from a metaphysician seeking to totalize the whole of Being and, more powerfully, a Nazi trying to spread the Aryan cultures of the *Heimat* to the whole of the world through the heroic endeavor of a leader.[3]

---

[3]Max Horkheimer is a frequent proponent of this reading of Heidegger, but in many places the references are subtle and omit the use of Heidegger's proper name. Jürgen Habermas is another notable example although his occasionally polemical attacks on these grounds cannot fail to illicit smirks

Irrationalism and Totalitarianism, however, miss the point in this case. A further clarification of "Saying" may be of service here. Consider a view of language that describes it as symbolic, conceptual, and uttered. Then, add to that view the additional view above that language is all that there is. A language user, one who speaks and writes a certain language, is permeated through and through with the language that she uses. She has grown up using it, her self-understanding has developed on the basis of her language and the way she uses it — the way her class, race, or gender uses it within her culture. Appropriating her culture and her way of life has been nothing other than her development as a particular member of this culture which involves an appropriation of the symbolic and conceptual orders of that culture. On the surface of it, this view may seem to include some form of realism. After all, there "really" are people and bodies and relationships upon which this appropriation is taking place. But this needn't be the case, one could easily claim that "bodies" and "relationships" are taken up as moments of the symbolic and conceptual orders, as components of the culture and historical epoch. Resistance to this view is strong. No one in their right mind would claim that the earth is only a member of a symbolic or conceptual order. It may be that, but it is also more than that. There is something about the earth, say, that endures beyond symbols and concepts, that overflows these schemes. The earth is real. This declaration of the reality of the earth that overflows symbols and concepts is one way of characterizing what Heidegger and Derrida are calling "presence."[4]

The real presence of the earth and whatever else is real is what is frequently considered the Other of language, the Other which grounds language, which reigns over it in the manner of guiding and ruling its meaning (i.e., its *arche*). Those who resist the universality of language

---

from a reader familiar with Heidegger's texts. I wonder how history will remember Habermas who endorsed the Gulf War on the grounds that Germany must stand by Israel, presumably because of past anti-Jewish atrocities committed by Germans. Such an endorsement based on tradition and without consideration for the validity of claims made by other positions (and the ideology involved in the aggression by the "United Nations") within the debate seems problematic from the point of view of a theory of communicative action.

[4]Werner Marx, in op cit., describes the traditional notion of presence (*parousia*) as substance (*ousia*) in terms of characteristics like eternalness, necessity, self-sameness, and intelligibility. The previously described position on language is roughly that of Hans-Georg Gadamer in *Truth and Method* (as is, I believe, the ambiguity of tacit naturalism).

tend to resist on this ground, the ground of permanence and reason—of presence. Insofar as the critique of metaphysics is a critique of the present Other of a re-presentative language, I will have to put off discussion of it until the matter of the non-question begging approach of the critique has been settled. We must take note of a distinction here, one that is ignored constantly in contemporary discussions of these matters (i.e., in Gadamer's view above and Rorty's indicated in chapter 2). The "Other of language" is not identical to the "Other of the essence of language." To claim that Saying has no Other is not to claim that language has no other. To some extent, this equivocation is at work in the contradiction from chapter 2. Language as Saying is all there is but language as a conceptual and symbolic order is not all there is. This only to *some extent* because "reality" as an Other to language—as concept and symbol—speaks only as a mode of Saying. "Reality" is intelligible to the (meta)physicist only because it is a mode of Saying, intelligibility as the presence of meaning is an effect of Saying. The Other of language is re-captured by Saying which assumes the appearance of a Totalitarianism guarding against escape, although for the moment it appears to have side-stepped part of the claim to Irrationalism.[5]

Saying, however, cannot be said to fall under the heading of some grand Totalitarianism. Saying circles over an abyss and this not because on the one hand there is Saying and over against it there is an abyss, a nothingness that stands as the Other of Saying. Rather, the circling of Saying is abysmal. All Saying gathers a withdrawal. Nothing circles along with Saying, Saying is equally a circling *of* nothing. Once again, the evasion of the charge of the totality seems to have driven us closer to the charge of irrationalism by accepting this seemingly contradictory relation within Saying. Totalitarianism and Irrationalism seem to be the Scylla and Charybdis of this Heideggerian project. Yet, Saying is not contradictory as this double circling of nothing and everything, it is

---

[5]I say part because, although the contradiction seems to have disappeared, the fact that Saying is neither conceptual nor symbolic continues to be irrational—though it is not necessarily the case that this form of irrationalism actually breaks the laws of reason despite its clearly positioning itself outside them. I might prefer to call it a-rational and before any criticisms are raised, an opponent might want to consider what sort of rational proof could be given for the validity of the laws of rationality. If no such proof could be rationally given (i.e., without begging the question of rationality's validity), it might be tempting to claim something like the a-rationality of the laws of reason as opposed to calling them irrational (perhaps the *a* priori of the axiomatic is essentially *a* rational?).

instead tension or striving itself. And this tension and striving recalls un-concealment and the world that opens there in its *a rational* hyphen (and also of the dif-ference and the *er-eignis)*. Consider the difference in this way: on the one hand, imagine someone who claims simultaneously the truth of *a* and not-*a* and, on the other hand, someone who is trying to decide between *a* and not-*a*. The first is clearly irrational, the second—the need to make such a choice, is at the foundation of all rationality. The tension of Saying is the tension of having to make a decision, not of contradiction. And this tension is doubled by the condition that the need to decide may be an unwarranted imposition. Either-or, either-or, either-or: perhaps the children of Copenhagen were being astute when they used this phrase to taunt Kierkegaard—the either-or taunts without offering solace. The either-or of a and not-a may be a prelude to a decision that invokes a question at the foundation of all metaphysics. As a question it ceases to function as an origin, however, since the origin must speak in the propositional language of an axiom.

Still, it is important to retain a sense of the dangers that prevail and I believe this is best accomplished by Irrationalism and Totalitarianism. Not only because they threaten this project, but because they threaten all of our lives and very frequently they operate together to do so: hell may be the impossibility of reason where Satan rules absolutely. The movement to dominate the entire world order is especially terrifying if it cannot be reasoned with, if it is so unrelenting in its project that it is beyond *new* or *other* considerations.

Saying says the Same, but this Same is also otherness, an Other, the nothing circles in the Same as the Other. The otherness of the Same is also the possibility of a tradition whose project it is to destroy the tradition. Perhaps tradition itself is this very destruction, where both indicate a face to face between one and the other in the manner of the Same. This means that when Derrida reads Heidegger (just as when Kant read Hume), he is faced with a decision. Derrida must decide how to read Heidegger, Heidegger presents Derrida with an enigma that he might be tempted to try and solve by making a decision. Believing in tradition is believing in a decision that has been made by every thinker relative to the works of past thinkers. When anyone questions concerning tradition, they are questioning concerning the nature of the decision and the nature of the enigma (one might even say that they are questioning concerning the question).[6]

---

[6]In so far as a question remains opened as a question, it is an enigma seeking solution in an answer. This must be considered relative to

It might be tempting to call the tension involved in having to make a decision a movement to and fro, a vacillation. The thinker facing the past texts of past thinkers vacillates on them. Back and forth, she is unable to make up her mind, to commit to a reading, to a clear position on them. She writes and writes in frustration, trying to make a decision on those matters she faces, on what exactly she is facing. This vacillation, this pacing before the matter of past thought, which is the activity of any great thinker, is both the moment of tradition and the moment of critique. And, more to the main point of this chapter, it is turning. Not turning from-to, but turning to and fro, back and forth: turning that continually turns, turning "itself" (*"ein aus sich rollendes Rad* "?). The inquiry has now come full circle in its relentless turning over the problem of the turn. A

Heidegger's project in *Being and Time* where the basic motive of reawakening the question concerning the meaning of Being is to pose the question as a question, to reawaken its questionableness. To that extent, the reawakening of the question is *both* the existential analytic of Dasein's temporality *and* the destruction of the tradition. These two projects of *Being and Time* can be thought as two components of one project, as belonging together, as the Same.

My position on this matter may offer something of a reassurance to those who think the fundamental move in deconstruction is to destroy the "canons" of history and traditional philosophy. It might seem that it is actually part and parcel of *metaphysics* to destroy (in the non-deconstructive sense that critics use) itself as tradition. In so far as the metaphysician seeks the truth, the prejudices of the past are irrelevant and it becomes necessary to set them aside for the sake of discovering the non-ideological truth. This move seems to be essential to traditional philosophy even if it doesn't become part of the doctrine until the Enlightenment (i.e., Aristotle's attack on Plato is lamented because of their relationship, but it is desirable in so far as Aristotle is a lover of wisdom — cf. Book I of the *Nichomachean Ethics*.). On the other hand, one might be tempted — and I frequently am — to read the deconstructive movement as an attempt to keep tradition and history alive. In deconstruction, the life and dynamic nature (perhaps, unfolding) of the traditional views are retrieved. What's more, as I shall show throughout the next few chapters, deconstruction is more interested in the being towards death of metaphysics rather than its actual death (to use the language of *Being and Time*). The latter of these two is something I would accuse any philosopher who was ultimately interested in getting it right, getting to the bottom of things, and thus making any future metaphysical inquiry unnecessary. Granted the deconstructive project changes the nature of the metaphysical project, but only so as to make it ongoing, always in the process of living its not-yet being over and done with. Cf. especially chapter 4 to discover just how radical a transformation of metaphysics this may be.

view of the turn has developed that is not essentially metaphysical and will not automatically implicate itself with certain traditions in the course of a critique aimed at those same traditions and all they imply. Maybe.[7]

The History of Metaphysics as Presence: the Tradition

After all that has been said thus far concerning Heidegger's project and the metaphysics opposed to it, the question remains as to just how we are to understand the relation of the two. Heidegger's project has been to display the nexus that withdraws in the traditional understanding of the claims made by that Same nexus of Saying that circles. The term "epoch" in fact means "to hold back" (*TB*, 9). Throughout this essay, I have used the term "epoch" to describe the historical modes of Saying as it is given over in the destiny of the Same that opens up in clearing. "Epoch," Heidegger tells us, derives from the Greek "*epoche*" meaning "to hold back." This makes it clear, as does the rest of the passage from *On Time and Being*, that "epoch" essentially refers to the history of Being as it has been presented by the Same in the Open. Because of this essential component of "epoch" as holding back, opposing metaphysics is not just another epoch of history. The opposition is the step back from the historically given Being into the withdrawing giving components of the Same. An epoch, therefore, is always historical and metaphysical. History always occurs in epochs and the essential (dynamic unfolding of Saying) is always withheld from epochs. Therefore, metaphysics can be viewed as this same holding back, as the receiving of the gift of the Same that denies the *giving* of the gift, that lets it withdraw in obscurity as the withheld component of thought. All of history, therefore, has been the history of metaphysics.[8]

---

[7]"Maybe" might be an English supplement for the German "*sei*" (present subjunctive of *sein* "to be") which doesn't otherwise exist in English. This, like the "and" in the title of this chapter, would be a supplement of Being and may recall the German *vielleicht* generally meaning "perhaps" or "maybe." But, as Krell notes in reflections upon his conversations with Heidegger, "*vielleicht*" also suggests "lightness" in the sense of "lightening" which also suggests "*Lichtung*": the clearing or lightening. Cf. Krell, op cit.

[8]It is necessary to point out in some way here that metaphysics, viewed in this way, is not some mistake resulting from the stupidity or the lack of rigor of two and a half (and more) millennia of thinkers. Instead, metaphysics—on this scheme—is viewed as a necessary component of the

Finally, as a reminder, recall that the history of metaphysics is the history of Being, since Being is what arrives in the sending giving of the Same.[9] The history of Being as metaphysics is possible only because it is, in essence, bound together with the Same which dispenses the message of philosophy (that is, metaphysics). The movement of the Same has been endlessly described as a tension of revealing/concealing. Metaphysics, in so far as it occurs in epochs that hold back the withdrawing giving dynamic of Being, is in oblivion to the withdrawing of the Same. Hence metaphysics is a correspondence to the Same that relates only to what is revealed in the Same as the presented Being of beings. The Being of beings that are present in the gift of the Same are grounded—within the discourse of metaphysics—in a unifying concept or substratum that guides and governs all that comes to presence. It is for this reason that Heidegger thinks of metaphysics as essentially the metaphysics of presence.

But this is already to oversimplify. Contrary to certain tendencies in contemporary "theory," the revelation of metaphysics as the history of presence and Being is not the final word on the matter, but is instead the opening of a problem. Being is given in the "*es gibt*" of the destiny of the Same, but it is not given as an answer to the Saying of the Same. This "answer," or perhaps it is better to call it the correspondence of the philosopher in his attunement to the Same, has been made in the form of Plato's *idea*, Aristotle's *energeia*, Kant's "position" or objectivity, Hegel's "absolute concept," and Nietzsche's "will to power" among others. Heidegger writes:

Saying of the Same. "However, oblivion of the distinction is by no means the consequence of a forgetfulness of thinking. Oblivion of Being belongs to the self-veiling essence of Being" (*EGT*, 50).

[9]This also raises, no doubt, the question of Marx's historical materialism and the critique of philosophy as ideology. It is certainly not Heidegger's point that history is driven by the ideas of an ordinary idealism, although it certainly is the case that philosophy has been such an idealism. Rather, the philosophers of each age (as I have said before in a slightly different context) have merely held the position of mouthpieces for the age, they are those who speak the word of Being, but that does not require that they are the only ones who hear it or the only ones whose lives are governed by it. The entire epoch is governed by that voice and the philosophers (and others too) are merely responding to what everyone is hearing. Later in this essay, I will take issue more directly with historical materialism and the extent to which Heidegger's remarks can be said to agree with as well as diverge from it.

Philosophia is the expressly accomplished correspondence which speaks in so far as it considers the appeal of the Being of being. The correspondence listens to the voice of the appeal. What appeals to us as the voice [*Stimme*] of Being evokes our correspondence. 'Correspondence' then means: being determined [*be-stimmt*], *être disposé* by that which comes from the Being of being. *Dis-posé* here means literally set-apart, cleared, and thereby placed in relationship with what is. Being as such determines speaking in such a way that language is attuned (*accorder*) to the Being of being. Correspondence is necessary and is always attuned [*gestimmtes*], and not just accidentally and occasionally. It is in an attunement [*Gestimmtheit*]. And only on the basis of the attunement (*disposition*) does the language of correspondence obtain its precision, its tuning [*Be-stimmtheit*].

As something tuned and attuned [*ge-stimmtes und be-stimmtes*], correspondence really exists in a tuning [*Stimmung*]. (*WP*, 75-7)

It is no accident that tuning carries with it a resonance of the "voice of Being." Being rings out of the stillness of the Same and is tuned in by the attunement of the philosophical thinkers of the history of Western metaphysics. The final sentence of the passage might likewise be translated according to this notion: "As something en-voiced and be-voiced, correspondence exists essentially in a voicing." It is the voice that unites the philosophical thinker and Being, the voice is their very belonging together. There is, on the one hand, the voice of Being and, on the other, the voice of the philosopher: these voices are in harmony, they speak in correspondence, as such.

This is not, of course, the traditional view of metaphysical thinking. When Aristotle argues against Plato's understanding of the *idea,* he does not do so on the basis of some shared subject matter that unites the thinking of the two as metaphysicians. The third man argument, for instance, aims at destroying the theory of forms as super-sensible mumbo-jumbo. Aristotle then turns to describe the Being of entities within the world in terms of substance or "*ousia.*" His claim might be that contrary to Plato's belief in a separate realm of forms, form is nothing other than an interwoven component along with matter and hence is irrevocably sensible. The realm of intelligibility, for Aristotle, is thus posited as a substratum that nonetheless only manifests itself in the sensible world of formed matter. No amount of philosophical abstraction will determine substance as a possible object for thought and hence the task of the philosopher, according to Aristotle, would be badly served in the sun-seeking mythos of Plato's cave dwellers.

Presumably no one knew Plato's thought better than Aristotle and yet Heidegger is claiming that this approach, this critical approach of Aristotle's, is fundamentally misguided. It covers over irretrievably the relationship that exists between the matter of which both thinkers are in pursuit.[10] Heidegger does not see Aristotle as a step forward or an improvement on Plato's thinking—neither would he reduce their relationship to a footnote. Rather Heidegger claims that each participates in a correspondent tuning to the Being of beings and that each of their discourses, each of their works, carries within it a coherence as well as a necessary relation to the matter at hand, the Saying of the Same as Being: "When philosophy attends to its essence it does not make forward strides at all. It remains where it is in order constantly to think the Same. Progression, that is, progression forward from this place is a mistake that follows thinking as the shadow which thinking itself casts" (*BW*, 215). That is, what Plato names with *idea* Aristotle names with *ousia,* they are the Same.

This is not to say that they are identical. Or even that the words *idea* and *ousia,* functioning as labels, append to the same referent. Instead, in both cases the philosopher is attuned to the voice of Being and this voice is speaking in a specific mode. Recall that one manner of describing this feature of the Same is in terms of the determined relations coming from an original relation that governs as their *arche.* That is, Plato and Aristotle already mark different epochs in the history of Being. On the one hand, Plato's world might be said to be a world of imitation whereby mimesis is the relationship that every existent entity has to the forms that determine its essential being. On the other hand, Aristotle's world might be that of definition where this is the determination of an entity in its Being as formed matter. The comparison here is between a world of imitations and a world of definitions with each totalized world determined in its Being by an all-powerful transcendental signified: *idea* and *ousia.* In both cases, the thinkers are concerned with beings in their Being, on the one hand, and the name of Being on the other.

Yet none of this comes to explicit notice in the works of either thinker: not in Aristotle with regard to Plato nor in Plato with regard to

---

[10]Notice that "irretrievably" refers to the Heideggerian notion of the retrieval or repetition that guides his reading of the historical thinkers of the West. The guide-word of the retrieve is to discover the unspoken in what is said by a thinker over and against what the thinker did say. What metaphysicians, and even pre-metaphysicians like Anaximander and Heraclitus, leave unsaid in their saying is precisely the Same that Heidegger is trying to suggest throughout his project.

his predecessors. This characterization of their relation was hidden from them in so far as their thinking was epochal, in so far as they failed to grasp the withdrawing sameness of their thought. Heidegger vacillates on what exactly to call this trait of metaphysical thinking: he refers to it as the oblivion of Being, errancy, forgetting the difference, etc. According to the aims of my project, I claim that this component of metaphysics is its failure to belong/hear in/as/through the Saying of the Same. But this can only be half right since these thinkers clearly belong together within the Same, but in such a way as to fail to make their belonging/hearing explicit.[11]

But this reminder fails to clarify; instead, it recalls difficulties strewn throughout the text. Let's try to lay it all out: the Saying of the Same circles as abysmal play. This sending or giving rings out as the voice of Being that undergoes a tuning in the epochs of metaphysics. Heidegger suggests in *Identity and Difference* an inversion of the metaphysical understanding of the principle of identity in virtue of a return to the belonging of *zusammengehören.* This same inversion requires a movement "beyond" Being which always asserts itself in the "as" structure characteristic of hearing. This implies that all hearing is in some sense metaphysical. I ask: how can all hearing be metaphysical while the inversion of the principle of identity requires a return to hearing as the proper site of thinking?

It seems that Heidegger has produced a morass (or I have in describing him). But we must recall that it marks a radical disruption of metaphysics to see in the attunements of Plato and Aristotle a correspondence with the voice of Being. To that extent, understanding the act of the philosopher as hearing, hearing the voice of Being, is already to catch sight of a structure that eludes metaphysical thinking. That is, the structure of Being's essence—where this suggests the dynamic unfolding

---

[11]Notice that the "not-yet" metaphysicians also fall into this category. Anaximander, Heraclitus and Parmenides all failed to think the proper dynamic of the Being that they somehow managed to experience more essentially than those who followed them in the history of metaphysics. I would like to venture here, in germinal form, the hypothesis that this is because the history of metaphysics is an absolutely necessary pre-requisite for the thinking of that proper essence which I have been calling the Saying of the Same: only a failure to experience the withdrawing of the giving of Being could eventually lead to the step back into that same withdrawal. Put in still another way, only when something has withdrawn substantially enough, can it be missed in a way that matters for thinking.

of Being in/as/through the giving of the Same. He writes:

> While we were just now thinking about Being, we found: what is
> peculiar to Being, that to which Being belongs and in which it
> remains retained, shows itself in the It gives and its giving as
> sending. What is peculiar to Being is not anything having the
> character of Being. When we explicitly think about Being, the
> matter itself leads us in a certain sense away from Being, and we
> think the destiny that gives Being as a gift. (*TB*, 10)

This is written in the context of Heidegger's effort to think the nature
of the It in It gives (*"es gibt"*). He first tries to think this It as Being and
discovers that this is not possible. Notice in these lines that Being is said
to "belong" to what is peculiar to Being. The essay in question, much
discussed in earlier chapters, goes on to discover that this "belonging of
Being" is the Saying of the Same as understood through the vehicle of *Er-*
eignis (which says the Same in virtue of the Same about the Same).

The voice of Being is heard in an attunement corresponding with
that same voice of Being. The philosopher that hears in this way belongs
to Being. The relation of the philosopher to Being is one of belonging,
they are the Same, they circulate in the Same, in the Saying of the Same.
Correspondence names this belonging together and reveals in concealed
fashion the *between* of the two terms "Being" and "metaphysical
thinking." There must be a double sense of hearing in this relation. On the
one hand, hearing is the hearing of the voice of Being, and on the other
hand, hearing is the belonging together that happens *between* the voice of
Being and its being heard. The relation precedes the relata, that much has
been covered completely. The relata as relata are related in a manner:
Being reaches out for thought and thought reaches out for Being. There is
something immanent to Being, to its voice, that involves the metaphysical
thinker and, likewise, there is something immanent to the metaphysician
which involves Being. They practice their movement in their opposition
to each other and to that extent they *are* the relata that they are. To the
contrary, we may discuss the relation out of which they come to touch
each other, they come to reach out to each other. This relation is a relation
of belonging and hence of hearing. This hearing is hearing "as such,"
belonging "as such." It is the nearness itself of the relation and therefore
it is stillness. It is, literally, a hearing that is not a hearing at all in so far
as it is stillness. It is a hearing that calls into question the very formulation
of the "as such."

Saying the Same is the pealing of stillness. Only because stillness
peals can there be anything like a voice of Being. Being is essentially

voice in this regard and all tuning that is a correspondence to Being is a hearing of the voice, which may be understood either in the sense of an objective or subjective genitive (the voice that is heard or the hearing that is voiced). The hearing that is the movement of belonging is no voice at all, it is hearing that has nothing at all to do with the voice. It is the belonging hearing of the Same that makes all voicing of Being possible. It is the hearing that is poised to hear stillness, it is the deaf hearing of silence, the silence that can only be heard in deafness, in the nearness.

In this way, metaphysics shows itself as *the* vocal form of hearing in so far as it is *the* attunement with Being. Yet, I have demonstrated that metaphysics, in a sense, fails to hear because it fails to understand its true nature as metaphysics; that is, as a hearing that hears the Same as the voice of Being. In this sense, metaphysics is a hearing that does not know that it hears, that does not make explicit the relationship of hearing that guides it from its essence. In so far as this is the case, metaphysics mishears. The proper hearing of the project described here is a delimiting of this mishearing in such a way as to posit an other hearing that does not in fact hear at all but instead ventures so deeply into its own dynamic unfolding that it no longer hears when it comes to reside in the striving tension of the ringing of stillness that characterizes all components of the Saying of the Same.[12]

Heidegger, therefore, claims the voice of Being essentially belongs to the metaphysics of presence, likewise all tuning. He writes: "What characterizes metaphysical thinking which grounds the ground of beings is the fact that metaphysical thinking departs from what is present in its presence, and thus represents it in terms of its ground as something grounded" (*TB*, 56). The introduction of ground, essential to all metaphysical thinking, is a move in the direction of presence and the present. The ground is present as ground in all that is present in Being as such. For example, in order for an imitation of an idea to be an imitation of an idea, the original, that is the idea, must be present in the imitation. An imitation can only be such in relation to the original. Hence the very

---

[12]It is precisely at this point where Derrida's relation to Heidegger is best visible. Heidegger could be seen as understanding the structure described here as the radical move away from the tradition of western metaphysics as presence. Derrida, on the other hand, *sometimes* sees this move of Heidegger's as *perhaps* the strongest defense of metaphysics as presence to date. Cf. Derrida's *Positions* p. 55 and all of his "The Ends of Man." This will become my focus in the sequel. Personally, I think this move by Heidegger is undecidable.

determination of an entity as an imitation already carries with it the presence of the grounding original. But presence not only suggests the presence of the ground in the beings grounded (recall that Heidegger referred to this as "taking account of the ground" by the entities that are grounded), but also indicates something about the Being of those entities themselves: that is, it indicates something specific about the nature of the ground itself. The ground must always be firm. There are numerous epochs in the history of metaphysics, each different and yet they are united in this feature: they each display a firmness of ground (which is really only a slightly useful fleshing out of the notion of ground itself). To explain this fully, recall the discussion of the thing in chapter 2: there are things gesturing in/as/through names bearing out world and granted by it. Such things are not very solid. Furthermore, things are ready and not ready to be named. They are slippery and elusive, never fully present or revealed, and always resting in a moment of repose within the sheltering clearing opening world. The presence of a thing was always a manner of its being obscured. This is not the case with entities grounded within the discourse of metaphysics, here the entities are firmly grounded in a present Being that anchors each of them with an "as such."

It has become clear to me that the notion of ground which is characteristic of metaphysics must, in some way, be related to the feature of metaphysics which is revealed in discussing its relationship to Being. Heidegger is clear when stating that Being functions as a ground in metaphysical thinking and that the ground is (and the principle of the ground that states "nothing is without ground or reason") universal to all metaphysics. In the phenomenon of hearing the voice of Being—whereby Being as the gift of sending is cut off from its withdrawing giving—a grounding occurs. Grounding is nothing other than this withdrawing, than this cutting off of giving, this taking to be immediate. The grounding axioms of a theory are self-evident and hence un-mediated by reasoning, they are the ground from which all reasoning takes off (the ground is *a rational*). The unmediatedness of the ground claims that the ground is not given by something else which is precisely what makes the ground capable of grounding (i.e., *cogito ergo sum*).[13]

---

[13]In this paragraph, it becomes evident to me that Being is in some sense doubled in a way other than the one given throughout this discussion whereby the attunement to Being in metaphysics is a kind of doubling of the voice of Being. That is, the voice of Being itself seems somehow doubled. On the one hand, there is Being that departs and gets cut off by a withdrawing while, on the other hand, Being cannot be cut off in its sending unless it were in motion to begin with. In the context of a discussion on metaphysics, Being shows

Thus far I have made an effort to draw metaphysics into a unity. Without dealing with specific metaphysical systems (save the briefly handled examples of Plato and Aristotle), I have made an effort to delimit the sorts of characteristics that determine a metaphysical mode of Saying over and against the Saying of the Same that has guided this project throughout. Yet in the course of this, metaphysics could not be radically separated from this project. Instead, it seems to mark a component of the way, an element in the developing economy. It would be false to say that metaphysics is an *other* to the Saying of the Same. Furthermore, the distinction as regards types of hearing does not leave me satisfied that metaphysics can be completely bracketed or separated from the Saying of the Same. Hearing as the hearing of silence or nearness or the ringing of stillness is essentially characterized by withdrawal. Metaphysics occurs in epochs because what withdraws is held back. In this essay, I have attempted to present what has withdrawn from metaphysics. The language of this sentence clearly reveals the problem that metaphysical thinking — and all other kinds — faces. By presenting what is held back in traditional metaphysics, I place what withdraws onto firm ground and thus enable it to be present in a theoretical investigation. Isn't this precisely what I have described as the *way* of metaphysics? Recall the acknowledgement in the previous chapter that the names for essential components of the bold claim are both adequate and inadequate to naming these components. In so far as this project has proceeded in language to name the Saying of the Same, it has operated within the Saying in a manner that seeks to transcend the limits of Saying. And all transcendence is characteristic of metaphysical delimiting of the ground present in all that is. It is, therefore, my concern that perhaps language itself is essentially connected to the Being of metaphysics (notice that historically language has always been understood primarily as speech or voice and thus is, by my reckoning, essentially connected to Being). Perhaps this

---

itself as both the closest link to the Saying of the Same which is in constant mediating and mediated motion and the breaking off from that same motion into an eternal ground of what is present as such. This makes it more clear why Heidegger initially refers to what I'm calling "the Saying of the Same" as "Being," "the Truth of Being," "the meaning of Being," etc. In all these cases, he is trying to enter into the sending of Being in such a way that it will reveal itself as sending, thus Being always remained in the proximity of this thinking. It is also because of this doubling of Being that Heidegger's replacement for "Being" is "Presencing" (*Anwesen*) which makes plain the sending component in its dynamic unfolding (*wesen*) along with its propensity to be cut of as the present (*Anwesen* literally means "present").

point can only be articulated in an essay by remaining silent, perhaps there is no way of speaking about the circling of the Same without causing its circling to cease and become present.[14]

One final clarification of metaphysics must be made before moving on to attempt to directly address this problem of the "overcoming of the tradition." The clarification concerns the supposed *unity* of metaphysics. This, unfortunately, will not distance metaphysics from deconstructive thinking so as to make the upcoming transgression any easier. Rather, it will bring the two still closer together.

In many of his discussions of the overcoming of metaphysics, Heidegger writes about an "end of philosophy." For example: "The old meaning of the word 'end' means the same as place: 'from one end to the other' means: from one place to the other. The end of philosophy is the place, that place in which the whole of philosophy's history is gathered in its most extreme possibility. End as completion means this gathering" (*TB*, 57). This understanding of "end" suggests nothing else but the place that is the place of all gathering, the clearing that is the open region of Saying the Same. The end of philosophy is not the point at which philosophy finishes with its possibilities as attunement to the voice of Being (i.e., where spirit realizes itself as such), rather it is Saying the Same which gathers philosophy together as such and allows it to belong together *as* philosophy attempting to Say the Same. In so far as the gathering place of philosophy is the clearing of the Saying of the Same,

---

[14]I am not in this passage accusing Heidegger of phonocentrism as the evocation of Derrida's project might suggest. Rather, I am trying to lay out the difficulty of "overcoming" metaphysics as it is developed in Heidegger's text. And, if anything, I think this indicates that Heidegger is more aware of the difficulties raised by the traditional understanding of language than Derrida gives him credit for. As the issue now stands, Heidegger is described as viewing the "overcoming" of metaphysics as an overcoming of the metaphysical understanding of language which is essentially voice. More on this in the following sections of the chapter.

It may also be added as commentary on this passage that the idea that I have carefully described in the Saying of the Same as untotalizable and abysmal is not an escape from this danger of turning the Same into a grounding of what is present. Wouldn't it still be the case that my presentation of the abysmal cuts what is groundless off from its sending groundlessness and hence turns it into a renewed kind of ground (perhaps an origin that is more springlike than groundlike — i.e., the German *Ur-sprung* indicating an original spring)? When Derrida writes, as in the introduction to *Margins,* of the remarkable power of metaphysics to recover any effort at "overcoming" it, it is precisely this sort of problem that he is suggesting.

it does not unify philosophy. Philosophy gathers at its end but that does not overcome the multiple determinations of philosophy that are its various epochs, nor does that suffice to breach an easily discernible distance between philosophy and the Saying of the Same that enables it to take place as tuning into the voice of Being. Instead, the end of philosophy places philosophy into a greater intimacy with its other, with the Saying of the Same heard in silence. I might claim, venturing into a grandiose circularity, that philosophy and Heidegger's project of "overcoming" it say the Same, they belong together.

This sheds new light on what has frequently been called Heidegger's "eschatology." It is ordinarily thought that the view of the history of philosophy as eschatology indicates that at one time thinking was not yet metaphysical (before Plato) and that now, as we approach the end of philosophy (which is the exhaustion of all its predetermined possible configurations), there will be a return to the first beginning whereby metaphysics will cease and the Saying of the Same shall reemerge in all its Anaximanderian grandeur.[15] This ultimate and extreme end of philosophy has therefore been tailored to resemble the second coming of Christ whose resurrection destroys the evil that has gained control over the earth in the interval of his absence. I emphatically reject this reading.[16]

---

[15]It is important that the figure of the eschatology is Anaximander since Anaximander's own fragment can be read as an eschatology of Being. The fragment speaks of the genesis and decay of things in accordance with the necessity dictated by Time. It is a fragment of endless circling, of the coming to be and passing away of all that is in accordance with the passage of time, boundless, which rules over everything. Thus everything in its inception is destined to decline, destiny itself is not only a coming to be but a passing away of necessity. "It belongs so essentially to the destiny of Being that the dawn of this destiny rises as the unveiling of what is present in its presencing. This means that the history of Being begins with the oblivion of Being, since Being-together with its essence, its distinction from beings—keeps to itself. The distinction collapses. It remains forgotten. Although the two parties to the distinction, what is present and presencing, reveal themselves, they do not do so as distinguished. Rather, even the early trace of the distinction is obliterated when presencing appears as something present and finds itself in the position of being the highest being present" (*EGT*, 50-51). Everything born is fated to die, even the oblivion of Being which has always been a Being toward its end, the end of philosophy.

[16] The best account of it that I know of is given by Werner Marx in op cit. Cf. Part IV. On page 165ff., Marx cites and discusses the same passage that follows in my text below. Essential to Marx's discussion is the idea of a

I quote in full with this new context:

> The antiquity pervading the Anaximander fragment belongs to the dawn of early times in the land of evening [the West]. But what if that which is early outdistanced everything late; if the very earliest far surpassed the very latest? What once occurred in the dawn of our destiny would then come, as what once occurred, at the last (*eschaton*), that is, at the departure of the long-hidden destiny of Being. The Being of beings is gathered (*legesthai, logos*) in the ultimacy of its destiny. The essence of Being hitherto disappears, its truth still veiled. The history of Being is gathered in this departure. The gathering in this departure, as the gathering (*logos*) at the outermost point (*eschaton*) of its essence hitherto, is the eschatology of Being. *As something fateful, Being itself is inherently eschatological.*
>
> However, in the phrase 'eschatology of Being' we do not understand the term 'eschatology' as the name of a theological or philosophical discipline. We think of the eschatology of Being in a way corresponding to the way the phenomenology of spirit is to be thought, i.e., *from within the history of Being.* The phenomenology of spirit itself constitutes a phase in the eschatology of Being, when Being gathers itself in the ultimacy

---

pre-destination of Being from its first beginning to its end which marks the coming of another beginning, and hence, another Being. The end of the first beginning, he argues, is not a telos that fulfills the potential of Being, but a demise or emptying of possibility (i.e., the first beginning runs out of things to be and so comes to an end where that end has been suggested by the potential present at the outset). The end, therefore, marks an identifiable moment in history and is significant as the end of history. Although the end is carried within the movement, it is ultimately something to be realized by a moment of closure which is itself the moment of another beginning. I should remark that this reading is very well substantiated by Heidegger's writing, but—as my reading of the passage in question should suggest—it fails to answer the question concerning the relationship between metaphysics and its other. This question is not answered when one says that the end of the first is the beginning of the other, especially if by that one suggests that until now there has been metaphysics, but soon hereafter there will be something other. This is the eschatology of Being and it makes Heidegger sound like he is waiting for a messiah (which is how he sometimes sounds). From my point of view, I can't see what basis Heidegger would have on this reading to claim that both moments were "beginnings." Furthermore, it would seem just as plausible for Heidegger to have thought that this sort of an end of metaphysics should be prevented rather than that it should be welcomed—and Marx readily admits that it is the latter reaction which is found in Heidegger's works.

> of its essence, hitherto determined through metaphysics, as the absolute subjecticity [*Subjektität*] of the unconditioned will to will.
>   If we think within the eschatology of Being, then we must someday anticipate the former dawn in the dawn to come; today we must learn to ponder this former dawn through what is imminent.(*EGT*, 18; emphasis added)

I do not deny that there is a strong indication here of the *overcoming* of metaphysics, or that metaphysics has not ruled the West throughout its history. I do claim, however, that the dawn of the West and that which is most early must both be understood as the Saying of the Same, whereas what is late is metaphysics. Notice that what once occurred will occur again *as* what once occurred. This is the departure of destiny, the destiny of Being, which we do not understand as history itself but as sending (and hence it is not to be identified with a certain period of time in the West, i.e., the age of Anaximander). The long-hidden destiny of Being is the hidden and withdrawing Saying of the Same that Heidegger has always claimed was overlooked in metaphysics. This repetition of the Saying of the Same, its circling, will occur at the end of metaphysics. This end of metaphysics, gathered in the clearing of the Saying of the Same, is the *eschaton,* the end. This "*eschaton*" is a gathering place, it is the end of philosophy. At the end of philosophy lies the dawn of philosophy understood as the Saying of the Same that circles. This does not mean that the Saying of the Same disappeared while metaphysics held sway, only that metaphysics itself is the ignorance of this end. Metaphysics, by definition, does not understand itself in its end. No doubt, eschatology is the coming to an end of metaphysics; but this does not mean that metaphysics will no longer continue to hold sway in the Open, only that it will be gathered there in such a way as to reveal its own gathering. This in turn recalls the gathering place from oblivion, so to speak (since it will no doubt continue to conceal itself), and thus marks the overcoming of metaphysics in/as/through a way.

Notice, furthermore, that it is an eschatology of Being and not of the Same that circles. Only Being and metaphysics can be placed together in an eschatology, since only these are cut off from their dynamic unfolding, restricted in their movement. This cutting off that is the establishing of the ground of the present carries within it the illusion of an eternal presence whereby the ground, never given, has ruled for all time and will continue to do so. Such a ground disregards its own essential nothingness or mortality (its being only an epoch). This exclusion of the nothing (recall that only "nothing is without ground or reason") is what subsumes the history of Being as metaphysics to an eschatology. It would not make sense to speak of the Saying of the Same as an eschatology since it carries its nothing with it in its circling, its circling is abysmal and hence the nothing cannot descend upon it; instead it always already emerges within as the sending in/as/through circling.[17]

With these remarks, the proximity of metaphysics to the Saying of the Same is almost absolute. This means that metaphysics becomes, in its end, the indication of something underneath or beyond metaphysics (i.e., its sending). But unfortunately, this indication takes place in what might be the most metaphysical of manners—as a revelation of the gathering place as a ground of all metaphysical thinking. It is at this point that we must begin turning.

Heidegger and Derrida: Turning on the Tradition

Early and late, Heidegger understood his project as twofold. But perhaps this already draws us along the way of an error. Perhaps Heidegger's project was never more than the one thought of the essence of Being which is carried out in a twofold manner. I refer, of course, to the early effort at a destruction of the tradition of philosophy together with the existential analytic of Dasein meant to reveal the meaning of Being in *Being and Time;* and the later effort of "The End of Philosophy and the Task of Thinking" which brings together the end of metaphysics and the uncovering of the sending of Being as the clearing of the Saying of the Same. So far I have tried to show that these two elements belong together. The claim that the destroying or destructuring of the tradition and the existential analytic toward the meaning of Being are one and the Same is analogous to the previous claim that the end of philosophy, the place where philosophy gathers, is the Same as the *sending* of Being that is tuned out in the hearing of metaphysics. In destructuring the tradition, or the thinking of the end of philosophy, I retrieve what is unsaid by the metaphysical thinkers of the tradition. The unsaid retrieved in their

---

[17]Perhaps this shows that the end of philosophy is an economy of death whereby the limit of philosophy, its gathering, becomes the matter for all thinking. This explains why "overcoming" philosophy has always been placed between quotation marks. It is not a matter of "overcoming" philosophy, but of thinking its end. This recalls the moment of authenticity in *Being and Time* which results from the Being-towards the End of Dasein where the end was death. This will be taken up in the sequel, especially chapter four.

thought is the Same. The epochs of philosophy gathered at its end are gathered in the Same. These two projects or two components of the one project fall together and become indistinguishable.[18] How should this be understood?

As a turning...

Heidegger writes in an essay usually thought of as "early":

> As insistent, man is turned toward the most readily available beings. But he insists only by being already ek-sistent, since, after all, he takes being as his standard. However, in taking its standard, humanity is turned away from the mystery. The insistent turning toward what is readily available and the ek-sistent turning away from the mystery belong together. They are one and the same. Yet turning toward and away from is based on a turning to and fro proper to Dasein. Man's flight from the mystery toward what is readily available, onward from one current thing to the next, passing the mystery by—this is *erring*. (*BW*, 135)

This comes from 1931 and has the mark of Heidegger's "earliness" all over it, in every word. "Insistence" is no doubt related to what I have been describing as the grounded present, whereas "ek-sistence" is the standing in the clearing evoked in the circling of the Same. The former a turning away, the latter a turning toward. What is important here for our purposes is that the turning toward and the turning away belong together, are the same. It is also important to point out that the errancy that this turning

---

[18]It may be of some service to the reader versed in *Being and Time* to go over more explicitly how this works. Heidegger's existential analytic of Dasein is performed in the service of reawakening the question concerning the meaning of Being. Dasein is chosen because it is an entity with a certain privileged position. That position has to do with Dasein's existence as a clearing where unconcealment or disclosure happens. In order to perform this ontological reading of Dasein as something more than a merely determined entity within the world, Heidegger has to contend with the traditional prejudice to view Dasein in terms of *subiectum* or *hypokeimenon* (subjectivity or substance). Thus the movement in the description of Dasein that goes from *res cogitans* to the clearing for Being's disclosure is not only an existential analytic but also a destruction of traditional metaphysics. It is therefore, at least in part, false to say that the destruction of metaphysics indicated in the introduction to *Being and Time* was never accomplished in the promised fashion.

away describes is essential to the being of Dasein and indicates a prior turning that enables *either* turning toward or away; this prior turning is the "turning to and fro proper to Dasein." The turning toward carries within it essentially a turning away, without the one there would not be the other. They belong together just as the revealing and concealing of *a-letheia* do. Only because Dasein can turn away is it able to turn toward. These mutually dependent turns gain their individual movement from the turning that enables them. Thus their belonging together can be called a prior turning. This prior turning that is the belonging together of this proper essence of Dasein later becomes the circling of the Same.

Consider the image of the hearing that goes on in the metaphysical tuning of the voice of Being. Here the metaphysical thinker is turning an ear toward the voice of Being, but this turning toward of the ear also turns away, since turning an ear toward the voice of Being so that it may whisper its truth involves the turning away of the face. In presenting Being with one's ear, one no longer faces Being. Likewise in turning one's ear away from Being, the voice is no longer heard, the deafness of the other hearing occurs as one faces what speaks. What one turns toward and what one turns away from is in both and every case the Same. What matters most of all in the two cases is whether the turning emphasizes hearing or facing.[19]

This turning which is both a turning toward and away, turning to and fro, occurs essentially as the circling of the Same where all circling—and especially this circling which opens in clearing—is turning. The turn is the arc of a circling and all circling is a double turning, a turning to and fro which continues indefinitely, without limit (i.e., the *a-peiron* from Anaximander's fragment). In a note to the essay "On the Essence of Truth" and appended—almost twenty years later—as section 9, Heidegger writes in explanation of the phrase "*the essence of truth is the truth of essence*" which guides the essay: "The answer to the question of the essence of truth is the saying of a turning within the history of Being. Because sheltering that lightens belongs to it, Being appears primordially in the light of concealing withdrawal. The name of this lighting is *aletheia*" (*BW*, 140). The movement from the first phrase "the essence of truth" to the second "the truth of essence" (handled previously and rendered "the un-concealment of dynamic unfolding") is a turning. I

---

[19]The movement here is toward the work of Emmanuel Levinas who understands the face as the face of the Other where this other is understood as infinitely Other. That is, as a radically withdrawn presence (viz. absence)—what is here called the sending/giving of Being occurring as the Saying of the Same. Cf. *Time and the Other*.

adopted this structure for the bold claim at the outset of chapter 2 and described the inversion as circling. Here circling is introduced into Heidegger's work as turning. Furthermore, this turning is displayed not only as the movement of *a-letheia* as the clearing of the Saying of the Same, but as the history of Being as metaphysics which circles within the turning of the Same and does so purely as the lighted side of the enigma (the mystery) which is revealed in presence. Metaphysics turns in the light as the metaphysics of light whereas the circling turning of the Same is the lightening and sheltering that both advances and recedes. Their turning belongs together.

There is a sense in which this turning is essential to the whole of the history of metaphysics and there is a sense in which it is not. Metaphysics continually turns toward and away from what speaks to its hearers in the Saying of the Same as the voice of Being, but it never turns toward this turning. This was described in the previous section as the failure to grasp hearing as such, metaphysics' failure to grasp its hearing as hearing the voice of Being and thus to see its project as the Same across epochs (i.e., Aristotle fails to grasp his essential relation to Plato and instead turns to criticize the master). A linguistic construction might help to make this point clear. Rather than saying that metaphysics in its turning fails to grasp turning as such (which would, as Derrida writes concerning the "as such," indicate a relationship to the turning similar to that of the principle of identity before it is overturned in Heidegger's essay in *Identity and Difference)*, I will say that metaphysics fails to grasp turning *and* circling, to grasp the turning that circles, to turn *and* to circle always understood as their belonging together that is the Same that circles and turns in Saying un-concealment, *er-eignis,* and dif-ference. This does not mean that metaphysics does not turn.

Heidegger writes: "To flee into the identical is not dangerous. To risk discord in order to say the Same is the danger" (*BW*, 241). This indicates that the linguistic construction that refers to turning *as such* is a construction from within metaphysics, from the point of view of the identical which is not dangerous. Rather, it must be described in terms of its relation to the Same, described in its turning as a turning which fails to grasp the turning *and* circling and thus does not risk discord (which in this context refers at least in part to the disagreement among thinkers regarding the meaning of "the Same," but also to the Latin *discordia* meaning strife and hence the economy of the Same in general). This failure to risk discord, to venture into the sending advent of the Same that plays in rampant discordance as strife, is characteristic of a certain kind of position on metaphysics: a view of metaphysics that takes its position from within metaphysics and hence fails to see anything like an end, its place of gathering (this is a position that doesn't see metaphysics' turning as oblivious to anything: a true first philosophy). The contrary view, the view that beholds metaphysics in its turning, is not outside metaphysics looking down. Rather it has moved within metaphysics to its end so as to stand in the gathering there where the turning takes place. This risky position is highly dangerous.

Heidegger understands the current epoch of the history of Being as the technological. I mentioned it before when discussing the extent to which the epoch determines both the messenger and the message. When the epoch is technological, the essence of technology is *Gestell* or enframing where the beings determined according to this mode of Being are *Bestand* or resources. The related roots of these two words (the one for Being the other for beings) indicates their relation: *stellen* on the one hand and *stehen* on the other. *Gestell* makes things stand, whereas *Bestand* is the manner in which they stand. Under the guise of the epoch of technology, there is a setting in order that labors. *Bestand* is not *Gegenstand,* the entities of technology are not objects for theoretical inquiry, they are resources for production. Under the reign of *Gestell,* the resources of the world are made to stand ready for the mastery and ordering of production. Even the laborers are subsumed to this ordering, they are a labor force (Cf. "The Question Concerning Technology").

Insofar as this is the contemporary epoch, it is not merely a matter of thinking differently that will bring this epoch to a close; as though we must only succeed in changing our world-view. Heidegger is not taking an idealist position similar to the one he believes Marx to have thoroughly destroyed in *The German Ideology.* Rather, the end of this epoch as well as the end of philosophy, is a matter for the destiny of Being. One epoch is only closed in the movement of the sending of Being. But should Enframing come to a close in the sending of another epoch, then we will have merely discovered a new mode of withholding, a renewed manner in which the oblivion of Being as presence can take place. Perhaps an analogy from Marx will help to make this point clear. In his display of the history of production in historical materialism Marx describes a sequence of stages of history marking hegemonic displacements of the past stage. The structure of history, where there is on the one hand a ruling class that possesses the society's wealth and on the other hand a ruled class which submits to the ruling class's ideology for the direction of society in its daily existence, is a constant rise of previously subdued groups that gain power through various social institutions and then eventually ownership on their way to gaining complete dominance within the society. This new dominance of a rising group marks a new stage in history. Strictly speaking, these hegemonic displacements cannot be called revolutions since none of them threaten the existing structure of society and the historical order that it reforms. A true revolution, Marx says even in his early works, is a radical transformation of this structure of society and thus an end of history in its degraded form and a beginning of "history" in a renewed, revolutionary (turning) form.

Revolution, in this Marxist sense, defines turning. The turning at the end of history and metaphysics in Heidegger is not one more epoch replacing the current one of technology, but a revolution that destroys the old structure. How then can we understand this turning in relation to the contemporary epoch? What is there about the contemporary epoch that enables this turning while the other epochs of history did not? The answer to these questions must lie within enframing itself since it would have to be here, in this mode of Being *as* a mode of Being, that turning gains its evident possibilities. And this must be so in a way that was not the case in previous metaphysical modes. Furthermore, why this feature of the current epoch does not contradict Heidegger's claims concerning an absence of progress in metaphysics will have to be addressed.

I begin by turning back to the essay on the principle of identity which discusses the epoch of technology. Here the calculating mastery of technology is explained in terms of a reduction to "man"[20] where "man" is understood as belonging together with Being in the history of metaphysics. That is, "man" has always belonged together with Being in the history of metaphysics as the fleshing out of the Parmenidean "For the Same are thinking and Being." In the epoch of technology, Being is no longer an apparent component in the sending of the epoch. The epoch of mastery and resources is an epoch devoted exclusively to man. It is where man comes to dominate the earth, to rule over it in the absence of Being. Heidegger understands the contemporary epoch as the voice of Being without Being (where the spectrum of Being's modification includes

---

[20]It seems perfectly appropriate to me to use the word "man" here since this is the concept of humanity or humankind during the epochs of the history of metaphysics. Man, as Heidegger writes in the *Question of Being* examined previously, is essentially tied together with Being and hence essentially connected to the history being described. Derrida refers to this same period as the period of phallogocentrism so as to highlight, among other things, the phallocentric nature of metaphysics. Doubtless, it would be somewhat controversial to claim this is Heidegger's reason for using the word.

privation). The epoch of technology, because it is without Being, is the epoch of nihilism.[21]

Nihilism, which is a mode of Being, makes itself present in the resources of the world in the form of a challenge to man as the ruler and master of all that is, the laborer and producer for whom all resources in nature must yield: "The name for the gathering of this challenge which places man and Being face to face in such a way that they challenge each other by turns is 'the enframing'" (*ID*, 35). Nihilistic Being is sent as a challenge. The earth as resource challenges man to be more productive and it challenges Being to accommodate everything that is as a resource. An entity is visible as a resource only if it is already challenging, already beckoning to be manipulated and put to use. This challenge that rules the world during the technological age displays the greatest danger the history of humankind has ever known. And this is not a result of technology being an atomic age threatening to incinerate all traces of history, rather technology is an atomic age *because* of this danger. The challenge of this age is the threat of all beings and this threat is the greatest danger. "The coming to presence of Enframing is the danger" (*QCT*, 41).

This danger—where Being is in complete oblivion—need not be compared to past epochs and modes of Being, instead danger is essential to the epoch itself. It is not a matter of Being becoming more eclipsed in this stage than in the others, although it is clearly Being's complete withdrawal into the challenge that confronts man in such a way as to reveal the danger. This danger should be viewed as essential to this mode of Being because of its unfolding as the nihilistic epoch. But the nihilism of this epoch is not the result of the progressive denial of Being of all the previous epochs. Each of the epochs is totally discrete.[22] Only separated

---

[21]*Gestell* names Being in this mode nonetheless. It is just that *Gestell* is almost exclusively conceived in terms of man and man's activity. It is also significant that this epoch of metaphysics is typically characterized by radical criticisms of metaphysics (i.e., positivism). Yet this positivism, which nonetheless hears the voice of Being in a manner of speaking, is just as equally characterized, according to Heidegger, as a metaphysical position. Could it be that the philosophical name of this epoch is "humanism"? It is also interesting to note the rise of cognitive science/artificial intelligence in the field of philosophy within this epoch.

[22]Although much has been said to distance Heidegger's conception of an epoch from the moments of the Hegelian dialectic (i.e., their externality to each other), there persists in all of the previous discussion a vague spectre of sequence proper to epochs. I have suggested that the epochs of Being eclipse each other such that there is little doubt that two may occupy the world at once. This is clearly not the case in Heidegger's thinking. Robert Bernasconi

epochs can gather at their end. The gathering only becomes visible if one takes a risk. Risk is a daily occurrence in the epoch of the greatest danger. Still more needs to be said to ally this risk as moving into discord with the danger of the challenge that is global technology.

The following has been quoted at length because of its importance for this issue:

> The coming to presence of Enframing is the danger. As the danger, Being turns about into the oblivion of its coming to presence, turns away from this coming to presence, and in that way simultaneously turns counter to the truth of its coming to presence. In the danger there holds sway this turning about not yet thought on. In the coming to presence of the danger there *conceals* itself, therefore, the possibility of a turning in which the oblivion of belonging to the coming to presence of Being will so turn itself that, with *this* turning, the truth of the coming to presence of Being will expressly turn in — turn homeward — into whatever is.
>
> Yet probably *this* turning — the turning of the oblivion of Being into the safekeeping belonging to the coming to presence of Being — will finally come to pass only when the danger, which is in its concealed essence never susceptible of turning, first coming expressly to light as the danger that it is. Perhaps we stand already in the shadow cast ahead by the advent of *this* turning. (*QCT*, 41)

(cf. *The Question of Language in Heidegger's History of Being.* Atlantic Highlands, NJ: Humanities Press International, 1985.) suggests thinking of the epochs of Being in the manner of periods of art such as romanticism, realism, impressionism, etc. The flourishing era of these periods can be said to follow in sequence, but they are not mutually exclusive. For instance, Heidegger is often accused of being a romantic despite his temporal distance from the age of romanticism. This sort of overlap is typical of such periodization of art. Furthermore, such epochs no doubt may share the world at a specific time and in fact do, although usually in conflict with one another. This also sheds light on the matter of various cultures inhabiting the earth together—perhaps in different worlds as they do so. The tragedy of imperialism and its destruction of other worlds thus becomes thematic in the critique of western metaphysics and its repression of dif-ference. The thematic is not one of world-views but of the dynamic sending of Being. This might also remind the reader of Kuhn in *The Structure of Scientific Revolutions.* (Chicago: The University of Chicago Press, 1970).

This passage poses few problems of interpretation in this context but it also offers few answers to our problems. The danger rules the mode of Being as enframing, but it has not been thought as danger just yet. The moment of turning is therefore the moment at which enframing as danger turns in such a way as to reveal the danger. Revelation of the danger is turning and circling. In revelation, a revolution in enframing occurs: it turns and circles. This is the case because the discord of the Same is a risk and the danger of enframing reveals the risk that is the discord of difference, un-concealment, and *er-eignis*.

In the essay "The Turning," Heidegger goes on to give many details about the phenomenon of revealing the danger. He cites Hölderlin's claim "But where danger is, grows/The saving power also" (*QCT*, 42). This gives hope that the danger of enframing can be revealed as such and that saving from the danger will ensue. In a wonderful passage, Heidegger links the notions of flashing and glance so as to describe the moment of grasping the danger as a lightning flash occurring in a moment of brilliance that recalls the moment as "*augenblick*" suggesting *er-eignis:*

> The in-turning that is the lightning-flash of the truth of Being is the entering, flashing glance — insight. We have thought the truth of Being in the worlding of world as the mirror play of the fourfold of sky and earth, mortals and divinities. When oblivion turns about, when world as the safekeeping of the coming to presence of Being turns in, then there comes to pass [*ereignet*] the in-flashing of world into the injurious neglect [*verwahrlosung* — loss of safekeeping] of the thing. That neglect comes to pass in the mode of the rule of Enframing. In-flashing of world into Enframing is in-flashing of the truth of Being into truthless Being. In-flashing is the disclosing coming-to-pass within Being itself. Disclosing coming-to-pass [*Ereignis*] is bringing to sight that brings into its own [*eignende Eraugnis*]. (*QCT*, 45)

This lightning flash that comes as the danger is unconcealed brings one into the gathering at the end of philosophy, the gathering that turns. This lightning flash is the setting turning and circling, the moment of turning is the entrance into the circling of the Same and the saving from the danger of enframing that unconceals its essence as danger in the same moment that saving occurs. The unconcealment of danger is the saving from that same danger—this is the turning and circling, the Saying of the Same that circles in the bold claim.[23]

Turning and circling as the insight into the end of philosophy, therefore, can be understood as a crossing over the line of nihilism. This crossing the line of nihilism that moves into the essence of technology as the danger is a turning into the clearing of the essence of Being that has determined the whole of the history of Western metaphysics. The crossing of the line of nihilism is the journey into the nothing of the *nihil* that gives to it its essence, in the nothing of the *nihil* lies the essence of nihilism: the nothing, the concealed nothing of the withdrawn Saying circling of the Same. The crossing of the line of nihilism is a crossing out of Being that unconceals a fourfold region of nearness and clearing: $\cancel{\text{Being}}$.[24]

In Heidegger's 1955 essay, *The Question of Being*—"Über "die Linie","" the crossing lines of nihilism become the matter for inquiry. This essay has been hovering in the background of many of the remarks made throughout my investigations, but as yet I have not focused on it. This latest gesture in its direction will not remedy this, but will help to clarify the eventual significance. Heidegger no longer understands "*über die linie*" as signifying "across the line" as it did for Jünger. Instead, Heidegger declares that this understanding of the phrase is linked to the Latin "*trans*" and the Greek "*meta*" both indicating metaphysical thinking. Heidegger asserts another, related, interpretation of the "*über*," the "*über*" as the Latin "*peri*" or "*de*" meaning roughly "on" or

---

[23] And in a sense, it is also Heidegger's attempt to say what is unsaid in his own thinking. That is, how is it that it is possible that there is a philosopher in the twentieth century who is able to give voice to the turning of the Saying of the Same. Perhaps this suggests why this element of the analysis is so difficult to grasp: the preconditions of the possibility of deconstruction—being performed in the work of the thinker—are unconcealing in the Saying of the Same.

[24]This X supplements Being as "and" and "maybe" have done already. Derrida writes in a way that will only come to make sense later: "The form of the chiasm, of the X, interests me a great deal......this is the figure of the double gesture...." (*P*, 70) and "According to the X (The chiasmos)(which can be considered a quick thematic diagram of dissemination)..." (*D*, 44) The X is the supplement because in nihilism it replaces Being and in the circling of the Same it is added on to it from out of its withdrawal. Can one add withdrawal? Doesn't the withdrawal that supplements Being challenge all thought of a neat opposition of presence and absence, addition and subtraction? Cf. the next section.

"concerning." He claims these two significations of "*über*" "belong together" (*QB*, 37). The metaphysical "across" joined together with Heidegger's "concerning" already begin to move in the direction of a turning of nihilism. A turning and circling that move "over" the line in such a way as to hover at the end of nihilism and gaze down/up into it so as to have an insight concerning its dynamic movement.

We now have a better idea as to what happens in the turning of philosophy that is the end of philosophy, but questions remain. The weight of the enframing is heavy, how is it lightened? Has Heidegger done all that was needed in exposing this lightning flash insight? What makes it possible for this lightning flash to occur? Is it the act of a lone thinker or must it be a broader revolution than that, a mass movement? What role do poets play in this lightning flash (after all, wasn't Hölderlin the poet for dangerous times)? Given that it is in poetry that this saving power that catches sight of the danger takes place in its turning and circling, how are poets possible at all?

Many of these questions will have to wait until the following chapters. For now, I will turn to the work of Jacques Derrida so as to address the matter of Martin Heidegger's relation to this lightning-flash insofar as it is possible at all given what was previously called metaphysics' immense power for subverting any discourse that attempts to disrupt it. The question that this inquiry must pursue is whether the turning may ever occur in circling, since the very nature of metaphysics has been the attempt to gain control over language in such a way as to disrupt even these words: turning and circling.

This passage marks Derrida's introduction into this essay, despite the fact that all of what has been said thus far bears a *certain relation* to his texts. To make this point emphatic, I will defer any attempt at discussing this "certain relation," perhaps indefinitely. It is only fitting that the contemporary thinker of *différance* should enter a text in the manner of this same *différance*.[25]

I noted in the discussion on Heidegger's use of the word "end," that there are a number of metaphysical senses that it would be problematic to attribute to Heidegger's thinking concerning the matter of the end. In other words, "end" is contained in numerous texts throughout the many epochs of the history of Western metaphysics. Derrida helps to clarify this

---

[25]As there is a footnote like this one in every text on Derrida (and even by Derrida), it is only fitting that there be one here if for no other reason than to mark this text as a text on Derrida. *Différance* suggests both to differ and to defer in a simultaneously (not yet) spatial and temporal sense. *Différance* is pronounced exactly like difference but it is written differently. It is always italicized (I don't know why).

point. He replaces "end" with "closure." But this replacement raises questions and does not lead to a simply presented reformulation of Heidegger's "end of philosophy." Instead, this replacement (better we should call it a displacement) is *the* problem of/at the end/closure of philosophy.

The significance that language plays in this displacement is not, of course, new to Derrida. Heidegger's discussion of Saying already begins along this way and since Saying was said to circle, we have already been exposed to the importance of Saying in the turning that is circling as the Same at the moment of metaphysics' end. That circling was of course the circling of the Same Saying un-concealment, *er-eignis,* and dif-ference. Derrida's move, differing from Heidegger's, comes through the recent linguistic tradition of Europe, most notably through Saussure. Like Heidegger, however, Derrida understands language as play. This combination leads Derrida to formulate language as the play of signifiers.

The play of Saying in its circling becomes more easily accessible in the concrete notion of the signifier borrowed from Saussure. Along with Saussure, Derrida accepts the claim that the signs in the structural web of language are not in any real existing sense connected to some necessary meaning. Rather, the signs are set apart, given their place in the network, only through the differences that exist between the signs. Each sign, therefore, carries within it the whole of the network in so far as it gains its signification from its differentiation (or context) from the other signs in the language. In the second chapter, I showed how Heidegger understood the relation of the thing and world—thing bears out world, world grants thing. If the world (the clearing where Saying circles) is the play of signs, the extent to which these descriptions are parallel is demonstrated. Each sign bears out the entire text or fabric of signs, whereas the text of signs (the whole play as the play of differentiations) grants the particular sign.[26]

But Derrida would find this use of the word "sign" problematic (as did Heidegger), and this is where he differs from Saussure. Unlike Saussure, who saw in every sign an essential link of signifier and signified (i.e., sound and concept), Derrida sees that every signified is in turn recaptured by the play of signifiers and thus enters into this game (and this is the case even if the signified is understood as a referent: recall that

---

[26]This all too briefly drawn parallel of world-thing and play-signifier will come to occupy a central role in the investigation in the chapters to come. In this relation and the special role the poet and thinker play in it, we will discover the implications this inquiry will have for dwelling.

the "thing" is an interplay of gestures—signifiers). There is no signified for Derrida. Rather, each signifier—in turn—signifies another signifier which in turn continues this procedure without cease.[27] It is play precisely because it does not know when to stop: all knowing is foreign to this kind of play. This displacement of the signified concept that marks Derrida's entry into a post-structuralism also allies him with Heidegger's description of the play of the Same. Derrida has placed all emphasis on the signifier within the structuralist text in an effort at setting language on this circling turning pathway; he has done so in such a way as to transform the nature of the signifier, making it into the signifier of a signifier. This secondarity, a secondarity still intimately connected to the structuralist (and hence metaphysical) text, denotes Derrida's transformative conception of language: writing.[28]

> In all senses of the word, writing thus *comprehends* language. Not that the word 'writing' has ceased to designate the signifier of the signifier, but it appears, strange as it may seem, that 'signifier of the signifier' no longer defines accidental doubling and fallen secondarity. 'Signifier of the signifier' describes on the contrary the movement of language: in its origin, to be sure, but one can already suspect that an origin whose structure can be expressed as 'signifier of the signifier' conceals and erases itself in its own production. There the signified always already functions as a signifier. The secondarity that it seemed possible to ascribe to writing alone affects all signifieds in general, affects them always already, the moment they *enter the game.* There is not a single signified that escapes, even if recaptured, the play of signifying references that constitute language. The advent of writing is the advent of this play; today such a play is coming into its own, effacing the limit starting from which one had thought to

---

[27]This sentence might suggest that the signifier is some self-identical thing. Hopefully, the abysmal nature of the signifier will become clear in what follows. That is, the signifier is nothing other than the gap or abyss opened up in its relation to the other signifiers in the language.

[28]The connection is no doubt to be found in the remarks made in the opening lines of Aristotle's *De Interpretatione* which read: "Spoken words are the symbols of mental experience and written words are the symbols of spoken words. Just as all men have not the same writing, so all men have not the same speech sounds, but the mental experiences, which these directly symbolize, are the same for all, as also are those things of which our experiences are the images" (*Basic Works of Aristotle.* New York: Random House, 1941. p. 40). The concept is signified by the signifying sound of speech while the written mark becomes the signifier of the signifier. Derrida sees this as the role given to writing throughout the history of metaphysics.

> regulate the circulation of signs, drawing along with it all the
> reassuring signifieds, reducing all the strongholds, all the out-of-
> bounds shelters that watched over the field of language. This,
> strictly speaking, amounts to destroying the concept of the 'sign'
> and its entire logic. (*OG*, 7)

Notice that writing suffers an advent, it clears in the manner of what Derrida elsewhere calls a "spacing," and that this advent is the advent of the play as well. This play is "coming into its own" today where that clearly recalls the owning of showing as Saying in *er-eignis*. Notice also that this advent effaces a limit that seeks to "regulate the circulation." By effacing such a limit, the circulation is freed, allowed to play without restriction, it enters into a circling that we can rightly call the economy of the Same.[29] This letting-play of the signifiers in the secondarity of writing is also said to reduce all that attempts to govern the "field of language" from beyond it. This clearly points out the same movement that Heidegger foresees in the end of philosophy, since what rules from beyond the field is nothing other than the Being of beings.[30] Finally, it is necessary to point

---

[29]This effacing of the limit that enables the play of signifiers to circulate freely (notice "free" designates clearing in Heidegger's text) indicates the difference between a restricted and a general economy. Cf. "From Restricted to General Economy: A Hegelianism without Reserve" in Derrida's *Writing and Difference*.

[30]It should be evident here and in the discussion of Aristotle and Plato in the previous section that the history of metaphysics is, to some extent, always a history of transcendental idealism. There is always a present Being beyond beings which rules categorially over the field of language here indicating the replaced or displaced field of beings. The removal of all such restrictions is therefore an affront to all transcendental idealism. The Same is in no way beyond the world and grounding it, it circulates in its play in/as/through the play of the world. See the remarks on the supplement in the following section. The distinction I continue to make between transcendental philosophy and the deconstruction of metaphysics depends on a fundamental element of Kant's critical philosophy that deconstruction sees throughout the history of philosophy: namely, the residual remaining outside the categories of the understanding. And by this I do not refer to the transcendent realm of the noumenal, but the realm of the given matter that is present there beyond the categorial intuition of the understanding—the matter given in intuition. I agree with Schürmann and others that the deconstructive move is made on a metaphysics understood in terms of transcendental idealism. But unlike Schürmann—who claims that the key move in Heidegger's deconstruction is

out the extent to which "destroying" occurs in this fragment of Derrida's text: the advent of the signifier of the signifier in its play *destroys* the concept of the sign.

There is more to be learned from this passage than that Heidegger's project can be repeated in French. Derrida appropriates the notion of writing that he uses to displace the metaphysical conception of language from the text of metaphysics itself. He notices in writing a secondarity (where that secondarity is the secondarity granted to the term by the discourse of metaphysics) that he wants to displace from, and then use to replace, metaphysics. Recall that metaphysics is the metaphysics of presence, the metaphysics of the ground of all that is present in its eternal presence.[31] The whatness (quiddity) of entities is grounded in such a way that is present within them, that presents them as they are. Writing is granted its secondarity in the economy of a metaphysics that grants the primary position in language to the voice, to speech as vocalized language. Derrida incessantly plays on the French word *vouloir-dire* which literally translated says "wanting to say." Meaning suggests volition and the voice, saying as vocal speech: the sound image which is the symbol for mental experience. What gives speech this priority is the presence of the speaker to himself in the moment of utterance. Speaking is always hearing-oneself-speak and therefore is always the absolute proximity or presence of oneself to oneself as the speaking subject. A whole string of concepts are therefore linked in this chain of primary valuation in metaphysical thinking: voice, meaning as volitional intent and concept, self-presence as self-consciousness, subjectivity and identity.[32]

Derrida is therefore able to conclude that the hierarchy in the

---

the move from categories attached to the activity of a subject to an ontological status—I think Heidegger maneuvers against a different central move of transcendental philosophy: the presence of an unquestionable given over and against the movement of "categories" (regardless of where they are "located").

[31] And more specifically for Derrida, metaphysics is history proper as the history of the effort to subsume difference to presence: "Dissemination treats-doctors-that *point* where the movement of signification would regularly come to *tie down* the play of the trace, thus producing (a) history" (*D*, 26). Dissemination is the multiplying and dividing of the self-present point whose domination of the play of the trace is history. This should become clearer in what follows.

[32] More will be said on these matters in the sequel. For now, I can only quickly refer to Derrida's discussion of Husserl's First Investigation on "Expression and Meaning" in his *Speech and Phenomena.*

metaphysical texts between speech and writing is exemplary of the hierarchy between presence and difference. Presence is only presence at the expense of difference. The origin, the self-present origin as the ground of all that is, that is the unique transcendental signified (*idea, ousia,* etc.) yields all differences within the sensible world of metaphysical thinking: difference is an effect of presence in traditional metaphysics. By capturing the signified concept, presence itself, in the play of signifiers, Derrida incites a revolution in/of metaphysics. By taking secondarity, displayed as writing, from the text of metaphysics and letting it loose as the play of signifiers, he sets that text circling and turning. In a sense, secondarity becomes original. But this is only in *a* sense since, as evident in the passage above, secondarity is directly opposed to all conception of the origin. By capturing the signified in the play of the signifier and thus granting secondarity its due, Derrida places metaphysics in a relation to the play of language that delimits its closure.[33]

But why closure and not end? Certainly here it is not merely a matter of two terms ordered in the metaphysical text in such a way as to incite a displacement of the kind seen in writing and speaking.

The word "closure" participates in many connotations. First, it may be related to Heidegger's dis-closure which early on functions in the lightening of the clearing. The sending of Being into the open is dis-closure. Perhaps, closure is the closing off of Being, the withdrawal of what appears in the open. And this in a twofold sense: (1) the end of an epoch described earlier in the discussion of technology. "Closure" informs us that it is something beyond merely human thinking that brings about the transformation in Being. (2) The withdrawal of the Same in the sending of Being. Metaphysics as the history of the oblivion of Being marks Being in its withdrawal as the circling of the Same. To that extent, we might speak of metaphysics as closure so as to indicate that it is intimately affiliated with this withdrawal. Second, closure suggests closed in the sense of a finite totality closed off in its totalization. As in the discussion from chapter 2, this indicates a trait of metaphysics as closed off from the opening of Saying. This totality of closure as the closure of metaphysics perhaps indicates its finite possibilities insofar as

---

[33]In what might be an unnecessary intrusion, I might just point out that this underlining of secondarity that goes on in Derrida's texts resembles an underlying of difference in much the same way that we saw in Heidegger's text throughout the first two chapters of this essay. It is no accident that in the passage where Derrida performs this turning all the significant notions from Heidegger are underlined: dif-ference, *er-eignis,* un-concealment, clearing.

they have been exhausted throughout the history of Being. The closure of metaphysics is thus the completion of its possible instantiations within history. Third, closure indicates a fence or a wall in the sense of a boundary, a limit: a limit that cannot be transcended, a line that cannot be crossed. Perhaps the closure of metaphysics merely marks its limitations, sets it apart from whatever else there is in such a way as to delimit and define it in its appropriate essence.

It would be a mistake to choose between any of these possible significations of closure. It would not be a mistake, however, to say that it is precisely because of these variations in the signification of closure that Derrida prefers it to "end." Relative to what has been said concerning writing and speech, we can point out that language, the play of signifiers, plays out of control. Intention, which belongs to the speech of metaphysics, is what enables speakers to put the reigns on the significance of words, enables them to maintain authority over meaning. In the supplement of presence (viz. writing), this authority is replaced too. When the "end" is invoked, it signifies out of control. It suggests Kant's noumenal realm and reason's *telos,* etc. This can not to be helped (unless of course one writes playfully which helps it only by making the lack of control extraordinary and hence dangerous). The move to closure, therefore, avoids these significations in favor of the others mentioned above. And still more.[34]

What more?: "The closure of metaphysics, above all, is not a circle surrounding a homogeneous field, a field homogeneous with itself on its inside, whose outside then would be homogeneous also. The limit has the form of always different faults, of fissures whose mark or scar is borne by all the texts of philosophy" (*P*, 56-7).

Earlier I mentioned the signification of closure as limit where limit no doubt is intimately related to the language of philosophy. Philosophy has always been concerned with limits, with delimiting, and even with the unlimited. Closure does suggest limits, but does so in such a way as to introduce the concept of limit into the chain of closure and the withdrawing circling of the Same. This overlapping of significations transforms the limit where this transformation occurs with the play of the signifier "closure" and makes it preferable to that of "end." The

---

[34]This reference to intentions and authority no doubt reveals one of the greatest problems in all of Derrida's texts. The matter of intention has been circumvented in favor of the play of the text's signifiers. But this seems to be coupled with the idea that there may be an intention to make the play happen in one manner over and against another. That is, doesn't it appear that a choice or decision has been made in the direction of one play (closure) over and against another (end)? It is not yet time to address this problem.

transformation occurs when the boundary of the closure is no longer able to stand as a solid line encircling the field of metaphysics. Such a limit divides metaphysics into an inside bordering an outside that is other (the circling of the Same). This opposition is no longer possible when philosophy, what is inside, reaches its limit, what is outside.

This is the case for a variety of reasons. First, the division of inside and outside is a division typical of metaphysics (i.e., Kant's pure forms of intuition and Descartes' *res extensa* over and against the *res cogitans)*. Such a limit conceived in the language of metaphysics is hardly effective for limiting metaphysics from the outside. Second, I already showed that metaphysics—according to Heidegger—will not allow a separate opposition to the Saying of the Same. Compare this to Derrida on the issue: "But—if the form of opposition and the oppositional structure are themselves metaphysical, then the relation of metaphysics to its other can no longer be one of opposition" (*S*, 117-9).

Therefore the limit must be allowed to transform itself along the links in the chain of the significations of closure. The clue for this is visible in the citation above from *Positions*. I repeat this time with emphasis: "*The limit has the form of always different faults, of fissures whose mark or scar is borne by all the texts of philosophy.*" This instance of limit sends us in the direction of another text which reads:

> This privilege [of presence] is the ether of metaphysics, the element of our thought that is caught in the language of metaphysics. One can delimit such a closure today only by soliciting the value of presence that Heidegger has shown to be the ontotheological determination of Being; and in thus soliciting the value of presence, by means of an interrogation whose status must be completely exceptional, we are also examining the absolute privilege of this form or epoch of presence in general that is consciousness as meaning in self-presence. (*M*, 16)

The limit that is not a boundary marking an inside off from an outside is a limit that can only be delimited, be asserted as a limit, in a solicitation of presence, a soliciting of metaphysics. Soliciting suggests for Derrida not only the familiar senses of persuade, petition, entice, or proposition but also the Latin *solliciter* meaning "to shake the whole." Our solicitous discourse will not only proposition and entreat metaphysics ("feed it lines"), it will also set it shaking and trembling (perhaps it fears for its virginity). And this so strongly that it will begin to crack and break. It is in this sense that the signification of closure is drawn toward the fissure and faults which will begin to mark and scar the texts of philosophy.[35]

When metaphysics is made to shake and tremble, its self-presence and eternal motionlessness begin to crack, the purity of its origin divides in a fissure that breaches a path (*bahnung*) through the whole of the history of metaphysics. The closure of metaphysics delimits philosophy by cracking it open to reveal the gaps that span and stretch out within it as though they were lines crossing their way over "Being." More specifically, closure indicates the letting play of signifiers that crack open in metaphysics as the breaking loose of secondarity from the degraded position granted to it by the history of philosophy. This secondarity is not surgically removed with precision, rather it does great damage to the body of the text of philosophy from which it is removed. Presence is demonstrated as an effect of the play of signifiers and not a property of the origin. For example, concepts—a mainstay of philosophical discourse—are displayed in Derrida's discourse as signifiers captured by the play and hence caught up in the circulating differences. What was once eternally present in essence, now begins to swim in the fluid play of secondarity (which is a good description of the leap from essence as quiddity to essence as dynamic unfolding). This is the closure of metaphysics. Metaphysics has begun to spin and tremble, to turn. Closure brings the limit into contact with the withdrawal of the Same that marks the departure of every epoch within the history of metaphysics. And it does so more generally than the "end of philosophy" functioning in the Heideggerian text as a kind of eschatology.

In the discussion of Heidegger we saw the turning away and the turning toward of Dasein as a belonging together in the turning to and fro that I claim is crucial to the clearing circling of the Same. The swarming of gestures in the revolutionary turning of Saying is a generalized movement of language whereby the principle of identity ceases to rule and the crack in the purity of self-presence resonates and resides in differences, gesturing things bearing out the world. When philosophy reaches its closure it, likewise, may be said to tremble and shake in the manner of this wild and weird gesturing where trembling is the opening up of an abyss within the sign, its beginning to gesture, resonate, and remain in residence. Closure, therefore, marks the double gesture of turning to and fro in the Derridean text:

---

[35]We could call this a drawing tight of the line so that it begins to shake as a bungy would if tightened and strummed. This is the mutual acceptance of movement *concerning* or *on* the line and movement *across* it that I am here describing as a movement *over* the line.

> I try to keep myself at the *limit* of philosophical discourse. I say
> limit and not death, for I do not at all believe in what today is so
> easily called the death of philosophy......In my readings I try,
> therefore, by means of a necessarily double gesture......by means
> of this double play, marked in certain decisive places by an
> erasure which allows what it obliterates to be read, violently
> inscribing within the text that which attempted to govern it from
> without, I try to respect as rigorously as possible the internal,
> regulated play of philosophemes or epistimemes by making them
> slide — without mistreating them — to the point of their
> nonpertinence, their exhaustion, their closure. To 'deconstruct'
> philosophy, thus, would be to think—in the most faithful, interior
> way—the structured genealogy of philosophy's concepts, but at
> the same time to determine—from a certain exterior that is
> unqualifiable or unnamable by philosophy—what this history has
> been able to dissimulate or forbid, making itself into a history by
> means of this somewhere motivated repression. (*P*, 6)

This double gesture of turning toward and away from the discourse of
metaphysics is the project of deconstruction that sets out to delimit the
closure of metaphysics. The turning to and fro of the pacing deconstructor
of philosophy is an ec-static motion that makes everything tremble and
shake, that sets the whole structure of philosophy shaking not so as to kill
it but so as to make its death immanent in the body or corpus of the
tradition. That is, the shaking delimits the death of philosophy not as
death, but as the cracking fissure of the structure that realigns the text in
accordance with the play of signifiers. The double gesture overruns
philosophy with the secondarity of its past history and, since life was
always privileged along with the presence of the subject to itself in living
self-consciousness, with a sort of death. This double gesture neither
transcends philosophy nor succumbs to it, but does both at once so as to
capture philosophy in the play of what it has historically determined as
outside alien to the purity that is its privileged subject.

On the last few pages of "The Ends of Man" Derrida describes this
double gestured turning as an undecidable option between two strategies,
both of which, on their own, will fail to reach the closure of metaphysics.
On the one hand, there is the strategy "to attempt an exit and a
deconstruction without changing terrain" whereby one uses the tools of
metaphysics to deconstruct it, here a certain "autism of the closure" is
risked. On the other hand, there is the strategy "to decide to change
terrain, in a discontinuous and irruptive fashion, by brutally placing

oneself outside, and by affirming an absolute break and difference." Here the risk is that one will naively reinstate the problems one has attempted to escape (Cf. *M*, 135). Both options fall short of the deconstruction of metaphysics. Deciding either to exit on the same terrain or by changing terrain is to fall into error. The double gesture, therefore, is the withholding of the decision; instead, it employs both strategies as demonstrated in the cases of "writing" and "closure."

This double gesture is frequently called "writing under erasure" where on the one hand (rather *with* the one hand) one writes, while erasing with the other hand what is being written. What remains in this double act is the trace of writing: writing under erasure is tracing. Trace, as the tracing of writing, suggests the secondarity of writing that was dismissed in philosophy's search for the ground. For Derrida, every gesture at the closure of metaphysics is a double gesture, a writing under erasure. Recall the demonstration in chapter 2 where the thing and its name were described as gestures. If the signifier gestures and the play of signifiers unleashes a play of gestures, then the gesture doubles as the signifier does (world-thing and text-signifier). This doubling is the undecidability emerging in/from the two strategies, and not two clearly presented options each of which can be defined in its singular self-identity. The double is the equivocation of the tension of duality and the twofold. Every gesture is double in so far as world grants thing and thing bears out world. That is, they reside in their dif-ference, belonging together *there.* The signifier signifies playing while it plays, its play is the play of the Saying of the Same.[36] This already incites the step to the next section.

The Tradition Begins to Turn: an Economical Exchange.

Soliciting the tradition, shaking the whole that gathers in its closure, recalls all the traits (*Zug*) of Saying the Same: the vibrations of *er-eignis,* the strife of *a-letheia,* and the tension of dif-ference. The cracking open of the pure and simple presence of the tradition is the interdiction of dif-ference into the ground, the making abysmal of the solid ground (*Grundriß*). The image bears developing: the solid ground is made to shake, it quivers and quakes in this deconstruction delimiting closure. There is no end to the trembling once closure is effected, since that would

---

[36]This renewed understanding of language requires that all the lines of metaphysical texts be reread, since this dividing of the line would be as much as to rewrite them all under erasure.

indicate a recovery of the ground. Nor is there an end to the *solidness of the ground* that shakes in closure, since that would amount to the death of philosophy in the way Derrida has rejected. Rather, it must be said that the shaking of the ground is perpetual, better it is indefinite. This shaking is not the prelude to an emerging circling of the Same, rather the circling of the Same circles and turns in/as/through the shaking of the solid ground at/in its closure. In trembling, there is double gesturing, a turning.

Trembling dislodges the ground (effaces and erases it), at least it dislodges it in so far as it robs it of its firmness and the security of its solid foundation. It is a matter of life and death for philosophy, but it would be a mistake to choose to call it the death of philosophy. When death comes to inhabit the ground in such a way as to endure along with it in its every possibility, the ground is the impossibility of a ground: an abyss. This is not because the ground stands above the abyss like a ledge, but because any ground inhabited by such shaking can no longer remain solid; it swims and circles in the abysmal Saying of the clearing, it dies. This summary of Heidegger and Derrida on the dying ground reveals a trait of their proximity. It is time to investigate their nearness with specific reference to Derrida. This is required because it marks a moment in what might preliminarily be called a "tradition of the death of philosophy." Examining this in its various facets will shed light on the notion of tradition in general as well as the turning of the tradition that continues at/in philosophy's closure.

In a questionable move, I am not going to focus explicitly on the remarks Derrida makes directly concerning Heidegger and his own relation to the project opened up by Heidegger's thinking. Although I will occasionally refer to those remarks in other contexts, I will not make this section into an ordinary...on Derrida on Heidegger discussion. In fact, I will claim that such approaches are flawed in principle and that even Derrida's own remarks specifically addressing Heidegger sometimes participate in this same error. When Derrida turns toward Heidegger in an effort to deconstruct and delimit the closure of philosophy, he does exactly what he says he will not do (in a violently disregarded context): "We are not going to emprison all of Heidegger's text in a closure that this text has delimited better than any other" (*M*, 123).[37] Put simply, when

---

[37]The phrase "all of" may rescue Derrida from this error and it is this "all of" that may eventually force me to focus more and more on the direct relation as it appears in Derrida's writing. This "error" in Derrida should not cover over the fact that I think that his texts have done more than anyone else's to suggest the reading of Heidegger performed throughout my project.

Derrida writes *about* Heidegger, he occasionally runs the risk of objectifying a text that has called all such objectification into question. But no doubt this raises suspicions concerning my own essay. It is in these suspicions that the question concerning the "tradition of the death of philosophy" acquires its full gravity.

Derrida's project moves in the direction of the play of the world or clearing as it plays in its play (it is possible to call this play an economy so long as we understand that such an economy is totally without restriction, a general economy). In "The End of Philosophy and the Task of Thinking," Heidegger describes clearing as *spielraum*. This is a word that, strictly speaking, says "playspace" although leeway, free space, or free play are more commonly used in the various translations. As descriptions, Heidegger is frequently claiming that his works come up short. At the end of some of the essays (like *On Time and Being* and "The Onto-Theo-Logical Constitution of Metaphysics"), he withdraws from what has preceded by alluding to the failure of his language to remain adequate to the matter discussed in the essay. Derrida's project attempts to remark on precisely this point in Heidegger's discourse. Derrida is trying, in a radical way, to depart from the presence of an inscription that follows upon any ordinarily conceived description. It is his task to erase the marks made in such a project so that the inscription remains a trace of the erased mark that frees play without constraining and restricting it with the presence of a definitely intelligible mark.[38]

> Is not Nietzsche's thought a critique of philosophy as an
> active indifference to difference, as the system of adiaphoristic

---

Derrida's name, no doubt, must be written in the margins of the entire last twenty years of Heidegger scholarship.

[38]The trace remains, withdraws, and so the movement in the circling of the Same or "writing" is one that is not characterized by perfect calculations or accounting (where everything that is can be accounted for by the ground, where the ground is that which accounts for everything that is). Where existence is limited to what can be accounted for, the economy of movement is restricted. When something remains over and above what lies in the accounts, it is general. Furthermore, the economy of exchange, economy where all circulation occurs on the basis of exchange (is accounted for by exchange), is restricted economy. Derrida says in *Given Time* in reference to Marcel Mauss' book *The Gift* that economies where there is a remainder, where not everything can be accounted, are economies of the gift (that is, a general economy). This is also where Derrida makes an explicit connection between the gift understood as remainder and Heidegger's discourse on *Ereignis*. Cf. especially, chapters one and two.

reduction or repression? Which according to the same logic, according to logic itself, does not exclude that philosophy lives *in* and *on différance,* thereby blinding itself to the *same,* which is not the identical. The same, precisely, is *différance* (with an *a*) as the displaced and equivocal passage of one different thing to another, from one term of an opposition to the other. (*M,* 17)[39]

This is in the context of reading Nietzsche as a member of the "tradition of the death of philosophy," a reading that it is not possible to perform here. At the closure of metaphysics, the presence privileged throughout its history will be shown to rest on the repression of its own dynamic unfolding. That is, in a sense, there never was any presence as metaphysics proposed it. The closure of metaphysics delimits the fissure surrounding metaphysics as its limit since the beginning. Derrida gives a name to this fissure of metaphysics' closure: *différance.* In/as/through a way, *différance* circles metaphysics as its limit; and does so always already, not as something that only begins in the end, but that has always been playing with the history of metaphysics.

This may suggest that *différance,* the crack in the foundation, is some kind of origin, the primal source of the discourse of the West now some two and half millennia old. This logic of the origin is no doubt necessary for the first few steps on the path of delimiting the closure of metaphysics, but we must not be fooled into taking these steps too quickly. The logic of the origin permeates Heidegger's first awkward steps along this way (i.e., *Being and Time*). Heidegger, in that work, seems to be seeking out the primordial or originary ground of Being (i.e., its sense or meaning). But even there, Heidegger is aware that the ground

---

[39]The passage continues: "Thus one could reconsider all the pairs of opposites on which philosophy is constructed and on which our discourse lives, not in order to see opposition erase itself but to see what indicates that each of the terms must appear as the *différance* of the other, as the other different and deferred in the economy of the same (the intelligible as differing-deferring the sensible, as the sensible different and deferred; the concept as different and deferred, differing-deferring intuition; culture as nature different and deferred, differing-deferring; all the others of *physis-techne, nomos, thesis,* society, freedom, history, mind, etc.—as *physis* different and deferred, or as *physis* differing and deferring. *Physis* in *différance.* And in this way we may see the site of a reinterpretation of *mimesis* in its alleged opposition to *physis)*. And on the basis of this unfolding of the same as *différance,* we see announced the sameness of *différance* and repetition in the eternal return" (*M,* 17).

is going to be very unusual, very different from what has come to be expected historically from the ground. Ecstatic temporality, a temporality that stands outside of itself in all its dimensions (and therefore moves even when standing still), hardly resembles a simple ground. It is not governed by purity or presence and the dynamic, in it that enables whatever exists to be, is essentially inhabited by nothingness. Time makes a slippery ground: it flows as a source making the earth muddy. It might be possible to begin deconstructive investigations by thinking of *différance* as an origin, but *différance* eventually elides this possibility. As a ground, it provides no solid footing.

Différance recalls writing as described in the previous section. Derrida calls any writing that inhabits the ground while transforming it "archi-writing," since *arche* suggests "origin" while writing incites the secondarity from the origin, the being-removed from what is original. Archi-writing names the movement of *différance* understood as the opening of the open, the play of language that takes place in *différance* as an archi-writing. This same movement is still further named by the archi-trace. The movement of *différance,* the archi-tracing, and the archi-writing all say the Same.

> For example, the value of the transcendental *arche* must make its necessity felt before letting itself be erased. The concept of archi-trace must comply with both that necessity and that erasure. It is in fact contradictory and not acceptable within the logic of identity. The trace is not only the disappearance of origin—within the discourse that we sustain and according to the path that we follow it means that the origin did not even disappear, that it was never constituted except reciprocally by a nonorigin, the trace, which thus becomes the origin of the origin. From then on, to wrench the concept of the trace from the classical scheme, which would derive it from presence or from an originary nontrace and which would make of it an empirical mark, one must indeed speak of an originary trace or archi-trace. Yet we know that that concept destroys its name and that, if all begins with the trace, there is above all no originary trace. (*OG*, 61)[40]

---

[40]Derrida's claim is that philosophy must make its way to the thinking of the trace through the medium of a certain transcendental idealism. The Being of the sensible is first thought in terms of a transcendental signified that governs the whole economy of the world that it transcends. Once this is thought, for instance in Kant and in the early Heidegger, the transcendental signified is ready to be erased. Only once it has been thought properly can it be erased. This erasure occurs in the manner of a supplement: the

But these names all run the risk of objectifying what they name, of reifying the ground into one more master name in a still further sending of Being as an epoch of metaphysical history. And yet all these names run this risk together. Derrida grants innumerable names to the movement of *différance* that cracks the ground of metaphysics. Trace, *différance,* interdiction, hymen, spacing, supplement, and so on and on. All these names say the Same, and in so doing they say nothing. They never make their meaning present because their meaning always indicates a further fleshing out in another naming. Trace indicates *différance* which suggests interdiction which invokes the hymen which moves in the direction of a spacing which still further gestures toward supplement. The meaning is always deferred, the chain of signifiers is continually deferring, never ceasing, maintaining its play throughout the texts of Derrida. This dynamic, this play of *différance* and the Same, points us in the direction of the circling in Heidegger's discourse. We can never rest comfortably, as though we were in complete understanding; rather, meaning and understanding are always just over the next hill, just past the next signifier. This is the play of *différance.* Its playfulness, offering no security, threatens us with the greatest danger, it threatens to drive us mad.

But why should we accept this play? Why should we believe that the presence of all that has been said in Western metaphysics has been enmeshed in an endless play all this time and only the repressive regime of signifiers enabled philosophers to understand this history as firmly grounded (or the history of a firm ground)? In a very important sense, this is the work of deconstruction. Deconstruction's task at the closure of metaphysics is to inhabit the texts of the history of philosophy. When Derrida goes to work on Plato, or Descartes, or Husserl, he very carefully explores their texts in an effort to discover the cracks and fissures in them.

---

transcendental signified is supplemented and as supplement (or trace or *différance,* etc.) it cannot *be* a transcendental signified anymore, it cannot *be* anything at all, it remains only differing and deferring itself. "The supplement comes in the place of a lapse, a nonsignified or a nonrepresented, a nonpresence. There is no present before it, it is not preceded by anything but itself, that is to say by another supplement. The supplement is always the supplement of a supplement. One wishes to go back *from the supplement to the source:* one must recognize that there is *a supplement at the source*" (*OG,* 303-4). Such a supplement must, of necessity, elide the givenness of the given so as to make it questionable, to circulate it in questioning (i.e., the Saying of the Same) Cf. further on in this section when the matter of the supplement is addressed.

He looks to Plato's degradation of writing only to find that there is a writing in the soul that grounds the presence of the soul to the forms, he looks at Descartes and discovers that the self-presence of the *cogito* (true in the self-presence of each instance of its being uttered) depends on a journey through madness in hyperbolical doubt, and he reads Husserl to discover in the living present of the transcendental reduction a trace structure of temporality that calls that same reduction into question.[41] Derrida proceeds very carefully to show that the values of *différance* et al. are demoted to secondary roles in texts emphasizing certain originary values that are possible only on the basis of some capacity for differentiation.[42]

In doing this, Derrida deconstructs the primary metaphysical texts of the history of philosophy. He deconstructs them, he shows that they rely on *différance* to make their points and yet in making these same points displace *différance,* banish it to a "fallen" role. Deconstruction cracks the foundation of the origin in the texts of metaphysics, cracks the Being of beings dominating the texts ruling metaphysical discourse. Deconstruction brings about the same closure that it reveals, it makes it happen by showing that it has always already happened. This active and passive role of deconstruction is the movement of *différance.* "*First, différance* refers to the (active *and* passive) movement that consists in deferring by means of delay, delegation, reprieve, referral, detour, postponement, reserving" (*P*, 8).[43]

----

[41]Cf. "Plato's Pharmacy" in *Dissemination,* "Cogito and the History of Madness" in *Writing and Difference,* and *Speech and Phenomena.*

[42] In my experience of discussing Derrida's project with philosophers trained in the recent Anglo-American Analytic tradition, I have noticed an overwhelming prejudice on their part to force all discussion of deconstruction into the realm of evaluating a theory. And this is usually done instead of actually addressing and engaging the specific readings that Derrida performs of traditional philosophical positions. Of course, I argue that Derrida is not developing a theory and so will be fundamentally misunderstood when he is engaged in these terms. When, in these discussions, I have recounted the actual moves made by Derrida in his reading of thinkers like Plato and Descartes, I find that those with whom I am speaking find it much more difficult to wave aside his view with some pat phrase about how Derrida "isn't doing philosophy."

[43]Cf. also: "The gram as *différance,* then, is a structure and a movement no longer conceivable on the basis of the opposition presence/absence. *Différance* is the systematic play of differences, of the traces of differences, of the *spacing* by means of which elements are related to each other. This spacing is the simultaneously active and passive (the *a* of *différance* indicates

These indications point to the beginning of the discussion on Derrida, where the signifier was delimited in its play as both signifying other signifiers and embodying the whole of the text's *différance* so as to give it the force of its signification. This post-structuralist view of language, the circling of the Saying of the Same, is no doubt the most important component of philosophy's deconstruction. Only with such an understanding of language can deconstruction move, deconstruction's movement is this Saying of language.

It may be asked at this point, carefully, whether or not there is anything at all besides the closure of metaphysics? Even carefully, however, any asking after the other of metaphysics that seeks to reduce metaphysics out of the picture in a clean and simple way is going to make an error similar to the ones Derrida described while asserting the necessary double gesture of deconstruction. The closure of metaphysics is a site, a spacing opening in clearing where metaphysics reaches its limit, inhabiting it indefinitely. "What is held within the demarcated closure may continue indefinitely" (*P*, 13). and "Transgression implies that the limit is always at work" (*P*, 12). We are, no doubt, over the line in the way that one can be said to be "over a barrel" (perhaps balancing on a *tight* rope?). Clearly, since thought of the transgression will no longer assist us in the deconstruction of metaphysics, we are going to have to relearn thinking. Derrida says this very clearly in a passage that echoes Heideggerian reverberations:

> The constitution of a science or a philosophy of writing is a necessary and difficult task. But, a *thought* of the trace, of *différance* or of reserve, having arrived at these limits and repeating them ceaselessly, must also point beyond the field of the *episteme*. Outside of the economic and strategic reference to the name that Heidegger justifies himself in giving to an analogous but not identical transgression of all philosophemes, *thought* is here for me a perfectly neutral name, the blank part of the text, the necessarily indeterminate index of a future epoch of

this indecision as concerns activity and passivity, that which cannot be governed by or distributed between the terms of this opposition) production of the intervals without which the 'full' terms would not signify, would not function. It is also the becoming-space of the spoken chain—which has been called temporal or linear; a becoming-space which makes possible both writing and every correspondence between speech and writing, every passage from one to the other" (*P*, 27). This passage also recalls the argument in the introduction for the manner of proceeding in my project. "Systematic play" is almost a paradox and yet its movement governs deconstructive movement.

> *différance. In a certain sense, 'thought' means nothing.* Like all openings, this index belongs within a past epoch by the face that is open to view. This thought has no weight. It is, in the play of the system, that very thing which never has weight. Thinking is what we already know we have not yet begun; measured against the shape of writing, it is broached only in the *episteme. (OG*, 93)

This new task for thinking already signifies what must come to meet us at some point along the way of this project. For now, I can only emphasize the importance language plays in this thinking. The problem that followed us into this section was the problem regarding the extent to which language dictated the impossibility of metaphysics' closure because of the metaphysical conception of language which has ruled the history of the West. This task for thinking will occur necessarily in the midst of language. I have already shown that Derrida understands deconstruction as exemplified in the rigorous and specific readings of the texts of Western metaphysics. Deconstruction discovers and reveals the fissures in these texts by examining the way that language has been used throughout the history of philosophy. It is no surprise that for the most part deconstruction has been understood as a literary strategy for precisely these reasons. But literature is not here, as it was for Aristotle, opposed to thought since the duality of language and thought is essential to metaphysics. In the reading of deconstruction, thinking takes place. Therefore, when metaphysics reaches its closure in the deconstruction of its texts, something is happening (coming to pass) in language and in thinking. The deconstruction of metaphysics is always the deconstruction of its texts and hence a deconstruction of its language, its thought, and the difference between them. The soliciting of the history of metaphysics is a shaking of the *whole* of metaphysics.[44]

The transformation from speech to writing enables this shaking. This does not mean that only written words matter in the task of thinking or that only cultures with written languages can be said to think, but that writing as the movement of *différance* is the way language dynamically unfolds. This holds true whether that language is written or spoken or

---

[44] Aside from suggesting that deconstruction is always the deconstruction of metaphysics (which will be discussed more clearly later on), this also suggests the manner in which the ongoing systematic structure of the "nothing other" is dissolved in turning. One cannot say that there is nothing other than metaphysics because there is deconstruction. Likewise, one cannot say that there is nothing other than deconstruction, because there is metaphysics. Furthermore, one cannot even say that there is nothing other than the deconstruction of metaphysics because—quite to the contrary—this is something other.

whatever. Writing becomes the most general economic term, so that all regional economies or play occur in/as/through the movement of *différance* expressed in writing. *Différance,* the word, already gestures in this direction when it is noted that the difference between *différance* and difference cannot be heard or spoken, but can only be recognized in writing or in the deferred spoken gesture (i.e., "with an 'a'" or "with an 'e'"). Writing becomes the name of that thinking which must be worked out as a task: "The *a* of *différance,* thus, is not heard; it remains silent, secret and discreet as a tomb: *oikesis.* And thereby lets us anticipate the delineation of a site, the familial residence and tomb of the proper in which is produced, by *différance*, the *economy of death"* (*M,* 4).

The economy of the Same is the economy of death as this was explored previously concerning the closure of philosophy. The Greek *oikesis* indicates "tomb" while *oikos* indicates "house." *Oikos* is combined with *nemein* meaning "to manage" to form "economy." Here is a point of proximity between Derrida and Heidegger: Derrida understands the economy as the site of the closure of metaphysics governed by the "proper" suggesting presence. The tomb marks the grave site and is inscribed with writing in some way: an epitaph. Economy, therefore, names deconstruction in so far as deconstruction brings about the closure of metaphysics, delimits it by placing it within its tomb, by marking its grave with an inscription.[45] In Heidegger's "Letter on Humanism," economy plays a major role as well. Of course, this is where Heidegger formulates the famous catch phrase "Language is the house of Being." House suggests *oikos*. In this same essay Heidegger makes mention of *nemein* claiming its traditional understanding to be that of "law." He replaces this traditional meaning with "assign" and goes on to say that "*Nomos* is not only law but more originally the assignment contained in the dispensation of Being" (*BW,* 238). Economy therefore becomes the home of this assignment of Being's dispensation. Economy economizes as the Saying of the Same that is the language housing Being in its sending opening clearing. Adding to this Derrida's meaning as the economy of death in the tomb of the proper at metaphysics' closure, there is an excellent starting point for the investigation into the relation of Derrida and Heidegger.

---

[45]The inscription is a "silent a" which displaces the metaphysically thought "a" of *a-peiron, a priori, a* rational, and even *a letheia.* The displacement occurs in the "a" always sounding an "e" in the moment of its being written "a": a double gesture.

Derrida's meaning supplements Heidegger's, where supplement is understood as a trait in all deconstruction and the movement of *différance* as turning and circling. Derrida's meaning supplements Heidegger's by adding to it *and* by replacing it. It is both an addition *and* a substitution: supplement carries out both of these significations. "The supplement adds itself, it is a surplus, a plenitude enriching another plenitude, the *fullest measure* of presence" (*OG*, 144). "But the supplement supplements. It adds only to replace. It intervenes or insinuates itself *in-the-place-of;* it fills, it is as if one fills a void" (*OG*, 145). For Derrida to supplement Heidegger he must be added to him *and* he must take his place. It would be a mistake to choose between these two options of supplement, it would be better to think the equivocation of these meanings. Doing so recognizes Derrida's relationship to Heidegger as supplementary suggesting both addition and replacement. This supplementarity is the "tradition of the death of philosophy," and it is the deconstruction of tradition itself.

All tradition operates as supplement. Perhaps when certain traditionally minded philosophers try to reduce the whole of philosophy to a footnote, it is precisely this sort of supplementation that they have in mind. Aristotle and the rest of the West, from the Epicureans onward, supplement Plato. There is, strangely enough, some truth in this claim. But only if we recognize that Plato too is only a supplement. The very idea of the corpus of a philosopher is a supplementary notion. A text is always a fabric work, a play of signifiers operating in the manner of *différance.* For this reason, a corpus—which is a text—is always supplemental. It is never present anywhere in and of itself; thus no one body of work can stand at the origin of philosophy, at philosophy's origin there is only supplement (which is not to say that anyone would be wanting more).[46]

Metaphysics has always been late in getting started, it has always begun in retrospect: even its name suggests this. Perhaps it is for this reason that the name of metaphysics is coupled with the names of history

---

[46]The body has been traditionally viewed as supplement, the *res extensa* outside the certain realm of the *cogito*, and this characteristic connects the body with the materiality of the physical world in its secondarity. No doubt this move toward the supplement, where the body supplements the mind that is the essential identity in the history of metaphysics, is a crucial feature linking this discourse to the Marxian. Yet I have to be careful to avoid merely performing a metaphysical displacement of the *res cogitans* in this move: I am not going to accept a mind-body binary so as to reduce one to the other. The logic of the supplement is a move to the undecidability *between* these two terms in the binary. This will be explored in more detail in the following chapters.

and tradition. This is, at least in part, because traditions occur in their being passed on from one generation to another; tradition always takes place *between* generations, in the movement from one generation to another. As such, traditions are always arriving too late, are always taking place too late in their repetition by another generation — in their being supplemented (notice that two of the significations of supplement suggest the presence and absence of the beginning, respectively). Metaphysics, tradition, and history all fall into this retrospective structure in such a way as to suggest that they are each without foundation, without beginning or origin. All are, at bottom, supplemental.

At this time it is appropriate to recall that curious "all of" which Derrida adds to his statement about emprisoning Heidegger in the closure he has delimited. Derrida's remarks concerning Heidegger always have this strange equivocation. Consider the remarks, mentioned earlier in the chapter, concerning Derrida's claim that he "sometimes" thinks that Heidegger is "perhaps" the greatest defender of presence. Why sometimes? Why perhaps? Derrida can never make up his mind about Heidegger, he can never decide how to read him. I could easily be banal and claim that he always maintains a *certain* undecidability regarding Heidegger. At every turn, Derrida places Heidegger within the proximity of the history of metaphysics and as no less caught in the movement of that same tradition although he is never able to nail shut the casket. He always seems to retreat a little from his claims, he does so in *Of Grammatology* and he continues to do so in the essays in *Margins*. This turning to and fro of Derrida in relation to Heidegger, this failure to make a decision, appears to be bad philosophical judgment when understood in terms of the logic of identity. Thought within the logic of the supplement, it makes perfect sense. Derrida cannot make up his mind, he adds to Heidegger, he replaces him. Derrida cannot make up his mind concerning the entire history of philosophy: he adds to it, he replaces it; his supplement brings it to its closure. It is possible to make these same claims regarding Heidegger.[47]

---

[47]These remarks are informed by a multitude of current studies on this issue. Cf. Caputo's *Radical Hermeneutics* where he discusses the "almost" that follows every particular critical discussion of Heidegger in Derrida's texts. Cf. also Herman Rapaport's *Heidegger and Derrida* (Lincoln, NE: The University of Nebraska Press, 1989) from which I have taken the image of the to and fro (*fort/da*) with regard to Derrida's relation to Heidegger. One might also check the remarks made by Derrida in the discussion after David Wood's paper entitled "Heidegger after Derrida." These remarks were

Supplementarity becomes the logic of the economy opened at the closure of philosophy. Time's movement supplements, history's movement supplements: so too nature, culture, world, man, space, entities etc. Everything once ruled by the propriety of metaphysics is released in the supplemental movement of the Same in/as/through *différance*. Supplementarity becomes the turning, the circling of language as Saying the Same. But this supplementarity is disseminated in the moment of Saying. The logic of the supplement is not a logic, properly speaking. It multiplies and fans out in the moment of Saying (writing). The supplement suggests *différance* and dissemination and trace and spacing, and, and, and... — indefinitely. Supplement is not a label given to a present thing that stands at the origin of Western thought. It is, like all signifiers, a double gesture that doubles and redoubles, that multiplies and differs in its deferring.

In this matter, an additional way that Derrida supplements Heidegger is demonstrated. The bold claim worked out in the first two chapters must be supplemented by Derrida. The claim where Saying takes place supplements indefinitely. Saying even disappears in favor of what is added to it. The text, the trace, discourse, the supplement, writing, etc. all weave their way into the claiming of the bold claim so as to add to and take the place of the naming that happens there: "Dissemination *affirms* (I do not say produces or controls) endless substitution, it neither arrests nor controls play ('Castration—in play always...'). And in doing so, runs all the risks, but without the metaphysical or romantic pathos of negativity" (*P*, 86).[48] The risk that occurs in the supplement recalls the

---

reprinted in *Research in Phenomenology,* vol. XVII.

[48]Not just any terms can play in this endless substituting. Only terms that are what Derrida calls "undecidable" can be implemented in this supplementarity. These are the terms that delimit the leeway (*spielraum)* of metaphysics, where the classical binary oppositions of metaphysics gain their determination. This undecidability recalls Heidegger's "belonging together." *Ousia* could not be supplemented in this chain since it works within its own chain of signifiers recalling the proper names of the transcendental signifieds. Substance (*ousia)* participates in a relation with the subject, they belong together just as *res cogitans* and *res extensa* do. These oppositional terms cannot be made to signify in the chain of supplementarity although "belong together" can along with *a-letheia,* dif-ference and *er-eignis.* This "restriction" on language is not a restriction, it is the play of language as turning circling. The claim that language signifies in supplementary chains does not reduce to the claim that any signifier can function in any signification. This movement of *différance* is what I am calling the logic of

danger of technological nihilism. We have arrived, after all, at the dangerous supplement.

The supplement, endlessly substituting and risktaking, is dangerous. "The supplement is maddening because it is neither presence nor absence and because it consequently breaches both our pleasure and our virginity" (*OG*, 154). The danger of the supplement comes in the course of a reading of Rousseau. Without going into the details of that reading (which would take us too far from our current theme), I will mention that in the course of this reading Derrida discovers the danger of the supplement described in Rousseau's work. It "is dangerous in that it threatens us with death" (*OG*, 155). The relation between the supplement and death weighs still heavier on thinking and shall require a detailed discussion. Hopefully, this can be deferred a little longer. For now it is enough to venture one more point of proximity between Heidegger and Derrida: the danger of the supplement that risks everything in venturing into the closure of philosophy.

(It should at least be noted, however, that this danger of the supplement is its danger to philosophy. Philosophy as the metaphysics of presence is threatened and endangered by the supplement which marks its death. This threat of the supplement explains the consistent degrading of writing, *différance,* etc. The pure origin of philosophy degrades the supplement because it fears it, because it threatens the rule of philosophy, threatens it in its foundations. The important question for Derrida and the deconstruction of philosophy is, why philosophy has been threatened all along by supplementarity and why philosophy has sought to protect itself through the secondarity of *différance*? The question is deferred most convincingly when it is asked in the most misleading way: is deconstruction the psychoanalysis of philosophy? the examination of philosophy so as to confront its repressed motives?)

At this moment, beyond the dangerous parentheses, all objectification is supplemented. The entity understood as an object can no longer stand present in its presence to a subject, but begins to trace in the *différance* of a continually deferred presence. This captures the object in the play of the world and strips it severely from its isolation standing opposite the subject. This rending free of the object from its objectivity happens in the cracks of metaphysics, as its cracking open. I have suggested before that this is the thing: "The field of the entity, before being determined as the field of presence, is structured according to the

---

supplementarity while realizing that there is a double gesture at work in calling this logic (the two senses of *logos).*

diverse possibilities—genetic and structural—of the trace. The presentation of the other as such, that is to say the dissimulation of its 'as such,' has always already begun and no structure of the entity escapes it" (*OG*, 47). This field of supplementarity and the trace (clearing) cannot be comprehended in the "as such" that is proper to all entities, including the objectivity of the object. The turning that occurs in the turning between Derrida and Heidegger is the turning of this field of the entity. This between and this field cannot be considered as any kind of determined entity, object or otherwise. No objectification of the field (opening) is characteristic of the clearing. Of course, I could say this over and over again until I have filled several volumes, but the words do not counterbalance the tendency of language to carry out this objectification. The deconstruction of metaphysics cannot be merely semantic, it must be syntactic as well. The predicate structure of the sentence, I have mentioned this before but its new context supplements the discussion, adheres to a certain hearing of Being in its grounded sending. We cannot bring about the closure of metaphysics without challenging the extent to which metaphysics even inhabits our grammar.[49]

This informs the suggestion earlier regarding Derrida's sometimes professed relation to Heidegger and the same issue regarding my project's relation to both Heidegger and Derrida. For Derrida to slide into some kinds of discussions about Heidegger is to objectify what ought to be maintained as a supplement. When Derrida objectifies Heidegger, he is most definitely not supplementing him. Derrida sometimes refers to his own turning to and fro relative to Heidegger as a "deconstruction" and no doubt it is just that at times. But it is also not that at all. For example, when Derrida turns his attention to Heidegger's discussion of *ereignis* in his essay "The Ends of Man," he criticizes Heidegger on the basis of proximity and the proper in so far as it participates in the logic of

---

[49]There are numerous places where this sort of issue can be found, not only in Derrida and Heidegger but in Nietzsche as well. This issue will be the focus in what follows. There are all sorts of ways to avoid propositional language within the techniques of rhetoric. As should have become apparent in the course of the last two hundred or so pages, I am attempting to do so through tropic development. "Trope" suggests circles, tricks, turns, metaphors, etc. To write or think tropically is to develop themes without explicitly stating them, but by making a suggestion, then moving on, and then circling back through the use of a related trope (or the same trope in a related context, or a new context). This approach is familiar in novels and poetry but not ordinarily thought as the dominant motif in philosophy. When deconstructors say that philosophy is literature, they might be understood to mean that the themes in the work develop in this same tropic way.

metaphysics and identity. Nearness also holds a key role in this critical reading, in so far as the proximity of nearness is supposed to suggest presence. But surely Derrida is aware that even, in a specifically Derridean sense, presence fails to suggest presence. That is, presence is supplemented at the closure of philosophy. Therefore, it is possible to speak of a constituted presence that doesn't even embody the privilege of the present proper to metaphysics. To merely say that Heidegger's notion of *er-eignis* and nearness participate in a metaphysics of presence without an examination that seeks the extent to which they turn these very notions into a Saying circling of the Same, is to fail to deconstruct him just at the moment when Derrida says most strongly that he *is* deconstructing him. That is, Derrida does not consider the extent to which Heidegger draws the relation that *er-eignis* and nearness have to dif-ference and the Same.[50] Nonetheless, in the moments when Derrida takes up a deconstructive relation to Heidegger he is brilliant.

Regarding my project in its relation to the two figures of deconstruction, it no doubt fails at being supplementary on a variety of levels. The previous paragraph, for example, allows the extent to which objectification occurs in handling these two figures to surface in the clearest way. Derrida is placed alongside Heidegger in sentences such as "When Derrida objectifies Heidegger, he is most definitely not supplementing him." The objectification of Heidegger is predicated of Derrida who acts as subject in the sentence, agent and author of the activity. This objectification stands the two up next to each other in a clearly delimited relationship of presence. Of course, this obvious occasion of objectification does not consume and exhaust the text in this place or any other — that would be contrary to the principles at stake here. The citation circles within language in so far as the whole language emerges in the signification of the sentence. No doubt the metaphysical grammar of my project thus far makes it yield frequently to an obvious display of metaphysical relations and the objectification of its subject matter. Even still, even at its most metaphysical moments, this text surrenders to deconstruction.[51]

---

[50]It is interesting that Derrida is aware of these sorts of plays in Heidegger's texts with regard to the use of "Same" which no doubt suggests a certain identity. It is therefore quite impossible to try and give a *reason* for Derrida's strange readings.

[51]For the moment this deconstruction takes the form of the sentence "The cited sentence circles within language in so far as the whole language emerges in the signification of the sentence." This is insufficient, but acts as

In the wake of supplementarity, in the trace it marks/makes as it moves along the way of *différance,* the turning of circling in Saying the Same takes place. This turning is not something that happens beyond the tradition of Western metaphysics nor as a tradition beyond the history of philosophy. Rather, it is the tradition itself which begins turning in this playful economy. Tradition succumbs to the supplement, is supplemented by it, and thus begins its turning at the moment *(augenblick)* of closure. Tradition is made to shake and its trembling takes place *(ereignet)* in the endless chain of the supplement. Strictly (and, hence, properly) speaking, there is no "tradition of the death of philosophy." Instead, we must speak of the supplement which supplements tradition at the moment of its closure. In the dangerous supplementary realization of philosophy's closure the tradition as such is overwhelmed by its death (which is not to say that it dies: perhaps I am evoking a moment of *angst)*. Death—the other that lurks in the shadows of all the movement of *différance*—is inscribed in the heart of philosophy as its death. This inscription on the tomb of philosophy marks the burial of its tradition and no doubt all the great monuments of its history will be turning over in their graves.

---

a clue to what would come next. The sentence in question circulates within language save for two words which seem to have been wrenched from language: "Derrida" and "Heidegger." Essential to the sentence's objectification is the dependence of the propriety of the names "Derrida" and "Heidegger." The deconstruction would have to move in this direction and would perhaps already take us in the direction of what has been demonstrated in this section of the essay. After all, as I already mentioned, what is there to either of these two names but their corpus, their body of works — all the texts signifying in their names? Perhaps, this essay — frequently presenting itself in the manner of objectification—is also embarking upon its own deconstruction? In so far as this can be said to happen, I have to admit that this is how it always takes place. All texts deconstruct themselves, make themselves tremble. This further supports the ongoing theme of language's play being beyond the control of anything like an author's intention (i.e., in the case of the "choosing one word over another") and supplements the argument that the play has its own rules and cannot be restricted by some one region or participant in the game. All writing, including this essay, is therefore an offering of one's body or corpus to the dance and play of Heraclitus' "ever-living fire" which burns the pages on the funeral pyre of the text.

Hermes and his Rogues: a Messenger of Death and the Abyss.

Plato gives us one of the oldest examples of a Western thinker who dismissed writing, and difference, to a secondary role in matters of truth and wisdom. In "Plato's Pharmacy," Derrida recounts the manner in which this is done in the dialogue with "Phaedrus." After discussing the crucial use Socrates makes of the Egyptian myth of Theuth who brought writing (among other things) to the King of Egypt, Thamus, only to have it rejected because the king thought it would allow the people to grow forgetful by supplementing their memories, Derrida turns his attention completely to this bringer of poisonous gifts. The interlude marks the multiple names of this God: "The Filial Inscription: Theuth, Hermes, Thoth, Nabû, Nebo."[52] We have encountered this demi-god before in Heidegger, but always under the guise of its Greek name, Hermes, the message bearer of the gods who brings the word into the open.[53] I can now round off the discussion of the turning and circling of Heidegger and Derrida by following Derrida closely in his description of this mytheme in Plato, he does so under the name of Thoth.[54]

---

[52]Cf. *Dissemination,* pp. 84-94 for this section and pp. 61-171 for "Plato's Pharmacy."

[53]Cf. "Dialogue on Language" pp. 29-32, 40, 54 in *On the Way to Language* and chapter 2 above.

[54]It is no doubt significant to both Heidegger and Derrida that many of the crucial moments in Plato's arguments take the form of myth, especially because the history of metaphysics ordinarily understands myth in opposition to the rational understanding of the *logos* (the traditional understanding of Heraclitus subservient to the principle of identity and translated into Latin as *ratio*). How could the first thinker of rationality (if we can really understand Plato in that way) so regularly perform his arguments in the form of a *mythos*? It must, at this point, be left an open question whether this demonstrates the deconstructionist claim that every text trembles at the closure of philosophy or that it just proves that whatever else is the case, Plato is not the first thinker of the history of metaphysics. There is textual evidence in both Heidegger and Derrida supporting both of these views: 1) that Plato's text is in tension with itself and 2) that Plato's text is to be distinguished from neo-Platonism which is properly speaking the foundation of metaphysics. This pair of possibilities is undecidable and—most likely—it is precisely Plato's tensions that enable neo-Platonic metaphysics *and* the deconstruction at its closure.

> No doubt the god Thoth had several faces, belonged to several eras, lived in several homes. The discordant tangle of mythological accounts in which he is caught should not be neglected. Nevertheless, certain constants can be distinguished throughout, drawn in broad letters with firm strokes. One would be tempted to say that these constitute the permanent identity of this god in the pantheon, if his function, as we shall see, were not precisely to work at the subversive dislocation of identity in general, starting with that of theological regality. (*D*, 86)

Thoth has no identity because he is the god of non-identity. He is the god who introduced the plurality of languages. And what is more, he is the god of difference within language according to Plato's *Philebus*. Reigning over the difference between languages and the difference within language, Derrida claims, "are inseparable" (D 89). What's more, this god of difference and non-identity who brings the gift of writing that poisons memory is a mediator. He is a messenger for a greater and higher god whose word he carries. This god is Ammon-Ra, the sun god of Egypt. Thoth is his messenger and his eldest son. He needs a messenger because he is hidden: Ammon is similar in sound to the Egyptian word for "to hide" "to conceal oneself" (Derrida cites S. Sauneron's *Les Prêtes de l'ancienne Egypte* p. 127). Ammon-Ra is the great falcon that is both origin of the egg and the egg itself as origin of everything. The concealed egg, Ammon-Ra who is the origin of all that is, summons his eldest son Thoth one day and bids him to replace him and thus be called: "Thoth, he who replaces Ra" (*D*, 89: Derrida cites A. Erman's *La Religion des Egyptiens)*. As supplement for Ra-Ammon, Thoth bears the message of this creator: in this way, Thoth comes to be the god of the moon who replaces the sun when it is hidden and which bears the message of its shining.

The supplemental nature of Thoth puts him in the company of much scheming and trickery going on in the world. He is the "clever intermediary, ingenious and subtle enough to steal, and always to steal away" (*D*, 88). And he also "frequently participates in plots, perfidious intrigues, conspiracies to usurp the throne" (*D*, 89). He is the patron god of sons who kill their fathers, brothers who gang up to kill their fathers, and brothers who kill their brothers: all in an effort to become king, to replace the reign of the old *arche*. Thoth is also a god with the power of calculation and thus the institution of the calendar. As such, he assisted the goddess Nout in her battle with Ra who blocked the sun from her and thus robbed her of all time. Thoth gave her a supplementary time that enabled her to have children who would later become king in place of Geb favored by Ra. Osiris, one of the children, became king only to be dethroned in a plot by his brother Seth with the aid, of course, of Thoth. Osiris was dismembered and scattered to the winds while his body was locked in a trunk. But Thoth, ever the opportunist, later helps to grant back to Osiris his power to rule. "In the course of the fight, Thoth separates the combatants and, in his role of god-doctor-pharmacist-magician, sews up their wounds and heals them of their mutilation" (*D*, 90).

More than just two-faced, Thoth plays on all sides of every dispute. He is capable of supplementing just about every position imaginable. Likewise, as the universal supplement, "[he] was naturally also capable of totally supplanting them and appropriating all their attributes. He is added as the essential attribute of what he is added to, and from which almost nothing distinguishes him. He differs from speech or divine light only as the revealer from the revealed. Barely." (D 90) As the supplement, the guiding god, of all usurpation, he is a usurper himself. And he is also the patron of the scribes and a scribe himself no less. He is the keeper of the books and "master of the divine word" (Erman). Interestingly enough, these two positions of Thoth—the usurper and the scribe—are joined in Plato himself. Plato, a scribe perhaps, speaks in his writings in the name of Socrates and all the many interlocutors. In writing, the scribe may supplement, writing is the supplement that supplements and Thoth gazes over all as the god of the supplement.

What's more, Thoth with his power of calculation is employed in Hades opposite Osiris at the scene of the last judgement "to record the weight of the heart-souls of the dead" (*D*, 91, from J. Vandier's *La Religion égyptienne)*. And it is fitting that this should be the case because, more than just an employee, Thoth—the god of writing—is also the god of death. "In all the cycles of Egyptian mythology, Thoth presides over the organization of death. The master of writing, numbers, and calculation does not merely write down the weight of dead souls; he first counts out the days of life, *enumerates* history" (*D*, 92). The role of writing and the role of death often intermingle in the persona of Thoth. Only the dead are allowed to look at the sun (Ammon-Ra) which Thoth replaces as supplement and there are books of the dead containing formulas for enabling them to do so. Frequently, the dead are simply identified with Thoth, "*the strongest of the gods*" (*D*, 92 from Erman). Death might be nothing else but a final transformation into the figure of Thoth.

Derrida sees Thoth continually operative within an entire system of oppositions: son/father, subject/king, death/life, writing/speech, night/day, West/East, moon/sun, etc.

> The system of these traits brings into play an original kind of logic: the figure of Thoth is opposed to its other (father, sun, life, speech, origin or orient, etc.), but as that which at once supplements and supplants it. Thoth extends or opposes by repeating or replacing. By the same token, the figure of Thoth takes shape and takes its shape from the very thing it resists and substitutes for. But it thereby opposes *itself*, passes into its other, and this messenger-god is truly a god of the absolute passage between opposites. If he had any identity—but he is precisely the god of nonidentity—he would be that *coincidentia oppositorum...*
> (*D*, 92-3)

In his role as the passage between opposites, he becomes undecidable.[55] He is the god of nonidentity because he is a son who is a father, a subject who is a king, death that is life, etc. He becomes the god that hovers at the moment of decision where the opposites come into a boiling tension, their belonging together shakes and trembles indiscernibly in this logic of the supplement governed by Thoth. Thoth imitates that which he sets himself up against and, in so doing, begins to represent its other, conform to it, and ultimately replace it—sometimes even violently.

> He is thus the father's other, the father, and the subversive movement of replacement. The god of writing is thus at once his father, his son, and himself. He cannot be assigned a fixed spot in the play of differences. Sly, slippery, and masked, an intriguer and a card, like Hermes, he is neither king nor jack, but rather a sort of joker, a floating signifier, a wild card, one who puts play into play. (*D*, 93)[56]

---

[55]Cf. footnote 43 above where Derrida's P 27 is cited at length. This "passage" that is Thoth recalls the *a* of différance.

[56]The role of Thoth as father, son, and himself reminds me of Stephen's theory of Shakespeare's *Hamlet* from the ninth chapter of Joyce's *Ulysses*. Stephen makes the argument that Shakespeare is his own grandfather, since he has fathered Hamlet the son, the son of king Hamlet the father appearing as a ghost and portrayed in the first productions of Hamlet by Shakespeare himself, in order to make amends for a wrong done to Shakespeare by his brother the usurper sleeping with Shakespeare's wife. Shakespeare fathered Hamlet so that Hamlet could father Shakespeare in the moment of tragedy when the heavens will be restored to their proper order. The conclusion is, of course, that Shakespeare is his own grandfather—he is the father, he is the son, and he is himself. Interestingly enough, one of the epigraphs from this

This card game imagery recalls that Thoth is the god of games of chance. Plato mentioned in *Phaedrus* that, along with writing, Theuth brought certain games of chance to the king of Egypt (i.e., dice and draughts).[57] Thoth is a gambler and the god of rogues making their living off the tricks of the trade in pool halls and floating crap games.

Finally, in a remark that brings the interlude to a close and returns the discussion to Plato's *Phaedrus,* Derrida adds that the final function of Thoth is to be found in medicine. Plato's use of the myth reflects the difference in significance the word *pharmakon* has with Theuth on the one hand and the Egyptian king on the other: *pharmakon* means both poison and remedy and this is the point of disagreement that leads the king to reject the gift of writing coming from the messenger of the gods (i.e., rather than cure the people's failing memory—as Theuth claims for the gift—the king says that writing will poison the memory of the people).[58] "Science and magic, the passage between life and death, the supplement to evil and to lack: the privileged domain of Thoth had,

---

section of Derrida's essay comes from Joyce's *Portrait of the Artist as a Young Man* where a younger Stephen is described in terms of the Thoth in him: "A sense of fear of the unknown moved in the heart of his weariness, a fear of symbols and portents, of the hawk-like man whose name he bore soaring out of his captivity on osier woven wing, of Thoth, the god of writers, writing with a reed upon a tablet and bearing on his narrow ibis head the cusped moon" (*D*, 84). Note that it is Stephen's aim to *write* the epic novel of Ireland.

[57]Recall Nietzsche's frequent focus on the roll of the dice as fate in the context of *amor fati*.

[58]Dose, as in dose of poison or medicine, comes from the Greek *didonai,* meaning to give. A dose of poison or an antidote is always given, it is a gift received. It is not that the gift frequently turns bad or poisons, but that gift giving is always both poisonous and therapeutic. In Mauss' *The Gift,* the way in which each gift bestows a heavy burden on the recipient of the gift is the focus of his observations of a variety of different societies from different geographical regions. It is, oddly enough, precisely on this point that Derrida takes issue with Mauss in *Given Time*. A gift that burdens or obligates the receiver is not a gift at all. The gift must be given without restrictions which, Derrida claims, requires that the donor and donee forget immediately that the gift has been given. The possibility of the gift is its impossibility. The poisoning that occurs in gift giving is, therefore, the poisoning of memory. This will come back in the last chapter when memory becomes a theme for dwelling and thinking.

finally, to be medicine. All his powers are summed up and find employment there. The god of writing, who knows how to put an end to life, can also heal the sick. And even the dead." (D 94) I am reminded here of the life of Chekhov who practiced medicine as well as writing. The story goes that he took to writing in order to make a living while playing the role of physician in the provinces where he lived: Chekhov believed it was immoral to take money for medical work. For Chekhov, writing was the true supplement, it supplemented his income so that he could practice medicine—a true child of Thoth.[59]

In addition to this little anecdote, Hermes—the Greek name of Thoth—is the "god of commerce, invention, cunning, and theft, who also served as messenger and herald of the other gods, as patron of travelers and rogues, and as the conductor of the dead to Hades." (American Heritage Dictionary) These messengers are the safekeepers of the dead and of travelers along their *way*. The supplement that always appears instead of an identity for this god is an economic concept that suggests magic and trickery, dethroning and intrigue. In French, the word for trickery, which by the way is frequently associated with the behavior of these same rogues who are guided by the patronage of Thoth and Hermes, is the same as the word for "turn" and "trope": *tour*. In addition to their trickery, rogues are often characterized as turn-coats and, furthermore, the word "rogue" comes from the Latin *rogare* meaning "to ask" or "to beg." These rogues, these magicians of trickery guided by Thoth, are also questioners, inquirers. And, recalling the introduction of this chapter, they are those who are not afraid to beg the question in their circling of undecidability.

As questioning turn-coats, rogues are thinkers of the turn—they are quick to turn on their colleagues and thus send them reeling—and they are usurpers of the throne assisted by Thoth. The logic of the supplement suggesting the play of differences named Thoth is the roguish logic of deconstruction bringing about the closure of Western metaphysics. No doubt, it replaces that same metaphysics in a movement that repeats it, imitates it, doubles it, and eventually makes it out to be a passageway that is undecidable between itself and its other. All rogues are master magicians, where the sleight of hand of magic is a double gesture—a writing that erases, a display that conceals (*a-letheia*), and a

---

[59]I have not heard of any stories of people who took to certain professions along with their writing because they thought it would be immoral to accept money for writing (although Spinoza's biography comes close). Chekhov's oversight in this matter may indicate the link between writing and matters of economy.

demonstration. And this sorcery of Thoth's is also necromancy, it summons the spirits of the dead in a movement at the closure of philosophy—bringing it about in a moment of necrophilia. The thinkers of closure, no longer philosophers but necrophiles, conjure the spirits of the dead thinkers of metaphysics in the deconstruction bringing philosophy into the abyss. And what greater rogue than a necrophiliac!

No doubt this essay has now ventured into an abyss. It embraces Derrida and Heidegger as the rogues of Thoth/Hermes and the messengers of death at philosophy's closure. This life of the messenger as inquirer and "lover of death" and the abyss takes place in the flash of insight at the turning of philosophy's closure. Turning, we turn our attention to the message bearer, the thinker of death and the abyss, in a discussion that will—it is to be hoped—make us shake and tremble with fear, the same fear that confronted Dedalus in his glimpse of the Thoth within that begged him to soar as the flying scribe master of death who shall not be burned by the heat of the sun.[60]

---

[60]It would be interesting at some point to carefully work through this labyrinth of associations between Dedalus/Icarus, Dedalus/Bloom (the father figure of *Ulysses*), Shakespeare/Hamlet, Thoth/Ammon-Ra, and their ordering through the Oedipus myth and the trinity. No doubt it would be interesting to play with the addition of Heidegger/Derrida to this list. This cannot be carried out in the present essay although I might briefly mention that Derrida at least sees the move to the undecidable as a move away from the logic that governs metaphysics: the logic of identity (only in a search for identity can an endless psychoanalyzing take place, only within the logic of identity can the trinity be a supreme mystery, etc.).

Chapter 4
Spinning Human Yarns
the ins and outs of mortality

E gypt, the traditional home of Thoth (who provided the basis for future European thothianism: hermeneutics), is also the site of the pyramids. These pyramids, like Africa itself, have been given a distinct place in the metaphysical history of the West. Not only have they been placed *outside* the West, beyond its boundaries as its exterior, but they have come to stand for (to symbolize) the exterior itself. Furthermore, these exterior symbols of the exterior have come to stand for the symbolic itself, to *symbolize* the symbolic. This secondarity of the Egyptian pyramids relative to the idealist metaphysics of Europe and the West is subject to the deconstruction at philosophy's closure. The trembling of philosophy at its closure calls all degradation of the secondary into question. In the case of the pyramid this provokes inquiry into the significance of all standing for... Can the pyramid stand for anything on such shaky ground?

The pyramid is important for its double structure, one part of which rises magnificently to the sky while the other descends into the depths of the ground in a labyrinth of secret passages. This architectural groundplan suggests a further symbolic one: the pyramid contains within it a hidden compartment totally submerged and invisible beneath the wonder of the visible part. In one way of thinking, the subterranean compartments are the crypts where the dead are laid to rest. It might be concluded that the visible outer structure of the pyramid is the living truth of its meaning whereas the concealed underground parts are the catacombs of death and the hidden. Another way to think of this is that the pyramids themselves are signs of great spirituality with inner recesses serving as shrines to the immortal soul in need of a luxurious surrounding for its sojourn into the eternal netherworld. The labyrinths of the pyramid provide a spiritual environment for the rebirth of the soul. The invisible underparts of the great wonders cannot be associated with an absence connoting death, but with the absolute and pure presence of an eternal living soul ascending from the sensuous world of human imperfection. At first glance the pyramids offer a perfect image for the thinkers of the West because it is here that the dualisms of mind and body, invisible and visible, etc. gain their first articulation. Because of the purity of this foundation—the spiritual life of the Pharoah who rules the community and the people— the pyramids appear to be as firmly grounded as a physical apparatus can be.

Yet the spirit that gives this firm foundation to the pyramids is essentially foreign to it. Ultimately, the physical sensuous being of the pyramid separates it infinitely from the spirituality that immigrates into it and occupies it as a stranger. The soul may give meaning and life to the stone structure but it does so from across a great divide that cannot touch the inner walls of the tomb too deeply. The connection of the upper structure to the soul that inhabits it is, in a sense, arbitrary, and the presence of the soul nevertheless fails to transform the pyramid into anything but a mass of dead rock, a gravestone. It is in this way that the pyramid stands for the purity of the eternal soul that inhabits it, its sole reason for standing is to house the spirit of the Egyptian people—their pharaoh. Nevertheless, it is hard to see this representational nature of the pyramid as anything but firmly grounded since nothing can be more solid than such a spirit.

Derrida has discovered this role of the pyramid in Hegel's texts on semiology. The pyramid and its double structure becomes, for Hegel, the sign for all signs as they function within metaphysics. The hidden inner meaning of the sign is the concept or signified idea that lies in the catacombs beneath it. Thought thinks the idea and places it, as a stranger inhabiting a tomb, into the body of the sign. The sign itself is exterior to the spirit but as such is able to provide a mediation for the spirit's return to itself in reflection, in its effort to realize itself as spirit. Hegel, like many other metaphysicians, sees the life of the sign in its concept or idea. The signifier is a bodily representation of the living idea that gives rise to it. Speech, as the making of signs, is the breathing of life into dead words: expression. Speaking is meaningful when the concepts of thought are placed within the vault of a signifier.[1] As a marker for the idea, the

---

[1] And it is for these reasons that language is refered to primarily as speech. The substance of speaking is breath which disappears quickly when uttered whereas the physical marks of writing remain much longer, etched as they are into stone, papyrus, etc.. The upshot is that speaking is more invisible than writing and hence retains a greater proximity to the soul, spirit, or concept. In French, *soufflÈ* already suggests spirit as does the German *atmen* thereby furthering the idea that the immediate presence of the spoken word to the speaker in the act of hearing oneself speak maintains a greater

signifier is a tomb. Derrida cites Plato's *Cratylus* which includes a remark
by Socrates linking the body, the tomb, and the sign:

> [Regarding the body(*soma*)] some say it is the tomb (*sema*)
> of the soul, their notion being that the soul is buried in
> present life; and again, because by its means the soul gives
> any signs which it gives, it is for this also properly called
> 'sign' (*sema*). But I think it most likely that the Orphic
> poets gave this name, with the Idea that the soul is
> undergoing punishment for something; they think it has the
> body for an enclosure to keep it safe, like a prison, and this
> is, as the name itself denotes, the safe (*soma*, prison) for
> the soul until the penalty is paid, and not even a letter needs
> to be changed. (*M*, 82)

No doubt we associate the tomb with death, the marker with the
grave and its resting corpse, the mortal remains of an expired life. The
tomb, here, is essentially a living marker; but a living marker of death.
That is, the sign and its concept, the tomb and its corpse, the body and its
soul all reveal a relationship where the essence of life is manifested in a
sign of death. There is a necessary relation of life and death as contraries
in this way of thinking. In the opposition, it is clearly death that serves
life, that assists life in the maintenance of its present: death keeps life safe.
Derrida writes:

> The tomb is the life of the body as the sign of death, the
> body as the other of the soul, the other of the animate
> psyche, of the living breath. But the tomb also shelters,
> maintains in reserve, capitalizes on life by marking that life
> continues elsewhere. The family crypt: *oikesis*. It
> consecrates the disappearance of life by attesting to the
> perseverance of life. Thus, the tomb also shelters life from
> death. It *warns* the soul of possible death, warns (of) death
> of the soul, turns away (from) death. This double warning
> function belongs to the funerary monument. The body of
> the sign thus becomes the monument in which the soul will
> be enclosed, preserved, maintained, kept in maintenance,
> present, signified. At the heart of the monument the soul
> keeps itself alive, but it needs the monument only to the
> extent that it is exposed—to death—in its living relation to
> its own body. It was indeed necessary for death to be at

---

proximity for thought's embodiment with itself: self-consciousness. Cf.
Speech and Phenomena and "La Parole Souffle" in *Writing and Difference*.

> work......for a monument to come to retain and protect the
> life of the soul by signifying it. (*M*, 82-3)

Death, marked here by the tomb, the body and the signifier, becomes the highest monument to life and the living. We can speak of these monuments as dedicated (in memorium) to the living that they mark: the tomb preserves the dead in the memories of the living. By enclosing what lives (a memory, a soul, an idea), the tomb, body, and signifier carry out the function within the world of that which lives beyond its representative.

In order to continue clarifying this understanding of death, we must recall that what has been said thus far is within the text of the history of metaphysics and is yet to work through its deconstruction. The concept as signified by the signifier was captured in the play of signifiers that Derrida posited over and against the structuralist conception. This remarking of the concept, so that it carries out play like the signifier, also has its way with the remains and the soul that lie beneath the analogous notions of tomb and body. The supplementary signifier remarking the concept so as to circulate it in an economy of the Same now circles in/as/through the additionally degraded notions of death and the body. These secondary components of metaphysics must be caught up in the circling of the Same in Saying. The traditional hierarchies of metaphysics, where the concepts aligned with presence are given the upper hand in an order of rank, are no longer capable of standing on their own: life and the soul join the concept in the movement of presence and, residing there, are made to tremble in the interruption of their purity by the spacing of *différance.*

In this way, there may still be an emphasis on the pyramid but its spirituality may be supplemented. We can begin to read the hieroglyphic writing on the wall so as to see that the upper structure of the pyramid stands over a labyrinth while viewing the whole thing as a tomb. Rather than placing the significance of the tomb on some inner spirit, we recognize in the tomb spirit itself (so to speak). The spacing and circling at (instead of) the "origin" in the manner of a generalized economy is the tomb of Being as presence and derived from the dynamic unfolding that makes any such presence possible. In so far as this economy is Saying, I might venture to add that Saying is the tomb of Being while keeping in mind that the Greek *oikesis* meaning "tomb" suggests "economy" and the "managing of a household or dwelling place." This might shed some light on Heidegger's "Letter on Humanism": "Language is the house of Being."

The addition of these two traditionally secondary components tells us as much about the circling of the Same in Saying as this latter topography tells us about the components themselves. Death humanizes, so to speak, the Same at the moment of its closure; whereas the body gives flesh to its skeletal structure (making a fine figure out of the form). In the tomb, the monumental tomb that marks the circling of the Same without aiming to hold a place for some living presence positioned beyond it, we find the true life of language. And no doubt this tomb that suggests the body and the sign, also suggests the trembling of the closure of philosophy. The transformation of death into a monument of life makes the distinction between life and death shaky and unclear. Life can no longer be understood as a simply present phenomena, or even as merely the manifestation of world in a certain manner. Rather, life itself takes on the character of a deathly movement.[2] Each and every moment of life is a living death, and this not because living creatures are essentially morbid, but because they are born already containing—as the essence of their living being—the inevitability of their death: they are mortals.

Death, as an ongoing modification of life itself, is therefore comparable to closure as an essential modification of philosophy at its end. In this way, I understand the reference to the death of philosophy quite literally. Philosophy's death, its inevitable self-deconstruction, is its Being-towards-death, its total saturation with its own finitude. And as philosophy is here being invoked as a synonym for metaphysics, I can speak of the closure of metaphysics as its death. Death, the death of a living mortal creature, circles within the Same as a component of the Same. What is more, the same can be said for the body and the sign. Death as the characteristic of all that lives as living therefore gives body to the trembling of the economy of *différance*.

In this chapter I will discuss the role of death in the economy of the Same. This will mean a discussion of the nature of the sign and its textuality as tomb. This focus on the corpus of writing will help us to see the deathly nature of language, world, and things. I will then discuss mortals in so far as they embody a living death. Such matters will raise

---

[2]This offers a way of reading Heidegger's notion of Being-towards-death in *Being and Time*. In the moment of anxiety, Dasein comes face to face with the nothingness of its own Being, the nothingness of Being. This ultimate impossibility of possibilities for Dasein reveals to Dasein that the meaning of its entire Being is in its finiteness, its essentially impending death. Insofar as Dasein appropriates a genuine understanding of its death, it is saturated by that death throughout its life. The existence of Dasein and its impending death become identified. The opposition between life and death is no longer able to stand. More on this in what follows.

questions regarding the traditional conceptions of human being now captured in this new economy; namely, the creature who has ideas and intends meanings by breathing life into spoken words. Through a discussion of death we will discover numerous components of the traditional conception of language and its essential relation to a metaphysics of desire. The turning that occurs as this tumbling into a tomb with trembling flesh will demonstrate an important connection between the circling economy and the metaphysics that has developed historically out of it. By fleshing out the circling of the Same, we will therefore come to see how the reification of the various epochs of metaphysics was not only possible but necessary, given the nature of things and the circulation itself.

Glas: There is Death in Every Thing

In *Being and Time,* Heidegger understands presence in terms of falling.[3] The metaphysics of presence as the Being of beings within the history of philosophy that is, for Heidegger, the history of the West in terms of its epochal understanding of what is, is a mode of the fallenness of what Heidegger calls "Dasein." Dasein, the clearing of unconcealment, is frequently associated with human being and a renewed type of humanism that overturns the philosophy of subjectivity (*ousia, hypokeimenon,* substance, *subiectum,* etc.) in favor of a realigned notion of the self.[4] Aside from the commonly referred to ontological nature of

---

[3]In the opening sections of Schurmann's book (op cit.), he argues that Heidegger must be read backwards. Or, that the early Heidegger must be read through the later Heidegger. I agree with this position not only for reasons of understanding the development and progress of Heidegger's thought (i.e., that the germs of an idea can best be viewed when one starts with the full-fledged depiction of it), but also because it seems like it isn't even a choice that a reader can make. Reading is always reading backwards just because writing is always writing forwards. Perhaps, then, reading retraces the steps of writing. And then, perhaps when one reads/writes under erasure one moves to and fro in the circling of the Same.

[4] I think this is Gadamer's reading in *Truth and Method* (New York: Crossroad, 1985.). It may also have been what Husserl was thinking when he called the book "philosophical anthropology." More recently, this reading is very clearly presented—in a way that is quite attractive to readers who have

"understanding" that Heidegger develops in the manner of the clearing or disclosing of Being, this reading of the early Heidegger may be supported by the role death and *angst* have in the phenomenological account, since these are both "obviously" human ailments.

The turning to and fro of Dasein discussed in the previous chapter can be, in this context, thought as the falling and recovering of Dasein as it moves between a confrontation of the nothingness its death reveals and a mode of escape that seeks diversion from the gravity of such a revelation. Here the image is of an individual human being shaken to the core by a confrontation with her mortality and doing whatever it takes to escape this awareness, to retreat into oblivion and forgetfulness. In this case, Dasein turns away from that event which individuates it, it "turns away from itself in accordance with its ownmost inertia of falling" (*BT*, 229). Its falling is the inertia of turning away, and the force of this inertia is increased through the inevitable pursuit of that which it tries to escape. In all its activities, that from which Dasein has turned away continues to exert an *overwhelming* influence. I might say that all its activity is an effort to outstrip that which has already found it. Dasein is going to die, it is anxious in the face of its ownmost death, and its anxiety pushes it ever onward in the manner of escape or "fleeing." Its fleeing is a continual admission of what pursues it, it continues to reveal the inevitability of its death in every attempt it makes to outrun it.

In this way, all falling is also a kind of turning toward in that it continues to acknowledge, in some way or another, the continuing gravity of what it seeks to escape.

> From an existentiell point of view, the authenticity of Being-one's-Self has of course been closed off and thrust aside in falling; but to be thus closed off is merely the *privation* of a disclosedness which manifests itself phenomenally in the fact that Dasein's fleeing is a fleeing *in the face of* itself. That in the face of which Dasein flees, is precisely what Dasein comes up 'behind'. Only to the extent that Dasein has been brought before itself in an ontologically essential manner through whatever disclosedness belongs to it, *can* it flee *in the face of* that in the face of which it flees. To be sure, that in the face of which it flees is *not grasped* in thus turning away in falling; nor is it experienced even in turning thither. Rather, in turning away *from* it, it is disclosed 'there'. (*BT*, 229)

---

not read much Heidegger — by Hubert Dreyfus in his *Being-in-the-World* (Cambridge, MA: MIT Press, 1991).

So the "there" is not grasped explicitly in the avoidance that is falling, but it is disclosed nonetheless. Dasein, the particular human being, even when it flees the most strenuously from its dynamic unfolding (that nothing which it has anxiety in the face of), continues to turn both to and fro. Following the figure of the last chapter, I might say that Dasein's turning in falling is still a turning *and* circling within the economy of the Same.

What see here in the *person* of Dasein repeats what we saw previously in the history of metaphysics as presence. The crack in the foundation of metaphysics that is the closure of that tradition is what the history of philosophy has consistently and continuously thought to elude, desired to escape. It may appear, and Derrida is aware of this, that deconstruction is to philosophy what psychoanalysis is to the anxious person fleeing in the face of herself. Derrida admits that it looks this way and goes on to say how and why: "The *symptomatic* form of the return of the repressed: the metaphor of writing which haunts European discourse, and the systematic contradictions of the onto-theological exclusion of the trace. The repression of writing as the repression of that which threatens presence and the mastering of absence" (*WD*, 197). He could have just as easily finished off with "the repression of that which threatens life and the mastering of death" since it is no doubt consistent with Heidegger's understanding of Dasein's anxiety over death to claim that it is related to a conception of life that is based on presence and death that is based on absence with the former no doubt being privileged in value over the latter.[5] Deconstruction appears like psychoanalysis because it seems to be interested in philosophy's tendency to repress. Although Heidegger says often that the condition of philosophy is one of forgetting and oblivion; and, despite the fact that repression usually occurs as an attempt to forget something painful or overly suggestive of an essential trait, this does not correctly describe the historical condition of philosophy. To put it in Heidegger's terminology: such a psychologistic representation would be ontic, whereas the problem with philosophy is ontological.

---

[5]For Plato and for Descartes, death is something that happens to the body. The soul is immortal, it does not die. The body that dies is a cave dweller or a fuzzy instrument of deception and, in either case, is incapable of providing the philosopher with knowledge. In so far as the pursuit of truth is the highest goal of all philosophy, the value of the body is limited. Death, as something that happens to the body is equally worthless. It is interesting to note, that it is a rather recent event to connect life with the body. Immortality, I believe, is still associated with the eternal life of a non-corporeal thing.

Derrida conveys this in the introductory passage of his essay on "Freud and the Scene of Writing" by saying that

> Logo-phonocentrism is not a philosophical or historical error which the history of philosophy, of the West, that is, of the world, would have rushed into pathologically, but is rather a necessary, and necessarily finite, movement and structure: the history of the possibility of symbolism *in general* (before the distinction between man and animal, and even before the distinction between the living and nonliving); the history of *différance,* history as *différance* which finds in philosophy as episteme, in the European form of the metaphysical or onto-theological project, the privileged manifestation, with worldwide dominance, of dissimulation, of general censorship of the text in general. (*WD*, 197)

As in *Being and Time* with regard to falling and "On the Essence of Truth" with regard to errance, Derrida wants to recognize metaphysics—the metaphysics of presence that "censors" *différance* which is its economy of movement—as an essential and even "privileged" manifestation of that economy's dissimulation. In making this claim, Derrida is acknowledging the importance of the turning away that happens in all philosophy of presence. This does not mean that on its own, falling constitutes an essential way of being for thought, but that thought wouldn't be itself, wouldn't come upon its closure, without being *both* a falling and a recovery. In so far as deconstruction works/plays at the *closure* of metaphysics, it works/plays at the closure of *metaphysics.*

Like Heidegger, who saw an essentially disclosive character in Dasein's falling, Derrida sees such a trait in metaphysics. The anxiety that sends Dasein on its way, fleeing from a confrontation with itself, is the "ground" of Dasein making Dasein the "null basis of a nullity" (*BT*, 330-1). In this way, Dasein comes to grasp death as its utmost possibility that is not to be outstripped and therefore learn to live with death. This seemingly psychological transformation of Dasein that occurs in its "indefinite certainty of death, [its opening] itself to a constant threat arising out of its own 'there'" (*BT*, 310), is in fact an ontological transformation. This transformation is marked by a limit that is the "not-yet" of every Dasein. The "not-yet" is that part of Dasein which is missing, which is *not yet there* and which, masquerading as an absence, pursues the fallen Dasein that is preoccupied by presence. But "[w]hen we use this expression we have in view that which indeed 'belongs' to an entity, but is still missing" (*BT*, 286). The "not-yet" is a component of

Dasein's being, but a component which challenges the very opposition between present and absent components, it is a component whose presence is absence, whose absence is presence: "That which makes up the 'lack of totality' in Dasein, the constant 'ahead-of-itself', is neither something still outstanding in a summative togetherness, nor something which has not yet become accessible. It is a 'not-yet' which any Dasein, as the entity which it is, has to be" (*BT*, 288). This "not-yet" *solicits* Dasein, it is Dasein's explicit turning to and fro that is the shaking of Dasein's very essence in an anxious being before the nothingness of Being: it is Dasein's limit saturating the whole Dasein and making it tremble with anxiety. *"But the state-of-mind which can hold open the utter and constant threat to itself arising from Dasein's ownmost individualized Being, is anxiety"* (*BT*, 310).

In the preceding, as opposed to the whole of the last chapter, I have been perfectly willing to read "Dasein" as a pseudonym for an individual human being, as in fact representative of human being as such. Some will say that this is as Heidegger intended it. This essay, however, is not an effort at describing the psychological states of Martin Heidegger; it is rather a textual reading which does not take it upon itself to assume any kind of unifying coherence in the works of "Heidegger." This text is a soliciting of his text, a letting become text of his text. Most of the import of these remarks will have to wait a little for elaboration, but suffice it to say that at this point "I" am not making these remarks as an attempt to yield a glimpse of "my own" psyche to the reader in need of learning my intentions. Rather, these remarks suggest a link between the deconstruction of metaphysics (deconstruction per se) and the Being-in-the-world of a personally understood Dasein. The turning to and fro of Dasein is the deconstruction of Dasein, Dasein's making itself tremble by the coming to pass of its "not-yet" as a trace in Dasein's structure. Furthermore, Dasein can be said to deconstruct itself, Dasein is its own deconstruction, deconstruction happens (*er-eignet*) to Dasein when falling Dasein comes up behind itself and makes itself shake with anxiety. To the extent that this is what happens to the metaphysics of presence in its moment of closure (when *différance* sneaks up on it from behind and inscribes a trace within presence; in fact, when it reveals itself to always already have done so), closure can be understood in terms of Dasein. By this I do not mean that the closure of metaphysics is an individual human event, but that Dasein is something Other than the individual human being, it is the Saying circling of the Same. By demonstrating the parallels between closure and Dasein, the decision between human being and

Being becomes very difficult; I might even say that an economy of *différance* saturated with undecidability is initiated.

I demonstrated this in chapter 2 by showing the way in which the circling of the Same (world) occurs in the manner of the thing. The relation of thing and world is not the relation of a ground to its determinants, but they belong together in the way characteristic of circling itself: the Same circles in the thing, the thing thinging is the bearing out of this circling. Therefore, Dasein as the essence of human being deconstructs subjectivity (and this is not the only place where Dasein is relevant to the overcoming of metaphysical ideas). In fact, this kind of cordoning off of regions is typical of a specifically metaphysical thinking that is not ultimately at work in the project of deconstruction. The deconstruction of subjectivity therefore makes itself felt throughout the entire apparatus of Western thought and that includes the kind of thinking that places individual human beings in opposition to Being. This is no doubt because of a pervasive constitutive unity within every metaphysical text and it is precisely this unity that is the "subject" of deconstruction: "But I have never believed that there were metaphysical concepts in and of themselves. No concept is by itself, and consequently in and of itself, metaphysical, outside all the textual work in which it is inscribed" (*P*, 57).

This claim already assumes much of the work of deconstruction in that it already claims to see a certain textuality or trace structure in the concepts of metaphysics where those concepts, by their very nature, preclude the originality of such a textuality. Therefore, we must backtrack so as to show more explicitly what it means to say this. The purpose of this step back is multiple and will take care of a variety of needs in one discussion. An example here will show: (1) the extent to which the deconstruction of subjectivity is the deconstruction of metaphysics generally. (2) The manner in which metaphysics is the privileged and essential falling of Dasein. (3) The way in which death functions as that which is trying to be outstripped and mastered in falling and the inevitability with which death will continue to pursue the fleeing subject so as to make it tremble. (4) And finally, the extent to which all three of these matters say the Same. No doubt this all gestures toward demonstrating that the metaphysics of presence which flees all textuality is in fact a text (that the Dasein that flees death lives its death). The discussion, therefore, will be concluded with an examination of the textuality of the text.

The exemplarity of the subject is found frequently in both Heidegger and Derrida when they use it to frame their discussions of the nature of metaphysics more generally, claiming that the subject is a typical way of understanding the being of the human individual within the history of philosophy. When I say that it is typical, I mean to imply that it is representative of the general tendency of metaphysics; subjectivity is a representative concept within the body of metaphysical concepts. What then does the subject represent? Perhaps this way of phrasing the question already skews the direction that the inquiry will go. No metaphysician would ever think to ask a question concerning what is represented by the subject. And then again, this is precisely the question that structures most of metaphysics. In a manner of speaking, Descartes is precisely interested in what exactly it is that the subject represents, but then again he would never concede that the subject represents anything at all. Representation and the subject, classically conjoined, do not admit of a certain relation. And this *certain* relation of the subject to its representations is the organizing feature in the philosophy of most thinkers.

The polysemy of "represent" shakes this paragraph, makes its point unclear, makes it fail to represent a distinct meaning. "What does the subject represent?" doesn't make sense, or rather it makes too much sense. It forces us to move to and fro between a variety of meanings without being able to fix on any one of them. But of course I am being overly playful here, decidedly unphilosophical, lacking any seriousness in the matter. It is obvious that there is an essence of "representation," a meaning that it clearly represents: the problem of representation, this is a familiar slogan. Of course we know what this means, there is no problem here unless one wants to create it with childish games. Serious philosophers would not only chastise a deconstructor his childishness in this situation, but would be doubly put off by the specific word set shaking in this example. After all, if "representation"—which is of course the foundation of all language—can be made meaningless (or made to overflow with meaning since where meaning is concerned an excess is just as damaging as a shortage), then perhaps the whole of language is at risk. That is, to the extent that we cannot speak of a single representative meaning of "represent," we are in danger of losing the entire notion of language based on representation. Representation can only be representation provided there is a single, pure, self-present concept that is signified in every act of representation.

> This hypothesis or this desire [the singular meaning of the word 'representation' which is only representative of language as such] would be precisely that of representation, of a representative language whose object would be to represent something (to represent in all the

senses of the delegation of presence, of reiteration rendering present once again, in substituting a presentation for another *in absentia* and so on); such a language would represent something, a sense, an object, a referent, indeed even another representation in whatever sense, which would be an anterior and exterior to it. Under the diversity of words from diverse languages, under the diversity of contexts or of syntactic systems, the same sense or the same referent, the same representative content would keep its inviolable identity. Language, every language, would be representative, a system of representatives, but the content represented, what is represented by this representation (a meaning, a thing, and so on) would be a presence and not a representation. What is represented would not have the structure of representation, the representative structure of the representative. Language would be a system of representatives or also of signifiers, of place holders (*lieutenants*) substituted for what they say, signify, or represent, and the unequivocal diversity of representatives would not affect the unity, the identity, indeed even the ultimate simplicity of the represented. (*SOR*, 303-4)

No doubt this passage does not restore confidence that the matter of representation is going to be taken seriously. Yet Derrida does claim to be putting forward the position specific to the metaphysics of presence as regards a language of representation. What guarantees the certainty of meaning in the use of words is the relation that exists between the representation and the represented. Language, the signifier, stands for a signified (either concept/meaning or thing/referent), "stands for" in the sense that the signifier is there for the speaker in place of the referent as its representative. A present thing that is perhaps absent at the moment is represented in the representation that language has for it. Furthermore, this representative has been sent to represent the object present somewhere else as some momentarily absent presence, it has been sent to the house of representatives—the subject of all representation.

In the language of representation, reference signals a fleeing in the face of... Here the representative gestures away from itself and toward some idea or entity within the world. The representative's function here is to deflect attention from itself, to direct the focus toward the represented object or idea. The sign has no agenda of its own, instead it seeks only to represent the missing referent toward which it points. The signifier represents the entity and it does not do so for its own sake but for the sake of a subject. Two distinct regions open up along with the language of representation: on the one side, the region of the subject and, on the other side, the region of the entities represented by the signs— objects (Or: on the one side the conscious subject and on the other side the self-conscious subject aware of its ideas through representing them to itself).[6] Therefore, when we consider the matter of fleeing, we must think not only of the sign involved in reference but the whole philosophical apparatus that such reference implies, the subject and object of reference. We must say, however, that such insistent reference of the sign toward some object is a fleeing in the face of the sign quality of the sign where that is understood in the manner of the trace structure or economy of *différance*. In its fallenness, the referring sign is a relation between two realms, a mediating factor. But this relational quality is ultimately one determined by the established or intended presence of the opposing components of the relation. That is, such signs are not constitutive of a mediating sphere understood in the manner of the clearing in the economy of *différance*. Instead, these signs are conceived in the manner of speech as spoken language subservient to the dictates of the present object being represented to/by the present subject.[7]

---

[6]Although self-consciousness as the representation of oneself to oneself is the epitome of subjectivity, it is pretty clear here that even subjectivity in its essential moment of self-representation must view itself as some kind of object. Cf. Jacques Lacan, *Ecrits: A Selection*, (New York: W.W. Norton & Company, 1977. p. 164-5): "'I think, therefore I am' (*cogito ergo sum*) is not merely the formula in which is constituted, with the historical high point of reflection on the conditions of science, the link between transparency of the transcendental subject and his existential affirmation.

"Perhaps I am only object and mechanism (and so nothing more than phenomenon), but assuredly in so far as I think so, I am absolutely. No doubt philosophers have brought important corrections to this formulation, notably that in that which thinks (*cogitans*), I can never constitute myself as anything but object (*cogitatum*)." On this basis, self-consciousness is always a constitution of the objectivity of the subject, I will frequently talk of subjectivity only in terms of its relation to an object where that object might be the representation of a real entity in perception *or* the representation of thought to the subject (the making present of the subject to itself in self-presence).

[7]Presence here might clearly function as the transcendental, the pure reality that only materializes in the phenomenality of a representation that brings its purity into question. Presence, therefore, need not be understood in empirical fashion since sometimes the empirically present is deemed the least present of all.

The goal of such representation is to make the object present in the subject, present to the subject. Because of this objective of representation, any inscription of *différance* or exteriority within the representation is an interruption of its presence to the subject.

> The ideality of the object, which is only its being-for a nonempirical consciousness, can only be expressed in an element whose phenomenality does not have worldly form. *The name of this element is the voice. The voice is heard.* Phonic signs ('accoustical images' in Saussure's sense, or the phenomenological voice) are heard [*entendus* = 'heard' plus 'understood'] by the subject who proffers them in the absolute proximity of their present. (*SP*, 76)

Language as speech is therefore essentially linked to the apparatus of the representational sign relating subject and object. The goal being to close the gap between the two realms and not to "mediate" them, the goal par excellence of classical epistemology, it is necessary for the sign to erase itself without a trace in the act of representation, to retreat in favor of the representation that presents the subject with the ideality of the object. The breath of speech, *soufflé,* works in just this way. Breath, aside from being immediately recapturable by the subject in its exhalation (immediately hearing itself speak), is also spirited away (*soufflé)* in the moment of utterance: it disappears into the air without a trace.

It is for just this reason, as I claimed without much explanation in the preceding chapter, that writing is demoted to the level of the secondary. Writing leaves a trace, marks an inscription, and what's more, enables that mark to continue signifying in the absence of the subject, the object, and even the initial context within which the marks were made. In this way, the presence that is the goal of all representational signifying, is essentially disrupted by the spacings of writing. As a result, Derrida points out the frequent hierarchy constructed on the basis of the spoken sign. To the extent that a written language represents the spoken sign— uses a phonetic alphabet, the writing is less disruptive. There is no greater threat to the representational model of language than the Chinese language, or the hieroglyphics of the Egyptian pyramids and artifacts.

The idea is the presence of the object to the subject in representation and as such it constitutes a knowledge of the object. In this way the making-concept of the outside world is the greatest task of inquiry and experience. As external, the world is beyond the subject: unknown, uncertain, unclear. Whether the project of the inquirer be one of experience or of thought, the goal is the same: to capture the outside world in the mind of the inquiring subject either *a priori* or *a posteriori.*

Representation is the manner in which this is accomplished and it is of
little significance for our purposes whether the generated ideas are
preceded by some sort of substantially determined subject or just a tabula
rasa.[8] In one way or another, most all philosophy from Plato to Hegel and
beyond has lived with an obsession for the idea, for the transplantation of
the world into the representational form of the object through an
experience or reason that enables thought to represent this to itself.[9]

The deconstruction of subjectivity takes place through the inquiry
into the representational nature of the subject and therefore through the
manner in which the sign is interpreted within the history of metaphysics.
The sign is that embarrassing mediation that must exist as a relation
between two presences and, for this reason, metaphysics works as hard as
it does to reduce the sign to as minimal a role as possible. The
representational sign threatens the understanding of the world as
representable, it calls into question the subject as such and the object in
itself. The representation, in its very essence, is supposed to bring the
objects of the world to stand opposite the thinking (representing) subject.
The representation subdues the objects of the world by making them into
the ideas of man, by making them present to man and existent only as
such. Understanding the Being of entities as representable allows the
representative to be the single controlling factor of what *is* in the world.

Here to represent [*vor-stellen*] means to bring what is

---

[8]On this note, the two major poles of the early modern philosophical
project can be linked while displaying an essential relation of empiricism and
rationalism. Although they differ regarding the specific origin of ideas and
hence the essence of the subject, they accept the general field of inquiry
which is, by and large, structured by the notion of "representation" as the way
of being of ideas and hence the mode natural to the relation between subject
and object. What's more, the two—at least in the figures of Descartes and
Hume—are in agreement as to the impurity of the exterior and the threat that
it holds for all epistemology requiring the self-presence or fixation of ideas.

[9] Stupid sentences like this last one suggest one of the main differences
between the works of Derrida and Heidegger, on the one hand, and my own,
on the other (although one does find sentences like it in both Heidegger and
Derrida). That is, this sort of a thing should not (and, deconstructively,
cannot) be said so assertively. The work of deconstruction is the working
through of any and every text so as to demonstrate just this trait. I call the
sentence "stupid" because it seems that stupidity is the making of claims
without doing the work required to make them, without demonstrating them
or even caring to.

> present at hand before oneself as something standing over against, to relate it to oneself, to the one representing it, and to force it back into this relationship to oneself as the normative realm. Wherever this happens, man "gets into the picture" in precedence over whatever is. But in that man puts himself into the picture in this way, he puts himself into the scene, i.e., into the open sphere of that which is generally and publicly represented. Therewith man sets himself up as the setting in which whatever is must henceforth set itself forth, must present itself, i.e. be picture. Man becomes the representative of that which is, in the sense of that which has the character of object. (*QCT*, 131-2)

Objects are all that there is in the world, everything is an object, and objectivity is the Being *things* come to have as they are represented. Therefore, the representational capacity of man (or *ousia)* is the overall guarantor of all that is, that assures and gathers the Being of what is as such. Since the subject is an essentially representing subject and the world is essentially a representable object, the being of the representation is the manner of all that is. To the extent that the representation must lie between the realms that it structures and to the extent that representation is something other than the real object and the subject, it creates a risk that there will be a failure on the part of the representation to represent what it presents to the subject. Knowledge in the project of epistemology becomes essential to any philosophy of representation.

Epistemology thus far has been taken to be an inquiry into the procedures and practices of the subject. The subject, as that which represents and guarantees the being of what it represents, is in need of a clarification so that the subject will be certain that his representations will adequately relate subject and object—this has been historically understood as a problem for the one, the agent, who carries out the representation and not for the representation itself as the *relation* between realms.[10] In fact, it is the quest for a guarantee of the adequacy of

---

[10]Anyone who wanted to claim that the projects of Quine in *Word and Object* (Cambridge, MA: MIT Press, 1960) and Davidson in *Inquiries into Truth and Interpretation* (Oxford: Clarendon Press, 1984) are somehow similar to that of recent post-structuralist French and German philosophy, would have to read them with this sort of point in mind. Whatever criticism they each make of empiricism and realism in the naive sense, they seem to be concerned with the same sense of ontology that has dominated metaphysics for two and half thousand years: the attempt to delimit the conditions for

representations that is the construction of subjectivity as the manner of understanding of the Being of human beings. Heidegger says that until Descartes *subiectum* was thought as the underlying foundation of the thing as it is in its fixed qualities, a characteristic more commonly known as "substance." The substance or *hypokeimenon* of an entity was that absolute foundation that supported all its accidents (traits or qualities). For much of the history of philosophy that meant "God" where "God" was the creator of all that exists and the granter and guarantor of all creation. At a time when there was a growing distrust of the faith that this doctrine required, it became the task of philosophy to assert human being as the basis for what exists and it was essential to such a humanist revolution that the *subiectum* of what is, the underlying foundation, be conceived as certain and thus able to guarantee the Being of what is. The manner of certainty of the *subiectum* became, in the philosophy of all moderns, the *cogito ergo sum*. In this way, the subject of all philosophy became the thinking ego and metaphysics became epistemology.

Philosophy had firmly fixed the subject in place as that which was responsible for the Being of what is by representing all objects in their being as such. But in the same moment that the subject gained this certain relation to the representation, as the certain foundation of each representation (as the representation of an object to a subject), a problem was raised that threatened the mastery of the present at work in the assertion of subjectivity: solipsism. The representations were guaranteed in the Cartesian project, but the represented entities were not. In fact, they were banished to an unbridgeable distance from the subject. What was present to the subject was the representations, the real objects represented were covered over by the veil of our ideas: Hume's work is the necessary outcome of the pathway begun by Descartes.[11]

The problem here is that the relation that must hold sway in the region between the subject and the world (or the transcendental subject and its phenomenal self-consciousness) is a region characterized by

---

mediating between language/thought and reality/world through a controllable and precise representative realm, even if that realm does cease to function (in different ways for each thinker) in a directly referential relation.

[11]Notice that although it is the subject that is the *solus ipse* of this skepticism, solipsism as it has been suggested here is not really a problem whose solution can be found in the nature of the subject as such. Instead, I am claiming that the nature of the relation between the subject and its world is what makes the problem of solipsism a necessary one for all modern thought.

presence. This should give us a clearer meaning of what Heidegger and Derrida call presence.

> The 'problem of Reality' in the sense of the question whether an external world is present-at-hand and whether such a world can be proved, turns out to be an impossible one, not because its consequences lead to inextricable impasses, but because the very entity which serves as its theme, is one which, as it were, repudiates any such formulation of the question. Our task is not to prove that an 'external world' is present-at-hand or to show how it is present-at-hand, but to point out why Dasein, as Being-in-the-world, has the tendency to bury the 'external world' in nullity 'epistemologically' before going on to prove it. The reason for this lies in Dasein's falling and in the way in which the primary understanding of Being has been diverted to Being as presence-at-hand—a diversion which is motivated by that falling itself. If one formulates the question 'critically' with such an ontological orientation, then what one finds present-at-hand as proximally and solely certain, is something merely 'inner'. After the primordial phenomenon of Being-in-the-world has been shattered, the isolated subject is all that remains, and this becomes the basis on which it gets joined together with a 'world'. (*BT*, 250)

When the relations of the world are understood in terms of presence, the real world (which might be a world of ideas) mediated by the signifier is "buried" in absence in its moment of representation to the subject. But because representation is understood as presence to the subject, it is essentially disjointed from the absence it means to represent in the same moment that it attempts to do so. The only way that the representational sign may be allowed to function in mediation between what is present and what is absent is for it to lose its function as representation and become a tracing structure that truly mediates presence and absence. But, in so doing, it would fail to be able to stand present to the subject and thus the foundation of the subject as the certainty, the immediate presence of the essence of what is, of the object, would be erased. In order for the representation to represent, it must become trace, and when it does so it ceases to represent anything at all. At that moment, the subject—as the setting for all representation—ceases to be the subject; and the real objects, as no longer standing opposite a subject, cease to be represented and therefore cease to be objects. The adequately letting represent of the representation that happens in trace is the destruction of representation itself. And that is why, representation—on its own—poses a threat to the subject and its objectivity.

Representation marks a certain falling, it is the downfall of the subject. The *différance* of the sign understood as trace depends on a deep furrow breached in the midst, dispelling the purity, of presence. In its representational nature the subject has sought to set itself up as the master of all that exists in its presence and, what's more, to set presence up as mastery. The certainty of the *subiectum* would place all the world before the subject, at its disposal, for it to use and manipulate as it needed and wanted. Nothing would have been able to escape the subject; everything that is could have been used and deployed in the service of the subject. The extent to which the subject is subject to the ways and means of something larger, something greater and more persuasive, would have been dispelled. In the representational nature of the subject, the subject seeks to flee its own fragility, its ownmost dependency and vulnerability on the ways of the world. By laying the world out at its feet, the subject would have built itself a rock solid dwelling to protect itself from the hostile world: (representational) language is the house of (human) being.

But representation contains within itself its own closure, as does subjectivity which is the scene of representation.

> To think the closure of representation is thus to think the cruel powers of death and play which permit presence to be born to itself, and pleasurably to consume itself through the representation in which it eludes itself in its deferral. To think the closure of representation is to think the tragic: not as the representation of fate, but as the fate of representation. Its gratuitous and baseless necessity.
>
> And it is to think why it is *fatal* that, in its closure, representation continues. (*WD*, 250)

It is only in fleeing from death, from the abysmal nothingness of the circling Saying of the Same, that representation stands forth as that mode of language which stands for presence itself and the presence of all that can be made to stand on its own at the scene of presence, the subject. The tragic play that is the history of metaphysics is the futile turning away from the inevitable end that sets upon all representative beings from the outset.[12] Insofar as this fleeing comes across difficulties resulting from

---

[12] In this sense, metaphysics as the history of philosophy really is just a

the errancy of fleeing in the face of itself (i.e. to the extent that the presence posited in representation makes representation as the signifying relation of presences untenable as a relation between spheres of being), it continues to turn toward that which it seeks to escape, it continues to come up behind itself and discover its own vulnerability, and this no doubt makes it tremble (rather I should say, this is the trembling itself). Representation is the resistance by presence to its essential (*wesende)* tracing. As a mode of resistance, it is a tension at the core of all metaphysics establishing its being as metaphysics. Furthermore, as a mode of resistance it is a tension in strife—it is trembling.[13]

   For Derrida, falling (*tombe)* is always falling into a tomb (*tombe)*, it is always falling as a way of dying.[14] Contrary to the idea sometimes

---

footnote to Plato. The *logos* that guides the investigation of the inquirer is flawed and, in a sense, not up to the task of achieving the purity of truth desired in the investigation. The death of philosophy as the actual death, the death that the philosopher seeks in so far as s/he wants to get it right, or find the truth, is a repetition of Socrates move in *Phaedo* where he says philosophy is the preparation for death so that knowledge can be attained when the philosopher is finally able to shed his/her body. The death philosophy seeks in attempting to discover the truth, is the eternal life of truth.

[13]This does not imply that representation fails because it fails to present the present to a presence in the form of thought or knowledge, etc. It is not the case that first there is presence and then its failure. Derrida writes: "No doubt life protects itself by repetition, trace, *différance* (deferral) [i.e. signification as representation in closure]. But we must be wary of this formulation: there is no life present at *first* which would *then* come to protect, postpone, or reserve itself in *différance.* The latter constitutes the essence of life. Or rather: as *différance* is not an essence, as it is not anything, it *is not* life, if Being is determined as *ousia,* presence, essence/existence, substance or subject. Life must be thought of as trace before Being may be determined as presence. This is the only condition on which we can say that life *is* death, that repetition and the beyond of the pleasure principle are native and congenital to that which they transgress" (*WD*, 203). In other words, there never was any presence. Representation is a determination of the relations of *différance,* as a relation understood in the manner of presence, it is the (metaphysically speaking) phenomenality of representation that posits the presence of a subject and an object. But since the presence of the relation is constituted upon *différance, différance,* the crack in the foundation upon which presence is built, will continue to threaten the superstructure of presence.

[14]In French, *tombe* suggests both the third person singular conjugation of "to fall" and the noun "tomb." This word play is strewn widely throughout

attributed to Heidegger, there is not on the one hand, an authentic primordial way of being and, on the other hand, a fallen and inauthentic way of being.[15] This distinction is itself a distinction within the history of

---

the whole of Derrida's *Glas* in both the essay on Hegel and the family and the essay on Genet and the name. In so far as both "falling" and "the tomb" are heard to resonate in the *tombe,* this labyrinthine work by Derrida tolls a ringing of the stillness of language. Derrida, in what must certainly recall Heidegger's phrasing of the Saying of language, suggests the ringing of the death knell, the *glas,* that marks the closure of metaphysics, that marks the trembling and echoing of metaphysics at the moment its death has been signaled. And this death knell also signals the falling of Jean Genet, the signature that falls into the tomb of the Genet corpus, into the unfathomable depths of his texts. The residence of "gl-" in the sounding of the *glas* also transports the family in Hegel's *Philosophy of Right* outside the presence of its spiritual abode.

These remarks must remain in lieu of a reading of this nearly unreadable text. It is nowhere near sufficient to say only this: the ringing of the death knell that resounds throughout the closure of presence, buries itself in the falling of Dasein that is always a falling into a tomb — buried *there, Dasein is encrypted in the earth.*

[15] For example, Dreyfus in op cit. But this is a very popular view and has gained a major place in the writing surrounding the "Heidegger Affair" since Adorno's discussion of the matter in *The Jargon of Authenticity* (Evanston, IL: Northwestern University Press, 1973). Also see Michael Zimmerman's *Heidegger's Confrontation with Modernity* (Bloomington, IN: Indiana University Press, 1990) and Richard Wolin's *The Politics of Being* (New York: Columbia University Press, 1991). The view is usually that authentic Dasein is appropriately responding to the call to arms through its historical understanding of itself as fulfilling a moment of destiny while following a great and heroic leader. But since this historical account of National Socialism seems so widely at odds with its propaganda, it would seem like a more convincing strategy to describe Heidegger's essential philosophical allegiance through a constant turning to and fro of authenticity and inauthenticity (i.e., so as to account for the fact, as Hannah Arendt has put it, that National Socialism and the Germans who promoted and followed it was essentially banal).

I should say that, although I have not as yet been convinced of Heidegger's "essential" relation to National Socialism, I do think that it is an important concern for any reader engaging his works. Rather than considering this a horrifying dilemma, however, it is the key motivation for my thinking Heidegger as an ethical thinker to the core: thinking the ethical is breached by the relationship of fascism and the contemporary age.

metaphysics, a distinction of the real and the illusory, the true and the copy or image; it is a distinction that can be found even within representation where the representation is the image of an original entity. It is on the basis of such a distinction that representation (essential to the world of the subject and also exterior to the subject and incapable of adequacy) is risky for the subject. Therefore, when I say that representation is the falling of Dasein and yet maintain that representation will always carry with it its own trembling closure, I am beginning to deconstruct the distinction between falling, on the one hand, and the primordial on the other. Falling is always already motivated by the anxiety over death and thus death remains as a trace within the movement of falling. Falling is the terminal condition of the world while presence is the effort to grab on to something on the way down. In a manner of speaking there never was any presence, presence is a mode of turning within the economy of *différance.*

The deconstruction of subjectivity is therefore the demonstration that unconceals the textual nature of the subject seeking to display itself in presence and as the master of all that is present (presiding over it, president of it). In this deconstruction, we discover that presence is not just an incidental quality of *différance,* an accidental error that occurred in the history of philosophy's effort to elude *différance.* Rather, presence is the turning away of Dasein from itself, of the Same from itself, in its moment of circling. It is the manner of the Same's resistance to itself, its tension with itself, that is the turning and circling of the Same, that is the belonging together of all that belongs together, that is the Same that circles in Saying. The trembling discovered within the being of representation is the always already becoming trace of representational language, this trembling is the textuality of the world.

> What does interest us is the fact that the textile that always represents never represents anything. And we like it so: the simulacrum of the represented is the lightness of Death. There are only representatives. Death is nothing. And yet representatives are even less than nothing. And yet everything is written for Death, from Death, to the address of the Dead. (*G,* 78)

In the closure of representation there is the materialization of the fabric of all that comes to pass in the world. Things, as what bears out world in their gesturing, are not static representable objects but interwoven gestures of signification. "This interweaving, this textile, is the text produced only in the transformation of another text. Nothing, neither among the elements nor within the system, is anywhere ever simply present or absent. There are only, everywhere, differences and traces of traces" (*P*, 26). There is no present or absent origin of the world, no present or absent world that is the origin of things. Rather, the world and the things granted and borne out there, are always already interweaving in a motion that never began, that never suffered a moment of presence.[16] We cannot understand the economy of *différance* as a transcendental origin or set of conditions upon which all that exists within the world is founded, rather the economy of *différance* is the coming to pass of things in the world. The fourfold world is a fourfold marking of death: dying mortals, the withdrawing gods, the sheltering earth, and the darkening sky. Heidegger says it in no uncertain terms when delivering a speech on the thingness of the thing in front of a group of scientists: "Science always encounters only what *its* kind of representation has admitted beforehand as an object of possible science.... Science makes the jug-thing into a nonentity in not permitting things to be the standard for what is real.... The thingness of the thing remains concealed, forgotten" (*PLT*, 170). Concealed in the scientific being of all the representations of the modern world is the thing, and the thinging of the thing is what pushes forward and erupts in the deathly trembling that disrupts the security and rigidity of the object. Just look around, there is (*es gibt*) circling and turning everywhere, a fourfold world in every thing.

Heidegger's thinking of the thing bore it out as a bearing out, a carrying out, of the world. And this "bearing" nature of the thing recalled the notions of gestation, giving birth, bearing, and gesture. "Thinging, [things] gesture -gestate—world" (*PLT*, 200). "Concerning which," Derrida writes. "*Mimique* [a text by Mallarme] explains that that text describes a gestural writing dictated by nothing and pointing only toward its own initiality, etc." (*D*, 202). The Mallarmean text on imitation (which recalls the action of the representation in copying or providing an image for an original presence), transforms imitation into an imitation of nothing, a gesturing which gestures in the direction of nothing. The gesture no longer refers, but instead shows that all reference is at bottom suggestion, the evocative tracing of the nothing: the gesture can be said to "float":

Each time it appears, the word *floating* suggests what

---

[16]"Already (*déjà*), such is the name for what has been effaced or subtracted beforehand, but which has nevertheless left behind a mark, a signature which is retracted in that very thing from which it is withdrawn" (*S*, 39). There is already death in every thing.

> Mallarme calls suggestion: barely revealing at all, on the
> point of disappearing, the indecision of that which remains
> suspended, neither this nor that, between here and there,
> and *hence* between this text and another, along with their
> ether, a "gas... both invisible and present" (Mallarme
> *Mimique* 736) (*D*, 238-9).

Floating is the suggesting of a gesture within a text. Gestures move
without pointing to some original entity or idea, but by suggesting. What
they suggest are other gestures, a play of gestures that move in tension as
a text, an interwoven array or assemblage of marks each marking its place
in the whole economy of the thing. In this way, the gesture is always a
double gesture, a gesture that evokes other gestures *and* that evokes the
nothing that suggests the texture of all gestures. The gesture plays in an
economy which yields a position to the gesture only through its *différance*
from other gestures in the economy (which is what lets the gesture suggest
other gestures).[17]

"Things be-thing—i.e., condition or determine—mortals. This now
means: things, each in its time, literally visit mortals with a world" (*PLT*,
200). "Literally visit," visit them with the letter of writing, and so mortals
(as those who die) occupy the place of the thing "in its time," suggest the
thing in its deathly determination (be-thinging). The suggestion of the
gesture determining mortals recalls Heidegger's remarks on the message-
bearer that carries out the message of Saying in "A Dialogue on
Language." The gestation of the world in Saying is its being carried out
by gestures, its being borne in such a way as to be borne into the
neighborhood of mortals where it can visit them. The play of the world in
things is dynamically unfolded in the "carriage" of the message bearer.
To the extent that the message bearer is the human being in its closure, I
must demonstrate the way in which human beings carry themselves, their
comportment (German: *verhalten,* "to relate"). I will come back to this
later in the chapter and again in the following one. Here it must remain as
only a suggestion for reading what follows: the thing as text bears out
relations with the human being as text within the material world. Texts
reading texts writing texts, etc.

> In the extent to which what is called 'meaning' (to be
> 'expressed') is already, and thoroughly, constituted by a

---

[17]The way of thinking in the manner of metonymy so frequent in this
essay and in the works of Heidegger and Derrida is an example of this. A
word has a position relative to the entire text of a language and yet also
suggests a multitude of specific other words.

tissue of differences, in the extent to which there is already a *text,* a network of textual referrals to *other* texts, a textual transformation in which each allegedly 'simple term' is marked by the trace of another term, the presumed interiority of meaning is already worked upon by its own exteriority. It is always already carried outside itself. It already differs (from itself) before any act of expression. And only on this condition can it constitute a syntagm or text. Only on this condition can it 'signify.' From this point of view, perhaps, we would not have to ask to what extent nonexpressivity could signify. Only nonexpressivity can signify, because in all rigor there is no signification unless there is synthesis, syntagm, *différance,* and text. And the notion of text, conceived with all its implications, is incompatible with the unequivocal notion of expression. (*P*, 33-4)

Expression is the manner in which representational language represents an idea that is purely present to a thinking subject. Derrida claims that "thought" is not present as pure and absolutely existent ideas that are represented in language. Instead, the textual trace structure of language is the manner in which any such "thought" is able to take place. The trace structure related in the tissue or text of differences without signified concepts present to them, is the relational structure of the world carried out in *différance* and Saying. Thinking, as the thinking of a subject, is first and foremost textuality. The subject is absorbed in the economy of *différance* along with the objects of representation.

In the essay on Freud he writes:

[In Freud] Psychical *content* will be *represented* by a text whose essence is irreducibly graphic. The *structure* of the psychical *apparatus* will be *represented* by a writing machine. What questions will these representations impose upon us? We shall not have to ask if a writing apparatus... is a *good* metaphor for representing the working of the psyche, but rather what apparatus we must create in order to represent psychical writing; and we shall have to ask what the imitation, projected and liberated in a machine, of something like psychical writing might mean. And not if the psyche is indeed a kind of text, but: what is a text, and what must the psyche be if it can be represented by a text? For if there is neither machine nor text without psychical origin, there is no domain of the psychic without text.

> Finally, what must the relationship between psyche, writing, and spacing be for such a metaphoric transition to be possible, not only, nor primarily within theoretical discourse, but within the discourse of psyche, text, and technology? (*WD*, 199)

Derrida's reading of Freud focuses on Freud's deconstruction of the subject as a self-present thinking thing characterized by its certainty as a foundation for the world. The becoming text of the psyche in psychoanalysis (in the science of the interpretation of the subject which would only need interpretation if it wasn't in fact a subject at all) is to be found in Freud as an inscription of writing upon the "mind" (a letter into the unconscious is the way Lacan saw it [in French: *lettre* (letter) sounds just like *l'etre* (being)]). Yet, the very texture of Derrida's description of the project to come already suggests the impossibility of the project as Freud understands it in certain passages of his work. The textuality of the psyche is carried out by Freud in the representation of the mind as a machine, a writing machine. This symbolic machine represents the textuality of the psyche. The symbolic, no doubt, is what stands for something else, a representation that stands in for that which it represents. The mystic writing pad operating in Freud's text as the symbol for the psyche suggests the representational realm of language at odds with itself in Freud. The text eludes fixation, it erases all presence and leaves only traces in the tensions of the signifiers differentiating each other. For Freud—as for Husserl, a certain priority is granted to the psyche, a certain original representable position. And this is not a position that completely materializes the notion of textuality for which Freud claims to be searching.

The elaboration of this problem in Freud moves us in the direction of the technological which, as we saw in the last chapter, poses the greatest danger. Technology is dangerous because it threatens to totally annihilate *différance,* the withdrawing sending of Saying. Danger is understood as a reversal of the way I've depicted it in the discussion of presence. And yet technology, as an epoch of Being as presence, is a turning away from the danger that is the inscription of *différance* within the purity of presence. But recall that it is in the danger of technology, where the saving power lies. The danger that technology poses in its effort to outrun the danger of closure and death, to make the world succumb to the total presence of the *Gestell,* un-conceals within the essence of technology the necessary risk that *différance* requires. Since technology reveals the danger of all efforts to secure presence, it reveals the necessity of taking the risk that technology has been working so hard to avoid.[18] This can be seen more thoroughly by returning to Freud and the use of a machine to represent the psyche.

The mystic writing pad is a machine that represents the workings of the psyche. The problem for Freud is how the psyche has new experiences, understood *as* new, while at the same time having memories with an ongoing role in the psyche? What must the mind be like if it can perform both of these operations? His answer is that it is like a mystic writing pad where there is a slab of wax covered by a thin sheet which is attached to the slab at one end and loose at the other. Actually there are two sheets, a transparent one on top of a translucent piece of waxed paper. Any inscription makes a mark that can be erased by lifting the sheets. The mark disappears at the surface but the wax slab beneath the sheets retains a trace of the inscription. Freud concludes his discussion of this machine by saying that the perfect representation of the psyche would be writing with one hand while the other hand periodically lifts the sheets to erase what has been written. This machinic writing under erasure is a textual understanding of the psyche.

Notice that Freud, like Plato in *Phaedrus,* views writing as subservient to memory. The writing machine *represents* memory, stands in for it, falls away from it in presenting it in its ideal essence. Writing is exterior to memory and this just as much for Freud as it was for Plato who went on to claim that writing was harmful to memory. But Freud is not Plato and Freud's thinking of the machinic would not be possible for Plato who would never have thought that memory was a machine with anything to do with writing, not even as representable by such a machine: "The 'subject' of writing does not exist if we mean by that some sovereign

---

[18]This reminds me of the relationship existing within the capitalist West since the political instantiation of a certain brand of Marxism. Marxism poses a threat that Capitalism must commit all its capabilities to thwarting. Marxism is a threat, and yet it is precisely within the auspices of Marxism that Capitalism is presented as the greatest historical attack on the general interest of the world community at large. Like technology, of course, Capitalism may reveal the essence of this twofold threat in the very moment that it seeks to outrun that which threatens it. Imagine, as an example, that the means necessary for Capitalism to ward off the threat of Marxism led to a deepening in the problems within the structure of Capitalism (i.e., a growing division between the owners of Capital and the dispossessed—no longer—laborers) thus forcing the consciousness of a large portion of the working class within the Capitalist societies to form in opposition to the dominant ideology promoting and propagating the Capitalist economic structure.

solitude of the author. The subject of writing is a *system* of relations between strata: the Mystic Pad, the psyche, society, the world. Within that scene, on that stage, the punctual simplicity of the classical subject is not to be found" (*WD*, 226-7). This representation of the psyche threatens subjectivity as the representative and ruler of Being. Thinking of the psyche on the basis of a writing machine makes any such notion as authority impossible, the author of such writing is always coming from somewhere else; and, if we look throughout the whole of the social setting of various psyches, we will never find a first author, the beginning of the dictation that constitutes conscious mental life. Thus, the machine is not run by anyone at all, does not have a specific source of energy outside of it. That is not to say however that it runs all by itself, it is "a mechanism without its own energy. The machine is dead. It is death. Not because we risk death in playing with machines, but because the origin of machines is the relation to death" (*WD*, 227).[19]

But it is precisely at this point that Freud backs off from this machine as the representation of the psyche. The machine, like the representation, is death. Unlike the psyche, according to Freud, such a machine, such a representation, does not run by itself. And this, Derrida says, repeats a very Platonic move in relation to writing. "Only the writing of the soul, said the *Phaedrus,* only psychical trace is able to reproduce and to represent itself spontaneously" (*WD*, 227). The mystic writing pad falls into Cartesianism when it is no longer representative of the psyche itself, but is only a piece of wax. Derrida thinks Freud, who understood as well as anyone that life and death are not strictly opposed (i.e., *eros* and *thanatos)* should have been led to ask other questions, more deconstructive questions concerning the nature of technology.

Derrida thinks Freud should have pursued the manner in which the machine, in its resemblance to the psyche, testifies to the finiteness of the spontaneity of memory supplemented in experience. Insofar as the psyche is represented by a machine, a certain death and finiteness inhabit the psyche: "The machine—and, consequently, representation—is death and finitude *within* the psyche" (*WD*, 228). More so, Derrida thinks such a machine describes the machinic origin of memory, the origin of memory in death and finitude.

---

[19]Recall the section in *Civilization and its Discontents* (New York: W.W. Norton & Company, 1961) where Freud describes the contemporary life of humanity as the effort at making human beings into prosthetic gods. By making machines or cyborgs out of human beings, we construct an apparatus that resists death, or so we think.

> Here the question of *technology* (a new name must perhaps
> be found in order to remove it from its traditional
> problematic) may not be derived from an assumed
> opposition between the psychical and the non-psychical,
> life and death. Writing, here, is *techne* as the relation
> between life and death, between present and
> representation, between the two apparatuses. It opens up
> the question of technics: of the apparatus in general and of
> the analogy between the psychical apparatus and
> nonpsychical apparatus. (*WD*, 228)

For Derrida something essential may be said about technology. The machinic being of the psyche is its ownmost death, is the making finite of the psyche and the radical exteriority of it as thought within the closure of metaphysics. That is, a written psyche is a technical psyche, a psyche that no longer carries the mark of interiority but the inscribed mark of an exteriority that has traditionally been held for the material of the technical text.

It seems that Derrida has embraced the manner of Being of technology as a component in the closure of metaphysics. But Derrida's interest in technology is on a par with Heidegger's. He too thinks that something saving is unconcealed in technology along with its overwhelming threat to all that is. The technological poses the greatest threat to the world because in many ways the technological, although still operative within the realm of presence, reveals the structure of the textual. The machine is death and, as such, it is on a par with the representation. To the extent that the machine represents the psyche, even going further than Freud and really letting the machine do so, the psychic gets caught up in an economy of the technological and the textual at the same time: and this through the exteriority of the machine. In the age of technology, unlike the other ages of the text, the machine as the traditionally pure exterior, has now been given a certain value with regard to the presence of the present. In the epoch of technology, presence stands in the manner of the purely exterior and all relations in this age are relations of exteriority.

The energy for such machines in the epoch of technology always comes from somewhere else and will be exhausted eventually. The essence of the machine is a network of machines. The nature of all technological machinery is a global workshop where the machines are brought into a contextual relation with each other. No longer can the age of machines be considered a world where individual and individuated objects are, through the process of representation, cordoned off from the rest of the world in a purely singular presence to itself and to the representing subject. The machinic network is a presence of a different kind, a different epoch of presence from the early modern. Here the technological more closely approximates the text, only rather than materializing a text in the structure of the trace, it constructs an apparatus that continues to propagate the division between presence and absence.

In "No Apocalypse, Not Now (full speed ahead, seven missiles, seven missives)," Derrida investigates the technological under the rubric of "speed." Derrida's characterization of the nuclear age as one of speed no doubt recalls Heidegger's characterization of this same age in terms of proximity. In a manner of speaking, it might be tempting to say that speed is a sort of *spacing* and that the nuclear age is the perfect representative of an age of spacing; and, hence, the capitalist mode of economics that governs this age, that governs and directs the age of speed, is an economy of *différance* extraordinaire. Yet, we must recall Heidegger's warnings regarding the proximity, manifested through airlines and radio, that seems to reduce distances on the earth so that nothing/everything gains a certain proximity. This is a proximity without nearness in the sense elaborated in the first two chapters, a proximity where the dogma of the familiar covers over the nearness of Saying. Derrida echoes this position when he says that the speed of technology is a speed without spacing, without *différance.*

The technological age is the age of the apocalypse, of the nuclear holocaust. But this nuclear holocaust is always and essentially a "not-yet." It is a war, a technological war, that has not yet happened and this is its essence. "For the 'reality' of the nuclear age and the fable of the nuclear war are perhaps distinct, but they are not two separate things" (*NANN*, 23). Since the nuclear war is a holocaust, an apocalypse, it will have always-already-not-yet occurred. And this for good reason, it is—as the apocalypse—the limit of all that can occur, it is the death of all possibility.[20] In talking about nuclear war

> [t]here is nothing but *doxa,* opinion, 'belief.' One can no

---

[20]The nuclear holocaust is a decidedly human event, but it is essential to the nuclear age that the arrogance of humanity in its view of itself as the center of the universe allows it to understand a puff of smoke in some distant corner of the universe as "the end of the world." The grandiose role this human event plays in the human awareness of the world further allows the movement toward closure since the human affinity for grandeur in matters of its own position in the scheme of things enables it to comprehend the grandeur of the scheme of things in the moment of closure.

longer oppose belief and science, *doxa* and *episteme,* once one has reached the decisive place of the nuclear age, in other words, once one has arrived at the critical place of the nuclear age. In this critical place, there is no more room for a distinction between belief and science, thus no more space for a 'nuclear criticism' strictly speaking. Nor even for a truth in that sense. No truth, no apocalypse. (As you know. Apocalypse means Revelation, of Truth, *Unveiling.*) No, nuclear war is not *only* fabulous because one can *only* talk about it, but because the extraordinary *sophistication* of its technologies—which are also the technologies of delivery, sending, dispatching, of the missile in general, of mission, of missive, emission, and transmission, like all *techne*—the extraordinary sophistication of these technologies coexists, cooperates in an essential way with sophistry, psycho-rhetoric, and the most cursory, the most archaic, the most crudely opinionated psychagogy, the most vulgar psychology. (*NANN*, 24)

The missile that is a crucial component of technology for apocalyptic nuclear war is the missive or mission of the delivery mechanism. The sending of a dispatch that Heidegger described, through the use of the *Geschick/schicken,* orders the mode of Being of modern technology. Technology is therefore essentially the technology *of* Being. The economic structure of technology most closely approximates that of the economy of *différance,* but it does so with a difference. The critical discussion of this age is the discourse of crisis, this is the age of the crisis. And the crisis is a sort of division in the foundation, a crack in the foundation. In the spread of technology, the nuclear apocalypse holds sway for all the world and not just the nuclear powers, a technological textuality is disseminated throughout the earth and occupies the earth like a foreign power, a threat to the earth's life.

"The nuclear age is not an epoch, it is the absolute *epoche;* it is not absolute knowledge and the end of history, it is the *epoche* of absolute knowledge" (*NANN*, 27). As such, it is the suspension of judgment, it puts the last judgment out of play. In this way, the nuclear apocalypse organizes all that occurs within the age, it acts as the absolute referent of the age, to which the economy of the technological text is geared and to which it is disposed (*Bestand).* All that is, in the age of technology, is standing in reserve for this final occurrence, gathered together in anticipation for this future event. The context of the whole of modern life is focused around the singularity of this not-yet occurring event. This event is without a name since it cannot be named, it cannot be evoked in so far as it is the essential not-yet of naming. This nameless event of the apocalypse that so closely resembles the textuality of the text in the economy of *différance,* is the quintessential transcendental signified that organizes all economy that occurs, in its nameless name, around it.

The not-yet of this transcendental signified not only organizes the whole of the technological, but guarantees its presence. Through the not-yet of the apocalypse, we can be certain that all that is, that is standing and waiting for the bringing on of the apocalypse, is present here now. Because the apocalypse is not now, it guarantees the presence of the now, it guarantees the continued presence of the technological driven toward apocalypse. Therefore, like in all closure, "the end has always already begun."[21] "The end is near."

Now we must recall that Derrida has frequently told us that the way to the trace structure of textuality in the economy of *différance* lies through transcendental idealism, through an economy of the transcendental signified. This machinic order of the technological governed by the overarching transcendental occurrence of the apocalypse is just such a way-station. We must, therefore, learn to think the closure of such transcendental idealism through the supplement of the trace at the end. This means, strangely, coming to think the end of the end.[22]

> Perhaps you will be tempted to call this the disaster, the catastrophe, the apocalypse. Now here, precisely, is announced-as promise or threat-an apocalypse without apocalypse, an apocalypse without vision, without truth, without revelation, *of dispatches* (for the 'come' is plural in itself, in oneself), of addresses without message and without destination, without sender or decidable addressee, without last judgement, without any other eschatology than the tone of the 'Come' itself, its very difference, an apocalypse beyond good and evil. 'Come' does not announce this or that apocalypse: already it resounds with

---

[21] Jacques Derrida, "Of An Apocalyptic Tone Recently Adopted in Philosophy," trans. J.P. Leavey, Jr. *Semia* 23 (1982), 81.

[22]Obviously "end" in this paragraph is thought in the manner of a presence to come. In *Being and Time,* Heidegger makes the distinction between "Being-towards-the-end" and "Being-at-the-end" (*BT*, 288 ff.) where the first is the anticipation of a not-yet and the second is the future moment that will come to be present. Therefore, "to think the end of the end" is nothing other than thinking the closure of presence.

a certain tone; it is in itself the apocalypse of the
apocalypse; *'Come'* is apocalyptic.[23]

"Come," for Derrida, is "beyond being," it is the arrival of the trace
structure, and it arrives most vividly in the manner of a missile that brings
all dispatching of missiles to a close. Derrida can only be thought, so too
Heidegger, as a philosopher of the apocalypse (a mystic as some would
call him) if the apocalypse that he bids Come be understood as the most
radical and extreme apocalypse possible, the apocalypse of even the
apocalyptic. This is philosophy at its closure, a philosophy that has not
died, but has accepted its death as a non-yet which will never be present,
which can only be said to Come.[24]

Technology represents the closure of philosophy and, as machine (a
mystic writing pad) it represents the technological textuality of the
psyche. It has then been the task of this section of the essay to show that
the closure of philosophy may begin its trembling in the transformation
of this representative of closure to the long fated closure of representation.
This death of philosophy decenters the subject in a textuality that is no
longer technological where the technological is the most sophisticated
and complicated defense of presence against the lurking economy of
différance yielding its falling. Beyond the presence of Being, beyond the
Being of presence, in the closure of the present, in the closure of
representation, the ringing of stillness that is the death knell of
metaphysics and Western history as presence will no longer be
represented as a bell, that, at the moment of death, begins to toll. Instead,
the ringing of stillness that is the resonance of the echoing bell tracing
through the air in its always already having been rung, reverberates and
vibrates in every thing. The event character of the ringing bell, of the
death knell, signals the closure of representation.

I write for the dead, [Genet] says everywhere.... But he
specifies: for the dead who have never been alive. The *glas*
is for (no) one. (No) one. It announces or recalls nothing.

---

[23] Derrida, "Apocalyptic Tone," 94.

[24]It is difficult to avoid linking the term "Come" with "dissemination" as
it will be discussed in the second half of this chapter. I do not know if the
connection exists explicitly in the French, but its suggestion in the English
would certainly appeal to all that Derrida has to say about both "coming" and
"disseminating." It is interesting to me that "Come" initiates a triangulation
of French, German, and English: comes-to-pass translates *Ereignis* and
suggests what comes in/as/through the future of deconstruction.

> It hardly sounds, it sooner resounds, before ever having
> touched the material of any sign. That sounds. Why call
> that death? Why call for one's death? Because that has
> already taken place. (*G*, 78-9)

There is Nothing but Tissue in the Body

Death, which befalls the representation in its effort to secure the
presence of the subject to itself in thought, is also the falling of the body
into a tomb. Not the tomb that is a monument surrounding a living source
of breath, but the falling tomb at the closure of representation, the tomb
that encrypts the corpse that remains at the end of the metaphysical
corpus. This closure, this becoming corpse of the body, is a dissemination
and germination of renewed life in the manner of the materialized tissue
of flesh: a flesh that no longer represents anything, that no longer stands
opposite the interiority of the mind, that no longer cringes before the
putrification of the flesh in desire dubbed disruptive of all rationality. The
flesh, the tissue of the body, is beyond Being, within the textuality of
différance that plays beyond presence and absence, that is neither here
nor there.

The body was already inserted into the mind through representation.
This is not because the body is the mind or soul's representative here on
earth—as Plato said in *Cratylus,* but because representation is always
bodily, it is the making phenomenal of thought in the representation of
the world to the subject. The thin, barely there, breath that is nonetheless
inserted like a sheaf between the desired presences of the metaphysical
subject, is a rhythmic breathing of a body's excretion through expression
into the extended realm of the exterior deemed secondary along with all
the other marks of the fallen. The breath (*soufflé*) that is spirited away
(*soufflé*) nonetheless leaves a trace beyond the presence of the subject.
The other hears the voice of the speaking body and steals the words in an
inscription of *différance* as the otherness of the subject.

> I must first hear myself. In soliloquy as in dialogue, to speak
> is to hear oneself. As soon as I am heard, as soon as I hear myself,
> the I who hear itself, who hears me, becomes the I who speaks
> and takes speech from the I who thinks that he speaks and is heard
> in his own name; and becomes the I who takes speech without
> ever cutting off the I who thinks that he speaks. Insinuating itself
> into the name of the person who speaks, this difference is nothing,
> is furtiveness itself: it is the structure of instantaneous and original

> elusion without which no speech could ever catch its breath
> [*soufflé*]. (*WD*, 177-8)

Hearing is always a hearing of the other, a differentiating described by Heidegger where hearing, even hearing oneself, is participation in the overall economy of Saying.

> As pure auto-affection, the operation of hearing oneself speak seems to reduce even the inward surface of one's own body; in its phenomenal being it seems capable of dispensing with this exteriority within interiority, this interior space in which our experience or image of our own body is spread forth. This is why hearing oneself speak is experienced as an absolutely pure auto-affection, occurring in self-proximity that would in fact be the absolute reduction of space in general. (*SP*, 79)

This is no doubt how it seems, how it appears, how its phenomenality is manifested in the gaze of a vision, a *theorein*. But it does not move this way. Auto-affection, Derrida says, is always a *relation* to oneself. The *différance* that inscribes this relation in the apparent self-presence of auto-affection has always already been there as an inscription and "[i]n this pure difference is rooted the possibility of everything we think we can exclude from auto-affection: space, the outside, the world, the body, etc." (*SP*, 82). The bodily *voice* that guarantees self-presence in the hearing oneself speak is just that, a *bodily* voice that cannot do what it intends, it cannot mean what it says.

In French, meaning is essentially saying, spoken, a voice that tries to reduce all exteriority in the moment of re-presentation. *Vouloir dire,* to want to say, to intend to say, gestures in the direction of a meaning that is ideal and whose ideality in its presence dominates the exteriority of the phenomenal world in the manner of the voice: "*The phoneme is given as the dominated ideality of the phenomenon*" (*SP*, 78). The meaning of the exterior world is guaranteed by the presence of the ideal within it. The meaningfulness of the body, its substantive everyday action, is guided and controlled by the embodied ideality of the mind. This apparatus of a body driven by a mind like a ship by a pilot is on a par with the effort at reducing everything material from the sign, previously described as a desire to make present the subject to the object so as to flee the inevitability of death. Meaning as "wanting to say" is essentially the desire to represent. Furthermore, the notion of meaningful action as "willing to speak" is essentially the desire to make present that which is conceivably absent.

When meaning comes to a closure along with representation, therefore, the body that represents the soul begins to tremble with desire. The claim is not that in the deconstruction of the body, all is desire. Rather, the body, which left to itself will only desire—will fail to incarnate a rational will, as the metaphysical locus of desire begins to shake *with* desire so as to elude every possibility of being a desiring body. Desire is the trembling of the rational will, it is a failure of reason to become embodied concomitant with the failure of the body— representative of the mind, to continue to desire. The trembling of the body with desire is the trembling of the body *with* desire, both the body and desire begin to tremble in the closure of metaphysics. Desire, the exteriority of reason attributed to the exterior body, disrupts the interiority of the mind (drives the mind crazy with desire) and then loses itself as desire; when it loses its opposition to the rational will, desire loses its meaning, it begins to tremble along with the body: "Without the possibility of différance, the desire of presence as such would not find its breathing-space. That means by the same token that this desire carries in itself the destiny of its non-satisfaction. Différance produces what it forbids, makes possible the very thing it makes impossible" (*OG*, 143).

We must read this passage from Derrida's reading of Rousseau carefully. "The desire of presence" signals both that it is presence that is desired and that desire is how presence acts. Desire and the desire for presence are also inextricably linked to the economy of presence, to the economy of the turning away and fleeing. The "breathing-space" that makes desire possible is made possible in turn by *différance*. For there to be a desire for presence there must first be a distance, a space within which desire can grow. Desire is produced by a lack, by a missing presence. To the extent that this space opened up by *différance* is "breathing" space it is a place where the voice may be said to whisper (*soufflé*), seductively. In so far as *différance* produces the desire for presence, it also produces a desire that will proceed by pursuing what is missing. The production of presence through absence is, therefore, the production of desire itself. Presence, as the turning away and fleeing in the face of death and *différance,* is essentially desire.

The "desire of presence," dependent on *différance,* is the desire of death, death's desire for its own death.

> Coming to terms with desire (the desire for the proper), and taking
> into account the contradictions among its forces (for properness
> limits disruption, guards against death, but also regards death
> closely; absolute property, one's undifferentiated proximity to
> oneself, is another name for death; the space of property thereby
> also coincides with the 'dead surface'), the text, quite squarely,
> makes the stage spin. Expropriation operates by violent
> revolution. (*D*, 331)

Once again, we must read with care. "Proper" here suggests the self-present, absolute presence to self, the essence of a thing is its own proper being. We should reread the passage without all the parenthetical asides: "Coming to terms with desire, and taking into account the contradictions among its forces, the text, quite squarely, makes the stage spin." That is, understanding desire involves understanding its nature as a text, as *différance.* "Squarely," in the context of an essay on Sollers' essay *Numbers* which ends with an extended reference to Heidegger's fourfold, suggests to me that Derrida is trying to emphasize a way that desire may be de-fetishized and remarked in an economy of *things* (over and against objects). The "violent revolution" of the next sentence then suggests that Derrida's understanding of the circling of Saying is of a violent transformation of its present economy.

The long parenthesis inscribed in the middle of the passage suggests an affinity with death. Desire is the desire of death in that the desire to guard against death, so as to insure the longevity of the proper or present, becomes ultimately a desire for death as the dissolution of the *différance* that spans out in life, marks the very finitude of *différance,* and brings about its presence to itself; presence is viewed as death's desire for its own death: the absolute finitude of the finite. "Absolute proximity" is the end of all *différance,* the total absence of differentiation, and this means that the desire for presence is the desire for the finiteness of *différance,* the coming to an end of all differentiation. Finitude is inscribed in *différance* as death, to desire the finitude of death and to desire death are one and the Same. In the moment and economy of desire, desire shakes and trembles to such an extent (it desires presence so forcefully) that it desires death as the finitude of *différance.* Death takes on at least two different meanings here: on the one hand, death is the absence of the present while, on the other hand, death is the trace structure of *différance.* In the desire for presence we must read both the metaphysical meaning and its closure in a reading that is a double gesture: "Différance does not resist appropriation, it does not impose an exterior limit upon it. Différance began by *broaching* alienation and it ends by leaving reappropriation *breached.* Until death. Death is the movement of différance to the extent that that movement is necessarily finite" (*OG*, 143).

The new terms within which desire comes to have its new name is the language of resistance. Desire is the resistance of death. But insofar as this resistance is the desire for presence and thus the arresting of death and its incarceration in the prison of the body, it is resistance to resistance, it is a resistance that is frustrated by its own nature as resistance. Desire is the desire to resist death in the appropriation of an immediate presence purified of *différance,* but this resistance to death is essentially desire and thus a spacing between the desire and presence. Desire and presence are both equally constituted in the *différance* of desire, and, as such, the resistances of presence are (con)textualized within the economy of the *between* that differs the contrary elements in the moment of constitution. Desire that has not yet begun to tremble and tumble in its becoming tomblike is a bodily desire for the interruption of *différance* in its economy (a desire for penetration). Desire, as resistance, desires to interrupt resistance, desires its own death—desires its own closure. For desire to have this character, it must be a fleshly desire, a deathly desire for the flesh which would cease to be the desire for presence as such or in itself and would become desire in the closure of the body that trembles in the wake of its textuality, of its essentially resistant unfolding. Resistance that resists either some presence or some absence is not yet resistance. Resistance dynamically unfolds in/as/through trace and text, an economy of resistance.[25]

Desiring bodies, therefore, may be thought in the tissues of the text. The textuality of the economy of *différance* incarnates itself as flesh, materializes as, among other *things,* the tissues of the (what was once) body. This tissue that is the flesh of the body in its closure plays in/as/through *différance* where that is the multiple and multivalent tension of resistances. When desire falls in upon itself in its closure, becomes enclosed in its tomb, its essential resistance fragments and unconceals itself (materializes in the most "literal" sense) as a play of resistances, of

---

[25]Michel Foucault writes in *The History of Sexuality, volume I: An Introduction* (New York: Vintage Books, 1980): "Hence there is no single locus of great Refusal, no soul of revolt, source of all rebellions, or pure law of the revolutionary. Instead there is a plurality of resistances, each of them a special case: resistances that are possible, necessary, improbable; others that are spontaneous, savage, solitary, concerted, rampant, or violent; still others that are quick to compromise, interested, or sacrificial; by definition, they can only exist in the strategic field of power relations" (p. 95-96).

tensions, of play. The fleshing out of this event in the texts of Derrida occurs in a revealing way when Derrida, in *Dissemination,* goes right for the genitals. More specifically, the hymen bands erect in the Derridean text as the essential tissue of the trace.

"'Hymen'... is first of all a sign of fusion, the consummation of a marriage, the identification of two beings, the confusion between two. Between the two, there is no longer difference but identity" (*D,* 209). From here, the hymen motivates an extended discussion of the oppositions that are brought into a "fusion": presence/absence, desire/fulfillment, distance/non-distance, etc. But Derrida does not mean to participate in the reductivism of metaphysics that brings all oppositions to rest in a single original cause or present source. He describes the extent to which a meditation on the hymen leads to the suspension of the presence of the opposed elements in favor of the space between them, the middle ground which stretches out across the distance between them.

> What is lifted, then, is not difference but the different, the differends, the decidable exteriority of differing terms. Thanks to the confusion and continuity of the hymen, and not in spite of it, a (pure and impure) difference inscribes itself without any decidable poles, without any independent, irreversible terms. Such difference without presence appears, or rather baffles the process of appearing, by dislocating any orderly time at the center of the present. (*D,* 210)

The middle across which the hymen stretches its tissue is a middle that lies between nothing and this holds as much for two so-called points in space (one here, one there) as for two so-called moments of presence (one future, one past). This veil is not something that reveals or conceals anything in particular, but rather the fabric of the veil is itself the milieu of revealing/concealing: the medium of the Same ("(medium in the sense of middle, neither/nor, what is between extremes, and medium in the sense of element, ether, matrix, means)" (*D,* 211)).

The hymen, the piece of flesh that marks consummation, is the fabric of life and death and the fabric of all that lies between, every presence that is penetrated by an absence.

> Rightly or wrongly, the etymology of "hymen" is often traced to a root *u* that can be found in the Latin *suo, suere* (to sew) and in *huphos* (tissue). Hymen might then mean a little stitch *(syuman) (syuntah,* sewn, *siula,* needle; *schuh,* sew; *suo).* The same hypothesis, while sometimes contested, is put forth for *hymn,* which would thus not be a merely accidental anagram of *hymen* [*hymne/hymen*]. Both words would have relation with *uphaino* (to weave, spin — the spider web — machinate), with *huphos* (textile, spider web, net, the text of a work — Longinus), and with *humnos* (a weave, later the weave of a song, by extension a wedding song or song of mourning). Littrè:... "according to Curius, `*úmnos* has the same root as `*uphao,* to weave, `*uphe,* `*uphos,* textile; in that long ago era when writing was unknown, most of the words used to designate a poetic composition were borrowed from the art of the weaver, the builder, etc." (*D,* 213)

The textuality of the hymen, which is also a marriage, suggests the song of mourning, perhaps sung alongside the ringing of the death knell. The tissue of the flesh is modelled on the fabric of the hymen, and this is not only the case because the hymen is the most tissuelike member of the body. The hymen is essentially such a text as a being *between.* The between in Heidegger and in Derrida demonstrates the medium of the Same and the between of the textuality of the hymen lies between the differends in an opposition. Between desire and its fulfillment lies a text, between presence and absence lies a text: a hymen. For Derrida, such textuality between elements suggests something more: *entre* — between is the entering of a text.

> The hymen enters the antre. *Entre* can just as easily be written with an *a.* Indeed, are these two *(e)(a)ntres* not really the same? Littrè: "ANTRE, s.m. 1. Cave, natural grotto, deep dark cavern. 'These antres, these braziers that offer us oracles,' *Voltaire, Oedipe* II, 5.2. Fig. The antres of the police, of the Inquisition. 3. *Anatomy*: name given to certain bone cavities.—*Syn: Antre, cave, grotto. Cave,* an empty, hollow, concave space in the form of a vault, is the generic term; *antre* is a deep, dark, black cave; *grotto* is a picturesque cave created by nature or by man. *Etym.* Antrum, *antron;* Sanscrit, *antara,* cleft, cave. *Antara* properly signifies 'interval' and is thus related to the Latin preposition *inter* (see *entre).* Provenc. *antre;* Span. and Ital. *antro.*" And the entry for ENTRER ["to enter"] ends with the same etymological reference. The *interval* of the *entre,* the in-between of the hymen: one might be tempted to visualize these as the hollow or bed of a valley (*vallis*) without which there would be no mountains, like the sacred vale between the two flanks of the Parnassus, the dwelling-place of the Muses and the site of Poetry; but *intervallum* is

> composed of *inter* (between) and *vallus* (pole), which gives us not
> the pole in between, but the space between two palisades.
> According to Littrè. (*D*, 212)

And, since this is so important, to continue reading a few lines later:

> The hymen, the consummation of differends, the continuity and
> confusion of the coitus, merges with what it seems to be derived
> from: the hymen as protective screen, the jewel box of virginity,
> the vaginal partition, the fine, invisible veil which, in front of the
> hystera, stands between the inside and the outside of a woman,
> and consequently between desire and fulfillment. (*D*, 212-3)

The two poles between which the textuality of the hymen spans are no
doubt, given the second graft (citation), the phallus and the hystera
involved in (in the middle of consummating) coitus. It is only fitting that
flesh trembling with desire and the body should begin its movement in
the figure of the sexual members.

For the moment, we shall follow Derrida in his development of these
components between which the textuality of the flesh materializes in the
tissue of the hymen. The textuality of the hymen, although it is pulled
tight in its spanning between, is the folds of its tissue. Flesh itself is the
folding of flesh, there is no flesh without the fold, just as the hymen folds
over in its manner of spanning a gap. The hymen is a fold, the hymen is
dynamic unfolding, and the conceivable singularity of the fold—as of the
hymen—must always be rethought in the manner of a divided singularity,
a oneness that is never single: a folding that is always a folding between
one and two.

> The necessity of folding the page of the hymen does not
> involve, after the fact, a secondary procedure. You will not have
> been required to flex back upon itself a surface that was at first
> smooth and flat. The hymen, "at the cleft," does not come to
> adopt, here or there, some fold, indifferent as to whether you are
> imposing it or refusing it. In the morgue of all Pierrots [a character
> in Mallarme that Derrida has been discussing], you have been
> able to read that the folding was being marked *in* the hymen, in
> the angle or cleft, in the *entre* by which, dividing itself, it related
> back to itself. Yet neither (is it) a fold in the veil or in the pure
> text but rather in the lining which the hymen, of itself, was. But
> by the same token *is* not: the fold in a lining by which it is, out of
> itself, in itself, at once its own outside and its own inside; between

> the outside and the inside, making the outside enter the inside and
> turning back the antre or the other upon its surface, the hymen is
> never pure or proper, has no life of its own, no proper name.
> Opened up by its anagram, it always seems torn, already in the
> fold through which it affects itself and murders itself. (*D*, 229)

The folding of the hymen means that it is always already a tearing, a rift
and a cleft. The hymen does not need to be penetrated from some exterior
in order to be doubled, to be impressed by *différance*. The hymen, as the
folded between, contains within itself the possibility of all tearing
asunder. When I referred to the phallus and the hystera I, contrary to the
suggestion in Derrida's text, referred to the differends of the relation
despite their being overrun by the relation itself, by the reduction to the
différance occurring in the hymen. The hymen is consummation not
because it is torn asunder by the penetration of the phallus, but because it
contains within itself its own consummation, its own being divided, its
own folding over.

Although the hymen indicates a heterogeneity in the fold, it does not
make essential nor even essentialize heterosexuality. To enforce
heterosexuality upon the hymen, to rape the hymen, would be to
understand desire in a metaphysical sense of a presence that is desired, a
presence that would mark the absence of the hymen. The hymen is an
important piece of flesh because it suggests both the metaphysics of desire
and its closure. Desire and fulfillment, absence and presence, all equally
understood from the point of view of the differends where the absence of
the vagina is desired and the fulfillment of that desire is the presence of
the phallus with the vagina. Insofar as the hymen stands in the way of this
desire, enables this desire to reach out and across the gap between absence
and presence, it suggests a certain metaphysics. But it also confuses (as
Derrida points out), it turns the phallus into an absence, it turns desire into
an absence, and enables consummation on the basis of finitude. That is,
because the hymen is absent in the presence of the phallus and present in
the absence of the phallus, the hymen as that which stands between the
phallus and the hystera confuses the *being* of the phallus, confuses the
desire of the phallus, by refusing any simple presence of what lies
between.

Discarding any heterosexuality conceived on the basis of two
present differends, we can nonetheless recall that the hymen evokes the
person of the woman, a woman that is flesh all over. Recall the first
chapter when, in comparison with Parmenides' poem, I remarked that
Heidegger's *a-letheia* was a woman with a vagina. I now see that I meant
to say, "a woman with a hymen": and to what extent should the hyphen
that supported the claim then be treated in the manner of a hymen? "The

play of silhouettes which is created here by the hyphen's pirouette serves as a sort of warning to us to keep our distance from these multifarious veils and their shadowy dream of death" (*S*, 49). The turning of the hyphen is the dance Derrida wants to associate with the seductive effort of woman to lure one nearer. This dance is the historically infamous dance of the veils. Women can dance the dance of veils because women themselves are veils, are the hymens that fold in the manifold nature of their unfolding. "The fold renders (itself) manifold but (is) not (one)" (*D*, 229).

Woman is the seductress, the one who lures through a dance into the nearness, who incites the desire to tear the veil asunder but whose essence is only that of the veil and so admits of no such event. Surely this must be an essentialization of woman even if it is in the name of sidestepping an essentialization of heterosexuality. Recall that Derrida all along has advocated the double gesture of deconstruction that occurs in the materialization of the textuality of what has previously, metaphysically, been considered a pure presence or a simple object. The double gesture has involved the positioning of the secondary within the text of metaphysics so that it takes up arms, or begins to strongly oppose that which has primary value (body and mind, absence and presence, writing and speech, etc.). Then, with this movement of the secondary within the text of metaphysics, Derrida advocates a dis-placement. So, first the emphasis on the secondary makes the traditional hierarchy uncertain, begin to tremble; and then the displacement of what is secondary enables a new site, a new economy of *différance* to be materialized. Just as I have done this with body and mind, representation and presence, etc., now I begin to do it with woman and man. Metaphysics, for Derrida, is not only logocentrism (privileging the present in terms of thought, voice, etc.), but phallogocentrism (privileging the phallus) which included a male dominated desire.

The unveiling of woman as the dynamic unfolding of the flesh is the incarnation of the human within the economy of *différance,* the un-concealment of woman as the unfolding of the hymen is the un-concealment of woman as the unfolding of the human, as the unfolding flesh of humanity. Therefore, the making hymen of woman is only the first step in a double step whose second step must be the displacement of "woman" as she has been historically understood. First off woman as she has been historically constructed must overturn the privilege of the masculine, and then she must displace that very overturning power with a second turn. Derrida calls this second turn "dissemination."

> The hesitations of the "veil" [*voile*], the "flight" [*vol*], the "leap" [*voltige*], as they condense down toward the point of an idea or of a dancer's toe,... are always, *in addition,* descriptions/inscriptions of the structure and movement of the literary textile, a "hesitation" turning into writing. In folding it back upon itself, the text thus *parts* (with) reference, spreads it like a V, a gap that pivots on its point, a dancer, a flower, or Idea. (*D*, 239)

This spreading out is the spray of dissemination: the spreading out of semes [seeds and signs]. But, as if it needed to be said again, the seeds are not concrete singularities, they are traces and gestures where gestures are significative suggestions of texts and tissues. The point upon which the pivot of the V is made is the *stigme* of the sign where such a point can no longer live with the stigma of purity. Rather, dissemination informs us that

> in turning incessantly on its point, the hieroglyph, the sign, the cipher moves away from its "here and now," as if it were endlessly falling, forever here en route between here and there, from one here to the other, inscribing in the *stigme* of its "here" the *other* point toward which it continually drifts, the other pirouette that, in each vaulting spin, in the whirls of flying tissue, is instantly remarked. Each pirouette is then, in its twirling, only the mark of another pirouette, totally other and yet the same. (*D*, 241)[26]

The incessant turning that materializes the text is the dissemination of the sign/seed in the second turn executed on the figure of woman in the history of metaphysics brought to its closure.

The fan, often used in the seductive fan dance, is the figure that draws together most of the imagery so far. The folded fan fans out in an unfolding that spreads across in spacing manifesting the full fabric of its weavings and designs. The fanning out of the fan is a spreading of the fold that disseminates the fabric of the fan. But even folded the fan's fabric is woven in a way. The fan is not first closed and then open, its folds are the condition of its being, its unfolding a matter of spacing admitting of degree.

---

[26]"Point" in French can mean both "point" and "not" while "Pas" can mean both "step" and "not." The turning that occurs in dancing is a kind of dance step or step taken with the planting of the foot or toe at some point on the floor.

> All this in the movement of a fan. The polysemy of "blanks" and "folds" both fans out and snaps shut, ceaselessly. But to read Mallarme's Èventail [fan] involves not only an inventory of its occurrences (there are hundreds, a very large but finite number if one sticks to the word itself, or an infinite number of diverse possibilities if one includes the many-faceted figure of wings, pages, veils, sails, folds, plumes, scepters, etc., constituting and reconstituting itself in an endless breath of opening and/or closing); it involves not only the description of a phenomenological structure whose complexity is also a challenge; it is also a remark that the fan re-marks itself: no doubt it designates the empirical object one thinks one knows under that name, but then, through a tropic twist (analogy, metaphor, metonymy), it turns toward all the semic units that have been identified (wing, fold, plume, page, rustling, flight, dancer, veil, etc., each one finding itself folding and unfolding, opening/closing with the movement of a fan, etc.); it opens and closes each one, but it also inscribes *above and beyond* that movement the very movement and structure of the fan-as-text, the deployment and retraction of all its valences; the spacing, fold, and hymen *between* all these meaning-effects, with writing setting them up in relations of difference and resemblance. (*D*, 251)[27]

A folded fan is a phallus whereas the open fan is the unfolding vagina, the play of *différance* that moves in the fanning of the fan is therefore the stretching of the hymen. And this fan can organize the discussion of the dissemination of woman in that the unfolding of the fan, the folding of the fan, is a manifold folding (multi-pli-cation). The fan, here presented as a kind of coordinating figure for a long chain of other figures in the text of Mallarme, operates by way of dissemination in a multiple sense: first off it disseminates the signs in the text of Mallarme, while secondly it carries within its folds the dissemination of its fabric.

Through the fan we see that the unfolding of the fabric, which is an interweaving of signs/seeds (*soma/sema* suggesting signs/seeds/body/tomb, etc.), is not the becoming multiple of a

---

[27]I suspect that a similar point is being made in Derrida's discussion of Nietzsche in *Spurs* with the exception that the figure of the fan is filled by the umbrella that Nietzsche says he has forgotten, in what is a nearly contextless fragment from the *Nachlass*.

singularity.[28] It is an already multiple that, in unfolding, fans out, disseminates. "Dissemination skims and froths the flight and theft of the seminal: a vain, blank loss in a wet dream in which the masthead, *pour qui le lit* [*for one that reads/for which the bed exists*], blots itself into abysses of lost veils, sails, and children" (*D*, 267). The frothing forth of sperm, of seeds, is the swarming of signs in the advent of closure, but here materialized in the germs of living creatures. The between of the hymen is the between of birth and death that is the mortal life materialized as a spraying of seeds. The milk of life (*lait* in French suggests the *lethe* of *a-letheia*) carries out the insemination of the fabric and tissue of life, finite mortal life that is always already death.

Dissemination is inseminated into the folds of the hymen and, therefore, occurs as the textuality of all the womanly flesh that the hymen once was thought to represent. Because the woman of metaphysics was the veil, the folded and seducing fabric of the fan, she cannot stand on her own essential grounding in the revaluation of man/woman that occurs in the first gesture of the double gesture. Woman, the fan dancer and veil weaving one, disseminates in the very moment of her unfolding, her unfolding is always already a dissemination. And this is precisely the meaning of the oft used phrase "always already," the dissemination of woman that occurs in the initial overturning of her oppression to man, is the dissemination of the singular phallus that the epoch of man, of phallogocentrism, represents.

---

[28]In a footnote Derrida writes: "No more than can castration, dissemination-which entails, entrains, 'inscribes', and relaunches castration—can never become an originary, central or ultimate signified, the place proper to truth. On the contrary, dissemination represents the affirmation of this nonorigin, the remarkable empty locus of a hundred blanks no meaning can be ascribed to, in which mark supplements and substitution games are multiplied *ad infinitum*. In *The Uncanny,* Freud—here more than ever attentive to undecidable ambivalence, to the play of the double, to the endless exchange between the fantastic and the real, the 'symbolized' and the 'symbolizer', to the process of interminable substitution—can, without contradicting this play, have recourse both to castration anxiety, behind which no deeper secret (*kein tieferes Geheimnis*), no other meaning (*keine andere Bedeutung*) would lie hidden, and to the substitutive relation (*Ersatzbezeihung*) itself, for example between the eye and the male member. Castration is that nonsecret of seminal division that breaks into substitution" (*D*, 268). Here we can already see the early suggestion of *Spurs* where castration will take on the force of dissemination in Derrida's reading of Nietzsche.

> As soon as one has recognized, from all the disseminated webs, the fold of the hymen—with all that this supplement is henceforth woven of—one has read not only the "nubile folds" in the *Tombeau of Verlaine* but also the endless multiplication of folds, unfoldings, foldouts, foldures, folders, and manifolds, along with the plies, the ploys, and the multi-plications ["pli" is French for 'fold']. Every determinate fold unfolds the figure of another (from the leaf to the sheet, from the sheet to the shroud, from the bed to the book, from the linen to the vellum, from the wing to the fan, from the veil to the dancer, to the plumes, to the leaflet, etc.) and of the re-mark of this fold-upon-itself of writing. It would be easy to verify the preceding demonstration for the polysemy of the fold: under the constraints of the differential-supplementary structure, which constantly adds or withdraws a fold from the series, no possible theme of the fold would be able to constitute the system of its meaning or present the unity of its multiplicity. If there were no fold, or if the fold had a limit somewhere—a limit other than itself as a mark, margin, or march (threshold, limit, or border)—there would be no text. But if the text does not, to the letter, exist, then *there is* perhaps a text. A text one must make tracks with. (*D*, 270)

The veil dance or the dance of the fan are not, strictly speaking, singular or individuated—essentially determinate objects; rather, they are gestures, they are the materialization of movement, of a spacing: an unfolding of a multiplicity. To think woman as essentially hymen is not to think her as an essence. In fact, as we journey into the folds of her nature, we discover the displacement of "woman" per se, we discover a multi-pli-cation of her maidenhood, a dissemination of her folds: seeking woman, there is (*es gibt*) nothing.

The fragmentation of the fabric of mortal life that occurs in the becoming flesh of the human hyman (is there an etymological relation? the Greek upsilon sounds like a "y") makes the body difficult to recognize within the gaze of metaphysics, within its *theoria*. That is why many readers of Heidegger have found it difficult to discover the body per se in his corpus: to the extent that the body does not appear in Heidegger's works, his work can be understood as circulating at the limit of philosophy. Derrida deconstructs this manifest absence of the human body in the corpus of Heidegger in the articles entitled "Geschlecht." *Geschlecht* means a number of things: sex, genre, family, stock, race, lineage, generation, etc. But Derrida's focus here is not an attempt to find in Heidegger a unifying sign of all these meanings of *Geschlecht* suggesting a body in Heidegger's thought; rather, he is looking explicitly at Heidegger's claims in the *Metaphysical Foundation of Logic,* roughly contemporaneous with the publication of *Being and Time*, that "Dasein" has been used to name the entity chosen for the existential analytic initiating the fundamental ontological inquiry into the meaning of Being because of its "neutrality." Dasein is neutral, neuter, without sex, Dasein is *geschlecht-losigkeit.*

This neutrality regarding the *geschlecht* is not indifference. "Dasein is neither of the two sexes *(Geschlecht),*" that's true, "[b]ut here sexlessness is not the indifference of an empty void, the weak negativity of an indifferent ontic nothing. In its neutrality Dasein is not the indifferent nobody and everybody, but the primordial positivity and potency of the essence" (*MFL*, 136-7). What is more, this not indifferent sexual neutrality that marks Dasein's being in its isolated originality as the Dasein that it is, is also a potency—a sexual potency perhaps, "which bears in itself the intrinsic possibility of every concrete factual humanity" (*MFL*, 137). Dasein never exists in its neutral and abstract form, Heidegger says, it always exists in the manner of a "factical concretion," a real in the flesh, living breathing being. This concrete being of Dasein, although in some ways understood as an isolated being, is not isolated in the existentiell sense, but only in the abstract metaphysical sense. In fact, Heidegger says, "Dasein harbors the intrinsic possibility for being factically dispersed into bodiliness and thus into sexuality. The metaphysical neutrality of the human being, inmost isolated as Dasein, is not an empty abstraction from the ontic, a neither-nor; it is rather the authentic concreteness of the origin, the not-yet of factical dispersion" (*MFL*, 137). Dasein's factical being is a not-yet, a mortal and finite being which spreads out in the world as flesh. In the fleshly origin of Dasein, Dasein swarms in the manner of a dispersed living body and Derrida is quick to point out the similarity of Heidegger's *Zerstreuung* and his own "dissemination."

This discussion of Dasein's body and sexuality comes from a period when Heidegger had not yet given up on the effort to conceive his project within the classical boundaries of metaphysics. He still saw himself as seeking to solidly ground the structures of metaphysics by finding a meaning of Being that would support the structure. In so doing, his language is still—in part, permeated with the assumptions of such a project, with the assumptions that seek to function like transcendental idealism. Yet Heidegger's project is not a simple form of transcendental idealism since he does not view the origin as tied up in the operations of cognition. The origin, for Heidegger, is the dissemination of all facticity, what he has called—in *Being and Time,* "thrownness": "The transcendental dissemination proper to the metaphysical essence of neutral Dasein, as the binding possibility of each factical existential dispersion and division, is based on a primordial feature of Dasein, that of *thrownness*" (*MFL*, 138). But in what sense can Heidegger mean transcendental here when he is talking of an originary dissemination that is the factical concreteness of Dasein which never exists in the neutral? Recently, a project is considered transcendental whenever it attempts to describe enabling conditions of possibility. Such enabling conditions function as the ground of all possibility. To that extent, the world is defined by its necessary relation to these fundamental conditions. Whatever is, must be definable in terms made possible by the enabling conditions of possibility. Whatever they happen to be.[29] Even when Heidegger understood his project in terms of transcendental language, he was unable to remain completely loyal to the project because of his insistence on drawing out a factical topology of the "essential" realm of Being. Such topology, the factical concreteness of Dasein's thrownness, already suggests the unconcealment of the "origin" in dissemination as a concrete spreading out, sowing of seeds. There is *nothing other* than what is spread out in manifestness.

Heidegger points out that this dissemination is important for the essence of Dasein because of Dasein's own manner of being alongside the entities within the world, and not merely a subject or ego that needs to transcend itself in order to have experiences or gain knowledge of the world. Heidegger says that "[thrown dissemination] is the presupposition, for example, for Dasein to let itself in each case factically be governed by beings which it is not; Dasein, however, identifies with those beings on account of its dissemination" (*MFL*, 138). That is, Dasein's thereness, the "there" of Being is *there* as opposed to "in here" because it is originarily strewn about *there,* multiplied and spread out all over *there.* And this holds not only for Dasein's being alongside entities within the world, but for its Being-with other Dasein. "The essentially thrown dissemination of Dasein, still understood as completely neutral, appears, among other ways, in Dasein's being-with with Dasein" (*MFL*, 139). Here it is clear that Heidegger understands the Being of the "there" of Dasein as

---

[29]This discussion clarifies further my position regarding the transcendental structure of all metaphysics. The master-name or transcendental signifier functions as a univocal enabling condition by providing the boundaries of possibility for whatever can be within the world. Such names describe the boundaries of the world and suggest that the worldhood of the world is a totality with its focus or center in the modification of Being relevant to the particular epoch: subjectivity, *Gestell,* etc.

something other than the Being of the world of entities, despite the fact that throughout *Being and Time* he identifies the two: Dasein is Being-in-the-world. The dissemination of Dasein makes it difficult to retain the distinction between an isolated Dasein (on any level: metaphysical or existentiell) and the world at large. The Being alongside the world of Dasein places Dasein in the world, saturates the world with Dasein and Dasein with the world.

After spending some time laying out the beginning of Heidegger's discussion of the originary dissemination of Dasein in its factical concreteness, Derrida turns to some remarks Heidegger made in *Being and Time* concerning Dasein's dispersion. Namely, the link that Derrida finds in an explicit connection between the intervallic tension of the *between* birth and death of Dasein and the notion of dispersion. "*Between* birth and death, the spacing of the *between* marks at once the distance and the link, but the link according to a kind of dispersion" (*G*, 77). The between draws together the dispersed components of Dasein's life. The life of Dasein is the life of the between, stretched out from one end to the other and it is a neutral dissemination within the drawn out expanse of the between. Dasein's life is the hymen: it is the unfolding dissemination of a tissue, of flesh. Heidegger may be speaking of the body in a fragmented fashion, not as a body that moves in the manner of a *res extensa,* but as a disseminated textuality that materializes concretely in all the manners of the *Geschlecht* but, in its origin, remains neutral to the *Geschlecht,* not as indifferent, but as the originary dispersion of all vital features, of all the living tissues of a history (histology).

The second essay called "Geschlecht," carries the subtitle: "Heidegger's Hand." Thinking concerning Heidegger's hand, recalls *Being and Time* and the distinction between the *vorhanden* and the *zuhanden* (or present at hand and ready to hand) as the primary modes of Being-in-the-world, but Derrida has some much more telling remarks in mind, remarks to be found in two of the major works of the 50s, *What is Called Thinking?* and *On the Way to Language.* Here the favored understanding of *Geschlecht* is going to be derived from the context of some meditations Derrida has done on "Philosophical Nationality and Nationalism." With this context and with Heidegger's ties with National Socialism, the meaning of *Geschlecht* as "race" strikes an especially loud note. But Derrida is quick to point out that *Geschlecht* may also suggest species, genus, gender, stock, family, generation or genealogy, and community. These meanings, aside from their apparent differences, share a common sense at least so far as Fichte understood the word *Geschlecht* in his *Discourses to the German Nation* which Derrida paraphrases: "*Geschlecht* is an ensemble, a gathering together (one should say

Versammlung), an organic community in a non-natural but spiritual sense, that believes in the infinite progress of the spirit through freedom" (*Geschlecht II*, 163). Derrida emphasizes, aside from Fichte's concern for the community's freedom and unity, his concern for the language of the people whose relation to the things in their world is mediated by a communally determined language. With regard to National Socialism, Derrida cites Heidegger's remarks regarding his own involvement with the Nazi party in order to show the extent to which Heidegger wanted to distinguish between the "National" and "Nationalism" (which he detested). The passage also makes clear that Heidegger's understanding of the "National" was in terms of a certain "gathering together" and not an affirmation of the Nazi Party's essential connection of the "National" with the biological and racialist ideologies of "Nationalism."

In the discussion of language in Fichte, Derrida stressed the sign as the kernel of language and essential to the people's relation to their surroundings. "Sign" becomes significant in light of the discussion of National Socialism only because of an effort on Derrida's part to think Heidegger's thought on the matter of the *Geschlecht* that, Heidegger claimed, divided him from the Party. That is, when Derrida goes to think the sign, he thinks a monstrosity, *un monstre,* a sign/monster. Now, the monstrosity of the sign, Derrida says, is not the monstrosity of National Socialism, but of the *Geschlecht*: *la monstre,* in French, signifies "a changing of gender, sex, or *Geschlecht.*" And what's more, "[m]onstrer is montrer (to show or demonstrate), and une monstre is une montre (a watch)" (*G II*, 166). Derrida is not letting this play happen because he is crazy, he is preparing to introduce the reader to a poem that Heidegger considers in *On the Way to Language,* Hölderlin's "Mnemosyne" which reads in German: *Ein Zeichen sind wir, deutungslos.* In French: *Nous sommes un monstre privè de sens* (roughly meaning: We are a monster/sign void of sense).

Derrida thinks this "translation" of *Zeichen* is enriching for thinking on the matter. In using *monstre,* the translator is able to suggest the crucial things Heidegger has to say in the book on language linking *Zeigen, Zeichen,* and *Sagen.* In *monstre,* we hear the sleight of hand that is involved in all Saying.

> The hand will be the (monstrous) sign [le monstre], the proper of
> man as (monstrous) sign, in the sense of *Zeichen.* "The hand
> reaches and extends, receives and welcomes — and not just things:
> the hand extends itself, and receives its own welcome in the hand
> of the other. The hand keeps. The hand carries. The hand designs
> and signs, presumably because man is a (monstrous) sign (*Die
> Hand zeichnet, vermutlich weil der Mensch ein Zeichen ist*)."
> (*WCT*, 16) (*G II*, 169)

The hand is the monster/sign that "we" are. The gathered together
community of man is a "we" that signs with a reaching hand, a carrying
hand, and so on. The hand is the proper being of man and separates him,
Derrida notes with reference to Heidegger, from every other *Geschlecht.*
The hand of man is the proper being of man and "[t]he hand cannot be
spoken about without speaking of technics" (*G II*, 169). Heidegger's
meditation on the hand is found in the lecture course *What is Called
Thinking?* and the signing/showing of the hand is indicative of the effort
Heidegger undertakes there to "learn thinking."

The question of learning to think immediately leads Heidegger to
wonder whether learning to think is on a par with learning to use tools for
handiwork. The question of thinking and the hand are drawn together in
a way that suggests the technical proficiency that may be accomplished
through the manipulation of things in the world occurring in learning how
to perform certain tasks. Handiwork, Derrida points out, is always in
danger of succumbing to a technics of the hand, a kind of manual labor.
All working with the hand raises the danger of the technological: "All
handiwork, all human dealings are constantly in that danger. The writing
of poetry is no more exempt from it than is thinking" (*WCT*, 14-15).
Thinking, like cabinetry, is for Heidegger a work of the hand. "Only a
being who can speak, that is, think, can have hands and can be handy in
achieving works of handicraft" (*WCT*, 16). The hand that signs, that
shows, implicates a being in Saying and therefore enables the being to
think. Derrida makes three remarks at this point: (1) He points out that
thought is a corporeal event according to Heidegger. (2) The hand is not
something to be thought, some object to be meditated about or studied,
but is thought, is thinking. (3) The final remark reflects back on the
political context with which the discussion began. That is, that
Heidegger's essential defense to the implication of himself in the
monstrosity of National Socialism was usually his meditation concerning
technology (that is, National Socialism as an incarnation of technology is
condemned).

Derrida is working at making Heidegger look like the quintessential
thinker of technology. The thinker on the hand who cordoned off human

being in opposition to Being, who reduced the thinking essence of human being to the showing/signing movement of the hand, and who therefore accepted a pragmatic understanding of entities that is characteristic of the *Gestell* of technology. And what is more, it is clear that Derrida is framing this discussion around the idea that Heidegger's incessant interest in the gathering together of the *logos,* etc. is a sign of all these technological and, therefore (perhaps), nationalist qualities of thought. When Derrida turns back to *Geschlecht,* one might expect to see how Heidegger's reading of that term in the poetry of Georg Trakl implicates and congeals all these points in a scathing attack on the thought of Heidegger. But that is not what happens. Rather, we learn, that "this genealogical composition of *"Geschlecht"* will be inseparable... from the decomposition of human *Geschlecht,* from the decomposition of man" (*G II*, 183).

Heidegger admits the multiplicity of the meaning of the word *Geschlecht* and embraces it over and against some kind of one track thinking that must see everything in one fixed manner. Heidegger draws the multiple meanings of the word together, gathers them together, but "[t]his unity is not an identity, but guards the simplicity of the same, even in the form of the fold" (*G II*, 184). The discussion that ensues in Heidegger's work on Trakl is an embracing of the multiplicity of language, an embracing that gathers the multiple in some way: weaves it together as a text. This happens most prominently in Heidegger's association of *Geschlecht* and *Schlag* (beat or strike). The association comes from a reading of Trakl's poem "The Occident" and can only be loosely derived from a peculiarity of the German language. The association is therefore a very specific, very German national association, a link dependent on the existence of the German community. But it is a link that dispels this same community when made. The gathering of the people in the language, the gathering of the senses of the manifold word *Geschlecht,* is a gathering together that decomposes the unity of all gathering, of all nationalism.

> "The striking (*Der Schlag*) whose imprint gathers together such a splitting in two in a simplicity of the *one* race (*der sie in die Einfalt des* 'Einen *Geschlechts' pragt*) and thus restores the stocks of the species (*die Sippen des Menschengeschlechtes)* and the species itself in the sweetness of the more serene infancy, that striking strikes (*eingeschlagen lasst)* the soul with an opening for

the path of the 'blue springtime'." (As translated from the citation in *G II*, 188)[30]

The striking that enters the race, that splits it, multiplies it, is the return to the "origin" of the species, to the blooming striking moment of difference that was elaborated in the first essay on Heidegger's *Geschlecht*. This stretching blow or "wingbeat" is the difference not only between races, but the difference between species as well, the difference between man and animal. The place of the gathering together in clearing is evoked in the movement beyond the singularity of the species or race. But Derrida further implicates Heidegger into a thinking of *Geschlecht* in its unity when he describes the unity of the site or gathering place. The thinking of *the* gathering place in Heidegger, Derrida suggests, is in opposition to the introduction of the "blow" into the *Geschlecht*. It is a second "blow," a second strike on the same order as that violent second strike that Heidegger wants to attribute to the thinking of metaphysics (and technology) that unifies the site in violent and beastial opposition. Derrida sees in Heidegger a repetition of the logic of presence (and thus exactly that which he claimed to be trying to escape in his move away from National Socialism) in Heidegger's own dispensing with presence.

Derrida is deconstructing Heidegger in this second essay on the *Geschlecht* and, therefore, is showing that the Heideggerian text is marked by tensions and turbulence. Heidegger's hand, which separates the human from the animal, continues to have a hand in the thinking of the *Geschlecht* even in the moment when he is trying to divide the *Geschlecht,* to multiply it and let its play go on and on undecidably. The essay on Heidegger's Hand ends with an invocation of the *envoi* or sending which Derrida here criticizes for its singularity in Heidegger. It is only natural, therefore, to want to read Derrida's "Sending: On Representation" immediately after the essay on the hand. To do so yields even greater confusion, since this essay draws to a close with a curious remark that completes Derrida's effort to read the *envoi* (sending or destiny of the Same) as a *renvoi* (sending back or circling back) and not just a *renvoi* but *renvois,* multiple circlings, circling that is the swarming and swimming of the manifold:

---

[30] The English translation at *OWL*, 195, reads: "The force which marks the tribes of mankind as the simple oneness of '*one* generation,' and thus restores them and mankind itself to the stiller childhood, acts by prompting the soul to out toward the 'blue spring.'"

> As soon as there are *renvois*, and its always already, something
> like representation no longer waits and we must perhaps arrange
> to tell this story differently, from *renvois* of *renvois* to *renvois* of
> *renvois*, in a destiny which is never certain of gathering itself up,
> of identifying itself, or of determining itself (I do not know if this
> can be said with or without Heidegger, and it doesn't matter).
> (*SOR*, 325)

A strange parenthesis, to say the least, especially since the whole of this essay, dedicated largely to a reading of Heidegger's "The Age of the World Picture," is saturated with Heidegger's tropes and figures. Derrida's entire reading of the singularity of the gathering place, of its ultimate unification of a multiplicity and hence its favoring the presence of an origin that is not always already dissemination, is resisted by other remarks made concerning the body in "Heidegger"—i.e., the first "Geschlecht" article. Such tensions are not a flaw, they are the becoming text of "Derrida," and they seem to surface in his strange parenthesis which wonders, although ultimately doesn't care, whether the swarming of the already multiple origin can be thought with or without Heidegger. But there is something missing from this reading, something that might have made the tension resonate still deeper and which would have reorganized the two essays around the incorporation of the body and the move against technology.

Heidegger's hand is ultimately no hand at all, it is the gesturing of language.[31] The hand as the signing/showing of language is not a single hand, as Derrida suggests, but a multiplicity of gestures.

---

[31]This is an interesting quirk to be found in Derrida. He is always very careful to warn the reader against hearing any particular term as an original signifier that organizes the whole economy that he wishes to elaborate. Even "economy" would have to be read as *supplemented* by *différance, hymen, text, writing, spacing,* etc. In fact, the multiplication of terms that on their own *disseminate* themselves is the greatest driving *force* in Derrida's thinking. Nevertheless, Derrida is unable to read Heidegger in this way, he fails to deconstruct Heidegger when such a deconstruction would be most influential for his own writing. Recall Heidegger's economy of the *Same, Saying, unconcealment, dif-ference, er-eignis, hand, clearing,* etc. de-*monstrated* in chapter one.

> But the hand's gestures run everywhere through language, in their most perfect purity precisely when man speaks by being silent. And only when man speaks, does he think—not the other way around, as metaphysics still believes. Every motion of the hand in every one of its works carries itself through the element of thinking, every bearing of the hand bears itself in that element. (*WCT*, 16)

The gesturing of the hand is the dissemination or dispersion of gestures throughout the *element* of thought where the "element" is that which bids thought to think. The "element" is thought's medium, the ether within which thought takes place, or the water within which thought swims, etc. Looking more closely at this citation, we see that the silent speech of "man" is carried out in the movement of the hand. Now, Derrida is right to point out that in this text Heidegger criticizes "writing" as a mechanized procedure, but he also inscribes the text with a silent speaking that is a tracing of the hand through ether. Heidegger has criticized writing as a writing of the hand in favor of a gestural writing that moves without the technical.

The becoming gesture of the hand, the gesturing of the hand, is its fleshy essence. Gesturing is the swarming of the world/Saying and, as I demonstrated in chapter 2, is not merely a character of hands, but things as well: "Thinging, things are things. Thinging, they gesture-gestate world" (*PLT*, 200). And Heidegger, as Derrida points out, does think the hand is a thing although he doesn't ever put it in quite those terms. The hand is a thing because it gestures, its suggestive showing and pointing is already a manifold of gestures, a text.

When we come to read in the hand a manifold of gestures, we begin to see that the hand, regardless of what Heidegger has to say about it, cannot *be* anything. The singularity and unity of the hand is dispersed in the *Geschlechtlosigkeit* of the neutral human Dasein discussed above. The gathering of the *Geschlecht* is a view of the *Geschlecht* that Derrida takes from Fichte and not from Heidegger. His slippery attribution of it to Heidegger occurs when Heidegger embraced a certain gathering together in National Socialism that would not be a "Nationalism." Here Heidegger is clearly embracing the gathering component of a movement while claiming to reject its emphasis on the *Geschlecht*. The strike (*Schlag)* that Heidegger attempts to deliver some years later in the reading of Trakl's *Geschlecht* remains consistent with Heidegger's acceptance of the *Geschlechtlosigkeit* of the gathering place of the destiny of the Saying of the Same. The gesturing hand in Heidegger is a hand beyond sexual difference, racial difference, and even species difference, it is the fleshly tissue of dissemination.

This discussion of Derrida's essays on Heidegger's swarming flesh, his corpse, has done little to develop the threatening technological that was brought up in the course of the discussion. Derrida wrote: "The hand cannot be spoken about without speaking of technics" (*G II*, 169) and I left it at that. But I can now come back to this after having shown that Heidegger is not speaking *about* the hand at all, but that he is gesturing in the manner of the hand. The clarification of these uses of the hand will double as the clarification of technology and the body's becoming flesh.

In *What is Called Thinking?*, Heidegger returns to Parmenides to discuss a fragment that is concerned with the same matter as the lecture course: that which calls thinking. *Cre to legein te noein to eon emmenai*, commonly translated as "One should both say and think that Being is" (*WCT*, 178), recalls the *Creon* of Heidegger's discussion of Anaximander. As in the essay on the earlier thinker, Heidegger emphasizes the meaning of *Cre* as "need" in the manner of what is needful, what one needs to do, what one should do. Only in this context Heidegger investigates the etymology with different connections in mind. He says that *Cre* "derives from *he keir* meaning the hand" (*WCT*, 186) and suggests *crao* or *craomai* meaning "I handle and so keep in hand, I use, I have use for" (*WCT*, 186-7). Heidegger is immediately concerned with distinguishing two separate ways of understanding this notion of "using":

> Starting with this use that is practiced by man, we shall try to point out the *nature* of using. It is not anything that man first produces and performs. "Using" does not mean the mere utilizing, using up, exploiting. Utilization is only the degenerate and debauched form of use. When we handle a thing, for example, our hand must fit itself to the thing. Use implies fitting response. Proper use does not debase what is being used — on the contrary, use is determined and defined by leaving the used thing in its essential nature (*wesen*).... To use something is to let it enter into its essential nature, to keep it safe in its essence. (*WCT*, 187)

Use in this way does not connote some kind of submitting of the thing to the ends and means of "man," exploiting a thing in the projects organized and produced by agents. Instead, use suggests an entering into relation such that this is a response to the thing, a response to the thing that guards and preserves it (*bewahren*), keeps it in the unconcealment of its dynamic unfolding. This kind of using is a gesturing with the hand that enters into the thing's own proper gesturing.

Using, Heidegger says a few pages later, as a "translation of the *cre...* belongs in the company of 'there is'" (*WCT*, 189). The movement of the hand that is the handling of the thing, that is the gesturing relation with the thing, is an unfolding of a kind of communication with the thing, a communion with the thing: a belonging together with the thing that is given over in the *es gibt* of the two. The "essential community" (*WCT*, 191) of the handling in using is contrary to any understanding of "use" that might include things like "rules of usage" or the mastery of a thing by putting it to good use. In Parmenides' fragment, the *cre* names the community not only between hand and thing, but between *legein* and *noein*. What is proclaimed in the opening of the fragment is that a community, a useful handling, occurs between *legein* and *noein*. We have already learned to hear in the *legein* a gathering that is not a bringing into singular unity. *Legein*, now clarified by the discussion of Derrida's notion of the textuality of the multiple gathering place, gathers together what lies in its disseminated multiplicity, it allows the gathering as a stretching out or spanning that weaves through the multiple layers of the gathering place. In *legein*, we must hear the weave of language that is the tissue of a text. *Noein*, recognizable as the verb form of the commonly used *Nous*, is interpreted by Heidegger as "a taking to heart." Ordinarily this word is understood as "perception" or "apperception" or something of the sort. Heidegger looks into its pre-socratic understanding in the not-yet philosophical work of Parmenides and finds that *noein* is a taking to heart because it is a concern for what is perceived but in such way that it "does not make over what it takes [*vernehmen* is the German for perception and indicates a 'taking']. Taking to heart is: to keep at heart" (*WCT*, 203). The heart no doubt furthers our fragmentation of the body in Heidegger's thought, but it also seeks to situate the community that arises in handling relative to the gathering that occurs in all taking to heart (i.e. the handling of things that is the taking in of things, the experience or perceiving of things).

Heidegger then goes on to a rather long discussion aimed at weaving together the notions of *legein* and *noein*, showing or suggesting their community, their belonging together. This is especially important to the context here because it shows the extent to which Heidegger wanted to interweave the gathering place of language with the tissue of the heart. Heidegger is very clear in claiming that the *legein* has a presiding role in relation to the *noein*. Only because things are gathered together and allowed to lie can they be taken to heart, he says. It is the task of the gathering to preserve the things that are laid out for the taking, but that does not mean, he cautions, that we should understand their relation in only a sequential manner. "*Legein* and *noein* are coordinated not only in series, first *legein* then *noein,* but each enters into the other. *Legein,* the letting-lie-before-us, unfolds of its own accord into the *noein*" (*WCT,* 208). The point he is gesturing toward is that although the taking to heart of (human) perception is determined by the gathering of Saying, it is nevertheless the case that the heart that reaches out to take what is gathered there is interwoven with those things that are laid out, they are unfolded and, recalling the discussion from *The Metaphysical Foundations of Logic,* multi-pli-ed *there.*

As was the case with the hand, the heart was not entering into relations with things that were transformed into terms that were endearing to the heart. This is not a heart of romantic love which colors and skews everything to the purposes of procuring and prolonging its throes of passion and delight. This heart, like the hand before it, takes the world to heart and wrestles with it there in its dynamic unfolding.

Heidegger's manner of reading the fragment from Parmenides proceeds in the same way that his understanding of the matter for thought proceeds in the fragment. That is, it proceeds in a supplementary fashion. Heidegger's reading is a constantly fragmented substitution on the basis of relations: Heidegger deconstructs Parmenides to the extent that he makes the fragment materialize as a text. Now, this "method" is interesting in that it also delineates the matter the fragment reaches out toward. That is, Heidegger is attempting to think (take to heart) what Parmenides has thought concerning thinking. To the extent then that substitution is his "method" it is also the "content" of the fragment. Thinking as deconstruction therefore materializes the textuality of a fragment where that has traditionally been understood as a method for referring to the content. The substitutions move from the *Cre* that is the handling of things to the *legein* that is their gathering to the *noein* that is their taking to heart. From there, Heidegger goes on to develop the *eon emmenai* that follows in the fragment and with which the fragment has to do, handling itself.

This explanation is a prelude to a substitution that I would like to make for the reading Heidegger performs in the essay in question. Heidegger goes on to say that the twofold nature of *eon emmenai,* its being a participle, etc. is its presencing unconcealment as twofold duality, and so on. We've seen much of this discussion already in the first two chapters. My point here is that the *eon emmenai* as that which in-cites the substitution at the beginning of the fragment, suggests the materialization of the supplementary notions in the matter (as the matter) of the duality unfolding. Furthermore, this materialization is always a multiplication of strands and threads of tissue. This holds for the fleshy heart and hand that gesture in the turning and circling of the Same just as it holds for the gestating things that likewise turn and circle in their bearing out of world.

Throughout the lecture course *What is Called Thinking?*, Heidegger associates technological thinking with "one-track" thinking where the "track" is supposed to suggest the railways for trains. The understanding of usage as handling in the *way* of dynamically unfolding gestures is, therefore, opposed to all univocity of understanding. Yet, I can't help but feel the technological import of the hand and its useful movement. What's more, I am alerted—since the discussion at the close of the first section of this chapter—to the possibility that this manner of substitution which clearly suggests an economy of relations, may very easily and very readily be forced into a framework that is unidimensionally organized and set to work in exploiting things as resources for whatever they're worth.

In technology, there are, strictly speaking, no hands. Rather, the hand becomes, along with the rest of the body, an implement of labor for the capitalization of surplus value in the productive action of a labor force or a laborer. In this usury/use of all hands in the labor force, Derrida points out in another text suggesting a reading of Heidegger, the wear and tear (*usure*) of the hand is used up as variable capital in the production process. This *usure* of the body for the sake of an overarching, life determining, capital is the employment of the hand in the manipulation of resources to be commodified and brought to market as incorporated and alienated labor. "Hand" here functions, no doubt, as a synecdoche of laborer in what is a metaphorical economy. As in the world of the catastrophe, the economy of capital approximates textuality without playing in the manner of its closure.

Just as a dead metaphor's wearing away, exhaustion of metaphoricity, is its overuse in a metaphysical economy of language, the hand's wearing away is its lifelong employment in the capitalist economy governed and organized by the life and cultivation of capital. Capital carries within it its own driving force of capitalization, of usury, of getting some kind of return on one's investment. There is no capital without capital gains and there are no capital gains without a wearing away of the hand (the slow and methodical alienation of the life of the laborer for the sake of capital's growth). All that is, in the life of capital, is subsumed under the univocal vision of its growth: trees are lumber, mountains are mineral deposits, and rivers are lines of transport and places to dissolve refuse. It orders the world so that there is one world, one people (a labor force), one slab of asphalt. And yet it does not do this from a centralized command post. It spreads out in localized zones so that it creeps into every nook and cranny of the world, its growth depends on its flexible capacity to appropriate at multiple local levels in a variety of ways and from a variety of points of view. The individual capitalist who sees himself as isolated in his efforts at commanding authority in his community (quickly transformed into a company town) is, through the mode of production, tied into a global network of suppliers, distributors, consumers, and markets spreading out between them. But these tendrils function in the reference to a transcendental organizing concept or signified that is capital, the gathering up and enframing of the world as standing reserve.

In the chapter on "The Working Day" in *Capital,* Marx says that the working day is 24 hours long minus whatever time the laborer will need to reproduce the labor expended during the working day so that he can come back to work tomorrow. Although the amount of time this actually leaves for the working day will vary on the basis of social and physical conditions, he says it is nonetheless the case that even the time spent away from work is structured by the time at work. Even leisure, the recreation of the worker for two weeks a year or two days a week or six hours every day, functions so as to reproduce the bodily energies that the laborer will require to return to work. The body, therefore, as the body of a laborer, is sold as a commodity on the employment market, and requires upkeep—like any machine would, to continue to contribute to the labor process.

> Capital is dead labor, that, vampire-like, only lives by sucking living labor, and lives the more, the more labor it sucks. The time during which the laborer works is the time during which the capitalist consumes the labor-power he has purchased of him.
>   If the laborer consumes his disposable time for himself,
> he robs the capitalist.[32]

It is the body that yields its blood, its life force, to the capital vampire. And just as a vampire does not want to drain its victim of all its blood immediately, lest there be none left to keep the body alive so as to regenerate more blood, capital must "care" for its life source in the same way.

This description from Marx varies somewhat from the description Heidegger gives. Heidegger would agree that the body is commodified (stripped of its "use-value" in favor of a market governed "exchange-value") in the labor of manipulating the *Bestand,* the resources, that are framed by the technological epoch, mode of withdrawing of the circling

---

[32] Karl Marx, *Capital*, vol. I, ed F. Engels, trans. S. Moore and E. Aveling (New York: International Publishers, 1977), 233.

of the Same (of the revolutionary economy of the Same); but he would want to include the additional claim that it is the dominance of "man," the mastery of humanity, over the world that is being asserted in this technological frame of mind. To what extent "man" can be master and yet labor force is difficult to fathom unless we recall that "man" within the age of technology understands Capital in terms of the individual capitalist. "As capitalist, he is only capital personified. His soul is the soul of capital."[33]

Capital personified. The person of the capitalist is a mask that capital wears. The body of the capitalist is the embodiment of capital, its incorporation. This is, of course, equally true of the laborer, although the laborer lacks "soul," he is merely capital. Both bodies, both masks that capital wears, embody capital although they do so in such a way as to mark a division within the economy of capital. Marx describes the division in terms of the relations each has to the productive process, to capital itself. Both are commodified, the markets of capital are as alien to the body of the capitalist as they are to the laborer. Capital governs the life of the capitalist, subsumes the capitalist's bodily energy to the project of capitalization, equally to that of the laborer. Yet the materialization of Capital occurs in the manner of a text (much could be done here with regard to Marx's favorite examples from the weaving of textile industry in the purchase of cotton to make yarn) where the fold or incision in the economy emerges as a class struggle *between* the bourgeoisie and the proletarian.[34]

---

[33] Ibid.

[34] A couple of remarks must be made regarding this discussion of Marx: 1. Marx suggests an Hegelian understanding of the division between capitalist and laborer when he refers to the capitalist as the "soul" of capital and hence implies that the capitalist has self-consciousness of his relation to the means of production. I have avoided this because a reference to self-consciousness accepts Marx's structure/superstructure distinction which is not to be found in Heidegger/Derrida's understanding of an economy, capitalist or otherwise. 2. In a related matter, the dialectical vision that Marx had of the economy poses certain problems. This is a terribly complicated issue and requires more room than can be given in this project, but in so far as dialectic refers to the interwovenness of an economy it is *similar* to Derrida's notion of the trace structure of the text and Heidegger's notion of the gathering place. Still, Marx has a unilinear and continuous conception of history that is not to be found in either Heidegger or Derrida. The distinction will no doubt be elaborated in a discussion of totality (and hence singularity) that Marx has for all economy in comparison with the dissemination and multiplicity that occurs in Derrida's economy. For Derrida, as we have been

The tissue of the flesh incarnates a textuality that is not technological. The fragmentation of the body in its closure in the sweeping manner of gestures gesturing toward other gestures gesturing... brings about a revolution in the economy of presence, sets it turning in the circling of *différance,* supplementarity, *and...* the Same. This fragmentation recalls some remarks made by Foucault near the end of the first volume of *The History of Sexuality* in the chapter on the "Right of Death and Power over Life." Foucault marks off two epochs, one characterized by the power over death the other by the power over life. He distinguishes a sovereign power that expresses itself by controlling the time of death of its subjects from a sovereign power that expresses itself in the disciplining of bodies for the ends of the sovereign power itself. The latter, the power over life, was incompatible with the power over death because "[h]ow could power exercise its highest prerogatives by putting people to death, when its main role was to ensure, sustain, and multiply life, to put this life in order" (*HS I*, 138)? [35] Death, therefore, marked a limit to what Foucault called "Bio-power."

---

noticing, the essential foldedness of *différance* means that its materialization or becoming text is always already a becoming many texts. 3. In a note on the similarity of the strategies of the three thinkers, it is interesting to mention that for Marx communism can be said to be the deconstruction of capitalism in that the inferior "class" gains footing within the old structure and then displaces that structure in its disappearance (along with the disappearance of all classes). Marx therefore saw capitalism as a necessary stage on the way to communism just as Derrida sees metaphysics as essential to closure and Heidegger saw technology as essentially linked to the saving power that emerges from it. Notice that in this way of thinking about it, the present and its beyond (whether capitalism/communism or metaphysics/deconstruction) cannot be thought in a "parasitic" relation or any kind of simple opposition.

Let this note stand for the opening of a questioning rather than the closing off of a solved problem.

[35]"In concrete terms, starting in the seventeenth century, this power over life evolved in two basic forms; these forms were not antithetical, however; they constituted rather two poles of development linked together by a whole intermediary cluster of relations. One of these poles—the first to be formed, it seems—centered on the body as a machine: its disciplining, the optimization of its capabilities, the extortion of its forces, the parallel increase of its usefulness and its docility, its integration into systems of efficient and economic controls, all this was ensured by the procedures of power that characterized the *disciplines*: an *anatomo-politics of the human body.* The second, formed somewhat later, focused on the species body, the body

Although I am taking Foucault out of context here, I want to suggest that it is just this tension that death marks for "Bio-power" (understood here rather roughly as the organization of all life's force toward the development of "capital") that I wish to inscribe into the "handling of things in community" that is the gestural tracing of the body at its closure: the tissue of the flesh. That is, the body's resistant materialization is a text that is not technological because it is always already not yet dead. Still, there is more work to be done because of the proximity suggested by this becoming corpse of the body and the living dead victim of the vampire. The distinction will have to come from an understanding of this condition as one of a beating heart brimming over with communion rather than as a bloodletting measured out periodically over the course of one's life. That is, the living death of the flesh must be thoughtful and poetic.

---

imbued with the mechanics of life and serving as the basis of the biological processes: propagation, births and mortality, the level of health, life expectancy and longevity, with all the conditions that can cause these to vary. Their supervision was effected through an entire series of interventions and *regulatory controls: a bio-politics of the population.* The disciplines of the body and the regulations of the population constituted the two poles around which the organization of power over life was deployed. The setting up, in the course of the classical age, of this great bipolar technology-anatomic and biological, individualizing and specifying, directed toward the performances of the body, with attention to the processes of life—characterized a power whose highest function was perhaps no longer to kill, but to invest life through and through" (*The History of Sexuality*, I 139).

Chapter 5
One, Two, Many Revolutions
The Poetics of Resistance

> Because I still like him, I can foresee the impatience of the bad reader: this is the way I name or accuse the fearful reader, the reader in a hurry to be determined, decided upon deciding (in order to annul, in other words to bring back to oneself, one has to wish to know in advance what to expect, one wishes to expect what has happened, one wishes to expect (oneself)). Now, it is bad, and I know no other definition of the bad, it is bad to predestine one's reading, it is always bad to foretell. It is bad, reader, no longer to like retracing one's steps. -Jacques Derrida, *The Post Card*

L et this epigraph serve as a warning and as a message of sympathy with those, impatient and frustrated, who have followed the demonstration of this project thus far. In the last four chapters a number of important matters have been delayed and deferred, at least it seemed that way. The bad reader will have long been waiting for the final payoff, wondering why it hasn't come already, perhaps. Maybe such a reader will have carefully worked his way through the introduction so as to try to find some hint as to what to expect in this last chapter, in this last crucial element of the demonstration where the practical component of the project will have been laid out. But all to no avail. There were no clear statements, no simple summaries of what the reader could expect. What a horrible situation this must be for such a reader, forced to be surprised, forced to come upon the unexpected, undetermined, non-predestined final maneuver in this long project. Maybe it is for this reason that I feel sympathy for such a reader. That is, providing such a reader is still with me, still waiting, still ready to be surprised. If so, then maybe this reader is not as bad as the epigraph has made him out to be, maybe there is still some hope left even for the bad reader.

In the previous chapter, subjectivity and desire were displayed in all their metaphysical glory and were linked to the transcendental organizing principles of technology and its capitalist economy. The bad reader who desires to subject himself to the pre-determined decision of a text that holds no surprises is a metaphysical reader extraordinaire. And it is noteworthy that Derrida links such a reader with the notion, that he cannot define in any other way, of the "bad." Metaphysics is bad, which must sound strange to a reader who has come to think that deconstruction is no longer capable of making such judgements. Why is metaphysics bad? What's so bad about it? Why should it be brought to its own closure by a deconstructive turn? Perhaps these questions are misplaced. In the third chapter, I demonstrated that metaphysics brings about its own closure, from within, as a part of its own economical dynamic. That is, metaphysics desires to outrun its own facticity, its own essential conditions, and is always frustrated in its attempt to do so. The security of the ground is always an illusion and will begin to shake and tremble if followed through to its necessary implications and conclusions; and nothing is better at doing just that than the technological.

Technology and capital bring the world into the guiding power of a totalizing principle and such a principle is hostile to the dynamic unfolding of world as Heidegger and Derrida have described it. Every effort at securing the dominance and mastery of the transcendental signifier will result in failure at the hands of the unstable things that bear out the world. Things are too wild, weird and unpredictable to be harnessed by the theories and frameworks of metaphysical epochs. It is therefore "bad" to desire to constrain things in this fashion. And what is more, it is even worse to be in a hurry to do so. We have seen both Heidegger and Derrida make reference to a technological emphasis on speed, where speed is supposed to make things nearer to human life, to reduce the distances between things. Such speed fails to bring things closer, instead it makes nearness impossible by way of alienation through universal imposition (*Gestell*) and decadence into commodities for exchange on an open market: things, under the auspices of speed, become less and less thinglike and farther and farther from human being. Technological "mankind" is always in a hurry, and its haste is spurred on by its failure to get near anything at all. The more human beings hurry, the more they must hurry, the more important it becomes for them to be even faster in their decision-making capacity and arrival at their pre-arranged destinations. We are an epoch of bad readers and our badness is self-escalated, making us worse readers until we eventually stop reading at all.

The previous chapter, along with the epigraph of this chapter, serves to warn the reader not to be quick to desire to subject himself to the restrictions and constrictions of the technological and capitalist epoch. Since such a failure to subject oneself and to desire a pre-destined decision is so totally unfamiliar to the current epoch, we are left reeling and spinning from the confusion that it brings. In this confusion, we may begin to feel the first hints of what has been demonstrated all along in the dynamic of this project. We have been made to reel and spin, to turn and circle, to break free from the moorings that have impoverished us as readers for the whole of the epoch that currently overwhelms us, for the whole of the technological whose gears grind and turn until they spin out of control in this terrible confusion. Such a turning and circling will also recall the dynamic of the second chapter which sought, so tediously and meticulously, to repeat (as if by circling back) the major moves of the first chapter. This circling back saturated the whole of the bold claim with the Saying of the Same, an economy of language. These four chapters must, in our reeling and spinning, work together in a singular dynamic that fails to admit of metaphysical determinations and the ghettoizations so common to most traditional theory. That is, we should guard against seeing each chapter in isolation, our confusion must allow the chapters to spin together, to interweave, and to begin to swarm, just as the dynamic was brought to lie. Very early on I showed that the thing and the world were inseparable. Furthermore, I circled the weirdness of the bold claim in a Saying that exposed it to a fourfold world taking place as language, as Saying. The thing's textuality bears out the textuality of the world. World and thing, thing and world, not a ground and its determinant, but a mutually circling dynamic without hierarchy. And then, more recently, the impulse of presence was inserted into this dynamic and the flesh of the human was demonstrated as a thinging thing also bearing out world.

This artificial summary is not a clue as to what the impatient bad reader can expect in what is to come, but a reward for the bad reader's confusion, what remains as residue and resonance in the confusion. This is the spinning of the bad reader's head, the thought that a now thinking bad reader may attain. One more time, more clearly (if that is possible): despite the pretensions of the project thus far, it is not the case that first we have the Saying of the Same, then the presence of metaphysics, then the flesh of the human, which (in what follows) will be shown to act. This structure, common to many metaphysical texts, would not have been subject to the deconstruction underway in this project's moment of closure. Instead, the human flesh is the Saying of the Same. Can that be said? Maybe. The presence of the metaphysical and the mastery of technology is the Saying of the Same. Maybe. And, alas, the practices of the human are the Saying of the Same. Maybe.

What is practice? Better: how does practice work? It circles, it spins in the manner of the Saying of the Same, it is the belonging together of *Er-eignis,* un-concealment, and dif-ference. Practice is the ringing peel of stillness, it is the closure of metaphysics, and it is the creeping flesh of human beings. All along I have been demonstrating the nature (*wesen* and *phusis)* of practice; which is to say, all along I have been demonstrating, gesturing with the hand, circling back upon the bold claim, elaborating weirdness, and, to an extent, resisting presence.

But perhaps I have overstepped my bounds, already rushed ahead in a decidedly "bad" fashion. No doubt. I have felt and been affected by the demands of the bad reader, by the issuing in of presence in the heart of this project. Despite my best efforts in the third and fourth chapters to convey to the reader the importance of waiting, I have failed to overcome this tendency in the writing. But for a tiny blank between a line, my failing is a falling. In my haste, I fall into oblivion, not the oblivion of the groundless, but the forgetfulness that seeks full disclosure.

In the previous chapter, the proximity of a certain technological textuality was un-concealed in relation to the material textuality of the Saying of the Same. These are not two separate dynamics, but a singular dynamic that takes hold over the current epoch. This proximity as "nearness" lies on the ground upon which I fall and is the aim of the demonstration. It is essential that I fall in this moment here now because it is crucial to disclose the proximity that only falling may reveal. The technological textuality is the utter nihilism of the post-modern. The philosophical and transcendental have fallen from view in favor of a boundlessness that is still held by a technology of movement. The calculus of this economy is capital's flexibility and imperial capacity for growth. All the world is the playground of such a postmodernism. The apocalypse of philosophy's end organizes and controls the movement of such an epoch. And this utterly cosmopolitan rootlessness saturates and explodes the totality of the world. But it still lies shielded, it is maintained with the rigidity of a groundless principle, of a transcendental signifier that signals an End of it all, a night where all cows are black and everything has been reduced to an even keel of equal worthlessness (which amounts to a universal measure of exchange through monetary value).

Disregarding the pleas to the contrary made by "theorists" everywhere, this is not the turning and circling of deconstruction. Such a deconstruction requires for its arrival the demolition of hierarchy, but it is not identical to it. There is no foundation, there is no transcendental principle or enabling condition in any shape or form, and this is a supplement of the dynamic unfolded in the postmodern nihilism that, despite appearances (or in agreement with them, as its critics would claim), rejects the technological and the capitalistic. And this not only in theory, but in practice as well. The possibility of this twofold rejection derives from necessity, because practice and theory have collapsed into each other, have become the belonging together of their relation in such a way as to dissolve the poles of the relation. And the Saying of the Same is nothing other than that. Not a theory, not a practice, but a concern for the Same, for the belonging together of the two and the tension *between* them. When we talk of a dynamic unfolding, of an unfolding and a dissemination, we speak of the emergence of world, but we also speak of the coming to reside in the open of things. And furthermore, we speak of our speaking and of our being alongside these things, we speak of our own emergence along with the things that flesh out our world.

Making this claim I both rush ahead and take a step back. I rush ahead because I clue the reader in on what to expect, but I also take a step back because I show the reader that we may have been reading this all along in the dynamic of the economy of the Same. And it is in this double gesture, both forward and backward, that I earn the title "post-modern" *and* "deconstructor," but they are not identical terms, rather two impulses that grow together in the course of the history of metaphysics and within the epoch of its closure.[1]

----

[1] The previous discussion is very controversial. Typically the line that is drawn within the postmodern is that between the postmodern and the post-structuralist, but even there the two are not taken as so radically different in kind as I claim they are. I am understanding the postmodern literally: the epoch that follows the modern; and, since the modern is the epoch of subjectivity, the post-modern, as follows from its interpolation with Heidegger, is the epoch of technology. Frequently, a criticism has been levelled against postmodernism, that it is politically reactionary, that it ultimately throws its hands up and lets the market and the global imperialist forces of the world take command over all that is. I suppose that I am accepting that criticism's view of the postmodern while at the same time excluding certain thinkers who these critics lump together with the postmoderns. I cannot offer at this time a reason for my doing this. But I do, in classical deconstructive fashion, ask the reader to be patient and wait for what is to come in the following pages. There it shall emerge that the practice of deconstruction is anything but an apologetics for the status quo of Western

Now we may turn our attention back to the questions concerning "practice" that were raised earlier. No doubt what follows cannot be a complete account of practice, but it will attempt to do a variety of things through a variety of means. The two most important points that I would like to mention in postmodern fashion prior to getting under way are: (1) The demonstration will try to further elaborate the sense in which this entire project has been permeated throughout with these concerns for practice: this will be done through a discussion of resistance and language/Saying as supplementary notions that are always already interwoven; and through a discussion of dwelling as the opening of the clearing in the world/thing economy. (2) It is also crucial that this discussion address the problems that the reader may have about its lack of commitment. The essential manner in which the deconstructor has been linked to the postmodern is through her lack of commitment. I will discuss how this issue separates the two figures and how postmodernism is without commitment because of the metaphysical necessity within the age of technology and, despite the desire to restate commitment as the cure for the technological universal imposition and dominance, that the deconstructor—still without commitment, offers another way (a pleonasm, no doubt, since the way is always other). I will show that commitment is a reactionary and conservative move in the face of postmodernism's threat and that deconstruction offers a better "alternative," where better is the opposite of something that is more "bad."

Resistance and Saying

The epigraph not only gives a clue as to what Derrida thinks of the "bad" but of what is opposed to it: "retracing ones steps."[2] Perhaps another way of putting this is "circling back" or "turning and circling" or "spinning texts." In a manner of speaking, or in many manners of

---

economic and cultural dominance.

[2]Walking, taking steps, has been described by physiologists as a falling and recovery, a falling concomitant with a recollection of one's composure so as to make the movement look fluid. This reminds me of the *fort/da* of Dasein's perpetual turning in the movement between authenticity and inauthenticity described in the fourth chapter.

speaking, this has been what I have been trying to do throughout this project. In the second chapter, this passage played an important role: "We are, then, within language and with language before all else. A way to language is not needed. Besides, the way to language is impossible if we indeed are already at that point to which the way takes us" (*OWL*, 112). Now, this suggestion only begins Heidegger's questioning concerning an experience with language, since our always already being within language does not imply our experience with language; but he does understand that if we seek a formula that will carry us forward along a way, we shall be looking in the wrong place for this experience. We must enter the way of language not by making haste to move forward into language, but by circling back into the language that has already claimed us (no doubt in the manner of a bold claim). Heidegger's suggestion for undergoing an experience with language was to retrace one's steps, to circle back, to begin turning within the loosened "web" of language.[3]

---

[3]In this movement, the meaning of repetition as it has been oft used throughout this project is filled out and unconcealed in its crucial role in the dynamic. Repetition, however, is not an uncontroversial notion and a few preliminary remarks may be inserted at this point (along with a gesture to a more complete handling in the third section of this chapter on commitment). I am very sensitive to the charge against repetition made by Herbert Marcuse in his article "Aggressiveness in Advanced Industrial Society" where he writes: "Hitler knew well the extreme function of repetition: the biggest lie, often enough repeated, will be acted upon and accepted as truth. Even in its less extreme use, constant repetition, imposed upon more or less captive audiences, may be destructive: destroying mental autonomy, freedom of thought, responsibility and conducive to inertia, submission, rejection of change. The established society, the master of repetition, becomes the great womb for its citizens." (*Negations*. London: Free Association Books, 1988. p 268) The context created around this passage is overwhelming in power as an objection to repetition. Marcuse connects repetition with the death instinct that is pandered to by the hegemonic powers of an industrial society to insure that the people of such a nation will participate willingly in their own repression and dehumanization at the hands of the technological scourge on contemporary life that Marcuse saw instantiated in both Nazi Germany and in the post-war Western nations of the world which have gained, in the course of their "victory" over fascism, an imperial control over all earthly life. One other important connection is made to the Orwellian tendency of such ideologies to dissolve the difference between opposites so that we are willing to believe that war is peace (both in the National Socialist as well as the recent United States military build up carried out in the name of peace and

preserving order), etc. Marcuse's article, as most of Heidegger and Derrida's texts, is a vicious attack on the technological and its leveling tendencies. Marcuse, however, unlike Heidegger and Derrida, wants to look to the humanist values of the Enlightenment for the overcoming of such a technological world. In fact, Marcuse seems to be making a case for seeing all non-humanist philosophical movements as cohorts of the fascist technological movement that dominate this century.

First off, I would say that where repetition is machine-like and based on a principle of identity, I agree with Marcuse. Secondly, I would agree and add that I too have elaborated the position that the death instinct which is the desire for death as the epitome of presence is used by such a technological epoch to promote acceptance of the people's dehumanization. Thirdly, I would also agree that where opposites are maintained as pure locales that come into opposition on the basis of presence, their wearing away and reversal is an insidious form of corruption that seeks to manipulate and destroy any possibility for thinking on the part of a receptive and coerced populace. My agreement on these three fronts already suggests that I think there is a great distance between the notions of repetition, death, the erasure of oppositions advanced in this text and those metaphysical technological notions that Marcuse criticizes so insightfully. It is the clarification of this distance that I leave off for the third section of this chapter. For now, I only want to make two points, one of which might not be opposed to Marcuse and the other of which is a criticism of him: 1. Along with or against Marcuse I claim that dehumanization is precisely the concern of the deconstructive turning of metaphysics. It is precisely the making of human tissue into the disciplined, machine-like bodies of technology that the disruption of presence seeks to solicit. As segue to the second point, however, it is the conception of the human that is at odds with Marcuse's characterization. 2. For deconstruction, the human—recalling Heidegger's phrase, must regain its evocation of the Earth. *Humus*, earth, is the unfolding of the human being in its living emergence and this is a dynamically un-concealed emergence. Marcuse, on the other hand, continues to see the human being as the free willing, autonomous individual that is restricted ontologically in its dynamic and subjected to the rational will to control characteristic of the Enlightenment. Even if one rejects Foucault's attack on the mechanisms of control stemming from Enlightened rationality and its constitution of subjectivity in *Discipline and Punish*, suspicions may remain for any who would look to the Enlightenment for a solution to the socio-historical problems of the technological age. Why should the ideals of nascent capitalism in its pre-industrial form be relevant to those who would resist contemporary problems (or, rather, in what way are historical intellectual

This same second chapter not only carried through on this circling back into the claim of that which claims us as language, but discovered in this circling back the opening up of a region or gathering place that, while reading Heraclitus, Heidegger understood as *logos*. I then described the regioning character of a world that always happens in the manner of granting things that bear out this world in a fourfold manner, a fourfold

---

movements historically effective)? Even if much could be learned from the study of this epoch, I can't suppose anyone would think those ideals applicable without massive revisions. And what would need to be revised? How do you know? Or are these the kinds of questions that stem from the very principles needing to be revised? In any event, no self-respecting adherent to deconstructive movement would deny the fruitfulness of engaging the Enlightenment in terms of its philosophical and ethical import, but even then the question remains as to whether such ideals can become effective without some kind of deconstruction delimiting the closure of metaphysics.

It should be clear that these remarks are directed as much against Habermas' Communicative Action Theory as against Marcuse. Habermas has, in a sense, shown a much more convincing way for the principles of universal reason to remain effective without succumbing to the dangers and excesses of instrumentalism, but I can't help but think he begins where he should come to a close. That is, he seems to think that the practical work of political action must begin with the principles laid down by the philosopher in his work, claiming that communicative action is nothing more than a formal procedure that is prerequisite for getting anything done. The argument with post-structuralism and deconstruction, therefore, occurs at the level of philosophical justification for laying out the epistemological conditions for such practice. But, although that is his project, he is not communicating with the other positions that he engages in works such as *The Philosophical Discourse of Modernity* since this is not the "conversation" writers like Foucault and Derrida are having (as I hope my project has shown). In what must be a brief attempt to make the deconstructive position comprehensible to the communicative action theorist (sic), I will venture to say that—on my reading—deconstruction attacks projects such as Habermas' when it claims that "procedures" for communication must be part and parcel of the political process. And what's more, there will have been positions excluded from discussion because they do not stem from the same set of rules or principles, and which have been deemed on that account irrational. Compromising as much as I am able so as to make this point clear: deconstructive practices and demonstrations find the incision of all communication in listening to the other in an open way that resists pre-supposing the other *is* saying the same *about* the same in terms of the same.

manner which later came to suggest Derrida's disseminating folds of the hymen that is human. I have continually recalled that the relation of world and thing is not first a world and then a thing. The thing, which trembles beneath the constituted objectivity of the moderns and the produced resources of capitalism, exploded all static reification of entities grounded upon the presence of some epochal understanding of Being. The thing is not something other than the circling of the Same in Saying or language, but is the same swarming and gesturing of this dynamic revolutionary economy. The discussion of the thing, recall, was framed with a discussion of naming, a name that bore out things, that set them spinning and gesturing in the manner Derrida came to call a text. In the materialization of the text, the thing things; and since the text is nothing other than its trace structure or supplementary dynamic, it incarnates (fleshes out) the granting world. An experience with language and an experience of the thing are both supplementary notions that circle back in the experience of the bold claim which is nothing other than the opening of the world in things.

Chapters 3 and 4, therefore, were also working hard to circle back within this same economy in so far as they tried to show in various ways how even presence and the metaphysical are steps taken within this same dynamic. Although I frequently made reference to Marx in these chapters, it is all too clear that Marx's emphasis on a superstructure that actually does rise up in presence from out of the underlying economy of a particular stage is not consistent with Derrida's notion of economy. The superstructure that is presence may be a modification of some kind of economic structure, but it does not rise up out of that economy; instead, it maintains a continual place in the regioning dynamic. To say, then, that presence (i.e. the transcendental) is a component of an imminent economy is not to reduce everything to an equal footing as many have understood the discourse of postmodernism to have done (and which I believe it will continue to do). Rather, presence becomes a constant threat to the circling of language. The bad reader, as Derrida describes him, can be seen as a dynamic essential to any textuality. Just as desire pushes forward to its own death to achieve the absolute stultification of its dynamic *différance,* the bad reader strives to bring an end to his reading, to bring about the death of the text, the presence of its end.

To speak, therefore, of these components immanent to the economy of the Same is already to have introduced the notion of tension and force. That is, the transcendental or metaphysical is a force within the economy. There is no rush to conclude that this turn in the elaboration of Saying is an introduction of some new component to deal with the overwhelming difficulties any practice of deconstruction must face. Consistent with the themes of this discussion of circling back, it is — or will be — clear that the language of force (and by inference, resistance) has been at work throughout this project. In the very first chapter, in the very first discussion of unconcealment as *a-letheia,* I showed the extent to which tension and striving played a role in the emergence or disclosure of unconcealment. Earth and world in the art work and *physis* in Heidegger's discussion of the pre-socratics were saturated with the language of force and tension. Later, in the third chapter, the very idea of deconstruction and the closure of Western metaphysics was described completely in terms of tensions and forces that were always at work in the text of metaphysics, cracking its foundations and unsettling its drive to dominate the economy of the Same. Even the thing in the various discussions of it, was characterized by the tensions and forces at work in the mirror play of the fourfold and the gesturing bearing out that came from the nearness, where nearness was that dynamic striving or strife that flexed between the poles of any apparently present relata.

Before continuing with this line of thought so as to draw out some of the details of the way in which Saying and tension merge and indicate an important emphasis on resistance, it is important to explain why it has been necessary to spring these connections at such a late moment in the project. Part of the reason should be clear from what has been said already concerning the bad reader: a writer is also a reader in the relations of materialization in a text that arrives within the dynamic of language. The patience that is at work in being a good reader, the retracing of one's steps that requires a meticulous concern for the goings on of any text, lets the dynamic unfold in all its richness before trying to close off the dynamic in a judgement concerning its inner workings and connections. Or perhaps this is already to overstep the bounds of the good reader. Rather, let the reader be warned that the circling back goes on perpetually since there is no judgment to be earned, the text continues, new connections arise, a good reader's patience can never be tried too much. Even now, we must relax a little and wait for more to be uncovered. It would be a mistake, contrary to all the guidelines of deconstruction laid out here and in other texts, to read these last paragraphs as the bottom line of this project, as the conclusion of a circling that has gone on long enough. A good reader will have taken a long time to have gotten to this point in the text and will no doubt have made many of the connections described above. And what's more, this same reader, this same dynamic that the text undergoes, will have become skeptical at the recent remarks and will hear them, read them as just that, re-marks, traces that extend the dynamic but fail (and perhaps don't even try) to put the text to rest, make it cease its spinning.

The tension will be there always, even the good reader is an essentially bad reader. The good reader comes to rest sometimes, desires to finish the book, draws conclusions that, having been drawn, do not get erased. Desire and representation, circling back once again (and again), become impulses to stop reading, to make things clear, to form judgments and make decisions as to the meaning of the text on the basis of connections already made so as to come to the end of these connections. A bad movie, like anything bad according to Derrida, is one in which the viewer can guess the ending as well as every twist and turn the plot is about to take, the connections are long since made and secured, the film maker desired to make a movie, and having made it, it ceased to be dynamic. A good movie never ends, its closure is the continual reworking of the movie, the viewer circles back constantly within it, why did all those things happen there, what did it all mean, how does it continue to shift and change as my recollections continue? And this movie blends in with more movies, it stays alive, it continues to connect and re-connect, its meaning is re-marked, its understanding is perpetually delayed. Everything made present dies, everything that eludes presence eternally recurs in an endless reforming and remarking that is its remaking.[4] This is so for great artworks of the past, it is so for great peoples and civilizations, and for great events. The trailing off into nothing of something great—in this manner of speaking—is either the realization of its presence (and hence badness) or the failure of a contemporary age to read. When the world is no longer legible to a people, it is hard to tell if it is the world that has become dead to materializing textuality or that an epoch has been overwhelmed by illiteracy. One thing, however, is clear, that in the age of technology as Heidegger understands it in Derrida's reading of him, no one reads anymore. And this text, written on a word-processor perched on a custom laminated table, has sought to tear through the veil of the epoch's failure to read. The structure of this text, its circling back, has been its attempt at exploding the bad reader in all textuality (of writers and readers), and forcing the reader to read well. Here I am

---

[4]Cf. Deleuze's understanding of Nietzsche's eternal recurrence in *Nietzsche and Philosophy*, translated by H. Tomlinson. New York: Columbia University Press, 1983.

attempting to let the text resist all the technological accompaniments that will prohibit its being read.

In the discussion of desire in the fourth chapter, I introduced briefly a language of resistance relevant to the desire for presence and the resistance it embodies toward death as well as the resistance death incarnates toward desire. Derrida wrote: "Différance does not resist appropriation, it does not impose an exterior limit upon it. Différance began by *broaching* alienation and it ends by leaving reappropriation *breached*. Until death. Death is the movement of différance to the extent that movement is necessarily finite" (*OG*, 143). The failure of *différance* to resist appropriation which here signals presence is its permitting desire to want to resist death. This failure of *différance* is its letting desire, and hence presence, resist the economy of *différance*. It is, Derrida claims, *différance* which yields this path of resistance to desire, allows it to breach a path, to open up the pathway of presence. Because it is *différance* that allows this breaching of a present pathway, *différance* also includes within this way the possibility of a reappropriation the boundary of which is marked and remarked by death which yields finitude to *différance,* its pathbreaking nature (in the sense of *wesen* which dynamically unfolds or disseminates).

But surely the resistance which resists by appropriating must oppose in some manner the resistance which reappropriates the guiding forces of *différance*. The two intertwine and collapse together, but yet also suggest a difference. I propose here, following Foucault (and explaining him), to understand the resistance of death that is an appropriation in the alienation of presence as a growing incorporation of positions within the confines of presence: subjects. This, again following Foucault, is the crystallization of resistance as presence — at least for all appearances. Call this "power," then. Resistance, as reappropriation, resists power in a manner of speaking and does so at power's source. I reserve and preserve the term "resistance" for this occurrence, but caution against a simple opposition of power and resistance in doing so. That is, just as I suggested a few sentences ago, the resistance which appears to oppose power in its relation to appropriation, to the taking possession of an alienated force, also shares in the dynamic of power. The opposition of power and resistance may be thought strategically. And this strategy is ultimately aimed at recognizing both the nature of power and its proximity (in the *nearness* of its striving and tension) with resistance. This nearness which, as the title of this book suggests, may be referred to as resistance, might also, more consistently with the material of this project, be thought as the spanning of a distance between that holds the *différance* in the middle of the two relata, like a hymen. Power and resistance are both modifications of this relation of tension or striving that bears out the world and its thinging things.

The gymnastics of this discussion result from the various discourses of contemporary theory which separate resistance/power from language/Saying. Even in Foucault, and certainly more so in other thinkers, power and discourse are thought in separate terms indicating that the important philosophical issue is how to rank order the two separate phenomena. This debate epitomizes the concerns of metaphysical thinking that always looks for something to ground the play of *différance* and rule or govern over its material instantiations. But this is a false path (a bad one), a mistaken matter for thought. The logic of the supplement developed in the previous two chapters and especially chapter 3, warns against making decisions or judgments based on this sort of privileging in the name of a revealed ground or first principle. The economy of Saying has often been described as supplement, as a webworking that does not permit the rankings and orderings so focal to the technological drive to attain mastery over the play of the world. To think the ground as a supplement is to resist its transcendentalization, to see in it a mutual interweaving of things and world, of texts and their materialization, of content and form, of substance and style. The supplementary terms that have painstakingly been laid out in a constant deferral of commitment to a singular origin (*aletheia,* difference, *ereignis,* Saying, *différance,* hymen, supplement, etc.) may be delayed once again so as to include the terms of resistance and power. Resistance, therefore, does not delimit some dynamic over and above the supplementary dynamic of Saying, but supplements that Same dynamic.[5]

Appropriation, therefore, in so far as it is the alienation of *différance* in its becoming present as object, commodity, etc. is therefore no different as a practice of producing laborers or inquiring subjects than is the act of uttering a statement that is meant to represent the object to the subject or that is meant to aid as a linguistic tool in the performing of certain technological objectives. In both cases (if there really are two), language and power show themselves to be equally at work in the delimiting of either a modern or a technological world. The performative speech act and the practice disciplined and shaped by power merge together as practices within a field of relations (a region of tensions or marks).

---

[5] Cf. My article "Carnival and Resistance" for a more detailed view of the argument concerning the problem of hierarchy in discussing post-structuralist concerns with power and language.

Appropriation, which recalls both property and possession as well as Heidegger's *Ereignis* as the event of appropriation, becomes an undecidable word on the limits of technology and deconstruction. When a practice is appropriated in coming into its own, it emerges from an economy of *différance* into an alienated world of entities. But it never does this cleanly and without tension since that world from which it comes and to which it arrives are both tense with the trembling of metaphysics upon its shaky ground. Heidegger gives the name of "whiling" to this phenomenon whereby the entity comes into its dynamic unfolding which is a tension between metaphysics and its deconstruction. The thing whiles on the verge of an alienated worldliness and its disruption. This whiling can be thought as the undecidability of the Event in so far as it permits, through its own movement, a reification in the open as a technological region. But to allow this to happen in calculating technological thought is to fail to grasp the event character of the event and, following the language of Saying that Heidegger evokes in the essay "The Way to Language," it is to fail to undergo an experience with language which reveals language as the Saying showing of the event of appropriation, *Ereignis*. Language as showing is the emergence of the event character of the event in its naming or gesturing (materializing textuality), whereas this same appropriation holds within itself the character of a reification not only of the thing (as an entity that is) but of the event as a static moment in the (a)history of Being.

This character of language as event and the resistant nature of *différance* in its appropriate movement suggests the language of resistance and power and yields a discourse on practices. Typically, the introduction of the prefix "er" to a verb in German adds to the unprefixed verb a sense of skillfulness or practiced capacity for doing something. For Heidegger, the event character of language already delimits it as a realm or region within which not only something like meaning takes place, but as something like a region within which practical possibilities can be carried out. The skillfulness of the *schicken* is intensified in the sending circling of the dynamic of language through Saying's economy as *Er-eignis* (and not only the Greek *Sophon* discussed in the "Logos" essay on Heraclitus). No doubt it could be imagined that when the event becomes the property of Capitalism such capacities and skills will quickly reify into the performances of agents who carry on their business within a technological economy. Practices are restricted and restrained in their being shaped in accordance with market forces that tell us our capacities and talents (to use the properly modern word for it) are useless unless they are developed and commodified.

As further elaboration and evidence for this view of language in Heidegger, I will turn to the word *"verhalten"* used in *Being and Time*. There the world is "significance" which is a contextual relationship of meanings and involvements. Furthermore, the guiding question of *Being and Time* is the question concerning the sense of Being in so far as that connotes its broadest possible intelligibility. Yet language—although seemingly central to understanding sense and significance or meaning, does not saturate Heidegger's concerns. Rather, the practices of a Dasein that is Being-in-the-world occupy that place. And what's more, these practices or comportments of Dasein are thought as *verhalten*. That is, relations of a relating being in the context of its active and meaningful existence. The relation is the basis for Heidegger's early understanding of both language and the practices of a Dasein that at least partially suggests human being in the world. The relation never leaves Heidegger's thought, never ceases to serve as the most important component of the dynamic that is the world/thing Saying the Same. This suggests that, later, when Heidegger is able to make a more sophisticated reading of language as Saying that opens up in/as/through world, the traces of a practice that guided his early thought still may be at work in the thinking of language. The addition to this of the proximity of *Er-eignis* to skilled practice (being fated for something) and the fated movement of a thing should put the finishing touches on this argument of practices' supplementation of language. All along there have been hints and suggestions of how big a mistake it would be to understand language as natural or ordinary language. In so far as "language" or Saying are supplemented in resistance and the tensions of a striving world/thing, it is no longer possible to clearly separate the dichotomy of force and language, or living and meaning.

The clearing, capable of appropriation but also resistant, signals the strife of un-concealment, dif-ference, *Er-eignis,* Saying, the Fourfold, world/thing, and all the supplemental terms from Derrida; and in signaling emerges as a region of tensions, tremblings, and forces. These resistances, like the clearing described in chapter 2, lay out the fields of interpretations and possible interpretations (messages and their being borne), and do so in such a way as to unconceal the language of practice in the practice of language. Clearing therefore encompasses within it a double movement, a movement of releasing and freeing up for economical *différance* as well as an opening up that is a closing off of possibilities, a having become open that now resists, stiff and unchanging—at least for a while. The double nature of this whiling, of what remains in the Open as a residue that has cleared, not only incarnates the dynamism of the flesh, it also incorporates the stasis of the body in appropriated power. This double dynamic, at work since the third chapter explicitly and really since the first awkward and metaphysical phrasings of that bold claim which gripped the project right at the outset, not only un-conceals a dynamic for practice/language but gives an extremely difficult suggestion for discerning, practically (i.e. poetically), the tensions within language/practice of the "good" and the "bad."

For those who still, uncontrollably, want catchphrases, I could say that good practice/language is eventful whereas bad practice/language appropriates. But for that impulse of the good reader that may still lie dormant this will not be enough, this will be one further delay and deferral of the movement at work here.

For yet a third time I will discuss the movement of the *fort/da* that is the turning and circling of Dasein. In the third chapter I linked this to Derrida's making metaphysics tremble and then in the fourth chapter I linked this to the twofold movement of the fleeing of Dasein in the face of itself that is its fateful falling, ultimately into a tomb that invoked and inscribed the closure of Dasein's existence. Now, all these occurrences of turning may be combined in the manner of that resistance that is the clearing of the world in the Saying of the Same carrying out practices in the thinging fourfold. Fleeing, the representation, or the inauthentic and then wanton Dasein, tries to outstrip its necessary being which is evoked all the more in such attempts at escape. I demonstrated that this falling was resistance to death that pursued Dasein as its utmost possibility. Fleeing was a fleeing into the world where Dasein's attention was taken up with certain concernful dealings with entities within the world and at the expense of the world as such. The un-concealment of Dasein's closure was, on this model, not Dasein's ceasing to concern itself with the world, but its renewed Being in an economy that moved at its closure, within its Being-towards-death. The practices of such a concernful Dasein are at work in both modifications of its Being, but they are transformed in accordance with Dasein's relation to its ownmost death. This is not Dasein's appropriation of its death as something that belongs to it in the sense of a mastery or possessed trait, but a transformation in the *heart* of Dasein. This language and practice of authenticity is troublesome for a variety of reasons, not the least of which is the maintenance of some entity Dasein that has existential structures that in some way or another exceed the dynamic of an uncontrolled Saying of the Same. That is, although the discourse of Dasein takes place in some explicit attempt at contrasting it with the humanist and subjectivist metaphysics of the modern epoch, it continues to alienate Dasein from the dynamic of what Heidegger then calls "Being." Yet there was a germ of thinking at work in this early text.[6]

Turning, understood through the language of the Saying of the Same now made resistance and practice, does not un-conceal as some quality of some entity that incorporates it and then becomes alienated from the economy at work in producing it, but as a component of that economy whose dynamic continues to play in/as/through the becoming flesh of the turning and spinning textile that is the flesh of human being, all interweaving or spinning is a continuing to interweave and spin. This flesh is not static but dynamic, meaning that it is at work: where "work" suggests the origin of the work of art and playing in the supplemental manner of *différance*. The materialization of the human being is a whiling that never ceases to be woven and to unravel in the carrying out of its turning with this economy. These "whiling" traces of the flesh are not then atoms or molecules of living tissue, but the remains of the holocaustal fire, the cinders that swarm as flesh consumed to the point of even consuming its own propensity for production and consumption.

With this step, I can display the turning of things (and human beings as things) as a carrying on or carriage that is always a speaking of Saying (*Die Sprache sprecht)* and the practices of this region of free possibilities. Turning is therefore a double turning in accord with the double movement of clearing and appropriating and *différance.* Turning away (viz. falling) is a turning in horror from the abyss of Saying's nothingness and turning toward is a turning away from the nihilistic horror of the exhausted meaning of the technological world that eclipses all experience of the dissemination of Saying.[7] This second turning away is a turning away

---

[6] It should be clear by now that I do not accept this reading of *Being and Time*. It requires that Dasein be understood (sic) as an entity. But Heidegger portrays Dasein as both a being and Being in so far as it is its disclosedness. In virtue of my understanding of Heidegger's project from early to late, this can only mean that Dasein is neither a being nor Being, but the belonging together of the two (i.e., the ontological difference).

[7] Notice the way in which this previous passage places the nothingness of the abyss over and against the nihilism of the technological. For Heidegger, nihilism is not an instantiation of nothingness, but an oblivion or forgetting of the nothing, a manner of Being in which the nothing has retreated into total concealment. It is perfectly consistent with this strange understanding of nihilism that in the epochs of nihilism everything seems to be running

toward the other of the technological, the deconstruction of its metaphysical Being. Both of these turnings are at bottom resistances, the first resistance appropriates life in its pure presence whereas the second releases the event structure of the event in its fully revolutionary unfolding. The opposite is revealed equally in each component of the turning. The first turning away turns from that which it reveals in not facing up to it, in trying to mechanize even the nothing in the technologically concernful dealings of the falling epoch. The second turning away not only turns back toward that which it has always sensed unconcealed "there" "behind" it, but also, in so doing, maintains its apprehension (and mis-givings) concerning that danger of the technological that it now resists in facing up to its ownmost eventful death.

It is for this reason that I have frequently emphasized the importance of resisting any effort at thinking a beyond to metaphysics or an overcoming of it. To turn in such a way as to think (to reckon or calculate) the total annihilation of the metaphysical is to continue to turn in the manner of the first turning, the manner of a fleeing and of an escaping. The main component of the second turning fails to be enacted when it overlooks the importance of the "behind," of that which hovers over one's shoulder as one's dynamic trait. The "behind" that in the second turning is the danger and horror of technological metaphysics cannot be controlled by some effort at harnessing it in the turn away that is a turning back. The logic of the "behind" is part and parcel of all turning and the failure to resist the impulse of presence, which claims that whatever is behind it is no longer present, is to naively repeat the dynamic of metaphysics in one's effort at turning away from it. It is precisely this that motivates Derrida's emphasis on a double gesture that always keeps an eye out for that which is "behind" and never rests comfortably in the harmonious region of some beyond. This, as should be obvious from the wording, is nothing other than a metaphysical gesture that believes itself to have escaped metaphysics. This delusion of thought is similar to the oblivion of the nothing that keeps the first turning moving in its attempt to escape. All escape fails to turn back toward, all escape falls naively

---

smoothly. In fact, it might even be the concealment of concealment that enables an epoch to see the world as running smoothly, as capable of running smoothly. The nothing that is turned from in horror is precisely that turbulence that has always been associated with revolutions where little is able to remain safe and sound from the disruption of the practical movement of the event. I'm grateful to Bill Vaughan for pointing this out to me in conversation.

into the illusory complacency of metaphysics. No matter how good one's motives may be, a turning away in escape will result in failure as that which it seeks to elude will eventually catch up with it in its appropriating taking possession. The utopia of a counter-culture is totally misguided and doomed if it thinks it can maintain its "style of life" without being eventually engulfed by the imperial movement of the technological. The truly resistant turning back and away from the metaphysical must always recall its essential double turning, its displacement (i.e. eventful clearing) must feed off of its ownmost movement of resistance to appropriation.[8]

The language of resistance begins to suggest the concomitant relation of practice and Saying that fleshes out the regions of *différance* coming to pass in/as/through the world/thing. Nevertheless, many important omissions are at work throughout this discussion. The messenger whose carriage is the bearing of the thingly message that opens up in the giving sending of the world, who practices his art there in an essentially double turning that makes him both message bearer and networker of information has been naively delimited in this discussion. "We" have continued to preserve the prejudices of a "we" whose autonomy from the economical forces is at least implicitly borne in the ongoing language and practice of this project. It is no small question to ask after the specifics of this carrier of messages who—along with all other things, bears the impossible weight of the double turning that constantly ebbs and falls within the ab-solute proXimity of metaphysics and deconstruction.[9] But, only at this point, can I give the discussion of

---

[8] Cf. note 3 above on Marcuse.

[9] "Ab-solute" here and in the phrase "ab-solute resistance" may not be thought as a term of eternal substantialization or objective dominance over the field of tensions (like that term "absolute proximity" called into question in chapter 4), but as a strategic unraveling of that same logic that yields talk of absolutes. Where the ab-solute is reserved for the proximity of the double turning to itself, of resistance to power, and of the relation that drives a rift into the between of a self-present identity become the Same (a leap away from the principle of identity), it becomes an ab-solute impossibility of the absolute where this phrase might employ the paradoxical logic of Kierkegaard in, say, "Fear and Trembling" which is meant to disrupt the totalizing capacity of the system that he takes as the horror to be turned away from. This kind of strategic double gesture, which inscribes the ab-yss into the hyphen of the ab-solute, should be familiar by now to the reader who has come to see the manner in which a deconstructive practice may inh(ab)it

this carrier, because only now is it possible to see the full relation of the notion of carrying here and the notion of, say, carrying out developed in the discussion of dif-ference in the first chapter. The carriage of dif-ference which came to circle within the Same is now un-concealed in its eventlike movement as the carriage of Saying that is language/practice. Or, to put it still another way, it is the experience of language that language itself speaks. This carriage may be inadequately named "poetic thinking."

The Poetic Thinker as Rogue and Mail Carrier

What makes Derrida such a great reader, and especially such a great reader of Heidegger, is his ability to show the ab-solute proXimity of metaphysics and deconstruction. This became apparent in the fourth chapter while looking at Derrida's reading of the *Geschick* or "sending." The multiplicity of language that Derrida pointed out in Heidegger's treatment of the *Geschlecht* in Trakl's poem, allows the sending of the Same to become a dissemination of sendings, a multiple unfolding of the fourfold world. The disclosure of the world for Heidegger is never singular, never *a Geschick,* but always many, just as the fold is always multiple, always a doubling of the singular, and so on. The discussion was inscribed by a discussion of the hand in Heidegger's *What is Called Thinking?* and revealed a twofold disclosing or gesturing of the hand as both technological and thoughtful. Although we caught sight of the technological in the hand, I have not gone very far in examining the

---

crucial components of metaphysics so as to solicit them and bring ab-out their economic closure. About face, play on maestro.

Furthermore, with regard to "proximity," it may be tempting to oversimplify Derrida's alliance of proximity (in Heidegger for instance) with the pure presence of metaphysics—i.e. the proper, property, Appropriation, proximity discussed in Derrida's *"Ousia* and *Gramme."* The oversimplification is the reduction of the playfulness that this word has in this project and, despite Derrida's claims, in Heidegger's text as well. That is, in the middle or midst of "proximity" the chiasmus of the X sounds and resounds, making all propriety of proximity tremble. The X of proximity is not a hyphen but it supplements the hyphen and draws the notion of proximity into the nearness of the ab-solute. Thus, be careful to reread: ab-solute proXimity.

thoughtful component of the hand, the manner in which the hand is essentially linked to the thoughtful practice called "deconstruction."

The hand is the "monstrous sign" that carries out the Saying of the world/thing in demonstrative gestures. As such a signing, the hand evokes the Saying of the Same which has been drawn into the practice of resistance and striving. The reaching of the hand, which Heidegger characterizes as a component of its carrying nature, recalls the reaching out of the Saying of the Same described in chapter 2 where I demonstrated the way in which "man" reaches out to that which reaches out to him. Thinking, in so far as it is the reaching of the hand that carries out Saying, is not a contemplative or theoretical endeavor, detached from all worldliness, but the carrying out of all worldliness, the within the world carriage of all gesturing creatures. On this account, thinking is conceived in the figure of practice and not in its characteristically metaphysical figure of cognition or intellect safe from the fray of the world.

The notion of "using" became important at that point for Heidegger's description of thinking. In that discussion I showed that Heidegger contrasted the notions of use as utilization and mastery to use as "to let [something] enter into its essential nature, to keep it safe in its essence" (*WCT*, 187) where essence is the way of the dynamic of world-bearing appropriate to the eventfulness of things. Recalling the essay "The Origin of the Work of Art," this characterization of thinking displays another ab-solute proXimity crucial to Heidegger's thinking on practice. That is, the letting come into its own of a thing is the "truthful" or "un-concealing" character of the work of art, the emergence of which is called *dichten* (usually translated as "to poetize"). This letting come into its own of the thing, is the preservation of the thing for a while through the poetizing forces of Saying. In Heidegger's lecture course on thinking, this poetic disposition of language is equated with the "taking to heart" of thinking.

Although this is largely repetition of an earlier demonstration, it also includes a slight variation on the theme. Namely, the poet or thinker are no longer being characterized as the agents underlying some practice. Rather, the coming to pass of the thing in poetry and thinking, in this taking to heart that is the reaching out of the hand that carries, is attributed to the Saying of language, or the practice of resistance. It would be a mistake to formulate a double characterization of the ab-solute proXimity of metaphysics and deconstruction in terms of, on the one hand, the dynamic of the world/thing and, on the other hand, the dynamic of the captain of industry and the poetic thinker. The emergence of the dynamic of the world/thing is the emergence of the dynamic of poetic resistance. The hand that gestures in thinking is the monstrous hand signing in the swirling circling Saying of the Same.

This demonstration, the de-monstering of "man" in favor of the monstrous sign that gestures in human fashion, is the deconstruction of subjectivity not only as some absolutely substantial component of reality, but also the deconstruction of "man" understood as something that can take place *beyond* the dynamic of Saying's circling. This reorientation of the human then breaks from the ill-named traditions of classical humanism (ill-named because it is not actually a concern for the human/hymen, but for "man") is therefore badly named "anti-humanism" and is better invoked in the naming of a remarking of the human. This humanity is very far from a liberal humanism that understands the human on the basis of an identity that lies in the essential quiddity of each individual living human creature, but is instead an emphasis on the dynamically unfolding sameness of humanity. That is, humanity's ownmost circling as its thinglike bearing out of world erases all simple identities in favor of the materialization of textual relations in the form of resistances and practices: the Saying of language in naming (gestating) the human. Only on this basis can human community be thought in so far as the community ceases to demand the sole and crucial locus of all its members' identities. The thinglike human community disseminates the human into a multiplicity of communities just as the sending of the circling of the Same is a multiplicity of sendings. I—so to speak—am not a member of one community, but as a communally emergent human, am caught up in the dynamics of many communities, some of which overlap, some of which do not, some of which abide nearby in proximity, and some of which do not.

Hostility, essential to the ab-solute proXimity of metaphysics and its deconstruction, is displayed in and across communities through the desire to identify and reify the community: to purge it of its textuality as *différance*. Within the community, within any dynamic, this desire is the attempt at escaping the dynamic multiplicity of all communal emergence. The attempt at appropriating the forces of the community for some crystallized power structure is the attempt of some hegemonic order gaining mastery over the community and presenting the community, subdued, as the picture of unity that supports the dominating interests. To reflect back on some of the sloppy language use in this very project, it is apparent that every statement of a "we" carries within it a dark threat over those who dare to resist the encompassing appropriation of the few who speak for the many. But any "we" is unstable, it vibrates within the unity of its forced identity and begins to shake apart into a multiplicity in the very echoing of its utterance. The "we" which can be made to carry within it the totemic power of the phallus that extends over the realm of the entire community, is an "I" in disguise. Or rather, the oligarchy of individuals — whose identity is brought to mastery, cast their nets over the community with the escalation of power to the "we." The "we" is, despite its hostile undertones, ripe for deconstruction because just that character which makes the "we" effective as a net, allows for its immanent dissemination and deconstruction. This same dynamic of the hostility within the community can be thought in the hostility that exists between communities. The net of the colonial powers, or an imperial power, or even the intrigues of an international community of political interests, can all be viewed as attempts at extending the realm of an already posited and stable community into further reaches of the world through the casting of a bigger and bigger net.

The image of the net, suggestive of a network, is powerful for its proximity to the mesh and webbing of the Saying of the Same, the economy of *différance*. The unconcealment of this ab-solute proXimity in the netting of a web, or the webbing of a net, further calls upon the necessity of thinking the nearness of the Saying of the Same, that nearness of withdrawal that is erased in the pure representation of the network. Thinking, as the dynamic of the Saying of the Same, can be characterized therefore as a human networking *and* as a human community or webwork. Thinking bears within itself the human in so far as it emerges as both technological utility and as deconstructive letting become text. Within thinking, therefore, the nearness of ab-solute proXimity is overwhelming and it is just such a nearness that characterizes thinking. The evoking of thought and that which evokes thought are the Same; they are the nearness that encircles in the practice of resistance.

Before going on with this discussion and looking more deeply into the meaning of this thinking that bears out the ab-solute proXimity of the nearness, it is worthwhile to turn to the frequently deferred relation of poetry and thinking. Since the third chapter of this project, it has been clear that the ab-solute proXimity of technology and deconstruction is crucial to their dynamic. Although I have shown that thinking bears out this proximity (at least I've been suggesting it), I have also shown a connection of poetry and thinking. Before venturing further (or perhaps as a roundabout way of venturing still further), I will turn to the relation of poetry and thinking in Heidegger's work so as to see if I can find a clue there for the journey into the nearness that is the practical resistance of technology in deconstruction.

In the discussion of Saying in the second chapter, I indicated that thinking and poetry *(dichten)* are two modes of Saying, in fact, two "pre-eminent modes." Before I return to the essay "The Nature of Language" which describes the relation of thinking and poetry, I will elaborate some of the topography of the discussion thus far. Technology and poetry came into ab-solute proXimity in Heidegger's "Question Concerning Technology" which discovered in the essence of technology the poietic emergence of Saying in the destiny of the Same:

> Because the essence of technology is nothing technological, essential reflection upon technology and decisive confrontation with it must happen in a realm that is, on the one hand, akin to the essence of technology and, on the other hand, fundamentally different from it.
> Such a realm is art. (*QCT*, 35)

And this recalls the artwork essay where the essence of art is called poetry. The inclusion of the *techne* of Greek thought in the *poiesis* of that same thought enables the thinker of the essence of technology to see in technology a *techne* that is essentially *poiesis,* the emerging destining of the Same. Because of the proximity of the *Gestell* of technology to the *Geschick* of destining or sending, and because of the proximity of the technological with the Greek *techne,* the poetic emerges in the nearness of the technological as its dynamic realm, the realm where it emerges but remains alienated. The nearness of poetry to technology no doubt recalls the nearness of thinking to technology described in the carrying of the hand.

Furthermore, recall the discussion in chapter 3 where poetry displayed itself as the saving power from the greatest danger presented in/as/through technology. Poetry's ability to venture into the nearness of technology is what empowers it as the saving of humanity from the technological. But not only the saving of humanity, but the saving of things from reification and commodification as technological resources. The poet lets the thing be as a thing and thus emerge from its technological constraints. This letting be is a saving in that it preserves or guards the thinging of the thing in its whiling within the Saying of the Same. Although this all functions as review, in this context it highlights the strange relation that evolves between poetry and thinking. Thinking, as thinking, ventures near to technology, while poetry does the same. Yet,

Heidegger maintains the distinction between poetry and thought. Carelessness in this matter may lead to a failure to think the nature of poetry or a failure to poetize the nature of thinking.

Some of Heidegger's commentators, like Richardson, have gone to great lengths to show the distinction and similarity of poetry to thinking. The apparatus in place in this project enables me to arrive at this relation without any more difficulty than I have had thus far in other such matters concerning the circling of the Same.

> Accordingly, when we speak of language we remain entangled in a speaking that is persistently adequate. This tangle debars us from the matters that are to make themselves known to our thinking. But this tangle, which our thinking must never take too lightly, drops away as soon as we take notice of the peculiar properties of the way of thought, that is, as soon as we look about us in the country where thinking abides. This country is everywhere open to the neighborhood of poetry. (*OWL*, 75)

Heidegger's language is very suggestive language here, it is the language of countries and neighborhoods. Up to this point in the essay, Heidegger has been showing that language does not yield to an attempt to think it through linguistic objectification. The objectification of language, speaking of or about it, is to venture into a tangle, a tangle that drops away, that falls away, when thinking notices what country it is in, what region it has come to reside when it attempts to think the nature of language. Nearby, in the neighborhood of this thoughtful region, is poetry. When thinking ventures into the region of language, into an attempt at undergoing an experience with language, it comes upon poetry.

Anyone who thinks, and it strikes me that there may be some who think this, that Heidegger is not carrying out a deconstructive relation to language, would do well to study the dynamic of this essay and the manner in which poetry and thinking are brought together. To be in the same neighborhood, of course, is to be in the nearness of something. When thinking ventures into the neighborhood of poetry it enters into its nearness, the nearness of Saying. But it is an error to think that first poetry was there and then thinking comes to join it. We saw in the earlier discussions of nearness that nearness is always an unfolding of a belonging together, a relation that is carried out in the striving tension between, say, revealing and concealing, and within the dif-ference, etc.

Once again, it would be wrong to hypostatize thinking and poetry as separate poles in a relation, it is their coming together in this neighborhood of Saying that is their mutual emergence, their belonging together there, which creates the neighborhood that they share.

The deconstructive component of this is unconcealed in the way in which Heidegger begins with an ordinary understanding of both poetry and thinking and begins to undermine this opposition in favor of its relation. "Neither poetic experience with the word nor the thinking experience with Saying gives voice to language in its essential being" (*OWL*, 80-1). If we think of poetry in the ordinary sense of the actions carried out by poets and thinking as the activities carried out by thinkers, we will fail to come upon language. Poetry does not speak language, nor does thinking speak it. Language speaks in the nearness of poetry and thinking, the speaking of language is the poetic thinking of Saying, the silent ringing out of the stillness in the nearness of Saying: Language speaks poetically and thoughtfully.

Traditionally, there have been poets and there have been thinkers and the two have been so ghettoized that they have never been permitted to live in the same neighborhood. Heidegger is warning us that this exclusive opposition of the two modes of Saying fails to see either in their relation to the Saying of language. Only thoughtful poetry speaks the emergence of language, only poetic thinking speaks the Same. "Perhaps the 'and' in 'poetry and thinking' will receive its full meaning and definition if we will let it enter our minds that this 'and' might signify the neighborhood of poetry and thought" (*OWL*, 81). Just as the title of chapter 3 brought this project into the neighborhood of the turning and circling of metaphysics and deconstruction, the "and" in the traditional understanding of poetry and thought does the same. The "and" ceases to signify the presence together of two separate and self-identical entities, but becomes the supplementary economy of their interweaving relation.

Those therefore who fail to see the supplementary nature of poetry and thinking are making the same kind of mistake someone would be making if they tried to think the relation of *différance* and trace and hymen and supplement in terms of the nature of each component's presence to the others. To try and clarify or present the relation of these supplementary notions in a way that fixes that relation is to reify the economy of the supplement in the moment that one tries to enter it. And this is on a par with the objectification of language that takes place in any metaphysical understanding of it, the process of inquiry permanently nullifies the goal of the inquiry, buries what it seeks before it sets out to look for it.

The neighborhood of poetry and thinking, the supplement of poetry and thought, is the tense striving of the nearness that opens up between them in the nontraditional poetic thinking. This tension not only reminds me of the essentially resistant practice involved in all such poetic thinking, but also points to the nature of the poetic as *dichten*. *Dichten,* in German, signifies both the writing of poetry in a more traditional sense deconstructed by Heidegger, but also suggests the act of stretching tight or making tight. What is tight, what is stretched to achieve tightness, no doubt begins to resonate and vibrate, begins to peel through the nearness of the tolling death knell of language. The trembling of metaphysics' closure is the stretching tight that occurs in all poetizing (where this word must, in the deconstruction made possible through the multiplication of the term's meanings, already suggest the tautness and vibrations of resistant poetic thinking). Poetic thinking, therefore, recalls that same tightening and stretching that I described in chapter 4 with regard to dissemination and the unfolding of the hymen. The emergence that is, singularly understood, the unfolding of the fold and the emergence that is, also singularly understood, the disseminating of seeds are, when considered in their supplemental nearness, the poetic thinking of the neighborhood where dwelling in nearness takes place.[10]

To the extent that the poetic thinker is stretching out within a neighborhood, it is also whiling away time in a human/hymen community. That is, in Heidegger's phrase, it is a dwelling within the fourfold region of the world. Dwelling is always dwelling in a neighborhood, and this means the nearness of a community. Because of the tensions in poetic thinking and because of the nearness poetic thinking has with the technological hostility of the network of people subjected to a principle of identity with the community, dwelling—and the exposition of it here, must function as a practice that resists the technological. Dwelling must show the way in which the nearness of poetry and thinking

---

[10]It is tempting, at least for me, to see thinking as dissemination and poetry as the unfolding of the hymen and although this may have certain strategic benefits, it is ultimately engaged in a dynamic that seeks the polarization of supplemental notions. To consider thinking, poetizing, unfolding, or disseminating as equal to anything, even to themselves, is to place them within a dynamic that is governed by the principle of identity and not the leaping of the Same, it is to try to bring the dynamic of this economy to a halt by inscribing it with present nodes that supersede the articulation of the relations of those structures.

emerges with the tense nearness of the technological. As such a demonstrative practice, dwelling must carry through on a renewed *ethos* implied by the Heideggerian and Derridean texts.[11]

Recall the following passage, discussed in chapter 2:

> The guide-word gives us a hint on this way [into the neighborhood of poetry and thinking], but not an answer. But that hint—where does it point? It points only to what defines the neighborhood of poetry and thinking as a neighborhood. Neighborliness, dwelling in nearness, receives its definition from nearness. Poetry and thinking, however, are modes of saying, indeed preeminent modes. If these two modes of saying are to be neighborly in virtue of their nearness, then nearness itself must act in the manner of Saying. Then nearness and Saying would be the Same. The demand to think this is still a flagrant imposition. Its flagrancy must not be softened in the least. (*OWL*, 95)

The neighborliness of poetry and thinking is the "dwelling in nearness" of the poetic thinker. The context of the discussion of these matters in chapter 2 led to the following claims being made: "[The nearness] is the striving where revealing and concealing are in tension thus enabling the

---

[11]*Ethos,* of course, is the Greek work Heidegger translates as *wohnen* or dwelling. Although it is correct to see in this word the origins of the metaphysical notion of "ethics," the word is not exhausted by such an account. Although the sequel will attempt to look deeper at this notion, the reader should be cautioned against referring to dwelling as Heidegger's "ethics" since Heidegger thinks this philosophical endeavor has been overwhelmed with metaphysical presuppositions and prejudices. In the language of Derrida, any ethics that is presented metaphysically will attempt to restrict the economy of *différance* so as to be sure of its ability to anticipate and pre-destine all the activity that ensues. It may be necessary in what follows to spend some time discussing the manner in which ethics, traditionally understood, has always attempted to control practice, to appropriate the actions of individual humans. Would metaphysical ethics be troubled with the question, is such a project on the part of ethics ethical? It is a strange position, I know, but one has to realize that in so far as metaphysics is allied with mastery, de-humanization, and totalizing, any ethics with its roots in metaphysics (and for Heidegger that means all ethics) is bent on just such goals. Let me ask the reader, once again, to resist the "bad" impulses of reading and reserve judgement on these matters, remain open to the possibilities that follow, and be willing to retrace your steps along the way.

world and earth to open up and come to rest upon each other in the strife."
It is now possible to realize that this resting upon each other is the thinging
of the thing that whiles away in the open. And furthermore, the strife and
tension of the nearness where the thing and poetic thinker reside or dwell,
is the practice of resistance. But only now am I ready to discuss the
"flagrant imposition" made upon the poetic thinker by dwelling in the
nearness. The flagrancy, Heidegger tells us, is so little something to be
overcome that it actually "must not be softened in the least." This
conflagration of nearness and dwelling must be retained, it must remain
as the residue and resonance of the opening nearness, of the ringing of
stillness with the Saying of the Same. In this flagrancy, in this
conflagration, it is necessary to hear the apocalypse of the apocalypse, to
see the all-consuming holocaustal fire that is technology's closure.

Pausing for a moment along the way of dwelling in nearness, of
neighborliness, I would like to interrupt the judgment that follows upon
this point. Retracing my steps, I would like to recall the extent to which
the ab-solute apocalypse of the apocalypse is the trailing off of all
apocalyptic thinking (practice) and that the holocaustal for Derrida is the
consumption of even the fire itself burning in every holocaust. To that
extent, this conflagration can be thought as the ab-solute resistance of the
apocalyptic and the holocaustal which characterize the epoch of
technology. Yet, this is done in a manner that recognizes the extreme
danger that the technological continues to bear. Heidegger's point must
be understood in this way, must be understood as a resistance of the
impulse to water down or oversimplify the dangers that constantly
threaten dwelling. The kinds of dangers that were earlier characterized in
the discussion of escape.

As an illustration, recall the manner in which things may be said to
run smoothly within the darkest of technological nihilisms. The tension
of a revolution disrupts the quietism of the status quo. Revolutionary
times are turbulent; and, if such times are turbulent in the manner of the
turning and circling inscribed in this project, then to attempt to decry the
"violence" of these rumblings is to defend the status quo whose exertion
of force has made the conditions right for the revolution to take place at
all. Consider a situation in which an "authoritarian" government with the
flimsiest semblance of democratic procedures is so brutal in its treatment
of the impoverished populace of its nation that many people join in a
movement to oppose this regime. To criticize this uprising in the name of
the well-oiled machine of the authoritarian leadership and their foreign
allies is to defend violence against revolutionary violence, it is reactionary

and conservative in the political *and* the metaphysical sense. It is the appropriating will of the technological powers that be that calls for the easing of tensions and the softening of all flagrant imposition to the status quo.

To continue with the discussion of dwelling, the question is raised as to how it is possible to distinguish dwelling residing in the revolutionary tensions of nearness from other kinds of apparently radical movements that may represent themselves as revolutionary but on the whole repeat the appropriating ideology of the technological.[12] First off, attention will be focused on some of the things Heidegger writes concerning the practices of dwelling.

The bad reader in every reader may yawn at the next step since they are totally unsurprised by the claim that the practices of dwelling are nothing other than the practices of deconstruction oft described throughout this project. Why not just stop here, the bad reader in me says; after all, isn't it painfully obvious by now what deconstruction is and that dwelling in the nearness that must work to resist technology as its nearness is just identical to that? And what's more, this desire says, isn't my conclusion based on the practices of the good reader in me who gains this knowledge of identity through a retracing of the steps the project has taken thus far and the manner of deconstruction that has been elaborated in them? Yet, already I sense the haste that prevails in this effort at a conclusion, the will to be determined and subjected to a singular position all of which is hostile to the practices of deconstruction.[13] Even in the supplementing of "deconstruction" with "dwelling" there must resonate a

---

[12]The previous discussion of the so-called "post-modern" and the deconstructive which, in very pedestrian terms common in the American academy, "all look alike" should show just how difficult this distinction appears to be. Once again this resemblance (so to speak) will not and should not be softened since it is the ab-solute proXimity of the two that enables the very possibility of dwelling in nearness.

[13]Notice here that even the notion of "position" elaborated in its deconstructive form previously shows a technological component. In English, the position is something that is posited, that is made to stand. There can be no position in the deconstructive understanding of position, there must always be positions. Derrida writes: "And if we gave to this exchange [that between Derrida and the interviewers], for its (germinal) title, the word *positions*, whose polysemia is marked, moreover, in the letter *s*, the "disseminating" letter *par excellence*, as Mallarme said? I will add concerning *positions:* scenes, acts, figures of dissemination." (*P*, 96)

nearness, a nearness that will circumscribe and inscribe the figures of Derrida and Heidegger into a supplemental tradition (cf. chapter 3, the section "The Tradition Begins to Turn: an Economical Exchange").

In his 1946 essay "What Are Poets For?," Heidegger, without mentioning dwelling, gives many suggestions for understanding it. The title comes from the poem "Bread and Wine" by Hölderlin which included the full line: "and what are poets for in a destitute time?" The destitute time for which the poet offers up poets as questionable is the epoch of technology in which everything seems to be running smoothly:

> Long is the destitute time of the world's night. To begin with, this requires a long time to reach to its middle. At this night's midnight, the destitution of the time is greatest. Then the destitute time is no longer able even to experience its own destitution. That inability, by which even the destitution of the destitute state is obscured, is the time's absolutely destitute character. The destitution is wholly obscured, in that it now appears as nothing more than the need that wants to be met. Yet we must think of the world's night as a destiny that takes place this side of pessimism and optimism. (*PLT*, 92-3)

This sounds familiar as Heidegger's notion of an inverted nihilism that governs the age of technology where the operations of the machinelike quality of life are so smooth and totalizing that the "nothing" beyond this epoch fails to emerge, withdraws into oblivion. The epoch is a time of nihilism and oblivion not because nothing matters, but because entities matter so much in their technological Being that there is no possibility of thinking the dynamism of their emergence, the "nothing" that is the Saying of the Same. The need that is felt at the absence of this "nothing," the nothing that is missing from technology, is interpreted technologically as the need for progress, etc.

Further on in the piece, after turning his attention to Rilke, Heidegger remarks: "The formless formations of technological production interpose themselves before the Open of the pure draft. Things that once grew now wither quickly away. They can no longer pierce through the objectification to show their own" (*PLT*, 113). Following Rilke, Heidegger refers to this as an "Americanism" in so far as America stands for the cutting edge of technological innovation and appropriation. Ultimately however, such an Americanism does not depend on the historical contingencies of one particular nation's dominance over the world market, it refers instead to a global technological epoch. An epoch where things no longer come into their own, but are commodified and objectified in the markets of a global capitalist economy:

> Self-willing man everywhere reckons with things and men as with objects. What is so reckoned becomes merchandise. Everything is constantly changed about into new orders. The parting against the pure draft establishes itself within the unstilled agitation of the constantly balancing balance. By its objectification of the world, the parting, contrary to its own intention, promotes inconstancy. Thus ventured into the unshielded, man moves within the medium of "businesses" and "exchanges." Self-assertive man lives by staking his will. He lives essentially by risking his nature in the vibration of money and the currency of values. As this constant trader and middle-man, man is the "merchant." He weighs and measures constantly, yet does not know the real weight of things. Nor does he ever know what in himself is truly weighty and preponderant. (*PLT*, 135)[14]

Here no doubt is left regarding Heidegger's clear connection between capitalism and technology; and, what's more, no doubt is left that he sees in this the pinnacle of destitution. The article has led to this discussion through a description of man's will in the epoch of technology, where man asserts himself as something above and beyond the "pure draft." The pure draft, as I showed in the discussion of *Bezug* in chapter 2, is the drawing in that occurs in the movement of the circling of the Same's opening up as fourfold world. The pure draft is that from which "man" is alienated in his self-willing and asserting, making himself and everything with which he is concerned an object of trade and consumption. This willing is a willing to outstrip the drawing in of the draft, the illustrating *Bezug* which would attempt to mark "man" within the remarking dynamic of a human hymen.

---

[14]Could it be that Heidegger is here merely concealing and repeating the ideology of National Socialism? The "merchant" that is "man" absorbed in the business of life may be the dehumanizing characterization of the Jew in Nazi propaganda. See the more careful examination later in this chapter where Heidegger's admittedly reluctant anti-Semitism (he doesn't, as we saw in chapter 4, want to buy into the racist metaphysics of "nationalism") results in Reb Derrissa's (the Rabbi/Moil of deconstruction) forced circumcision of the old German.

Because man's will, by making man autonomous, alienates him from the pure draft, Heidegger always associates it with metaphysics. In this work, technology is thought as the highest instantiation of the will as "the will to will." Total technological mastery becomes the willing of a will that dominates the world, that takes it over and, at least from the alienated perspective of man, makes man's will look like the master of all that is. Technology becomes the extended and totalitarian will of mankind and the progress that is desired in the need of the destitute time is the desire to extend the will for its own sake, the will to will. Man, in having this point of view however, fails to see the extent to which he himself becomes a component of the will's technological extension. Man dissolves into the alienated and alienating churning of the machine and becomes one further tool in the project of a global technology: human resources.

Although this destitution seems essentially dangerous to the essence of "man," it is precisely the obscuring of the danger that lies in wait for "man." Destitution's obscuring of its own destitution is the failure to take account of the danger. This danger then becomes associated with the pure draft that has been covered over in the technology of the epoch. Technology, threatened by the danger of the pure draft, attempts to shield all things in the objectification process. Alienation alienates things from the draft and shields them. This shielding appears in the manner of "need" and "want" and "will." Unshieldedness, therefore, appears as a danger that threatens all that is in its quiddity, its metaphysical essence. "Man" and all that he needs in the world is threatened by this unshieldedness. The poetic thinker, therefore, is the one who ventures into the unshieldedness where the danger lies. The poet is the one who wrestles with the danger, who risks all that is shielded for the sake of this danger. Such risking, for Heidegger, seems essentially linked to the very notion of "way" and being along the way.

> The word *Wage,* in the sense of risk and as the name of the apparatus, comes from *wägen, wegen,* to make a way, that is, to go, to be in motion. *Be-wägen* means to cause to be on the way and so to bring into motion: to shake or rock, *wiegen.* What rocks is said to do so because it is able to bring to balance, *Wage,* into the play of movement, this way or that. What rocks the balance weighs down; it has weight. To weigh or throw in the balance, as in the sense of wager, means to bring into the movement of the game, to throw into the scales, to release into risk. What is so ventured is, of course, unprotected; but because it hangs in the

> balance, it is retained in the venture. It is upheld. Its ground keeps
> it safely within it. (*PLT*, 103)

The wager risked in the venture is the playing of a game of draughts, granted to humanity through the messenger Thoth whose rogues play on in the dangerous and unshielded region of the pure draft. Poetic thinking is the movement of rogues in the play of the venture abiding as pure draft. The rogue is the one who takes the risk, who abandons the shieldedness of the technological form of exchange and sets out to make his way as a gambler. A conversion occurs here, a transformation. Heidegger tells us that there is a safekeeping in the draft, a manner in which things are guarded there. Although the rogue disrupts the security of shieldedness, she acquires a new home along the way. Her life takes on a new balance, or rather it is so set in motion that her life hangs in the balance with this same venture, she becomes an adventurer and is welcomed as such. There is a place in this game for every thing and every thing, no longer alienated in the shieldedness of its Being, can come to rest and reside there.

> Unshieldedness can keep us safe only when the parting against
> the Open is inverted, so that it turns toward the Open — and into
> it. Thus, what keeps safe is unshieldedness in reverse. Keeping
> means here, for one thing, that the inversion of the parting
> performs the safekeeping, and for another, that unshieldedness
> itself, in a certain manner, grants a safety. (*PLT*, 121)

Heidegger thinks the ab-solute proXimity of the venture into the pure draft in terms of the keeping that is *bergen* (from *Unverborgenheit* as unconcealment) suggestive of a coming to reside in the concealment of Being, in the circling of the Same disruptive of and displacing all metaphysical epochality. The unshieldedness that threatens the epoch of the technological is a keeping safe when turning into the opening of clearing takes place. Not only objects are ventured as things, but "man" enters into the venture as poetic thinker and rogue.[15]

---

[15]Heidegger says a few things in this essay that suggest that, although plants and animals are vulnerable to an alienation from the Open through the willing of man, they are not vulnerable to this on their own: "Plant and animal do not will because, muted in their desire, they never bring the Open before themselves as an object. They cannot go with the venture as one that is represented. Because they are admitted into the Open, the pure draft is never the objective other to themselves" (*PLT*, 110). This perhaps excludes animals

This venturing into the safekeeping of the draft is formulated by Heidegger as a movement into the dynamic of forces: "The gravity of the pure forces, the unheard-of center, the pure draft, the whole draft, full Nature, Life, the venture—they are the same" (*PLT*, 105). Therefore, poetic thinking is a resistance of the desire to will in the technological epoch, but a resistance that overcomes the resistance it previously had to unshieldedness. Furthermore, this resistance is thought as an "unheard-of center," a silent center, a center that is not, is nothing. The talk of the center, which must be unheard of in the pure draft which does not remain fixed and so, properly speaking, can have no center—at least no center to speak of, reminds us of the discussion of the heart in the fourth chapter where we saw that the taking to heart was the fleshly understanding of thinking. The heart, which is the center of the body (its core—*coeur*), becomes flesh and tissue so that, as a center, it becomes unheard of, a center that is no center to speak of, a silent center that turns into the openness of the play of the pure draft. This theme becomes important in this essay when Heidegger, near the end, contrasts the consciousness of the modern man with the heart's space dubbed as the center of all interiority.

The heart's space is the inner worldly character of the world that emerges in the opening of the Open. This conception of the "inner" cannot be understood in Heidegger's text along the same lines that one might use to understand the interiority of consciousness. Quite the opposite, the inner space of the heart where "everything is inward: not only does it remain turned toward this true interior of consciousness, but inside this interior, one thing turns, free of all bounds into the other. The interiority of the world's inner space unbars the Open for us. Only what we thus retain in our heart (*par coeur*), only that do we truly know by heart" (*PLT*, 130). The inner worldly space of the heart is even more interior than the interiority of consciousness. It is an interiority so severe that it loosens all the bonds that keep the interior on the inside and so as to release the inner "into the other." The dynamic here clearly repeats that of Derrida's deconstruction which pushes the interiority of the mind, for instance Husserl's notion of ideality, so far in its implications that it discovers

---

and plants from being rogues because a rogue must be able to turn back to the draft after having fallen from it. Plants and animals are not excluded from the Open, from the play of the draft, but they can never be said to leave the draft of their own will, thus they are not rogues.

there the in-scription of the other, of exteriority. So too does this happen in the venture into the inner worldliness of the heart's space where the tissue of human rogues plays in the drawing in of sheltered *(bergen)* things *(das beziehen der Bezug)*.

The place at the center of the heart's space, this is an interpolation of what has been said already, is an ab-yss: an unheard-of center, an empty center. The pure draft where the poet ventures is the abyss which "holds and remarks everything" *(PLT*, 93). The swirling absence of the ground in the middle of that destitute night where the poet is the one "among mortals who must, sooner than other mortals and otherwise than they, reach into the abyss, come to know the marks that the abyss remarks. For the poet, these are the traces of the fugitive gods" *(PLT*, 93). Marking and remarking is the play of the pure draft that goes on in the center of the heart's space, that materializes there in the manner of the world's textuality. The poet ventures there risking everything in the tracing of the fugitive gods, the gods that have withdrawn in the epochs of metaphysics and for whom Heidegger quipped, "Only a god can save us."[16] This inner space remarking the tracings of withdrawing gods is the place of the nearness, the neighborhood where the poetic thinker dwells:

> The poet thinks his way into the locality defined by that lightening *(Lichtung)* of Being which has reached its characteristic shape as the realm of Western metaphysics in its self-completion. Hölderlin's thinking poetry has had a share in giving its shape to this realm of poetic thinking. His composing *(dichten)* dwells in this locality as intimately as no other poetic composition *(Dichtung)* of his time. The locality to which Hölderlin came is a manifestness of Being and which, out of that destiny, is intended for the poet. *(PLT*, 95)

Hölderlin, like Rilke, is a poet for destitute times, but the poetic thinking of the rogue is the dwelling in the locality that spans in the tissues of the space at the unheard of center of the heart. And this is a stretch of the world that is there for the whole of humanity; at bottom, in their heart of

---

[16]From the interview referred to frequently as "Only a God Can Save Us" given to *Der Spiegel* in 1966 and, by Heidegger's request, only published posthumously. It has been translated into English in several places. Cf for example, Richard Wolin, *The Heidegger Controversy.* New York: Columbia University Press, 1991.

hearts, all humans are poets if only they are ready to take the risk into the venture and the forces of resistance at play there.

With all this as background, I can now venture into the resistant dwelling place where the human adventure will have been put into play. I showed that the essential component of dwelling is coming to reside in the safekeeping that is the drawing in of the pure draft or the circling of the Same and I uncovered frequent clues that this is the letting come to reside of things in the Open by poetic thinkers. Poetic thinking as dwelling in the nearness of the inner abysmal sanctum of the heart's space is thus opposed to all transcendental organizing principles (i.e. it is the deepest of any possible immanence), is nothing other than the letting materialize of the textuality of world/things.

It may be interesting to compare this description of Heidegger's thinking on the heart with a certain description given in Derrida's *Glas* of the Jewish

> tabernacle [that] gives its name and its place to the Jewish family dwelling. That establishes the Jewish nation. The Jewish nation settles in the tabernacle, adores therein the sign of God and his covenant. At least such would be believed.
>
> Now the tabernacle (texture of 'bands' whose excess we must continually reuse, Exodus 26) remains a signifier without signified. The Jewish hearth forms an empty house. Certainly, sensible to the absence of all sensible form, the Jews have tried to produce an object that gave in some way rise, place, and figure to the infinite. But this place and this figure have singular structure: the structure encloses its void within itself, shelters only its own proper interiorized desert, opens onto nothing, confines nothing, contains as its treasure only nothingness: a hole, an empty spacing, a death. A death or a dead person, because according to Hegel space is death and because this space is also an absolute emptiness. Nothing behind the curtains. Hence the ingenious surprise of a non-Jew when he opens, is allowed to open, or violates the tabernacle, when he enters the dwelling or the temple, and after so many ritual detours to gain access to the secret center, he discovers nothing—only nothingness.
>
> No center, no heart, an empty space, nothing. (*G*, 49)

The home of the Jew, the inner sanctum that determines the Jewish household or community is this empty place where nothing lies safe. For such a tabernacle to be a dwelling place for the Jew, the Jewish life must continue to interact within the ethical sphere laid out by the Law of such a tabernacle. The community of the Jew becomes an ethical community where things are made to reside in the open space of nothing holding sway. And not only things in the common sense, but things as the humanity of a human being that is also allowed to dwell there.

"*The fundamental character of dwelling is this sparing and preserving*" (*PLT*, 149). To save and to preserve a thing in dwelling does not mean to spare it from danger, but it "really means to set something free into its own presencing [*anwesen* or dynamic unfolding]" (*PLT*, 150). Dwelling is essentially linked in Heidegger's discussion of "saving" to the manner of mortals within the fourfold. Dwelling is the mortality of mortals and it is the "fourfold preservation of the fourfold" (*PLT*, 151). Mortals as one fold in the fourfold that bears out the dwelling of mortals occurring in the manner of preserving things in their gesturing bearing out of the fourfold. Mortality as the death of human beings is the becoming hymen of the human. To dwell is therefore to dwell within the preserving character of the sheltering (*bergen*) that is the concealment or death of what is.

The necessary component of dwelling as mortality recalls the materializing of the tissues of the human, it is the letting become text of things in so far as a thing's textuality is its coming into the safekeeping of the trace structure, the un-concealment of the text. To dwell is to preserve the textuality of things in the manner of a deconstruction of any metaphysical urge that seeks to place all things into the constraints of objectivity and commodification. Resisting the resistance that is needed so as to shield ourselves from the danger of deconstruction and the pure draft of dwelling, the deconstructor's letting materialize of things in their textuality is the letting play out of the thing in the adventure of the game. The desire in all practice is the desire to fix and stratify. The venture into the game of drafts is the resistance of all stratification and reification of things and hence the resistance of all subjection of things to their objectivity and the resistance of this desire to subject (the hostility of the technological epoch described above in terms of appropriation and the object of Marcuse's concern in "Aggressiveness in Advanced Industrial Society"[17]). When the gaze of the deconstructor resists reification, it lets the "object" twist and flex free of its fixed position and get up in the play of positions that is the place of dwelling. Dwelling is the perpetual

---

[17] See note 3 above.

deconstruction of the objectivity of objects so that they may be released into their thinghood, their thinging nature or dynamic unfolding.[18]

Releasing things into their thinging nature is thought in Heidegger's text under the name of *Gelassenheit*. Contrary to the haste of the technological, Heidegger associates *Gelassenheit* with waiting. Not a kind of waiting that a-waits what it is waiting for, that anticipates this awaited something as an expected future, the predestination of which is already delimited. Waiting, in Heidegger's sense, is a keeping open for, a remaining open for some future possibility. "In waiting we leave open what we are waiting for" (*DT*, 68). By waiting we are not already determined as to what it is that is coming to us in waiting. The coming itself, advent of coming, becomes the nature of all true waiting. Come! In this waiting, we are not merely carrying out some necessary chore the performance of which is a burden to be borne. Rather, more than a task, it is waiting which opens, the opening of the open is the waiting that leaves or lets open. It is not the case that first there is openness and then there is waiting or that first there is waiting and then the open comes. Waiting is the opening up of the open, it is the venture into the nearness. "Openness itself would be that for which we could do nothing but wait" (*DT*, 68). Waiting as thinking is the "coming-into-nearness of distance" (*DT*, 68).

This waiting that is the opening up of one's heart for surprise is the waiting of the Jew whose Christ never comes, whose arrival cannot be counted upon, the time before which cannot be measured. Waiting is the keeping of the secret that lies at the center of the household, a ritualized guarding of the sacred center that is nothing. The waiting of *Gelassenheit* that ventures into the regioning region or opening open is the Jewishness at the origin of all Christian metaphysics. It is the Jewishness that doesn't rush into accepting the savior that offers shieldedness in the world of His revelation. And what's more, this Jewishness is the keeping sheltered of

---

[18]Cf. Derrida's remarks in *Glas* concerning the Jew and the Christian where the Jew defers and delays the coming of Christ, the Jew is nothing other than the deferral of the coming of Christ since for the Jew Christ is always coming and yet never comes. In this way the "baby Jesus" remains within Mary's womb and the hymen remains intact. The coming of Jesus is the bursting of the hymen and the emergence into presence of the history of the West. For this reason, all Western history is Christian history and it is a mistake to lump together the Judeo and the Christian without taking into account their ab-solute proXimity.

a secret that preserves the covenant of the community, a community that arises from out of the neighborhood of the nearness: it might be said that the Jew, tracing out the fugitive gods, manages the household as a manner of waiting where the economy ('to manage the house') is not calculating, but waiting—Language as waiting is the house of Being, the tomb and tabernacle where waiting takes place.

Heidegger doesn't, in this context, bestow the name of patience upon this waiting, but it is clear that patience is necessary for all waiting. Without patience, waiting becomes a-waiting and the desire for the presence of a future now fixed in the mind of the impatient ones. Patience invokes a manner of practice in so far as it calls upon the practitioner to release herself to the openness of the possibility of all that comes into the Open. The coming open is the worlding of the world that grants and is borne out by things. Patience is always patience in the coming of things, patience for the advent(ure) of things in their thinging. In this way, patience is always a way-making and it is always a patience for the adventure that is the venturing into the drawing in of the draft. Patience is reaching into the draft, or letting it reach out into the human, and letting one's waiting be preserved there. Patience therefore replaces all mastery over things that impatiently wills them to bend into certain possibilities that have been preordained.

Patience, however, is not passive and this not only because it takes a great deal of power (resistance of haste) to be patient, but also because one must first be an agent in order to become passive. Passivity is always the negation of the agent's action and so always marks a willing not to will as the essential object nature of the metaphysical subject. The patient poetic thinker who dwells in waiting is such an ab-solutely resistant character that she resists becoming even an agent. Her patience, or passion, doesn't involve her in some immobile or docile subordination, but in an ab-solute movement the economy of which is the dynamic of all Saying, of all the turning and circling of the deconstructive movement in metaphysics.

Strictly speaking, *Gelassenheit*—usually translated as releasement, tells of a movement into the regioning region that then overwhelms the humanity of "man" and allows it to arrive neutral as a *Geschlecht* in the play of the draft. Such a releasement as moving into the nearness and dwelling there becomes a resistant perpetual holding Open for what comes, for the thinging of things as world. By going through the long pathway that elaborates the deconstructive nature of dwelling as a waiting for what comes with haste (i.e., a good reader), I carried out this discussion in deconstructive manner rather than in some metaphysical manner that merely lays down claims. Still, it remains to be seen what role the retracing of one's steps can have in the waiting of a neighborly dweller. *Gelassenheit* requires that waiting open up in the relation of the draft not only in the future to come, but in the past that comes as well. We must be patient with regard to the past as well as the future. Even the past can be recollected in the gathering place of the nearness, and in this recollection of the past there must be a patience for what comes: letting the past venture into the nearness.

Heidegger's notion of retrieval developed in the early work was always directed toward a hearing of the unsaid in what has been said. What has been said is what is past, what has already come to pass in the Saying of the Same, as metaphysics or otherwise. To be able to recollect the past in the nearness of its abiding coming to presence, one must have patience for the unsaid in what has been said and, in so doing, allow the whole of what has been said to be transformed by what was left unsaid. The history of philosophy as metaphysics, for instance, has left much unsaid according to Heidegger, but his own thinking on these matters was spurred on in a dialogue with that same tradition. Through his recollection of the tradition in retrieval, Heidegger achieved a patience with the tradition that enabled a venture into the nearness of its Saying and unconcealed the unsaid in what has been said. By retracing his steps, by going back over again and again the history of Western metaphysics, Heidegger was able to evoke the nearness of that history in the act of deconstructing it.

"Thought is in need of memory, the gathering of thought" (*WCT*, 138). The "all-gathering" nature of thought is its recollection in memory and, what's more, its thankfulness to the dynamic that calls upon thinking in this gathering of memory. What calls out to thinking, what gathers it up or collects it in its emergence as the destiny or sending of Saying's *Geschick,* is that which is recollected in the emergence of thinking. Thinking as opened up by the destiny of the Same's movement, is always a re-collecting, re-marking, and re-tracing of the movement, of the steps of the movement that is the evoking, or calling up, of thought. Thought is nothing other than its own thinking, its own emergence as thought, the gathering of the human in the pure draft that draws within its domain, the traces of disseminating thought, inscribes it there without alienation but saturated by dif-ference from which the call emerges and to which it comes and resides.

Thinking, then, is the thankfulness of the human for the gift given in the economy of dif-ference. This thankfulness emerges along with the recollection of the gift where this recollection is nothing other than the collection of the gift in the opening of its gathering, the thoughtful human community for instance. The gift is the calling out of the Same: "'to call' means to set in motion, to get something underway" (*WCT*, 117). Just like the poet's wager, the calling that calls upon the thinker is a setting in motion. A calling that draws the thinker into the draft of Saying, that lets the thinker emerge as the "text and texture of the question" (*WCT*, 116). To let oneself be called, is to allow oneself to reside in the calling of the Same as a thinker of what is worthy of thought: to let oneself be called is to accept the gift of the Same, to receive it and be thankful in a heartfelt manner for it. Thanking is always the heart's being overwhelmed by the gift, the letting oneself be called upon by the gift. Any thing which is given over in the *Geschick* of the gift, becomes worthy of thought, and becomes a thing for which the Same is thanked.

Thinking evoked by the calling of the gift, gives thanks for the gift. But the economy here is not the immediate return of the gift through thanks, but rather thanking is itself a gift given over in thinking. Thanking and giving are the Same, the gift is nothing other than the thanking for the gift. The thanking and the giving do not constitute an exchange, but are themselves the dialogue of giving. As such, thinking can be said to dwell in the adventure of the draft. It is drawn into this abysmal and unheard of center in the giving. As such it attains an ab-solute proXimity to poetry. "The essential closeness of poesy and thinking is so far from excluding their difference that, on the contrary, it establishes that difference in an abysmal manner" (*WCT*, 134). Thinking and poetry, so much alike, retain their differences. Yet, this is not the difference that subsumes difference to the separate presence of two poles in opposition. Poetry and thought are supplemental. "[P]recisely because thinking does not make poetry, but is a primal telling and speaking of language, it must stay close to poetry" (*WCT*, 135). One needn't be a poet to think, and one needn't be a thinker to poetize. Poetic thinking is the drawing near of the gathering and venturing of human thankfulness and residence in the tension of a poetic drawing tight. Poetic thinking becomes a near dwelling of poetry and thought in the nearness of the pure draft where even the technological can be said to emerge.

The relation of poetry to thinking on the one hand, and the poetic thinker to the technological that she resists becomes more than a singular tension, but a double tension, a doubling or folding of tensions that disseminate in being folded. Dwelling is always near-dwelling as a movement set in motion between thinking and poetizing. What is more, dwelling is always dwelling in the nearness where that signifies the absolute proXimity of deconstruction and metaphysics. Because of the two tensions, two forms of resistance in all dwelling, I can say that dwelling is always the near-dwelling in the nearness, being a neighbor within a neighborhood.

To dwell in such a manner is to re-collect in objects their dynamic thinging as things: to take up residence as the stretching out of the community within some region that is made to vibrate there in the openness opened up in the *Gelassenheit* of the thinker poet. Things are perpetually threatened by the overarching tendency of the nearby technological in this community. The threat of the technological is not to be outstripped and the possibility of a once and for all stripping away of presence is left open in the dwelling of the community's neighbors. Things enter into persistent tensions between the metaphysical and its deconstruction, deconstruction being the double gesture that recognizes and patiently practices within the essential fluctuations of things in their nearness not only to dwelling but to technology as metaphysics. Resistance is not once and for all carried out in a moment of appropriation of some power structure, but is the persistent resistance in the face of that which always threatens to shield things in the safety of an ordered power structure. Every effort at resistance comes upon the possibility of reification and, as such, must continue to resist itself in its resistance. Resistance must resist its own desire to end the strife of resistance so as to maintain its dynamic unfolding as resistance, resistance that disseminates as the opening of what lies near in the familiar world of deconstruction's tensions and forces.

Marx says in *The German Ideology* that "[c]ommunism is for us not a *state of affairs* which is to be established, an *ideal* to which reality [will] have to adjust itself. We call communism the *real* movement which abolishes the present state of things. The conditions of this movement result from the premises now in existence."[19] Leaving aside the problems the word "communism" holds for the current historical age, we should be careful to hear the movement at work in this passage and the extent to which that movement is a deconstruction resulting from the stage of capital and that abolishes the dominance of the present. Some Marxists have heard in these remarks an emphasis on the ongoing and perpetual nature of revolution, not *the* revolution that goes on and on forever, with purges and Gulags to consolidate the power of a new elite, but the

---

[19] Karl Marx, "The German Ideology," in *The Marx-Engels Reader*, 2d ed., ed. Robert Tucker (New York: W. W. Norton, 1978), 162.

perpetuation of revolution that hears in that the dissemination of revolution, revolutions that continue to disrupt any possibility of establishing an elite center of power.

The poetic thinker as community involved—"communist"—rogue, therefore, always retraces her steps in her patience for that which comes, for that nearness which is always in the near (in the neighborhood) but never comes to be present. The notion opposed, and developed by Derrida in *The Post Card*, in its proximity to the rogue is the mail carrier. The mail carrier, like the poetic thinking rogue, is a messenger of sorts, but a messenger carrying out an appointed route cordoned off to him by the postal delivery system which has mapped out the addresses and destinations all over the world. Every letter in the mail carrier's pouch has a specific destination inscribed across its face: an address. The calculating capacity of the address system ensures that almost every letter can be expected to reach its appropriate place. A system of sending and delivery, like the economy of the Same which is a destining into the openness of what lies near, the postal system delegates to the mail carrier a specific neighborhood. The mail carrier is the epitome of the technological delivery system, mechanized and efficient, yet flexible as the weather and ready to serve its function even in the worst of circumstances. Even still, the mail carrier and his postal employer cannot account for every eventuality. People move, forget to leave forwarding addresses, post cards and letters are addressed improperly, human error allows for mistakes in the sorting. Even in the smoothly running operations of the technologically superior postal systems of Western countries there can be no guarantees that every letter will arrive at its proper destination. Arrival is never a sure thing, sometimes we can be kept waiting indefinitely for the arrival of some special package, a gift from a friend abroad perhaps.

The neighborhood demarcated in the route of the mail carrier is nearby in ab-solute proXimity to the neighborhood of the rogue who ventures into the dangerous risk that her letters will not be delivered. The risk of the rogue is the gambling that is carried out in every attempt to drop a post card into the mail box on the corner, the risk that arrival will never come and that one's waiting will be in vain. The customer who awaits the mail carrier becomes irate when the anticipated response does not come, this customer demands the presence of the awaited item, demands a predictable control over the workings of the public post. The rogue risking her life in the post-structuralist movement of the deconstruction of metaphysics does not become irate, she works and plays at deconstruction, she waits, she is patient, she knows that the semblance of order in the postal system is a facade that obscures the underlying conflagration of its uncertainty and turmoil.

At this point, it is time to turn more carefully to the suggestion made a few pages ago that patience is a form of the passive. A passive waiting for the letter that doesn't come, a passivity in the face of the intimidating bureaucratic structure of the postal system and its backlog of undelivered mail. These patient addressees of the world's calling by way of post card, it might be argued, are the meek who lack commitment, who fail to become active at the most destitute of times and, in so doing, submissively allow the powers that be to maintain their control over the world, the post office to retain its domination as the monopoly in charge of all delivery and with full information on every address in the neighborhood. And what is more, it has occasionally been argued that Heidegger's emphasis on releasement as patience is evidence for his advocating a kind of totalitarian political structure to which and before which all of humanity is docile, herd animals waiting patiently in line at the post office to be treated badly and forcefully by a rude clerk.[20]

---

[20]Cf. Michael Zimmerman's *Heidegger's Confrontation with Modernity* as an example of this. Although Zimmerman has presented the most careful effort to date at linking Heidegger's thinking with National Socialism, I can't help but come away a little less than convinced. My problem fits into two major categories, both of which can only be presented in brief at this time.

1. The fact that Heidegger's "romanticism" corresponds to some extent to the romanticism of the Volkish movement is not enough to condemn him as a National Socialist in essence. Even if one allows Zimmerman this reading, one is left wondering about the connection between the ideology of a movement and its material instantiation—as I mentioned before. But, if Zimmerman insists on the point, claiming that it is the inability of the Heideggerian philosophy to grapple with concrete political connections thus allowing him to be drawn in by the Volkism of National Socialism and, therefore, making it useless as a deconstruction of traditional thought; then, I would feel pressed to ask what's so wrong about the Volkist ideal? And, thinking ahead to the second point in this note, I would warn any who would answer rashly to be careful.

2. If the romantic Volkish ideal is blameworthy because of its ability to uncritically sell technological imperialism to the masses, then the history of the United States and Western Europe is implicated as well. Leo Marx, in his *The Machine in the Garden* (London: Oxford University Press, 1964) traces the history of the pastoral ideal from Shakespeare's *The Tempest* to Melville's *Moby Dick* and beyond. His point is that western technology, like

The Dedication of Patience

It would be a mistake to hear in these postal tropes a simple opposition to the rogue. Derrida's *The Post Card* shows that the postal principle at work in Heidegger's thinking of the *Geschick* or sending that arrives in the epochs of Being—and which is addressed in one way or another—is thinkable through the technological apparatus of the postal system. Derrida seems to address the problem in Heidegger as to why it is that the epoch of technology has a special relation to the deconstruction of metaphysics. The fact that the Saying of the Same is a postal system full of deliveries and addresses may at first suggest that Heidegger, in a Derridean criticism, has mistakenly thought the deconstruction of metaphysics as a technological principle. That is, the emergence in disclosure of epochs in the Saying of the Same is a delivery system. But Derrida, in "Envois," pushes this trope to its extreme positions and discovers the adventure that is always risked in using the post. Regarding both Heidegger and Freud, Derrida writes:

---

the steam train and the whole pioneering relation to North America, was sold to settlers and Americans on the basis of a romantic vision of technology as poetic artifice in nature. He implicates no less than Thomas Jefferson and Daniel Webster in this act of praising the greatness of the countryside and agriculture in high sounding terms ultimately aimed (in some cases reluctantly by all involved) at pushing the country forward in terms of mechanical development. The pastoral ideal is a powerful force in contemporary life and has fooled many into rushing forward into the oblivion of spaceless communication in place of spacing communities. For an example, keep your ears open to discover how Time-Warner sells reluctant Americans on the idea of an information superhighway peering into their living rooms.

Needless to say, it is my hope that the circumcision of Heidegger that is taking place in this chapter will have been at least a partial anecdote for whatever absence of resistance to political ideals veiling atrocity results from a focus on Heidegger's life.

> The master-thinkers are also masters of the post. Knowing well how to play with the *poste restante.* Knowing how not to be there and how to be strong for not being there right away. Knowing how not to deliver on command, how to wait and to make wait, for as long as what there is that is strongest within one demands — and to the point of dying without mastering anything of the final destination. The post is always *en reste,* and always *restante.* It awaits the addressee who might always, *by chance,* arrive.
>
> And the postal principle is no longer a principle, nor a transcendental category; that which announces itself or sends itself under heading (among other possible names, like you) no longer sufficiently belongs to the epoch of Being to submit itself to some transcendentalism, 'beyond every genre.' The post is but a little message, fold, or just as well. A relay in order to mark that there is never anything but relays. (*PC,* 191-2)

The relay becomes a supplemental term in the dynamic of the economy of *différance* for Derrida. The little message that these master rogues knowingly fail to deliver, but for which they continue to wait and make wait, is always passed on, gets caught up in an economy of passing on, of coming to pass, and fails to arrive in so being relayed. This perpetual relaying of the public post is the *fort/da* of the mail system, the back and forth of the relay system that is correspondence by mail. How do I know my correspondent received my letter? Only when I receive hers? And what if the letter gets lost in the mail, or worse, returned to sender, how does it happen that my correspondent responds to such a failure to deliver?

The *Geschick* of the postal system is multiplied in the passing along of the mail. Like Heidegger's frequent emphasis in other works on the *Gestell,* the "Ge" of the *Geschick* is the multiplication of sending, its emergence in the manner of multiplying relays and deferrals to the next letter and delays for various reasons. The multiplication of post cards in any correspondence (which of course dissolves the univocity of any correspondence—of truth, of identity, of equality, etc.) is the gathering and venturing of the drawing in of letters to the inscribed but empty center of the delivery system that is the opening world granting and giving things. This multiplication also emerges in the "Ge" of *Gelassenheit* which releases itself to the multiplication of sending, of possible deliveries and deferrals, that releases itself to waiting for the mail to come.[21]

But the rogue is not the opposite of the mail carrier, instead she is herself a messenger, a carrier of relays who never gets anywhere, who promises to deliver but always delays the moment of paying off, of coming through on what has been promised, who always recognizes in her writing and reading of mail that one letter will never be enough and one destination will never be conclusive. The usury of the roguish carrier is her promising more than she is either willing or able to deliver. It is also the wear and tear that erodes the rubber on the soles of her shoes as she steps along the way carrying her messages. She is a usurer, but only to those who await her deliveries. I see her coming up the street, her uniform and bag call out to me, address me by name and promise me a coming letter or post card. I await her, see her come to the mail box on my stoop beneath my address. She takes, once again, the letter I have sealed and marked for delivery in the standard manner of the outgoing letter (raising a metal flag signaling the need for a pick-up and, no doubt, the hope for a delivery), but she leaves nothing in return. My hands fumble for it, this nothing left by the rogue, her impish relays demanding more than I too will be able to provide. When, in this receipt of nothing, this failure to arrive of what I have been waiting for, I don't notice the absence and begin to undertake the tracing of the missing, or perhaps purloined, letter, only then am I rogue enough, brave enough to venture that nothing has been sent, nothing has arrived to be fumbled with, to be opened: the opening up of nothing, nothing has been delivered. The risk is the risk of being a victim of usury. And this risk must be understood in a wholly economic sense.

What better usurer than a Jew? And not just any Jew, but Derrida and, allow me this recollection of the passages on the heart and the empty tabernacle of the community, even Heidegger. But such a usury, being jewed out of what one can rightly expect to take possession of, is essential to the point of view of the unshieldedness of the draft that is feared and

---

[21]This of course repeats the same dynamic with regard to the *Geschlecht* in chapter 4 where this word multiplied its meanings in its dispersion within the there of Dasein's thrownness. The gathering of the *Logos* is therefore not a gathering in the sense of a logic guided by the principle of identity which would clarify and resolve every message in its meaning, would make intelligibility arrive in each passage, but a gathering that is always a sending and resending of re-collected re-lays, a dispersal of meaning, of logic in favor of a leap into the Same that displaces all certainty and all decidability. Meaning never arrives, it is always deferred, relayed, and recollected.

escaped in all metaphysical economies, all Christian economies where the Jew is marginalized and allowed to survive only in the manner of the usurer or pawn broker (and just see how long such a Christian economy would dare to survive without its Jews in their ghetto). The deconstruction of the Western economy of the technological and capitalist in metaphysics is of course a wearing away, an exhaustion of this dichotomy of Christian and Jew, but a doing so by way of shifting the emphasis to the secondary figure of the Jew and then displacing Jewishness so that it becomes something other than the usurer of the Christian economy. The pure draft of the heart's inner space is the tabernacle at the heart of the community (nation of the covenant of Abraham) and it is the incision into the phallic center of the Christian dominated metaphysics of presence (i.e. its circumcision).

Notice the importance of the displacement in this movement. It is not the case that usury, as jewing another out of a rightful return on an investment, becomes the standard of life upon the fall of Christian dominance. Instead, the extent to which the Christian is essentially linked to this dynamic of the usurer is revealed in the playing out of the metaphysical possibilities presented there. The capitalist economy of the technological is the christianization of all things. The Christian falsely places the Jew in subordinate position of usurer so that the Christian may develop in moral secrecy the usurious economy extraordinaire. Consider for example Weber's thoughts on *The Protestant Ethic and the Spirit of Capitalism*. Weber attributes the rise of capitalism not to the Jewishness of a global economy, but to its basis in the Calvinist and Methodist principles of asceticism and the carrying out of God's work upon the earth. That is, the technological rationalizing of the world through the creation of a capitalist economy arose out of the desire to increase God's power and works on the earth. Also, the value work came to have as a working for the grace of God in humble submission to the creative power that is God. The protestant ethic didn't demand accumulation and appropriation for its own sake but for the sake of pleasing and increasing the wealth of God. Now, although Weber seems a little nostalgic for the good old days when being a capitalist meant something spiritually, he admits that the current bureaucratic form of capitalist rationalism that blindly rages on in the world is the doing of a Protestantism that has lost its spirit, that has, in a nutshell, failed to deliver what it has promised to deliver and instead delivered quite the opposite. Not God's kingdom on earth, but a mechanized hell.

Pushing usury to its limits does not then recognize the Protestantism of usury as capitalistic accumulation, but rather sees in the failure to deliver on the part of such accumulation a suggestion of the danger that has been covered over in the smooth running bureaucracy of the technological. The risk that ensues may seem to give in to this usury by failing to commit to some clearly defined and rational alternative, but that may be more a problem with the view from the metaphysical economy than with the positions that come into play in the danger that draws out the implications of metaphysics while drawing it towards its closure. To say that since there is no way to fulfill one's promises, to deliver what one has promised to deliver, it is therefore okay to be a usurer, is to continue to play in the metaphysical economy that accepts the opposition itself while denying the existence of the privileged term. Baudrillard's book, *Simulations,* a sort of standard in postmodernism, seems to me to do exactly that with regard to the relation of the imitation or copy and the original. There are no originals, therefore everything is a copy and we may proceed as such. Much of what I would call postmodernism could be seen to rest squarely on this metaphysical position. That is, it denies the privilege of the elevated term in metaphysics and accepts the secondary term, accepts secondarity, but does so without bringing about any kind of displacement or transformation of the term, thus leaving it in its metaphysical opposition and continuing to recognize the force the original term continues to have over the dynamic of the postmodern. It is only one gesture in deconstruction's double gesturing. A fleeing in the face that nevertheless allows that which it flees to sneak up on it from behind.

The criticism of deconstruction's lack of commitment is therefore best directed against postmodernism in so far as it might accept the terms of the debate. The postmodern might say commitment is opposed to play or whatever you like and then deny the possibility of such a commitment which then frees him up to play all he likes with the commodities and objects of the technological while continuing to write papers and going to conferences at which he plays at being a critic. After all what does it matter, what truth is there to these actions, etc. Not only does this behavior accept the definition of play and commitment as they have been determined by metaphysics, but it actively supports this metaphysical epochality of technology by failing to resist it in a thoroughly displacing and deconstructive fashion.[22] Dwelling as patience that roguishly carries

---

[22] I really don't know how to read Lyotard's *The Postmodern Condition* (Minneapolis, MN: The University of Minnesota Press, 1984) in any other way than as an apologetics for cybernetics. Even when he is critical of

the message of the danger that waits but never comes is the carrying out of this displacement. As such it is the opening up of a renewed, or replaced *ethos* (understood at the moment strictly in the Greek sense of a dwelling place but here adjusted to mean a dwelling re-place, re-marked, re-trace, re-trieved, etc.).

Should I say, then, that usury is the uncommitted practice of the deconstructing rogue? Usury suggests both using up and acquiring a surplus, both infinite expenditure and capital gains. In the first sense, there is no return on the investment, in fact, it isn't even an investment, it's waste, an extravagant expense without return, without residual. In the second sense, everything is done for the sake of what returns, what shall come to remain. The interest one has in one's investment is all for the sake of a return, a surplus. This surplus is not without exchange, it is not a remainder pure and simple, but rather it is the exchange value given to time. In exchange for time, there will have been a residual, interest to be paid, a return on the investment. Within this sense of usury, the meaning of time is the return on an investment—time is money, it is the most precious commodity. Under conditions of the commodification of time, the utility of time is thought as an investment where what has been sent will be returned later along with a surplus. In point of fact, there is no supplement here, every penny can be accounted for, every nickel and dime can be calculated in terms of its return years in advance. Such an economy of "surplus" is in fact a thoroughly exchange based economy where there is no loss or gain at all, a zero sum gain with every dollar the result of an exchange.

Only the usury that uses up leaves nothing. Only for this kind of use is there nothing left. But what of the use-value? Perhaps the using up of a commodity, its consumption, is an exchange of sorts. In exchange for consumption there is pleasure or benefit, etc. Something is gained from the consumption. This too would seem like a further form of utility. When I eat a potato, it may be used up but only as potato, my body—say—through the expenditure of calories will use that potato for various other functions. This form of usury, this using up that is merely an exchange of sorts, doesn't provide the secondarity essential for the deconstruction of the usurious Jew. We are in need of a true using up, a use that is a

---

technology, every word seems saturated with a titillation that ultimately affirms what it denies. This seems like the most influential move in postmodernist texts written in the last ten years: affirmation in the form of denial and denial in the form of an affirmation.

complete expenditure without return, without exchange, an expenditure after which nothing remains. This "gift" where nothing is received in return has been called an impossible possibility by Derrida and others. Rather than chase after the unmeaning of a contradiction, I will ask whether there is squandering? Is anything ever squandered? Is it possible to use something up without using it, without attaining some use-value from it?

Rather than being a question about the practices of deconstruction, or the action carried out by deconstructors, this is a question that drives rogues away from practice and action. These prodigal rogues not only waste every opportunity to take up action or to carry out a practice, they also seem to be in the process of wasting themselves, of squandering themselves, their potential, their capacity to achieve and succeed, their selves. How strange it would be to refer to this as a commitment to squandering!

Heidegger, in a citation given in the previous section, talks about the destiny of a place before optimism and pessimism. Derrida writes in *The Post Card* of the undecidability of our relation to the postal system and to the optimism and pessimism that it gives us. He refuses to take a stand, to come to a position with the dynamic of the for or against of the delivery system, within the dynamic of its technological presence upon the earth.

> They will never know if I do or do not love the post card, if I am for or against. Today they all chew up the work for the computer, they punch themselves in by themselves in order to step up to the cashier from one month to the next ["What counts in all of it is the pace, the step"]. For this one has to submit [commit?] oneself to bi-spoolarity, oppose here to there [*fort/da*], be for or against. You have surely noticed, among other subtle categories, that since last year some are camping on the position of "optimism," others are making a career in "pessimism," the ones are religious, the others not. And they take out their index cards, produce references, in the end other post cards on which they can no longer read anything except the perforation (B A, B A, O A, OA, R I, R I). What fatigue. (*PC*, 238-9)

And it is a mistake to view this failure to take a stand, to take up a commitment, as a failure to engage oneself in positions. Just as it is a mistake to understand Heidegger's "Only a God can save us" as the epitome of religiosity *or* as a dark and abysmal pessimism that emerges out of atheism. Derrida and Heidegger's indecision is not commitment or the lack of it, it is between the two. The polarity, the "bi-spoolarity," of these two options is an opposition within the technological that always demands and commands a decision, the smooth running nature of the technological depends on it. To fail to make a commitment in favor or against, a commitment to optimism or pessimism, etc. is to hold oneself in the distance between technology and its deconstruction, to hold oneself back from, to take a step back from, the essentially epochal dynamic of all technology. Only in the indecision of these positions, can one come to pass in the manner of the poetic thinking rogue who risks the danger, who resists the desire to make everything safe through the making of decisions and the coming to conclusions (or as in the case of the postmodern mail carrier—with a good haircut and a pair of trendy shoes no doubt, who plays at delivering the mail while recognizing how serious a job it is and how important it ultimately will be to play it safe).

The push back to commitment in the face of this postmodern play places the hard-line traditional Marxist in the same place as the conservative Heritage Foundation intellectual who clamors over the need to return to the classical greatness that is Europe and its monological control over the world culture disseminated in the academy and, no doubt, elsewhere. In both cases, a reactionary movement is pointing back to the abused and privileged paradigm of the epochs of metaphysical history. In both cases, the historical dynamic of the conservative that is the metaphysical favor of stasis and presence is being opted for. The deconstructive turning, its tropes, are moving in the manner of resistant waiting, resistance of all presence, resistance to the dynamic nearness that presence as metaphysics occupies, dwelling is the resistant waiting that lies in the nearness of the technological and resists its sway. This is not a committed position against metaphysics, that would be to oversimplify the danger. Rather, this is the taking up of positions in the danger that technology poses, it is making oneself ready for revolutions with the metaphysical, a waiting that patiently whiles away in the adventure of deconstructive squandering.

If the Jew is committed to the danger of the draft, if I say this with a deconstructive turning, I submit (commit) the Jew to Marcuse's criticisms alluded to above.[23] That is, the Jew committed to death, to play, to the wearing away of truth as univocal correspondence, and to the inversion of oppositions, is a Jew who has cast "his" lot ("his" because such a Jew,

---

[23] See note 3 above.

contrary to the other, is masculine, phallic, uncircumcised, and baptized) with the National Socialists, he is a postmodern in the worst possible sense (no doubt he is a Jew for Jesus). To describe a form of patience that is committed to its patience is to impatiently frustrate all possibility of patience as a waiting that is left open for what comes. The Jew committed to his patience struggles impatiently against his patience, absolves his impatience in his impatience to be patient. And this Jew does in fact convert the meaning of the terms while maintaining them in their metaphysical meaning.

Heidegger writes:

> Clearly no age has known so much, or had at its disposal such ready means for knowing everything swiftly and for cleverly persuading everyone, as our age. But clearly no age has understood so little of what is essential about things as our age. And there is so little understanding, not because this age has fallen victim to a general imbecility, but because this age —-in spite of its greed for everything—resists what is simple and essential and what promotes involvement and *perseverance*. Furthermore, this emptiness can spread because in the man of today the virtue of *patience* has ceased to exist.
>
> Patience—-that is the quiet anticipation in our persevering attention to what we should want, namely, that is be. Patience is the care which has turned away from all that noisy procuring and has turned to the whole of Dasein. Patience is the truly *human* way of being thoughtful about things. Genuine patience is one of the basic virtues of philosophizing—-a virtue which understands that we always have to build up the pile of kindling with properly selected wood so that it may at one point catch fire. Patience in the first and last instance—"patience"—this word has withdrawn from essential language. And we do not wish that this word become a slogan, but rather that we practice it and in practicing it gain a facility in it. It is in such practicing that we first attain to genuine measures of our Dasein and achieve the keen ability for differentiating what is offered to Dasein.
>
> But the impatience of the many—-who want to be finished already before they even begin, in order to be able to let go of their *abiding* impatience at the very first opportunity—-this impatience might overtake us already with our first groping step into the work that we want to effect.[24]

---

[24] Martin Heidegger, *Hegel's Phenomenology of Spirit*, trans. P. Emad and K. Maly (Bloomington: Indiana University Press, 1988), 73.

This other patience, this patience that waits for nothing to come, may appear to be a waste of time, the passing of time without spending it wisely. As such, it is the squandering of time. But this wasted expenditure of time un-conceals as time itself. That is, time is squandering, time squanders, it lays waste, it makes everything into nothing. By squandering in/as/through time, the patient Jew makes everything that exists into nothing. Such a Jew that squanders existence is dwelling amidst nothing, dwells in the midst of nothing. Hers is an *ethos* before metaphysics and ontology, before what is as nothing at all. No longer adjunct to a Christian economy, this usurer begins to squander profit. Deconstructing Jewish subordination and inessentiality tears the relation from its restriction within the Christian economy and turns it loose from any appropriate exchange.

The position of the adjunct is a squandered site. That is, the adjunct is always squandered and squandering. The Jew wastes her economic energy (mis-placed energy) on the inessential, she squanders her own resources. The Christian economy squanders the Jew to the extent that it wastes her energy on the inessential. The reciprocity of waste in the squandered object and squandering subject is the only exchange the Jew can know and this is only the trace of an exchange since both sides of the relation are squandered. It is an exchange of nothing. Squandering not only makes something into nothing, but all economy of squandering is the exchange of nothing, nothing can be exchanged because all that there is to exchange is wasted.

Squandering also suggests extravagance. It isn't only a waste of a thing, but the extravagant expenditure. A gift of sorts where the one who gives cannot afford such a gift. To give beyond one's means, to give everything away including one's capacity to give later, is to extravagantly squander one(self). In the squandering of wealth, it is precisely nothing that is achieved. The Jew gives away everything so that she may come to possess nothing. Notice that she begins with something, she starts in the position of a possessor without mentioning how she came to such a condition, she has it, and then she squanders it, turns it into nothing. This excursus into extravagant gift-giving is precisely an inquiry into the inessential event of squandering. One of the obsolete meanings of "squander" is "to scatter." Deconstruction, the dissemination of metaphysics, is the squandering of the tradition. What is squandered is scattered, it is scattered without order or reason, it is merely meted out into a fragmented world without aim or purpose.

The adjunct is the inessential supplement that squanders and is squandered, that turns into nothing, that scatters and fragments, that gives extravagantly. Has there ever been an adjunct who wasn't also a disciple of "Heidegger" (literally speaking)? And this marks the Jew's *ethos*, the site of all Jewish dwelling, of every deconstructed Jewish situation. When Jews in community engage in this mutual gift-giving (this adjunct behavior), they are not responsible, cannot be expected to give equally, and do not expect to arrive at the neat and orderly remainder that one has in the potlatch. She does not expect, she will have squandered that. Whatever there is (*es gibt*), whatever she gives, it will be squandered. Hear that! The Jew is not frugal or reserved, the only residual left for a squanderer is nothing.

As an adjunct rogue, this prodigal Jew has been driven away from the everyday concerns of the economy of exchange. And what's more this prodigality is an extravagant waste—not only because such an economy wastes the rogue's talents, but because the rogue herself wastes them, turns them into nothing, resists any desire to exploit and market them, resists any desire even to possess them. Such a prodigal will not have owned anything, will not have done anything, will not have achieved anything.

Opposed to the ideo-logic of property in the classical liberal views which hasten toward the political commitments of the universal and the natural, the deconstructing Jew's patience is a patience that builds a community where building takes on the significance of Heidegger's *bauen* signifying "to dwell." The community here is the people that waits together, that belongs together in its waiting, in its patient openness to what comes, and that lets whatever comes be squandered. This openness overwhelms the delivery of things as objects, of events as present moments of appropriation, in favor of a building of the community, a dwelling together in openness, a squandering of what is.

> What then, does *Bauen*, building, mean? The Old English and High German word for building, *buan*, means to dwell. This signifies: to remain, to stay in a place. The real meaning of the verb *bauen*, namely, to dwell, has been lost to us. But a covert trace of it has been preserved in the German word *Nachbar*, neighbor. The neighbor is in Old English the *neahgebur; neah*, near, and *gebur*, dweller. The *Nachbar* is the *Nachgebur*, the *Nachgebauer*, the near-dweller, he who dwells nearby. (*PLT*, 146-7)

To speak of the dweller's commitment to this dwelling place, this community or neighborhood, is to alienate the dweller from the dwelling place in the same way that all humanism alienates "man" from the draft that draws him into its danger. The dwelling of the dweller, being within a community, is not some action over and against the building of that same community which gets built as some archi-tectural apparatus that remains only after the building is complete. Instead, building is itself dwelling, the carrying out of a groundplan (*grund-riß*) which draws the builder into it, which builds the builder in the carrying out of the plan (*riß*). As such, it squanders any residual status for the builder. Building is squandering to the extent that it results in nothing (there is no result), builds a dwelling that is the residence of nothing, perhaps its resonance echoing off the walls.

To be committed is to be focused and centered upon one's willing, to be dedicated to one's willing over and against the peripheral movements and occurrences of life. Regardless of whether the peripheral will help or hinder this willing, it is blocked out and separated from the agency of the committed agent. Commitment is always a commitment to an ossified plan and, as such, it is always the exclusion of possibilities, it is always the carrying through on a solution to a posed problem. Where dedication is aligned with commitment it is always willing. Still, in dedication a trembling begins to hold sway. The deconstructor, as I showed in the fourth chapter, is not without dedication. The dedication of a memorial that re-collects the living dead of an event, the writing on the walls of Thoth's pyramid.

Where dedication suggests commitment, it suggests the exclusion of possibility and a closing off of the draft which draws all practices within it as illustrations. But in this dedication, memorials spring up and make the willing of a commitment tremble with its groundlessness. The dedication of the deconstructor is the carrying out of building in the coming to reside in the community that she inhabits. Her dwelling place is the memorial dedicated to her building, not built there as the symbolic presence of the community's identity, but saturating the community, filling out the community, making it into a neighborhood.

Some time ago, while visiting the concentration and death camp at Dachau, the group with which I was traveling was overcome by a tragic silence as it approached the gates. The camp is preserved as a monument in the neighborhood of Munich where once its crematoria wafted up smoke that spirited away in the burning cinders of squandered Jewish corpses. Inhaled and exhaled by the nearby German populace, this smoky spiriting away (*soufflé*) became the transcendental organizing principle of the German people bent on their movement of destruction. Then too there was a terrible silence with reference (dare I say reverence) to the camp nearby. There are neighborhoods in the suburb of Dachau, people living close by, across the street even, then as now. The silence of these visitors some years ago and the silence of the Germans living nearby carries a similar memorial to the events that occurred. Unlike then, however, the camp—left in tact to some extent, carries upon its grounds a monument with an inscription dedicated to the holocaust: *nie wieder,* never again. Perhaps some Germans somewhere uttered these same words, under their breaths, with regard to the manipulating practices of the usurious Jews who they were convinced had laid Germany to waste. "Never again will we let those Jews ruin our country." And now, never again will we... What? Let those Jews be burned in the holocaustal flames of the crematoria? Let the holocaustal fire burn on? In either case, the dedication of the memorial stands beyond the world outside where, as the thinking of the technological warns us, the holocaustal burns on and continues to consume, continues to produce in its leaping flames the power needed to keep the motors running in the machinic economy. As long as the dedication on the memorial in Dachau remains beyond the technological economy, it remains a monument where spirits live in an eternal netherworld, it remains alien from the world at large: a pyramid representing the past.

The dedication of the memorial must not be allowed to stand, it must be unfolded in its multiple positions, it must be squandered. Where silence reigns only in the presence of the memorial, it comes to stand for something, to symbolize something, it remains merely symbolic. The holocaustal must be elevated to the level where even the consumption of consumption is consumed in the fires that burn, where even the fire is consum(mat)ed in the burning. Only then can nothing remain, only then can there be cinders, and "cinders there are." When the silence of those committed to the flames of the holocaust is allowed to be silenced in the present silence of the memorial, silence fails to ring out, to peel in the stilling nearness. This silencing of silence in the presence of the memorial is the grinding of the gears of technology that has no place within it for the dedication of the memorial, instead the dedication is delegated to a place outside the community of networking individuals, to the national parks of Germany, Poland, Austria, France, et al. This is an economy where nothing is wasted.

Only when dedication is the re-collection of the cinders that float up and swarm in the aftermath of the blaze can there be talk of dedication in dwelling. A dedication that is not a willing, not an alienation of some agent from some project, or some monument from the community. The Jewish community after-Auschwitz, bent on a Zionism at whatever the cost to others, is dedicated to the preservation of monuments, and is not saved from this dynamic. Such a Jewish community is being Jewish within the overall economy of the technological, it is a false silence that pretends to revere the holocaust dead while commodifying them for use in technological projects.[25] Even the remnants of the Shoah may not be wasted in such an economy. The displacement of the Jew, her becoming wanderer itinerant deconstructing rogue entering into the relays of the message carriers, is the dwelling of the community within the memorial, dedicated to cinders and ashes that there continue to be, retracing her steps, stepping not beyond the place of the memorial, and recollecting the nearness in her dwelling.

To be committed has always been thought within the constrictions and limitations of the rational. One who is dedicated but not rational, who suffers from madness for instance, is in need of commitment and, to remedy the situation, is committed to the asylum where the dedication of the insane can be controlled and disciplined into some kind of orderly shape or gestalt. Commitment therefore is always a commitment to rationality and Enlightenment where rationality not only excludes all that is not rational as immoral or inhuman, but determines itself in accordance with a ratio that measures out and calculates causes and effects, means and ends. This ratio without recollection masters all that is in bringing it to light, only what is brought to light in reason's measuring and calculating is real and truly or legitimately human.[26] Such a ratio always

---

[25]Cf. Irena Klepfisz's article "Anti-Semitism in the Lesbian/Feminist Movement" in *Nice Jewish Girls: A Lesbian Anthology.* edited by Evelyn Torton Beck. Watertown, MA: Persephone Press, 1982. pp. 45-51. She writes: "I am a lesbian/feminist threatened in this country. I am also a European-born Jew, born during the Second World War, a survivor of the Jewish Holocaust. That historical event, so publicized and commercialized in the mass media, so depleted of meaning, has been a source of infinite lessons to me, lessons which I value" (p. 48).

[26] Even the universal rationality of Kant's ethics seems to fit into this description. For Kant, morality is a matter of discovering the principles that underlie one's act, applying a criteria for measurement to it (universalization, whatever that means) and determining whether it withstands the imperative of the law of non-contradiction in the process.

builds monuments to its rationality, the whole of the technological world as it stands ready to be used and exploited for gain and benefit can be understood as a monument to reason. Heidegger's description of the *Bestand,* the standing reserve of entities in the *Gestell,* suggests this readiness to be used, this commitment that prevails in the expectant waiting of the technological entity that desires its own implementation. These are the monuments of the Enlightenment, these are the monuments of reason. Dachau as much as agricultural farming, a monument to reason.[27]

---

[27]This remark suggests the famous erased sentence from Heidegger's "Question Concerning Technology": "Agriculture is now a motorized food industry: in its essence it is the same thing as the manufacture of corpses in gas chambers, the same thing as blockades and the reduction of a region to hunger, the same as the manufacture of hydrogen bombs." Most people would have little trouble in recognizing in this example the achievement of the Enlightenment and Enlightenment ideology in the technological age. The horror of most commentators is the supposed bad taste (or worse) of placing the gas chambers that "manufacture" corpses alongside industrialized agriculture. Commentators almost always point out the benefits and glories of such kinds of agriculture. And even those commentators who want to defend Heidegger as trying to think in terms of "essences" are willing to go along with this characterization. Unfortunately, they are wrong. A lot has been written in recent years about the politics of food distribution and famine and the role that big businesses which control the markets of agri-business have played in the perpetuation of famines across the third world. (Cf. for example Susan George's *Feeding the Few: Corporate Control of Food.* Washington, D.C.: The Institute for Policy Studies, 1985.)

Agri-business is that control over food supply that seeks to increase profits without necessarily feeding people; and, furthermore, it does so by heightened mechanization and productivity so as to consolidate control over food in fewer and fewer hands bringing about the destruction of the small farmer who can't compete with the financial resources for progress of the big companies (i.e., Archer Daniel Midlands). The motorized food industry has never been concerned with feeding the hungry and would rather see food rot or go to corrupt politicians within a famine stricken nation than see it given away to the starving. Heidegger's unpublished sentence actually finds adherents in the leftist political activist communities of environmentalists and anti-imperialists who see the politics of famine even in such circumstances as the cattle industry that irresponsibly utilizes better producing farm land for the sake of the higher profits yielded in the meat industry than in the selling of, say, beans and rice. Far from cold and unfeeling in reference to the suffering of millions at the hands of Nazis like Heidegger, these remarks suggest a multiplication of the thinking of the holocaustal that sees that holocausts are daily occurrences in the epoch of technology.

Heidegger's concern for "essences," for dynamic unfolding, is not an abstraction that crowds out the silent voices of suffering human beings, but is a concern for the material emergence of apparatuses that carry out this suffering and the neighborly resistance to them. Heidegger may have been a Nazi, but his thinking, made Jewish in its Derridean good reading, is a confrontation with the nationalism and multi-nationalism of the technological epoch.

This may all read like an apologetics aimed at rescuing Heidegger from his fascist political commitments as the Rector at Freiburg and the thinker who desired to be the official philosopher advising Adolph Hitler on how to lead the movement of the destiny of Being. But I am ready to admit that Heidegger may be very reluctant to submit to the reading I have given him in these last pages and, perhaps, in this project as a whole. That is, I am open to the possibility that Heidegger's thinking is National Socialist through and through from 1927-1976 and that it not only crowns the ideological head of that movement but even goes so far as to desire its implementation and material emergence. After all, could desire be anything other than totalitarian? Could commitment, political or social or theoretical, be anything else? No, I accept this reading. And I admit it so far as to say that Derrida may well have, in his good reading of Heidegger, tied the old German down so as to make circumcision possible despite the kicking and screaming. He wouldn't have wanted to castrate the man now would he?

In fact, I want to even go so far as to claim that it is Heidegger's desire for fascism and commitment to National Socialism that makes it possible for him to be the thinker of technology, the thinker who was able to leap into the economy of the essentially technological in such a way as to see the danger that swirls there, and the monumental nature of all that hangs in the balance. Heidegger may have been a Nazi, but "Heidegger" cannot *be* anything at all, Derrida has shown us that. And what's more, Derrida says this frequently, "Heidegger" has shown us that as well. Heidegger's becoming text through death is the ongoing turmoil of the Heidegger affair now couched in matters of ideology: who will get all the good jobs at the university, deconstructors or critical theorists? Since the deconstructors who like Heidegger are Nazis, the only prudent thing to do is to hire the critical theorists. The importance of resisting the opposition of committed standpoints is to be thought in the textuality of Heidegger/Derrida, the Jew and his circumcised other. And crazy as it might sound, it is precisely the nearness to fascism that must be thought, and "Heidegger —like Heidegger— continues to call upon us to do just that.

Where memory symbolically presents past images as representations, monuments are being built. These memories make the passage of time into a reasonable exchange where each moment passes with the arrival of an image that remains as a saved and filed moment in time. Time, in this view, is never wasted, it always leaves something to show for itself, every past instant can be preserved by the image that stands as its present monument, as its memory. Deconstructed time, the time of the Jew, is given, it is an extravagant gift where the giver gives too much and the receiver reciprocally gives the gift away. Nothing remains for this time, there is no present, no monuments, no memory. Such a time is squandered and squandering, it elides exchange. And what it wastes most of all is the very being of the giver, the gift, and the recipient. There is nothing at all remaining in/as/through this time.

Such is the time of the memorial, the dedication where everything is squandered. There are no images present to memory, but traces of time, time tracing its way along a pathway leading nowhere. Building, time that builds while leaving nothing, only its own resonance. The resonant sound of building lets nothing stand as a result or artifact for memory, what is built is instead resonance per se. This resonance is itself an *ethos*, a dwelling place for one newly re-situated in time, a residence in a neighborhood where nothing is exchanged and everything is laid to waste. At the center of the Jewish dwelling, a squandered site, a place where even the center itself has been wasted, is the silent ringing peel of a stillness that resonates through time. This eccentric community without idols persists as an ongoing residual memorial of its own squandered self.

Listen. Hear nothing. Nothing hears. A truly bold claim.

Two points that may belong together: (1) In the Jewish decalogue in Exodus 20, it would seem that there is a strong emphasis being placed on the forbiddenness of the "graven image." The second commandment reads: "Thou shalt not make unto thee any graven image, or any likeness of any thing that is in heaven above, or that is in the earth beneath, or that is in the water under the earth." The importance of this commandment is partially evident from its location on the tablet, but is further reinforced by a later claim:

Ye shall not make with me gods of silver, neither shall ye
make unto you gods of gold. An altar of earth thou shalt make
unto me, and shalt sacrifice thereon thy burnt offerings, and thy
peace offerings, thy sheep, and thine oxen: in all places where I
record my name I will come unto thee, and I will bless thee. And
if thou wilt make me an altar of stone, thou shalt not build it of
hewn stone: for if thou lift up thy tool upon it, thou hast polluted
it. Neither shalt thou go up by steps unto mine altar, that thy
nakedness not be discovered thereon. (Exodus 20, 23-26)

That the altar should be a gathering place upon the earth seems clear, that
it should avoid the construction of monuments and ideals also seems
clear. Notice also, that the second commandment does not only refer to
images of God, but to images of any *thing* at all. 2. Dwelling in the
memorial is building without the construction of entities, it requires a
situated relation to the movement of time that squanders everything that
is. As such, time retains traces of what is always already not yet past.
Because of this, it makes little difference whether I say that time dwells
or that human beings dwell, rather *there is* dwelling. The *philosophical*
conclusion that can be drawn from this is that the deconstruction of
metaphysics is ethical, it is the re-placement of metaphysics with ethics,
but not in such a way as to put ethics first (as some have done). Instead, I
would say that metaphysics and ethics belong together and their
difference is nothing at all — it is only the silent trace of a difference. The
deconstruction of metaphysics unconceals the *ethos* of time and thus
reveals that all metaphysics has always taken place in that *ethos* where
human beings dwell. Dwelling, therefore, resists metaphysics while
residing in its ab-solute proXimity.
    Arriving at the moment of ecstasy, there is a drive to squander. That
is, in ecstasy there is squandering, the drive to make something into
nothing: the drive a-way. The climax here is the becoming ethical of the
deconstructive economy, the circulation of Saying. This economy is no
longer one of a strict exchange, but an extravagant gift giving where all
the wealth of metaphysical riches in the history of ethics is squandered.
But not only that. Given the development of the demonstration thus far,
it is also a self-succumbing squandering, the waste of an opportunity. It
is my position that the description or demonstration of the post
metaphysical attack coming from the lineage of deconstruction has
provided an opportunity for the exposition of an *ethos*, an ethical

derivation of the practices of deconstruction. And this too must be squandered, must be driven a-way.

It is crucial that the reader, the good reader, not be led to conclude that... well, not be led to conclude. It's not over yet. The event arrives but its arrival has the character of an always already and any attempt to take advantage of this opportunity as though it were the payoff for a previous trial, as though it were a *telos* that the demonstration sought to reveal or achieve, would be to make an exchange with the reader in accordance with whatever patience he or she were willing to dedicate. But a dedicated patience will have squandered opportunities for payoff, will have neglected and wasted exchanges without residual or resonance. After all, should the matter for ethics be reduced to an epistemology as the tradition so tediously demands? What is the good and how can it be verified as such? These questions are not ethical in substance, or rather it is precisely in so far as they have substance that they elude the ethical. That ethical place where dwelling comes to pass is nothing substantive, it is a place of waste, a place littered with residue.

If memory is a collection of entities, then reminiscence or recollection is the squandering of entities. In recollection the gathering of objects is sacrificed for the sake of gathering itself, of situating oneself in the place where objects come to gather as things. So the lie told about the littered place is that there is something littered there, a discarded wrapper or beverage can or whatever; the litter that is the wasted space of ethics is the place where things lie, what remains exposed in the entity, what fails to gather in its objectivity or instrumentality. It is for this reason that Heidegger thinks the ethical as a listening that initially may have suggested an alternative to theory. What could have been more simple, where metaphysics relies on the eyes, Heidegger's approach turns toward the ears. But the listening that re-places theory is not an alternative to methods of inquiry into the sensible, but is a (dis)placing of oneself into the resonance that overwhelms things in their being. The ethical, therefore, is nothing and it is perfectly acceptable to say there is no ethics. All ethics is squandered.

Perhaps it is oversimplifying it to put it this way, but for Heidegger an attack on metaphysics situates human being in the world and thus establishes a relation between... Another way to oversimplify might be to say that there are never multiple (or singular for that matter) operational interests in action. That is, all human being is dwelling where the possibility of making a distinction between practical and theoretical is absurd. The biggest mistake in the entire history of philosophy was the principle that metaphysics, ethics, logic, and epistemology were distinct areas of inquiry. A judgment which makes them all epistemology, all areas of inquiry.

The twisting free of dedication from commitment is the venture into the nearness of the pure draft that is the postal concern of all post-structuralism. It is a prodigal deconstruction that recognizes in technology and metaphysics a constant threat. Not something that will just go away, or something for which one desires to turn back the clocks as a means of escape, technology as a supplement of the nearness comes to pass as that which dwelling resists. The desire for presence, desire and willing as presence, will always be present and can only be resisted in the step not beyond it which sets moving the deconstruction of metaphysics. Whether or not the power of technology can be resisted will have to become an undecidable non-pessimism and non-optimism of the poetic thinking squandering of dwelling that builds in/as/through communal and neighborly resistance. The ringing of stillness that peals in the "only a god can save us" or the refusal to be committed to a political agenda or architectural blueprint will have to come to pass in the patient dwelling of the community that squanders its monuments, in the nearness of the heart's inner space, in the tabernacle at the empty center of the secret Jewish covenant: the human people who wait for the coming of their god, who wait in the openness of the future. Maybe, Viel-leicht.

In a series of interviews with Dreyfus and Rabinow and published as an afterward to their book *Michel Foucault: Beyond Structuralism and Hermeneutics,* the following exchange can be found:

> Q: Do you think that the Greeks offer an attractive and plausible alternative [to contemporary ethical movements]?
> A: No! I am not looking for an alternative; you can't find the solution of a problem in the solution of another problem raised at another moment by other people. You see, what I want to do is not the history of solutions, and that's the reason why I don't accept the word "alternative." I would like to do a genealogy of problems, of *problematiqués.* My point is not that everything is bad, but that everything is dangerous, which is not exactly the same as bad. If everything is dangerous, then we always have something to do. So my position leads not to apathy but a hyper — and pessimistic activism.

> I think that the ethico-political choice we have to make every
> day is to determine which is the main danger.[28]

The context of the discussion of danger is saturated by the issues, as are frequently found in Foucault's writings, of techniques and practices. The techniques available for the "care of the self" or the materializing of the human hymen as I have demonstrated it, are dangerous. They threaten human tissue with the incorporation of a bio-power that operates "vampire-like" on the forming bodies and subjected egos of human life. These techniques are the threat of power; and resistance, as resistance to danger, is the only respite, it is all that remains. The patience of dwelling described above may suggest a similar phenomenon to Foucault's. We will never run out of things to do and our patience is the kind of waiting that enables us to carefully carry through with the handling of this squandering on the verge of the technological. What Foucault tries to describe through a mixture of hard work and pessimism, is what I have tried to de-monstrate in the preceding pages: a poetic dwelling in resistance that is neither pessimistic nor optimistic, that goes along the way of resisting metaphysics with dedication despite the impossibility of coming to an end. Intensely local in its vision of "practice," this notion of dwelling does not engage in idle utopian theoretical pursuits attempting to create *ex nihilo* a new vision of the state that would only detract from the work/play that we are called upon to perform within an ever materializing historical (con)text. But apathy is not the opposite of such theorizing, in fact, one of the instantiations apathy (or a failure to engage in the call to arms) may take is the idle engagement in certain kinds of theorizing. Dedicated to the way of resistance, dwelling does not offer an alternative, as Foucault puts it, another solution to some problem. Instead it becomes a perpetual questioning, a path of inquiry, a road for rogues to travel.

This hyperactivism of the dissemination ('Ge') of *Gelassenheit* in poetic resistance is what is and has been suggested in/as/through the claiming of Heidegger's line. Heidegger's place on the line is a barricade or march (margin) where the demonstration of Being's closure can take place, where metaphysics can be called into question. And what's more, this is not a line that anyone should refuse to cross. The crossing of the line, the crossing out of the line that is the crossing out of Being in its

---

[28] Hubert L. Dreyfus and Paul Rabinow, *Michel Foucault: Beyond Structuralism and Hermeneutics* (Chicago: University of Chicago Press, 1983), 231-32.

closure, is not some line over which one steps, moving from one side of it to the other (like some line in the sand that has been drawn and crossed); yet this movement is still a crossing *of* the line, a marking and remarking of the line across the face of Being and metaphysics. The crossing of the line is marching through the presence of Being so as to dis-seminate[29] it into fourfold regions, to spread it out in the opening up of a world struck through (*Schlag*) with an incision or break in the ground. Crossing is always a de-monstration of the metaphysics of presence. Heidegger on the line is therefore not some cross Martin bears in his waiting for the god who will save us, but his crossing through the danger that threatens, and *this* is the poetics of resistance.

---

[29]Dis-semination, hyphenated, suggests the nearness of dissemination to castration and death which is symbolically evoked in the Jewish ritual of circumcision. This no doubt recalls the indifference of Heidegger's neutrality claimed for Dasein. Dasein, in its concrete facticity is *Geschlechtlos,* neutral, and this neutrality was its dissemination, its castration. Heidegger's release of Dasein in the *Metaphysical Foundations of Logic* from the Phallogocentrism of Western metaphysics is not only his making Dasein a Jew, but his castrating the sexism of the West in favor of a neutral dynamic unfolding of the human hymen. The role of the father in this ritual, performed at the bris on the eighth day of the newborn boy's life recalls further the dynamic discussed at the end of the third chapter regarding the fathers and sons of Derrida's discussion of Thothianism.

Bibliography

Ackrill, J.L. "ΣΥΜΠΛΟΚΗ ΕΙΔΩΝ" in *Plato*. edited by G. Vlastos. Notre Dame, Indiana: University of Notre Dame Press, 1978.

Arendt, Hannah. Eichmann in Jerusalem: A Report on the Banality of Evil. New York: Penguin Books, 1977.

——. *The Human Condition*. Chicago: The University of Chicago Press, 1958.

Aristotle. *Metaphysics*. translated by W.D. Ross. published in *The Basic Works of Aristotle*, edited by Richard McKeon. New York: Random House, 1941.

——. *On Interpretation*. translated by E.M. Edghill in ibid.

Austin, J.L. *How to Do Things with Words*. Cambridge, Massachusetts: Harvard University Press, 1962.

Baudrillard, Jean. *Simulations*. translated by P. Foss, P. Patton, and P. Beitchman. New York: Foreign Agents Series-Semiotext(e), 1983.

Bernasconi, Robert. *The Question of Language in Heidegger's History of Being*. Atlantic Highlands, NJ: Humanities Press International, 1985.

Bernstein, Richard J. *The New Constellation: The Ethical-Political Horizons of Modernity/Postmodernity*. Cambridge, MA: The MIT Press, 1992.

Biemel, Walter. *Martin Heidegger: An Illustrated Study*. New York: Harcourt, Brace, Jovanovich, 1976.

Blanchot, Maurice. *The Writing of the Disaster*. translated by A. Smock. Lincoln, NE: The University of Nebraska Press, 1986.

Butler, Judith. *Gender Trouble*. New York: Routledge, 1990.

Caputo, John D. *Radical Hermeneutics*. Bloomington, Indiana: Indiana University Press, 1987.

——. "The Thought of Being and the Conversation of Mankind: The Case of Heidegger and Rorty." published in *Hermeneutics and Praxis*, edited by R. Hollinger. Notre Dame, Indiana: University of Notre Dame Press, 1985.

Daly, Mary. *Gyn/Ecology*. Boston, Massachusetts: Beacon Press, 1990.

Deleuze, Gilles. *Nietzsche and Philosophy*. translated by H. Tomlinson. New York: Columbia University Press, 1983.

Deleuze, Gilles and Felix Guattari. *Capitalism and Schizophrenia*.

Volume 1: *Anti-Oedipus*. translated by R. Hurley, M. Seem, and H.R. Lane. Preface by Michel Foucault. Minneapolis: University of Minnesota Press, 1977. Volume 2: *A Thousand Plateaus*. translated by B. Massumi. Minneapolis: University of Minnesota Press, 1987.

Deleuze, Gilles and Claire Parnet. *Dialogues*. translated by H. Tomlinson and B. Habberjam. New York: Columbia University Press, 1987.

Derrida, Jacques. *Spurs*. Bilingual edition. translated by B. Harlow. Chicago: University of Chicago Press, 1979.

——. *Speech and Phenomena: And Other Essays on Husserl's Theory of Signs*. edited and translated by D. Allison. Evanston, Illinois: Northwestern University Press, 1973.

——. *Of Grammatology*. translated by G.C. Spivak. Baltimore, Maryland: Johns Hopkins University Press, 1976.

——. *Writing and Difference*. translated by Alan Bass. Chicago: The University of Chicago Press, 1978.

——. *An Introduction to Edmund Husserl's "Origin of Geometry."* translated by J.P. Leavey, Jr. Lincoln, Nebraska: University of Nebraska Press, 1989.

——. *Margins of Philosophy*. translated by Alan Bass. Chicago: University of Chicago Press, 1982.

——. *Positions*. translated by Alan Bass. Chicago: University of Chicago Press, 1981.

——. *Dissemination*. translated by Barbara Johnson. Chicago: University of Chicago Press, 1981.

——. "No Apocalypse, Not Now (full speed ahead, seven missiles, seven missives)." translated by C. Porter and P. Lewis in *Diacritics*, vol. 14, no. 2 (summer 1984).

——. "Of an Apocalyptic Tone Recently Adopted in Philosophy." translated by J.P. Leavey, Jr. in *Semeia* no. 23, 1982.

——. "Economimesis." translated by R. Klein in *Diacritics* vol. 11, no. 2 (summer 1981).

——. "Living On: *Border Lines*." translated by J. Hulbert in *Deconstruction and Criticism*. New York: Seabury Press, 1979.

——. *Glas*. translated by J.P. Leavey, Jr. and R. Rand. Lincoln, NE: The University of Nebraska Press, 1986.

——. "Geschlecht: sexual difference, ontological difference." in *Research in Phenomenology*, 1983.

——. "*Geschlecht* II: Heidegger's Hand." translated by J.P. Leavey, Jr. in

Deconstruction and Philosophy, edited by Sallis. The University of Chicago Press: Chicago, 1987.

—. "Sending: On Representation." translated by P. and M.A. Caws in *Social Research*, volume 49 no. 2, summer 1982.

—. "The *Retrait* of Metaphor." translated by F. Gasdner et al., *Enclitic* 2, no. 2, 1978.

—. *Cinders*. translated and edited by N. Lukacher. Lincoln, NE: University of Nebraska Press, 1991.

—. *The Post Card: From Socrates to Freud and Beyond*. translated by A. Bass. Chicago: The University of Chicago Press, 1987.

—. "Shibboleth." translated by J. Wilner in *Midrash and Literature*, edited by G.H. Hartman and S. Budick. New Haven: Yale University Press, 1986.

—. *Memoires: for Paul de Man*. Revised edition. translated by C. Lindsay, J. Culler, E. Cadava, and P. Kamuf. New York: Columbia University Press, 1989.

—. *Of Spirit: Heidegger and the Question*. translated by G. Bennington and R. Bowlby. Chicago, IL: The University of Chicago Press, 1989.

Dreyfus, Hubert L. *Being-in-the-World*. Cambridge, MA: The MIT Press, 1991.

Frege, Gottlob. "On Sense and Reference" in *Translations from Philosophical Writings of Gottlob Frege* edited and translated by P. Geach and M. Black. Oxford: Basil Blackwell, 1966.

Freud, Sigmund. *Civilization and its Discontents*. translated and edited by J. Strachey. New York: W.W. Norton & Company, 1961.

Foucault, Michel. *The History of Sexuality, volume I: An Introduction*. translated by Robert Hurley. New York: Vintage Books, 1980.

Gadamer, Hans-Georg. *Truth and Method*. translated by G. Barden and J. Cumming. New York: Seabury Press, 1975.

—. *Philosophical Hermeneutics*. translated and edited by D.E. Linge. Berkeley, CA: University of California Press, 1976.

Gasché, Rodolphe. *The Tain of the Mirror*. Cambridge, MA: Harvard University Press, 1986.

George, Susan. *Feeding the Few: Corporate Control of Food*. Washington, D.C.: The Institute for Policy Studies, 1985.

Habermas, Jürgen. *The Philosophical Discourse of Modernity*. translated by F.G. Lawrence. Cambridge, MA: The MIT Press, 1990.

Harvey, David. *The Condition of Postmodernity*. Cambridge, MA: Blackwell, 1990.

Heidegger, Martin. *Identity and Difference*. Bilingual edition, translated by Joan Stambaugh. New York: Harper & Row, 1969. German title: *Identität und Differenz*. Pfullingen: Verlag Günther Neske, 1957.

———. *Early Greek Thinking*. Translated by D.F. Krell and F.A. Capuzzi. New York: Harper & Row, 1984.

———. *Basic Problems of Phenomenology*. translated by A. Hofstadter. Bloomington, Indiana: Indiana University Press, 1988.

———. "On the Essence of Truth" translated by D.F. Krell in *Basic Writings* edited by D.F. Krell. New York: Harper & Row, 1977.

———. *Being and Time*. translated by J. Macquarrie and E. Robinson. New York: Harper & Row, 1962.

———. *Poetry, Language, Thought*. translated by A. Hofstadter. New York: Harper & Row, 1975.

———. "Time and Being." translated by J. Stambaugh in *On Time and Being*. New York: Harper & Row, 1972.

———. "The End of Philosophy and the Task of Thinking." translated by J. Stambaugh in ibid.

———. *What Is Called Thinking*. translation by J.G. Gray. New York: Harper & Row, 1968.

———. *The Question Concerning Technology and other essays*. translated by W. Lovitt. New York: Harper & Row, 1977.

———. "The Turning" translated by W. Lovitt in ibid.

———. *On the Way to Language*. translated by P.D. Hertz. New York: Harper & Row, 1971.

———. *Discourse on Thinking*. A translation of *Gelassenheit* by J.M. Anderson and E.H. Freund. New York: Harper & Row, 1966.

———. *Existence and Being*. translated by D. Scott, edited by W. Brock. Chicago: Regnery, 1968.

———. *The Question of Being*. Bilingual edition. translated by J. Wilde and W. Kluback. New Haven, Connecticut: College and University Press, 1958. German title: *Zur Seinsfrage*. Frankfurt am Main: Vittorio Klostermann, 1956.

———. "Overcoming Metaphysics." translated by J. Stambaugh in *The End of Philosophy*. New York: Harper & Row, 1973.

———. *What is Philosophy?* translated by J.T. Wilde and W. Kluback. New York: NCUP, Inc., 1956.

——. *The Metaphysical Foundations of Logic.* translated by M. Heim. Bloomington, IN: Indiana University Press, 1984.

——. *Parmenides.* translated by A. Schuwer and R. Rojcewicz. Bloomington, IN: Indiana University Press, 1992.

——. *The Principle of Reason.* translated by R. Lilly. Bloomington, IN: Indiana University Press, 1991.

——. *Hegel's Phenomenology of Spirit.* Translated by P. Emad and K. Maly. Bloomington, IN: Indiana University Press, 1988.

Hofstadter, Albert. "Enownment" in *Martin Heidegger and the Question of Literature.* edited by W. Spanos. Bloomington, Indiana: Indiana University Press, 1979.

Horkheimer, Max. *Critical Theory: Selected Essays.* translated by M.J. O'Connell and others. New York, NY: Continuum, 1989.

Irigaray, Luce. "This Sex Which is not One" translated by C. Reeder in *New French Feminisms* edited by E. Marks and I. de Courtivon. New York: Schocken Books, 1981.

Joyce, James. *Portrait of the Artist as a Young Man.* New York: Penguin Books, 1976.

——. *Ulysses.* Corrected Text edited by H.W. Gabler, W. Steppe, and C. Melchior. New York: Random House, 1986.

Kierkegaard, Søren. *Philosophical Fragments.* translated by H.V. Hong and E.H. Hong. Princeton, New Jersey: Princeton University Press, 1987.

——. *Fear and Trembling/Repetition.* edited and translated by H.V. Hong and E.H. Hong. Princeton, NJ: Princeton University Press, 1983.

Klepfisz, Irena. "Anti-Semitism in the Lesbian/Feminist Movement," *Nice Jewish Girls: A Lesbian Anthology.* edited by E.T. Beck. Watertown, MA: Persephone Press, Inc., 1982.

Kockelmans, Joseph J. *On the Truth of Being.* Bloomington, IN: Indiana University Press, 1984.

——. (editor) *On Heidegger and Language.* Evanston, Illinois: Northwestern University Press, 1972.

Krell, David. *Intimations of Mortality.* University Park, PA: Penn State Press, 1986.

——. *Of Memory, Reminiscence, and Writing (On the Verge).* Bloomington, IN: Indiana University Press, 1990.

Lacan, Jacques. *Écrits: A Selection.* translated by Alan Sheridan. New York: W.W. Norton & Company, 1977.

Lacoue-Labarthe, Philippe. *Heidegger, Art and Politics.* translated by C. Turner. Oxford: Basil Blackwell, 1990.

Levinas, Emmanuel. *Time and the Other.* translated by R.A. Cohen. Pittsburgh: Duquesne University Press, 1987.

———. *Totality and Infinity.* translated by A. Lingis. Pittsburgh, PA: Duquesne University Press, 1969.

Lyotard, Jean-François. *Heidegger and "the jews."* translated by A. Michel and M. Roberts. Minneapolis, MN: University of Minnesota Press, 1990.

Marcuse, Herbert. *Negations: Essays in Critical Theory.* translated by J.J. Shapiro. London: Free Association Books, 1988.

Marx, Karl. "The German Ideology." published in *The Marx-Engels Reader.* edited and translated by R.C Tucker, 2nd ed. New York: W.W. Norton & Company, 1978.

———. *Capital, volume. 1.* edited by F. Engels. translated by S. Moore and E. Aveling. New York: International Publishers, 1977.

Marx, Leo. *The Machine in the Garden: Technology and the Pastoral Ideal in America.* London: Oxford University Press, 1964.

Marx, Werner. *Heidegger and the Tradition.* translated by T. Kisiel and M. Greene. Evanston, IL: Northwestern University Press, 1971.

Mauss, Marcel. *The Gift.* translated by W.D. Halls. New York: W.W. Norton, 1990.

Mosse, George L. *The Crisis of German Ideology: Intellectual Origins of the Third Reich.* New York: Schocken Books, 1964.

Norris, Christopher. *What's Wrong With Postmodernism.* Baltimore, MD: The Johns Hopkins Press, 1990.

Palmer, Richard E. *Hermeneutics.* Evanston, Indiana: Northwestern University Press, 1969.

Plato. *Sophist.* translated by F.M. Cornford in *Collected Dialogues.* edited by E. Hamilton and H. Cairns. Princeton, New Jersey: Princeton University Press, 1980.

———. *Symposium.* translated by M. Joyce in ibid.

———. *Phaedrus.* translated by R. Hackforth in ibid.

Rapaport, Herman. *Heidegger and Derrida.* Lincoln, Nebraska: University of Nebraska Press, 1989.

Richardson, William J. *Heidegger: Through Phenomenology to Thought.* ` The Hague, The Netherlands: Martinus Nijhoff, 1967.

Rorty, Richard. *Philosophical Papers Volume 2: Essays on Heidegger and Others.* Cambridge, Massachusetts: Cambridge University Press, 1991.

———. "Overcoming the Tradition: Heidegger and Dewey" in *Consequences of Pragmatism.* Minneapolis, MN: University of Minnesota Press, 1982.

—. "Philosophy as a Kind of Writing: An Essay on Derrida" in ibid.

Rossiter, Clinton. *Conservatism in America*. Cambridge, MA: Harvard University Press, 1982.

Russell, Bertrand. "On Denoting" in *Logic and Knowledge*. edited by R.C. Marsh. London: Unwin Hyman Limited, 1956.

Sallis, John. *Echoes: After Heidegger*. Bloomington, Indiana: Indiana University Press, 1990.

—. (editor). *Deconstruction and Philosophy: The Texts of Jacques Derrida*. Chicago: The University of Chicago Press, 1987.

—. (editor). *Heidegger and the Path of Thinking*. Pittsburgh, PA: Duquesne University Press, 1970.

Saussure, Ferdinand de. *Course in General Linguistics*. translated by W. Baskin. New York: McGraw-Hill Book Company, 1966.

Schürmann, Reiner. *Heidegger on Being and Acting: From Principles to Anarchy*. translated by Christine-Marie Gros in collaboration with the author. Bloomington, IN: Indiana University Press, 1987.

Searle, John R. *Speech Acts: An Essay in the Philosophy of Language*. Cambridge, MA: Cambridge University Press, 1969.

Sheehan, Thomas. editor. *Heidegger: The Man and the Thinker*. Chicago: Precedent Publishing, Inc., 1981.

Silverman, Hugh J. and Ihde, Don (editors). *Hermeneutics and Deconstruction*. Selected Studies in Phenomenology and Existential Philosophy, volume 10. Albany, NY: State University of New York Press, 1985.

Soper, Kate. *Humanism and Anti-Humanism*. London: Hutchinson and Co. Ltd., 1986.

Weber, Max. *The Protestant Ethic and the Spirit of Capitalism* translated by T. Parsons. New York: Charles Scribner's Sons, 1958.

Wheelwright, Philip, editor and translator. *The Presocratics*. Indianapolis, IN: Bobbs-Merrill Company, Inc., 1975.

Wolin, Richard (editor). *The Heidegger Controversy*. New York: Columbia University Press, 1991.

Wood, David. *The Deconstruction of Time*. Atlantic Highlands, NJ: Humanities Press International, Inc., 1989.

—. "Heidegger after Derrida" in *Research in Phenomenology,* Volume 17, 1987.

—. (editor) *Derrida: A Critical Reader*. Oxford: Blackwell Publishers, 1992.

Zimmerman, Michael E. *Heidegger's Confrontation with Modernity: Technology, Politics, Art*. Bloomington, IN: Indiana University Press, 1990.

Printed in Great Britain
by Amazon

51808536R00222